REFORMATION THOUGHT

REFORMATION THOUGHT

AN INTRODUCTION
THIRD EDITION

ALISTER E. MCGRATH

Copyright © Alister E. McGrath 1988, 1993, 1999

The right of Alister E. McGrath to be identified as author of this work has been asserted in accordance with the Copyright, Designs and Patents Act 1988.

First edition published 1988
Second edition published 1993
Reprinted 1993, 1994 (twice), 1995, 1996, 1997 (twice), 1998, 1999
Third edition published 1999
2 4 6 8 10 9 7 5 3 1

Blackwell Publishers Ltd
108 Cowley Road
Oxford OX4 1JF
UK

Blackwell Publishers Inc.
350 Main Street
Malden, Massachusetts 02148
USA

British Library Cataloguing in Publication Data
A CIP catalogue record for this book is available from the British Library.

Library of Congress Cataloging-in-Publication Data has been applied for

ISBN 0-631-21520-4 (hbk)
ISBN 0-631-21521-2 (pbk)

Typeset in 10 on 12 pt Bembo
by Best-set Typesetter Ltd., Hong Kong
Printed in Great Britain by MPG Books Ltd, Bodmin, Cornwall

This book is printed on acid-free paper

Contents

Contents

Preface to the Third Edition

The European Reformation of the sixteenth century is one of the most fascinating areas of study available to the historian. It also continues to be of central importance to anyone interested in the history of the Christian church or its religious ideas. The Reformation embraced a number of quite distinct, yet overlapping areas of human activity – the reform of both the morals and structures of church and society, new approaches to political issues, shifts in economic thinking, the renewal of Christian spirituality, and the reform of Christian doctrine. It was a movement based upon a more or less coherent set of ideas, which were believed to be capable of functioning as the foundation of a programme of reform.

But what were those ideas? How may their origins be accounted for? And how were they modified by the social conditions of the period? One serious difficulty – indeed, perhaps the most serious difficulty – facing today's historian of the Reformation is the strangeness of the ideas underlying it. Many modern students of the Reformation know little about Christian theology. For example, the great reforming slogan 'justification by faith alone' is incomprehensible to many today, as are the intricacies of the sixteenth-century debates over the eucharist. Why should these apparently obscure issues have caused such a storm at the time? There is an obvious temptation for the student of the Reformation to avoid engaging with the ideas of the movement, and treat it as a purely social phenomenon.

This book is written in the conviction that there are many who will not be prepared to rest content with this superficial engagement with the ideas of the Reformation, and wish to deal with them seriously – but who are discouraged from doing so by the formidable difficulties encountered in trying to understand its ideas. Christian theology will always hold a place of importance in the study of the Reformation. To fail to have at least some degree of familiarity with theology is to lack an understanding of the culture and self-consciousness of the Reformation era. Religious ideas played a large part in the development and expansion of the Reformation. To study the Reformation without considering the religious ideas which fuelled its development is comparable to studying the Russian Revolution without reference to Marxism. Historians cannot cut themselves off from the language and ideas of their era of study.

A further difficulty placed in the path of such a student is the remarkable advance made within the last forty years and more in our understanding both of the Reformation itself, and of its background in the late Renaissance, particularly in relation to late medieval scholasticism. Much of this work has yet to filter through to the student, and there is an urgent need for a work which will explain the findings of recent scholarship, and indicate its importance for our understanding of the Reformation.

The present work aims to do just that. It assumes that the reader knows nothing of Christian theology, and aims to provide an entry level guide to the ideas that proved to be so central to this movement in European history, while at the same time distilling the findings of much recent scholarship in its field. The book arose from many years' experience of teaching the field of Reformation studies to students at Oxford University, and I wish to acknowledge my complete indebtedness to those students. It is they who have taught me just how much about the Reformation, so often taken for granted, actually needs to be explained. It is they who have identified the points of particular difficulty which need special discussion. It is they who have identified the need for precisely this work – and if the reader finds it helpful, it is those students who must be thanked. I am also grateful to my colleagues from the Oxford University faculties of theology and history for many helpful discussions concerning the difficulties encountered in teaching Reformation thought in the modern period.

This book first appeared in 1988. It was immediately clear that it had met a real educational need. An expanded and revised second edition appeared in 1993. This new edition retains all the features which made those earlier editions so attractive to students, while incorporating additional material of direct relevance. In addition to general updating as necessary, reflecting scholarly developments since the last edition, the new edition offers substantially increased biographical coverage of major Reformation thinkers, and extends its coverage to include the thought of the English Reformation.

Alister McGrath
Oxford, January 1999

How to Use this Book

Three words sum up the aim of this book: introduce; explain; contextualize. The book aims to introduce the leading ideas of the European Reformation during the first half of the sixteenth century. It is like a sketch map, which indicates the main features of the intellectual landscape: notes and suggestions for further reading will allow the reader to add finer detail later. Second, the book aims to explain these ideas. It assumes that the reader knows nothing about the Christian theology which underlies the Reformation, and explains what terms such as 'justification by faith' and 'predestination' mean, and why they are of religious and social relevance. Third, it aims to contextualize these ideas by setting them in their proper intellectual, social and political context. That context includes such great intellectual movements as humanism and scholasticism, the alternative religious ideologies of the radical Reformation and Roman Catholicism, and the political and social realities of the imperial cities of the early sixteenth century. All these factors affected the thought of the reformers, and its impact upon their public – and this work aims to identify that influence and assess its effects.

A series of appendices deal with difficulties which experience suggests most students encounter as they read works relating to the Reformation. What do these abbreviations mean? How can I make sense of those references to primary and secondary sources? What does 'Pelagian' mean? Where should I go to find out more about the Reformation? These questions and others are dealt with at length, making this book unique. It will be assumed that the reader speaks no language other than English, and all Latin quotations or slogans will be translated and explained. Although the text of the work draws extensively upon foreign language scholarship, unavailable in English, a select bibliography of works available in English is provided for the benefit of such readers.

1

Introduction

Many students approach the Reformation in much the same way as medieval travellers approached the vast dark forests of southern Germany – with a sense of hesitation and anxiety, in case what lay ahead should prove impenetrable, or in case they should find themselves hopelessly lost. They are often like explorers venturing into new terrain, unsure what there is to find, at times bewildered by the unmapped wilderness, at others exhilarated by unexpected vistas and valleys. Like Dante, they find themselves longing for a guide who will be a Virgil to them – leading them through the intricacies of what is otherwise virtually incomprehensible, and certainly confusing. It is tempting for such students to ignore the *ideas* of the Reformation altogether, in order to concentrate upon its social or political aspects. The price of making the Reformation easier to come to grips with in this way, however, is both to fail to capture its essence as a historical phenomenon and to understand why it remains an essential reference point for much contemporary debate in the religious world and far beyond.

It is understandably difficult for a student sympathetic to the secularism of modern western culture to come to terms with a movement motivated by religious ideas. It is tempting to marginalize these ideas and approach the sixteenth century with the world-view of the modern period. Like any historical phenomenon, however, the Reformation demands that its interpreters attempt to enter into *its* world-view. We must learn to empathize with its concerns and outlook, in order to understand how these affected the great flux of history. The Reformation in Switzerland and Germany was directly based upon religious ideas which demand and deserve consideration. Even in England, where local conditions led to political factors having greater influence than religious ideas, there was still a significant core of such ideas underlying developments. This book aims to explain as clearly as possible what the religious ideas underlying the Reformation actually were and how they affected those who entertained them.

The present introductory chapter aims to deal with some preliminary matters, in order to prepare the ground for discussion of the thought of the Reformation in later chapters.

The Cry for Reform

The term 'Reformation' immediately suggests that something – namely, western European Christianity – was being reformed. Like many other terms used by historians to designate eras in human history – such as 'Renaissance' or 'Enlightenment' – it is open to criticism. For example, the twelfth century witnessed a comparable attempt to reform the church in western Europe – but the term 'Reformation' is not used to designate this earlier movement. Other terms might be thought by some to be more appropriate to refer to the sixteenth-century phenomenon under consideration. Nevertheless, the fact remains that the term 'Reformation' *is* generally accepted as the proper designation for this movement, partly because the movement was linked with the recognition of the need for drastic overhaul of the institutions, practices and ideas of the western church. The term helpfully indicates that there were both social and intellectual dimensions to the movement which it designates.

By the beginning of the sixteenth century it was obvious that the church in western Europe was once more in urgent need of reform. The cry for 'reform in head and members' summed up both the nature of the crisis and its perceived solution. It seemed that the life-blood of the church had ceased to flow through its veins. The church legal system was badly in need of overhaul, and ecclesiastical bureaucracy had become notoriously inefficient and corrupt. The morals of the clergy were often lax and a source of scandal to their congregations. Clergy, even at the highest level, were frequently absent from their parishes. In Germany, it is reported that only one parish in fourteen had its pastor in residence. The Frenchman Antoine du Prat, archbishop of Sens, turned up for only one service at his cathedral: moreover, his presence and role at this service was somewhat passive, since it was his funeral. Most higher ecclesiastical posts were secured through dubious means, generally relying upon the family connections or the political or financial status of the candidates, rather than their spiritual qualities. Thus Duke Amadeus VIII of Savoy secured the appointment of his son to the senior position of bishop of Geneva in 1451; if anyone had misgivings about the fact that the new bishop had never been ordained and was only eight years of age, they were wise enough to keep quiet about them. Pope Alexander VI, a member of the Borgia family (famous for its lethal dinner parties), secured his election to the papacy in 1492 despite having several mistresses and seven children, largely because he bought the papacy outright over the heads of his nearest rivals.

Machiavelli put the loose morals of late Renaissance Italy down to the poor example set by the church and its clergy. For many, the cry for reform was a plea for the administrative, moral and legal reformation of the church: abuses and immorality must be eliminated; the pope must become less preoccupied with worldly affairs; the clergy must be properly educated; and the administration of the church must be simplified and purged of corruption. For others, the most pressing need concerned the spirituality of the church. There was an urgent need to recapture the vitality and freshness of the Christian faith. Many looked back with nostalgia to the simplicity and excitement of the apostolic Christianity of the first century. Could not this Golden Age of the Christian faith be regained, perhaps by pondering anew the New Testament documents? This programme of reform was the wistful pipe dream of intellectuals throughout half of Europe. Yet the Renaissance popes seemed more interested in secular than in spiritual matters, and managed between them to achieve a hitherto unprecedented level of avarice, venality, immorality and spectacularly unsuccessful power politics. The words of Gianfresco Pico della Mirandola (often confused with his uncle, Giovanni), spoken in March 1517, sum up succinctly the thoughts which preyed on many educated minds at the time: 'If we are to win back the enemy and the apostate to our faith, it is more important to restore fallen morality to its ancient rule of virtue than that we should sweep the Euxine sea with our fleet.'

There were others, however, who added another demand to this list – the demand for a reformation of Christian doctrine, of theology, of religious ideas. To critical observers such as Martin Luther at Wittenberg and John Calvin at Geneva, the church had lost sight of its intellectual heritage. It was time to reclaim the ideas of the Golden Age of the Christian church. The sad state of the church in the early sixteenth century was simply a symptom of a more radical disease – a deviation from the distinctive *ideas* of the Christian faith, a loss of intellectual identity, a failure to grasp what Christianity really was. Christianity could not be reformed without an understanding of what Christianity was actually meant to be. For these men, the obvious decline of the late Renaissance church was the latest stage in a gradual process which had been going on since about the theological renaissance of the twelfth century – the corruption of Christian doctrine and ethics. The distinctive ideas which thinkers such as Luther and Calvin held to underlie Christian faith and practice had been obscured, if not totally perverted, through a series of developments in the Middle Ages. According to these thinkers, it was time to reverse these changes, to undo the work of the Middle Ages, in order to return to a purer, fresher version of Christianity which beckoned to them across the centuries. The reformers echoed the cry of the humanists: 'back to the sources (*ad fontes*)', back to the Golden Age of the church, in order to reclaim its freshness, purity and vitality in the midst of a period of stagnation and corruption.

Contemporary writings unquestionably paint a picture of growing ecclesiastical corruption and inefficiency, indicating how much the late medieval church was in need of reform. It is necessary, however, to enter a note of caution on the manner in which these sources are to be interpreted. It is quite possible that these sources document growing levels of expectation within the late medieval church as much as declining levels of performance. The growth of an educated laity – one of the more significant elements in the intellectual history of late medieval Europe – led to increasing criticism of the church on account of the obvious disparity between what the church *was* and what it *might be*. The growing level of criticism may well reflect the fact that more people were, through increasing educational opportunities, in a position to criticize the church – rather than any further decline in the ecclesiastical standards of the day.

But who could reform the church? By the first decade of the sixteenth century, a fundamental shift in power within Europe was essentially complete. The power of the pope had diminished, as the power of secular European governments had increased. In 1478 the Spanish Inquisition was established, with power over clergy and religious orders (and eventually also over bishops) – and the control of this system of courts rested not with the pope, but with the Spanish king. The Concordat of Bologna (1516) gave the King of France the right to appoint all the senior clergy of the French church, effectively giving him direct control of that church and its finances. Across Europe, the ability of the pope to impose a reformation upon his church was steadily diminishing; even if the will to reform had been there in the later Renaissance popes (and there are few indications that it was), the ability to reform was gradually slipping away. This diminishment in papal authority did not, however, lead to a decrease in the power of local or national churches, which continued to exercise major influence over nations. It was the ability of the pope to control such local or national power that declined during our period.

It is therefore important to notice the manner in which Protestant reformers allied themselves with regional or civic powers in order to effect their programme of reform. Luther appealed to the German nobility and Zwingli to the Zurich city council for reform, pointing out the benefits which would accrue to both as a consequence. For reasons we shall explore presently (pp. 21–4), the English Reformation (in which political factors led to more theological considerations being treated as of secondary importance) is not typical of the European movement as a whole. The continental Reformation proceeded by a symbiotic alliance of reformer and state or civic authority, each believing that the resulting Reformation was to their mutual benefit. The reformers were not unduly concerned that they gave added authority to their secular rulers by their theories of the role of the state or the 'godly prince': the important thing was that the secular rulers supported the cause of the Reformation, even if their reasons for doing so might not be entirely praiseworthy.

The mainstream reformers were pragmatists, people who were prepared to allow secular rulers their pound of flesh provided the cause of the Reformation was advanced. In much the same way, of course, the opponents of the Reformation had little hesitation in calling upon the support of secular authorities which felt that their interests were best served by a maintenance of the religious *status quo*. No study of the Reformation can overlook its political and social dimensions, as secular authorities in northern Europe saw their chance to seize power from the church, even at the cost of thereby committing themselves to a new religious order. Nevertheless, the fact remains that certain distinctive religious ideas achieved widespread circulation and influence within western European society in the sixteenth century. These ideas cannot be ignored or marginalized by anyone concerned with the study of the Reformation. It is hoped that the present work will introduce, explain and contextualize them.

The Concept of 'Reformation'

The term 'Reformation' is used in a number of senses, and it is helpful to distinguish them. Four elements may be involved in its definition, each of which will be discussed briefly below: Lutheranism, the Reformed church (often referred to as 'Calvinism'), the 'radical Reformation' (often still referred to as 'Anabaptism') and the 'Counter-Reformation' or 'Catholic Reformation'. In its broadest sense, the term 'Reformation' is used to refer to all four movements. The term is also used in a somewhat more restricted sense to mean 'the Protestant Reformation', thereby excluding the Catholic Reformation. In this sense, it refers to the three Protestant movements noted above. In many scholarly works, however, the term 'Reformation' is used to refer to what is sometimes known as the 'magisterial Reformation', or the 'mainstream Reformation' – in other words, that linked with the Lutheran and Reformed churches, and excluding the Anabaptists.

The unusual phrase 'magisterial Reformation' needs a little explaining. It draws attention to the manner in which the mainstream reformers related to secular authorities, such as princes, magistrates or city councils. Whereas the radical reformers regarded such authorities as having no rights within the church, the mainstream reformers argued that the church was, at least to some extent, subject to the secular agencies of government. The magistrate had a right to authority within the church, just as the church could rely on the authority of the magistrate to enforce discipline, suppress heresy, or maintain order. The phrase 'magisterial Reformation' is intended to draw attention to this close relationship between the magistracy and the church, which lay at the heart of the reforming programme of writers such as Martin Luther or Martin Bucer.

All three senses of the word 'Reformation' will be encountered in the course of reading works dealing with the sixteenth century. The term 'magisterial Reformation' is increasingly used to refer to the first two senses of the term (i.e. covering Lutheranism and the Reformed church) taken together, and the term 'radical Reformation' to refer to the third (i.e. covering Anabaptism). The present work is primarily concerned with the ideas of the magisterial Reformation.

The term 'Protestant' also requires comment. It derives from the aftermath of the Second Diet of Speyer (February 1529), which voted to end the toleration of Lutheranism in Germany. In April of the same year, six German princes and fourteen cities protested against this oppressive measure, defending freedom of conscience and the rights of religious minorities. The term 'Protestant' derives from this protest. It is therefore not strictly correct to apply the term 'Protestant' to individuals prior to April 1529 or to speak of events prior to that date as constituting 'the Protestant Reformation'. The term 'evangelical' is often used in the literature to refer to the reforming factions at Wittenberg and elsewhere (e.g. in France and Switzerland) prior to this date. Although the word 'Protestant' is often used to refer to this earlier period, this use is, strictly speaking, an anachronism.

The Lutheran Reformation

The Lutheran Reformation is particularly associated with the German territories and with the pervasive personal influence of one charismatic individual – Martin Luther. Luther was particularly concerned with the doctrine of justification, which formed the central point of his religious thought. The Lutheran Reformation was initially an academic movement, concerned primarily with reforming the teaching of theology at the University of Wittenberg. Wittenberg was an unimportant university, and the reforms introduced by Luther and his colleagues within the theology faculty attracted little attention. It was Luther's personal activities – such as his posting of the famous ninety-five theses (31 October 1517) and the Leipzig Disputation (June–July

1519: see p. 88) – which made waves and brought the ideas in circulation at Wittenberg to the attention of a wider audience.

Strictly speaking, the Lutheran Reformation began only in 1522, when Luther returned to Wittenberg from his enforced isolation in the Wartburg. Luther had been condemned by the Diet of Worms in 1521. Fearing for his life, certain well-placed supporters removed him in secrecy to the castle known as the 'Wartburg', until the threat to his safety ceased. In his absence, Andreas Bodenstein von Karlstadt, one of Luther's academic colleagues at Wittenberg, began a programme of reform at Wittenberg which seemed to degenerate into chaos. Convinced that he was needed if the Reformation was to survive Karlstadt's ineptitude, Luther emerged from his place of safety, and returned to Wittenberg.

At this point, Luther's programme of academic reform changed into a programme for reform of church and society. No longer was Luther's forum of activity the university world of ideas – he now found himself regarded as the leader of a religious, social and political reforming movement which seemed to some contemporary observers to open the way to a new social and religious order in Europe. In fact, Luther's programme of reform was much more conservative than that associated with his Reformed colleagues, such as Huldrych Zwingli. Furthermore, it met with considerably less success than some anticipated. The movement remained obstinately tied to the German territories, and – Scandinavia apart – never gained the foreign power-bases which had seemed to be like so many ripe apples, ready to fall into its lap. Luther's understanding of the role of the 'godly prince' (which effectively ensured that the monarch had control of the church) does not seem to have held the attraction which might have been expected, particularly in the light of the generally republican sentiments of Reformed thinkers such as Calvin. The case of England is particularly illuminating: here, as in the Lowlands, the Protestant theology which eventually gained the ascendancy was Reformed rather than Lutheran.

The Reformed Church

The origins of the Reformed church lie with developments within the Swiss Confederation. Whereas the Lutheran Reformation had its origins in an academic context, the Reformed church owed its origins to a series of attempts to reform the morals and worship of the church (but not necessarily its *doctrine*) according to a more biblical pattern. Although most of the early Reformed theologians – such as Zwingli – had an academic background, their reforming programmes were not academic in nature. They were directed towards the church as they found it in the Swiss cities, such as Zurich, Berne and Basle. Whereas Luther was convinced that the doctrine of justification was of central significance to his programme of social and religious reform, the early Reformed thinkers had relatively little interest in doctrine, let alone one specific doctrine. Their reforming programme was institutional, social and ethical, in many ways similar to the demands for reform emanating from the humanist movement. We shall consider the ideas of humanism in some detail presently (pp. 41–51); for the moment it is important simply to note that all the major early Reformed theologians had links with the humanist movement, which were not shared by Luther, who regarded it with some suspicion.

The consolidation of the Reformed church is generally thought to have begun with the stabilization of the Zurich reformation after Zwingli's death in battle (1531), under his successor, Heinrich Bullinger, and to have ended with the emergence of Geneva as its power-base and John Calvin as its leading spokesman, in the 1550s. The gradual shift in power within the Reformed church (initially from Zurich to Berne, and subsequently from Berne to Geneva) took place over the period 1520–60, eventually establishing both the city of Geneva, its political system (republicanism) and its religious thinkers (initially Calvin, and after his death Theodore Beza) as predominant within the Reformed church. This development was consolidated through the establishment of the Genevan Academy (founded in 1559), at which Reformed pastors were trained.

The term 'Calvinism' is often used to refer to the religious ideas of the Reformed church. Although still widespread in the literature relating to the Reformation, this practice is now generally discouraged. It is becoming increasingly clear that later sixteenth-century Reformed theology draws on sources other than the ideas of Calvin himself. To refer to later sixteenth- and seventeenth-century Reformed thought as 'Calvinist' implies that it is essentially the thought of Calvin – and it is now generally agreed that Calvin's ideas were modified subtly by his successors. (We shall explore this development in relation to the doctrine of predestination on pp. 140–3.) The term 'Reformed' is now preferred, whether to refer to those churches (mainly in Switzerland, the Lowlands and Germany) or religious thinkers (such as Theodore Beza, William Perkins or John Owen) basing themselves upon Calvin's celebrated religious textbook *The Institutes of the Christian Religion* or to church documents (such as the famous *Heidelberg Catechism*) based upon it.

An additional factor should be noted in connection with the term 'Calvinist'. The term dates from the 1560s, when a significant alteration in the political situation in the German territories took place. Germany had been seriously destabilized in the 1540s and early 1550s by conflicts between Lutherans and Roman Catholics, and it was widely recognized that such conflicts were damaging to the Empire. The Peace of Augsburg (September 1555) settled the religious question in Germany by allocating certain areas of Germany to Lutheranism and the remainder to Roman Catholicism – the famous principle often referred to as *cuius regio, eius religio* ('your region determines your religion'). No provision was made for the Reformed faith, which was effectively declared to be 'non-existent' in Germany. In February 1563, however, the *Heidelberg Catechism* was published (see p. 240), indicating that the Reformed theology had gained a firm foothold in this hitherto Lutheran region of Germany. This catechism was immediately attacked by Lutherans as being 'Calvinist' – in other words, foreign. The term 'Calvinist' was used by German Lutherans to attempt to discredit this new and increasingly influential document, by implying that it was unpatriotic. Given the original polemical associations of the term, it would seem appropriate for the historian to abandon it in favour of a more neutral term – and the term 'Reformed' unquestionably serves this purpose.

Of the three constituents of the Protestant Reformation – Lutheran, Reformed or Calvinist, and Anabaptist – it is the Reformed wing which is of particular importance to the English-speaking world. Puritanism, which figures so prominently in seventeenth-century English history and is of such fundamental importance to the religious and political views of New England in the seventeenth century and beyond, is a specific form of Reformed Christianity. To understand the religious and political history of New England or the ideas of writers such as Jonathan Edwards, for example, it is necessary to come to grips with at least some of the theological insights and part of the religious outlook of Puritanism, which underlie their social and political attitudes. It is hoped that this work will help with this process of familiarization.

The Radical Reformation (Anabaptism)

The term 'Anabaptist' owes its origins to Zwingli (the word literally means 're-baptizers', and refers to what was perhaps the most distinctive aspect of Anabaptist practice – the insistence that only those who had made a personal public profession of faith should be baptized). Anabaptism seems to have first arisen around Zurich, in the aftermath of Zwingli's reforms within the city in the early 1520s. It centred on a group of individuals (among whom we may note Conrad Grebel) who argued that Zwingli was not being faithful to his own reforming principles. He preached one thing, and practiced another. Although Zwingli professed faithfulness to the *sola scriptura* ('by Scripture alone') principle, Grebel argued that he retained a number of practices – including infant baptism, the close link between church and magistracy, and the participation of Christians in warfare – which were not sanctioned or ordained by Scripture. In the hands of such radical thinkers, the *sola scriptura* principle became radicalized (see pp. 150–61): reformed Christians came to believe and practise only those things explicitly taught in Scripture. Zwingli was alarmed by this, seeing it as a destabilizing development which threatened to cut the Reformed church at Zurich off from its historical roots and its continuity with the Christian tradition of the past.

The Anabaptists had good reason to accuse Zwingli of compromise. In 1522, he wrote a work known as *Apologeticus Archeteles*, in which he recognized the idea of a 'community of goods' as an authentic Christian ideal. 'No-one calls any possessions his own,' he wrote, 'all things are held in common.' But by 1525, Zwingli had changed his mind, and come round to the idea that private property was not such a bad thing, after all.

Although Anabaptism arose in Germany and Switzerland, it subsequently became influential in other regions, such as the Lowlands. The movement produced relatively few theologians (the three most significant are generally agreed to be Balthasar Hubmaier, Pilgram Marbeck and Menno Simons). This failure partly reflects the fact that the movement did not have any substantial common theological basis. It is, however, also due to other factors, not least of which is the forcible suppression of Anabaptism by the secular authorities.

A number of common elements can be discerned within the various strands of the movement: a general distrust of external authority, the rejection of infant baptism in favour of the baptism of adult believers, the common ownership of property, and an emphasis upon pacifism and non-resistance. To take up one of these points: in 1527, the governments of Zurich, Berne and St Gallen accused the Anabaptists of believing 'that no true Christian can either give or receive interest or income on a sum of capital; that all temporal goods are free and common, and that all can have full property rights to them'. It is for this reason that 'Anabaptism' is often referred to as the 'left wing of the Reformation' (Roland H. Bainton) or the 'radical Reformation' (George Hunston Williams). For Williams, the 'radical Reformation' was to be contrasted with the 'magisterial Reformation', which he broadly identified with the Lutheran and Reformed movements. These terms are increasingly being accepted within Reformation scholarship, and the reader is likely to encounter them in his or her reading of more recent studies of the movement.

Probably the most significant document to emerge from the movement is the Schleitheim Confession, drawn up by Michael Sattler on 24 February 1527. The Confession takes its name from the small town of that name in the canton of Schaffhausen. Its function was to distinguish Anabaptists from those around them – supremely from what the document refers to as 'papists and antipapists' (that is, unreformed catholics and magisterial evangelicals). In effect, the Schleitheim Confession amounts to 'articles of separation' – that is to say, a set of beliefs and attitudes which distinguish Anabaptists from their opponents inside and outside the Reformation, and function as a core of unity, whatever their other differences might be.

The Catholic Reformation

This term is often used to refer to the revitalization of Roman Catholicism in the period following the opening of the Council of Trent (1545). In older scholarly works, the movement is often designated the 'Counter-Reformation': as the term suggests, the Roman Catholic church developed means of combating the Protestant Reformation, in order to limit its influence. It is becoming increasingly clear, however, that the Roman Catholic church countered the Reformation partly by reforming itself from within, in order to remove the grounds of Protestant criticism. In this sense, the movement was a reformation of the Roman Catholic church, as much as it was a reaction against the Protestant Reformation.

The same concerns underlying the Protestant Reformation in northern Europe were channelled into the renewal of the Roman Catholic church, particularly in Spain and Italy. The Council of Trent, the foremost feature of the Catholic Reformation, clarified catholic teaching on a number of confusing matters, and introduced much needed reforms in relation to the conduct of the clergy, ecclesiastical discipline, religious education and missionary activity. The movement for reform within the Roman Catholic church was greatly stimulated by the reformation of many of the older religious orders and the establishment of new orders (such as the Jesuits). The more specifically theological aspects of the Catholic Reformation will be considered in relation to its teachings on Scripture and tradition, justification by faith, and the sacraments.

As a result of the Catholic Reformation, many of the abuses which originally lay behind the demands for reform – whether these came from humanists or Protestants – were removed. By this stage, however, the Protestant Reformation had reached a point at which the mere removal of malpractices and abuses was no longer sufficient to reverse the situation: the demand for the reformation of doctrine, religious ideology, and the church was now regarded as an essential aspect of the Protestant–Roman Catholic controversies. This point highlights the need to consider the religious ideas lying behind the 'magisterial Reformation', which became of increasing importance to the Protestant–Roman Catholic debate as the sixteenth century progressed.

The Importance of Printing

Recent technological developments in the field of data processing and transfer have revolutionized many aspects of modern life. It is important to realize that a single technological innovation destined to have an enormous influence over western Europe was developed on the eve of the Reformation. This innovation was, of course, printing. It is impossible to underestimate its impact on the Reformation.

Although originally developed centuries earlier by the Chinese, the first European printed documents which can be dated reliably originate from the press of Johann Gutenberg at Mainz around 1454. In 1456, the same press produced a printed Latin Bible. This was followed in 1457 by the so-called Mainz Psalter, which established the custom of identifying the printer, the location of the press, and the date of publication on the title-page of the work. From Germany, the technology was taken to Italy, presses being established at Subiaco (1464) and Venice (1469). Caxton set up his printing shop at Westminster, London, in 1476. The famous Aldine Press was established at Venice in 1495 by Aldus Manutius Romanus. This press was responsible for two important developments: 'lower case' letters (so-called because they were kept in the lower of two cases containing type) and the sloping 'italic' type (so-called in English-language works, on account of Venice being located in Italy; Aldus himself called the type 'Chancery').

Why would printing have such a major impact upon the Reformation? The following major factors point towards its importance in this matter.

First, printing meant that the propaganda of the Reformation could be produced quickly and cheaply. The tedious process of copying manuscripts by hand was no longer necessary. Further, the errors introduced by the copying process were eliminated; once a work was set up in type, any number of error-free copies cold be run off. Anyone who could read and who could afford to pay for books was in a position to learn of the sensational new ideas coming out of Wittenberg and Geneva. For example, in England it proved to be the literate and financially advantaged classes who knew most about Lutheranism in the third decade of the sixteenth century. Lutheran books, banned by the authorities as seditious, were smuggled in through the Hanseatic trade route to Cambridge via Antwerp and Ipswich. There was no need for Luther to visit England to gain a hearing for his ideas – they were spread by the printed word (see pp. 236–7).

This point is of interest in relation to the sociology of the early Reformation. In both England and France, for example, the first Protestants were often drawn from the upper strata of society, precisely because these strata possessed the ability to read and the money to pay for books (which, as they often had to be smuggled in from abroad, were generally rather expensive). Similarly, the greater influence of Protestantism at Cambridge that at Oxford partly reflects the former's proximity to the continental ports from which Protestant books were being (illicitly) imported.

Second, the Reformation was based upon certain specific sources: the Bible and the Christian theologians of the first five centuries (often referred to as 'the Fathers', or 'the patristic writers'). The invention of printing had two immediate effects upon these sources, of considerable importance to the origins of the Reformation. First, it was possible to produce more accurate editions of these works – for example, through the elimination of copying errors. By comparing the printed text of a work with manuscript sources, the best possible text could be established and used as the basis of theological reflection. In the late fifteenth and early sixteenth centuries, humanist scholars rummaged through the libraries of Europe in search of patristic manuscripts which they could edit and publish. Second, these sources were made much more widely available than had ever been possible before. By the 1520s, just about anyone could gain access to a reliable edition of the Greek text of the New Testament or the writings of Augustine of Hippo (a patristic writer particularly favoured by the Reformers).

The eleven volumes of the collected works of Augustine were published at Basle by the Amerbach brothers, after an editorial process lasting from 1490 to 1506. Although only 200 copies of each volume seem to have been published, they were widely used to gain access to the most reliable text of this important writer. Erasmus of Rotterdam produced the first published Greek New Testament in 1516. Entitled *Novum Instrumentum omne*, the work had three main sections: the original Greek text of the New Testament; a new Latin translation of this Greek text, which corrected inadequate existing translations, especially the Vulgate (see pp. 53–6); and finally, an extended commentary on the text, in the form of annotations. The work was widely used by those sympathetic to the cause of the Reformation. For the reformers – especially Luther and his colleagues at Wittenberg – the religious ideas of the Reformation drew largely on the Bible and Augustine. The advent of printing, linked with increasingly effective bookselling methods, meant that accurate and reliable texts of both these sources were widely available, thus facilitating both the initial development and the subsequent spread of these ideas. As Gordon Rupp once remarked:

The new tools, the new texts, crude as they were, uncritical and slipshod as their editors might be, made possible a concentration on the Bible, the results of which were startling and practical enough. The Reformers of Wittenberg, Zurich, Basle, Strasbourg and St Gallen knew what they were doing . . . There

is evidence how, in distant Cambridge and Oxford, the younger scholars went
to great pains because of them, and sought dangerously and eagerly these tools
of the new biblical learning. They laid the foundations of the religious, theological Reformation. Thomas Garrard the book agent, not Thomas Cromwell
the politician, struck the tinder that lit Master Ridley's candle.

The importance of printing in spreading the ideas of the Reformation
cannot be overstated. Surveys of the personal book collections of French bourgeois families point to the religious implications of this trend. Lefèvre's French
New Testament of 1523, pointedly addressed 'à tous les chrestiens et chresti-
ennes', along with his French Psalter of 1524, were read widely throughout
France, and were even distributed free of charge within the reforming diocese
of Meaux. Copies of these works, along with the New Testament commentaries of Erasmus, Melanchthon and Lefèvre himself, are frequently to be
found jostling for space on the shelves of *bourgeois* libraries in the late 1520s.
If these books were ever read by their owners – and the evidence strongly
suggests that they were – a considerable head of pressure for reform would
have developed.

An example will illustrate the importance of printing to the propagation
of the ideas of the Reformation abroad. A crucial turning point in the French
Reformation was marked by the publication of the French-language edition
of Calvin's *Institutes of the Christian Religion* in 1541. Suddenly, coherently
expressed and carefully justified radical reforming doctrines were available
within France in a language which most could understand (see pp. 244–8).

Someone seems to have pressed a panic button. On 1 July 1542, the
Parisian *parlement* directed that all works containing heterodox doctrines, especially Calvin's *Institutes*, were to be surrendered to the authorities within three
days. The visitation of bookshops became an important element of the official
attempt to suppress the growing heterodox movement. The following year the
Parisian Faculty of Theology, charged by the King of France with the maintenance of religious orthodoxy, drew up a list of sixty-five subversive titles
which were to be banned with immediate effect. Of the thirty-six which it
is possible to identify and date with anything approaching probability, twenty-
three were printed in Geneva.

Calvin's *Institutes* were thus seen as the spearhead of a Genevan assault upon
the French church, mediated through the printed word. On 23 June 1545, an
extended list of prohibited works was published. Of its 121 titles in French,
almost half were printed in Geneva. The reaction from the booksellers of Paris
was immediate: they protested that they would face financial ruin if they were
prohibited from selling such books. It seems that there was a major market
for works which were considered to be dangerously unsound by the Faculty
of Theology – further evidence of the importance of a literate and affluent

laity in promoting the ideas of the Calvinist Reformation. Indeed, Laurent de Normandie, Calvin's friend and bookseller, found the contraband book trade so profitable that he emigrated to Geneva, in order that he might publish such books, rather than just sell them.

This is not to say, however, that the Reformation was wholly dependent upon a technological innovation. The evidence available points to printing as an agent of change in the intellectual climate, whereas the cities were generally converted to the cause of the Reformation through the impact of specific religious preachers and personalities. We must remember that the pulpit was of decisive importance in influencing what was a largely illiterate public – and much of the output of the printing houses took the form of collections of sermons.

The Social Context of the Reformation

The northern European Reformation was based largely in the cities. In Germany, more than fifty of the sixty-five 'Imperial Cities' responded positively to the Reformation, with only five choosing to ignore it altogether. In Switzerland, the Reformation originated in an urban context (Zurich), and spread through a process of public debate within Confederate cities such as Berne and Basle and other centres – such as Geneva and St Gallen – linked to these cities by treaty obligations. French Protestantism began as a predominantly urban movement, with its roots in major cities such as Lyons, Orléans, Paris, Poitiers and Rouen.

It is becoming increasingly clear that the success or failure of the Reformation in these cities was dependent in part upon political and social factors. By the late fifteenth and early sixteenth centuries, they city councils of the imperial cities had managed to gain a substantial degree of independence. In effect, each city seems to have regarded itself as a miniature state, with the city council functioning as a government and the remainder of the inhabitants as subjects.

The growth in the size and importance of the cities of Germany is one of the more significant elements in late fourteenth- and fifteenth-century history. An extended food crisis, linked with the ravages of the Black Death, led to an agrarian crisis. Wheat prices dropped alarmingly in the period 1450–1520, leading to rural depopulation as agricultural workers migrated to the cities in the hope of finding food and employment. Denied access both to the trade guilds and to the city councils, discontent grew within this new urban proletariat.

The early sixteenth century thus witnessed growing social unrest in many cities, as demands for broader-based and more representative government gained momentum. In many cases, the Reformation came to be linked with these demands for social change, so that religious and social change went together, hand in hand. We must not think that religious concerns swamped all other mental activities – they simply provided a focal point for them. Economic, social and political factors help explain why the Reformation succeeded, for example, in Nuremberg and Strasbourg, yet failed in Erfurt.

A number of theories have been advanced to explain the appeal of the Reformation to the cities. Berndt Moeller argued that the urban sense of community had been disrupted in the fifteenth century, through growing social tension within the cities and an increasing tendency to rely upon external political bodies, such as the imperial government or the papal curia. By adopting the Lutheran Reformation, Moeller suggested, such cities were able to restore a sense of communal identity, including the notion of a common religious community binding inhabitants together in a shared religious life. Significantly, Moeller drew attention to the social implications of Luther's doctrine of the priesthood of all believers (see pp. 222–3), which broke down certain traditional distinctions within urban society and encouraged a sense of communal unity.

A second explanation was advanced by Thomas Brady, based largely upon his analysis of the city of Strasbourg. Brady argued that the decision to adopt Protestantism at Strasbourg was the outcome of a class struggle, in which a ruling coalition of patricians and merchants believed that their social position could be maintained only through alignment with the Reformation. The urban oligarchs introduced the Reformation as a subtle means of preserving their vested interests, which were threatened by a popular protest movement. A similar situation, Brady suggested, existed in many other cities.

A third explanation of the appeal of the Reformation to sixteenth-century urban communities centres on the doctrine of justification by faith (an idea explored in detail in chapter 6). In a study published in 1975, Steven Ozment argued that the popular appeal of Protestantism derived from its doctrine of justification by faith, which offered relief from the psychological pressure of the late medieval penitential system and an associated 'semi-Pelagian' doctrine of justification. As the weight of this psychological burden was greatest and most evident in urban communities, he argued, it was within such communities that Protestantism found its greatest popular support. Ozment argued that Moeller had vastly exaggerated the differences between Luther and the theologians of the southwest. The early reformers shared a common message, which could be summarized as the liberation of individual believers from the pyschological burdens imposed by late medieval religion. Whatever their differences, the magisterial reformers – such as Bucer, Zwingli and Luther – shared a common concern to proclaim the doctrine of justification by faith through grace, thereby eliminating the theological necessity of and diminishing the popular concern for indulgences, purgatory, invocation of the saints, and so forth. This theory is of importance to this work, as it illustrates the role of ideas in generating pressure for reform and change: the pressure for social change is, if Ozment is right, the *outcome*, not the *cause*, of new religious ideas.

Each of these theories is significant, and together they have provided an important stimulus to the more detailed study of the development of urban Protestantism in the first phase of the Reformation. Equally, each has been shown to have obvious weaknesses, as one might expect from ambitious global theories. For example, in the case of Geneva, as we shall see, the social tensions which eventually resulted in alignment with the Protestant city of Berne and adoption of the Zwinglian Reformation did not arise from class differences, but from division within a common social class over whether to support Savoy or the Swiss Confederacy. The pro-Savoyard Mammelukes and the pro-Bernese *Eiguenots* were both drawn from a single social group, characterized by a range of identifiable shared economic, familial and social interests. Similarly, Ozment's suggestion of a universal concern for the doctrine of justification finds little support in the case of cities within or linked with the Swiss Confederacy – such as Zurich, St Gallen and Geneva – and overlooks the obvious hesitations concerning the doctrine on the part of many Swiss reformers.

Nevertheless, some common features emerge from a study of the origins and development of the Reformation in major northern European cities such as Augsburg, Basle, Berne, Colmar, Constance, Erfurt, Frankfurt, Geneva, Hamburg, Lübeck, Memmingen, Ulm and Zurich. It is helpful to explore them.

In the first place, the Reformation in the cities appears to have been a response to some form of popular pressure for change. Nuremberg is a rare instance of a city council imposing a reformation without significant preceding popular protest or demand. Dissatisfaction among urban populations of the early sixteenth century was not necessarily purely religious in character; social, economic and political grievances were unquestionably present, to varying extents, within the agglomerate of unrest evident at the time. City councils generally reacted in response to this popular pressure, often channelling it in directions appropriate to their own needs and purposes. This subtle manipulation of such pressure was an obvious way of co-opting and controlling a potentially dangerous popular protest movement. One of the more significant observations which may be made concerning the city Reformation is that existing urban regimes were often relatively unchanged by the introduction of new religious ideas and practices, which suggests that city councils were able to respond to such popular pressure without radical changes in the existing social orders.

Second, the success of the Reformation within a city was dependent upon a number of historical contingencies. To adopt the Reformation was to risk a disastrous change in political alignment, in that existing treaties or relationships – military, political and commercial – with territories or cities which chose to remain catholic were usually deemed to be broken as a result. A city's trading relationships – upon which her economic existence might depend – might thus be compromised fatally. Thus the success of the Reformation in the city of St Gallen was partly due to the fact that the city's linen industry was not adversely affected to any significant degree by the decision to adopt the Reformation. Equally, a city (such as Erfurt) in close proximity to a catholic city (Mainz) and a Lutheran territory (Saxony) could risk becoming embroiled in military conflict with one or other of these interested parties, with potentially lethal results for the independence of that city. Furthermore, serious internal disunity as a result of a decision to introduce the Reformation could render the city vulnerable to outside influence – a major consideration in Erfurt city council's decision to half reforming activities in the 1520s.

Third, the romantic, idealized vision of a reformer arriving in a city to preach the gospel, with an immediate ensuing decision on the part of the city to adopt the principles of the Reformation must be abandoned as quite unrealistic. Throughout the entire process of Reformation, from the initial decision to implement a process of reform to subsequent decisions concerning the nature and the pace of reforming proposals, it was the city council who remained in control. Zwingli's Reformation in Zurich proceeded considerably more slowly than he would have liked on account of the cautious approach adopted by the council at crucial moments. Bucer's freedom of action in Strasbourg was similarly limited. As Calvin would discover, city councils were perfectly able to evict reformers from their precincts if they stepped out of line with publicly stated council policy or decisions.

In practice, the relationship between city council and reformer was generally symbiotic. The reformer, by presenting a coherent vision of the Christian gospel and its implications for the religious, social and political structures and practices of a city, was able to prevent a potentially revolutionary situation from degenerating into chaos. The constant threat of reversion to Catholicism, or subversion by radical Anabaptist movements rendered the need for a reformer inevitable. Someone had to give religious direction to a movement which, unchecked and lacking direction, might degenerate into chaos, with momentous and unacceptable consequences for the existing power structures of the city and the individuals who controlled them. Equally, the reformer was someone who was under authority, one whose freedom of action was limited by political masters jealous for their authority and with a reforming agenda which generally extended beyond that of the reformer to include consolidation of their economic and social influence. The relation between reformer and city council was thus delicate, easily prone to disruption, with real power permanently in the hands of the latter.

In the case of Geneva, a delicate relationship developed between the city's reformers (initially Guillaume Farel and Calvin, subsequently Calvin alone) and the city council. Conscious and jealous of its hard-won authority and liberty, the city council was determined not to substitute the tyranny of a reformer for that of a catholic bishop. In 1536, the city had just gained its independence from Savoy, and had largely retained that independence, despite the attempts of Berne to colonize the city. Geneva was in no mood to be dictated to by anyone, unless they were in a position to bring massive economic and military pressure to bear. As a result, severe restrictions were placed upon Calvin's activities. He was someone whose options were severely limited. The expulsion of Calvin from Geneva in 1538 demonstrates that political power remained firmly in the hands of the city council. The notion that Calvin was the 'dictator of Geneva' is totally devoid of historical foundation. Nevertheless, the city council found itself unable to cope with a deteriorating religious situation in Calvin's absence. In a remarkable act of social pragmatism and religious realism, the council recalled their reformer, and allowed him to continue his work of reform. Geneva needed Calvin, just as Calvin needed Geneva.

An important difference may be noted at this point between Lutheran and Reformed thought. Luther was the product of a small Saxon town under the thumb of the local prince, but the great Reformed thinkers Zwingli and Bucer were the product of the great free cities of Zurich and Strasbourg. Fro these latter, the Reformation involved the identification of 'citizen' with 'Christian', with a great emphasis upon the political dimension of life quite absent from Luther's thought. Thus Zwingli lay great emphasis upon the need to reform and redeem a *community*, whereas Luther tended to concentrate upon the need to reform and redeem the *individual*. Luther, through his doctrine of the 'Two Kingdoms', effectively separated religious ideas from secular life, whereas Zwingli insisted upon their mutual integration. It is therefore significant that the Reformed church gained its most secure power-bases in the cities of southern Germany and Switzerland, which were more advanced socially, culturally and economically than the northern cities destined to become Lutheran strongholds.

The social context of the Reformation is a fascinating subject in itself, but is noted here primarily on account of its obvious influence upon at least some of the religious ideas of the reformers. For example, there are excellent reasons for suggesting that many of Zwingli's ideas (especially his ideas concerning the societal function of the sacraments) were directly conditioned by the political, economic and social circumstances of Zurich. Equally, some of Calvin's ideas about the proper structures of a Christian church seem to reflect institutions already in existence at Geneva prior to his arrival in that city. We shall consider this issue at a number of points in the course of this work.

The Religious Ideas of the Reformers

It is appropriate to introduce the religious ideas of the reformers at this point. These ideas will be amplified and developed throughout this study, and the present section is intended to give the reader a preliminary overview. Just as a sketch map provides a broad survey of an area, in order that fine detail may be mapped in later, so the present section is intended to introduce the reader to the ideas to be encountered as this work progresses.

The fundamental conviction motivating the magisterial reformers was the Christianity could best be reformed and renewed by returning to the beliefs and practices of the early church. The first five centuries – often designated 'the patristic period' – tended to be regarded as the Golden Age of Christianity. The great vision of many sixteenth-century reformers was summed up in the Latin slogan *Christianismus renascens* – 'Christianity being born again'. How could this rebirth take place? The reformers pointed to the vitality of Christianity in the apostolic period, as witnessed by the New Testament, and argued that it was both possible and necessary to recapture the spirit and the form of this pivotal period in the history of the Christian church. It was necessary to go back to the New Testament and its earliest interpreters, in order to learn from them. These were the title-deeds of Christendom, the fountainhead of Christian belief and practice.

Standing in the great tradition of the Old Testament prophets, the reformers laid down a challenge to the religious leaders of their day. They saw the latter as guilty of condoning additions to and distortions of the Christian faith – alterations which reflected the interests of ecclesiastical fund-raisers and which fed popular superstition. The doctrine of purgatory and the related practice of selling indulgences were singled out as representing sub-Christian cults, exploiting the hopes and fears of the ordinary people. It was time to eliminate such corruptions through the consistent appeal to the beliefs and practices of the early church, which was held up as a model for the kind of shake-up and clean-out that the church so badly needed.

This great emphasis upon early Christianity as a norm or point of reference for the sixteenth-century vision of *Christianismus renascens* allows us to understand why the reformers placed such great emphasis upon the New

Testament and the early Christian writers usually known as 'the Fathers' or 'the patristic writers'. It was in these writings that a blueprint for the reformation and renewal of the church was to be found. Here could be found the original ideals of Christianity. Thus the production of the first Greek New Testament and the first edition of the works of Augustine (regarded by most reformers as *the* patristic writer) were milestones in the sixteenth-century programme of reform, and became widely available throughout Europe. For Martin Luther, the programme of reform could be summed up in a simple phrase: 'the Bible and St Augustine'.

The rise of Renaissance humanism was widely regarded as providential, in that the great advances made in Hebrew and Greek studies in relation to classical texts in western Europe paved the way for the direct engagement with the scriptural text, in place of the unreliable Latin translation of they Vulgate. The new textual and philological techniques pioneered by the humanists were regarded a holding the key to the world of the New Testament, and hence authentic Christianity. As the sixteenth century entered its second decade, there were many who felt that a new era was dawning, in which the voice of authentic Christianity, silent for so long, would be heard once more.

Simple though this programme of reform might seem, it was accompanied by formidable difficulties, which we shall be exploring in the course of this work. The agenda for the Reformation had been set, and the tools by which it might be achieved were being prepared. But we must plunge into the heady waters of fifteenth- and early sixteenth-century thought if we are to understand the backdrop to this drama in human history.

Yet not every part of Europe was equally influenced by the new religious ideas emerging from the crucible of the Reformation. In some cases, it was the social or ecclesiastical consequences of those ideas, rather than the ideas themselves, which were to prove the catalysts for change. For example, Germany was deeply affected, in a direct manner, by religious ideas; England was significantly less affected, with a more political style of Reformation developing. How are we to understand these developments? What is their significance? We will explore the situation in Germany and England in more detail, in an attempt to understand the different functions of religious ideas in these two contexts.

The Social Role of Religious Ideas: Germany and England

The sixteenth-century English Reformation under Henry VIII bore little relation to its German equivalent. The historian F. W. Powicke has remarked that 'the one thing that can be said about the Reformation in England is that it was an act of State'; and again, that 'the Reformation in England was a parliamentary transaction'.[1] There is enough truth in Powicke's generalization to draw attention to a key difference between the German and English Reformations.

In Germany, there was a protracted struggle between evangelical and catholic writers and ecclesiastics during the 1530s, as each attempted to gain influence in a disputed region. In England, Henry VIII simply declared that there would be only one national church within his realm. By royal command, there would be only one Christian body in England. The reformed English church was thus under no pressure to define itself in relation to any other Christian body in the region. The manner in which the English Reformation initially proceeded demanded no doctrinal self-definition, in that the church in England was defined socially in precisely the same way before the Reformation as after, whatever political alterations may have been introduced. This is not to say that no theological debates took place in England at the time of the Reformation; it is simply to note that they were not regarded as identity-giving.[2]

The Lutheran church in Germany was obliged to define and defend its existence and boundaries at the level of religious ideas because it had broken away from the medieval Catholic church – a church which continued to exist around Lutheran regions, forcing Lutheranism to carry on justifying its existence by defending its ideas. The situation in Germany became even more complicated during the 1560s and 1570s, as Calvinism began to make major inroads into previously Lutheran territory. Three major Christian denominations were now firmly established in the same area – Lutheranism, Calvinism and Roman Catholicism. All three were under major pressure to identify themselves. Lutherans were obliged to explain how they differed from Calvinists on the one hand and Roman Catholics on the other. And doctrine proved the most reliable way of identifying and explaining these differences: 'we believe this, but they believe that'. The period 1559–1622, characterized by a new emphasis on the need for purity of doctrine, is generally referred to as the 'period of orthodoxy'.

Lutheranism and Calvinism were, in many respects, very similar. Both claimed to be evangelical; that is, both argued that they were rooted in the gospel (Latin *evangelium*) itself, rather than in human traditions. Both rejected more or less the same central aspects of medieval Catholicism. But despite these obvious similarities, Lutheranism and Dalvinism needed to be distinguished from one another. German politics demanded that some simple way of identifying Lutheranism and Calvinism be developed; and doctrine proved to be the most reliable way of distinguishing these two otherwise very similar bodies. On most points of doctrine, Lutherans and Calvinists were in broad agreement. Yet there was one matter – the doctrine of predestination – upon which they were radically opposed. The emphasis placed upon the doctrine of predestination by Calvinists in the period 1559–1622 partly reflects the fact that this doctrine distinguished them from their Lutheran colleagues.

Niklas Luhmann, perhaps the most significant recent sociological writer to study the question of the social function of Christian doctrine, stresses that doctrine arises partly in response to perceived threats to the distinctive religious identity of a group, which may come about through encounters or conflict with other religious system. Doctrine is, according to Luhmann, the self-reflection of a religious community, by which it maintains its identity and regulates its relations with other such communities. The case of Lutheranism maintaining its distinctive identity within the German territories in the face of Calvinist and Roman Catholic opposition illustrates this principle well. It will also be clear why there was no need for the emerging reformed church in England to maintain its identity against any such internal opposition; there was none, on account of the Act of Uniformity.

The Henrician church in England thus regarded itself as sufficiently well defined as a social unit to require no further definition at the doctrinal level. The situation remained much the same under Elizabeth I. The 'Elizabethan Settlement' (1559) laid down that there would be only one Christian church in England – the Church of England, which retained the religious monopoly of the pre-Reformation church, while recognizing royal, rather than papal, authority. The phrase 'Church of England', as defined legally in Halsbury's *Laws of England*, makes no reference to its doctrine: the 'Church of England' is regarded as continuous with the church established in England during the period 597–686. Roman Catholicism, Lutheranism and Calvinism – the three Christian churches fighting it out for dominance of the continent of Europe – would not be tolerated in England. The social pressures which made religious ideas so important in the German context never really developed during the period of the English Reformation. There was thus no particular reason for the Church of England to pay much attention to doctrinal questions. Elizabeth ensured that it had no rivals in England. One of the purposes of doctrine is to divide – and there was nothing for the Church of England to divide itself from. England was insulated from the factors which made doctrine so significant a matter on the mainland of Europe in the Reformation and immediate post-Reformation periods.

Indded, the need to ensure that all English Christians (whether inclined towards some form of Protestantism or towards Roman Catholicism) felt reasonably at home in the Church of England led to the necessity of doctrine being played down: an emphasis on doctrine might lead to divisions within the new church, and hence internal weakness. As Elizabeth tried to ensure England's safety in the dangerous world of the late sixteenth century, the last thing she wanted was an England torn apart by doctrinal differences. A divided

English church would mean a divided England; and a divided England would be a weak and vulnerable England.

The social context of the Reformation thus has a significant influence on the extent to which religious ideas affected events. In Germany, such ideas proved to be enormously important; in England, considerably less so. It is only with the rise of Puritanism as a significant religious and political force in England towards the end of the sixteenth century that religious ideas began to become significant in the English situation.

Yet Germany perhaps provides a more reliable paradigm than England for understanding the enormous impact that religious ideas had within France, the Lowlands, northern Italy or Switzerland. Cut off from mainland Europe by the North Sea and the English Channel, England enjoyed an untypical isolation from the power of the religious ideas which were sweeping through Europe and occasionally evoking Wars of Religion in their wake. The student of the English Reformation may perhaps be excused for gaining the impression that religious ideas played a secondary role at the time; elsewhere, the story was very different. England cannot be allowed to be the controlling paradigm for an understanding of the role and influence of religious ideas at the time.

Having explored some preliminary issues, we are now in a position to engage with the Reformation. The most appropriate place to begin this encounter is by exploring the world of late medieval religion, to which we now turn.

For further reading

For useful overall views of the Reformation, see:

John Bossy, *Christianity in the West 1400–1700* (Oxford, 1987).
Euan Cameron, *The Reformation* (Oxford, 1991).
Owen Chadwick, *Pelican History of the Church*, Vol. 3: *The Reformation* (London, 1972).
A. G. Dickens and John M. Tonkin, *The Reformation in Historical Perspective* (Cambridge, Mass., 1985).
Steven E. Ozment, *The Age of Reform 1250–1550* (New Haven/London, 1973).

On the social context of the Reformation, see:

Hans Baron, 'Religion and Politics in the German Imperial Cities during the Reformation', *English Historical Review* 52 (1937), pp. 405–27, 614–33.
Basil Hall, 'The Reformation City', *Bulletin of the John Rylands Library* 54 (1971), pp. 103–48.

Berndt Moeller, *Imperial Cities and the Reformation: Three Essays* (Philadelphia, 1972).

Steven Ozment, *The Reformation in the Cities: The Appeal of Protestantism to Sixteenth-Century Germany and Switzerland* (New Haven/London, 1975).

On the impact of printing, see:

M. U. Chrisman, *Lay Culture, Learned Culture: Books and Social Change in Strasbourg, 1480–1599* (New Haven/London, 1982).

Elizabeth L. Eisenstein, *The Printing Press as an Agent of Change: Communications and Cultural Transformations in Early Modern Europe* (2 vols; New York, 1979).

For a superb collection of sixteenth-century illustrations relating to the Reformation, see:

Pierre Chaunu, *The Reformation* (Gloucester, 1989).

2

Late Medieval Religion

The backdrop to the Reformation is the late medieval period. In recent scholarship, there has been a growing emphasis upon the need to place the Reformation movement in its late medieval context and to bring together the insights of late medieval, Renaissance and Reformation studies. The separation of these fields – for example, through each having their own university chairs, journals and learned societies – has greatly hindered this process of synthesis and consolidation, essential to the correct understanding of the ideas of the Reformation. In the two chapters which follow, we shall examine in some detail the two most important intellectual forces in late medieval Europe: humanism and scholastic theology. The present chapter deals with some preliminary points about late medieval religion.

The Growth of Popular Religion

Older studies of the background to the Reformation tended to portray the later Middle Ages as a period in which religion was in decline. In part, this reflected the uncritical attitude adopted by these studies towards the literature of the fifteenth century which was critical of the church. Modern studies, using more reliable criteria, have indicated that precisely the reverse is true. Between 1450 and 1520, Germany saw a considerable increase in popular religious piety. This point was brought out with particular clarity by Berndt Moeller in an article entitled 'Piety in Germany around 1500'.[1]

Moeller drew upon a range of studies, which demonstrated that, on just about every objective criterion conceivable, there was a remarkable growth in popular religion in Germany on the eve of the Reformation. Between 1450 and 1490, the number of masses endowed by upper Austrian gentry increased steadily, reaching a peak in the period 1490–1517. The fashion grew of forming religious brotherhoods for the purpose of paying for a priest to say mass for their members when they died. These fraternities were basically poor men's chantries. Their existence was linked with a cluster of beliefs concerning death and eternity – ideas such as purgatory and the intercession of the saints. In Hamburg alone there were ninety-nine such brotherhoods on the eve of the Reformation, most of which had been established after 1450. Church building programmes flourished in the later fifteenth century, as did pilgrimages and the vogue for collecting relics. The fifteenth century has been referred to as 'the inflation-period of mystic literature' (Heiko A. Oberman), reflecting the growing popular interest in religion. And it is this popular interest in religion which led to criticism of the institutional church where it was thought to be falling short of its obligations. This criticism – treated by older studies as evidence of religious *decline* – thus actually points to religious *growth*. Interestingly, this growth in piety appears to be largely restricted to the laity; the clergy of the day show little, if any, sign of spiritual renewal. The scene was set for the rise of anti-clericalism, in that the clergy came to be seen as exploiting the new interest in religion, without contributing to it.

The Rise in Anti-Clericalism

An important aspect of fifteenth-century German religion was the phenomenon of anti-papalism and anti-clericalism.[2] One factor which contributed to anti-clericalism was the poor quality of the rank and file clergy. In Renaissance Italy, it was common for parish priests to have had virtually no training; what little they knew they gleaned from watching, helping and imitating older (though not necessarily wiser) colleagues. Diocesan visitations regularly revealed priests who were illiterate or had apparently mislaid their breviaries permanently. The poor quality of the parish clergy reflected their low social status: in early sixteenth-century Milan, chaplains had incomes lower than those of unskilled labourers. Many resorted to horse and cattle trading to make ends meet. In rural France during the same period, the lower clergy enjoyed roughly the same social status as vagabonds: their exemption from taxation, prosecution in civil courts and compulsory military service apart, they were virtually indistinguishable from other itinerant beggars of the period.

The clergy enjoyed exemption from most taxes. This exemption was the source of much popular irritation, especially in times of economic difficulty. In the French diocese of Meaux, which became a centre for reforming activists in the period 1521–46, the clergy were exempted from all forms of taxation, including charges related to the provisioning and garrisoning of troops – which provoked considerable local resentment. In the diocese of Rouen, there was a popular outcry over the windfall profits made by the church by selling grain at a period of severe shortage in the 1520s. Clerical immunity from prosecution in civil courts further isolated the clergy from the people.[3]

In France, the subsistence crises of the 1520s played a major role in the consolidation of anti-clerical attitudes. In his celebrated study of Languedoc, Le Roy Ladurie pointed out that the 1520s witnessed a reversal of the process of expansion and recovery which had been characteristic of the two genera-tions since the end of the Hundred Years War. From that point onwards, a crisis began to develop, taking the form of plague, famine, and migration of the rural poor to the cities in search of food and employment. A similar pattern has now been identified for the period in most of France north of the Loire. This subsistence crisis focused popular attention on the enormous social distance between the working class and the ecclesiastical establishment.

The vast majority of late Renaissance bishops in France were drawn from the nobility, a trend illustrated in diocese after diocese.[4] In Meaux, the higher echelons of the ecclesiastical establishment were drawn from the urban patri-ciate, as were the senior clergy throughout the Brie. A similar pattern can be established at Rouen, as it can at John Calvin's birthplace, Noyon, where the de Hangest family monopolized ecclesiastical affairs, exercising substantial powers of patronage as well as providing most of the bishops of the diocese over a period of more than a quarter of a century. In the province of Languedoc, the senior clergy were generally outsiders, often nobility imposed upon the dioceses by royal patronage. Rarely resident within their dioceses, these clergy regarded their spiritual and temporal charges as little more than sources of unearned income, useful for furthering political ambitions else-where. The noble background and status of the episcopacy and senior clergy served to distance them from the artisans and peasants and to insulate them from the economic subsistence crisis of the 1520s. It is this growing tension during the 1520s in the relationship between the senior clergy – largely based in the towns and cities – and the rural population which constitutes the back-drop to the origins of the Reformation in France.

The new emphasis upon education within humanist circles throughout much of western Europe in the 1510s and 1520s led to the ecclesiastical estab-lishment being viewed as reactionary, hostile to the new learning and threat-ened by both its progress and its emphasis upon the personal appropriation of faith. Literature began to appear in the 1520s suggesting that clergy had a vested interest in retaining the old, lax ways, which made few demands of them as teachers, as spiritual guides, or as moral examples or agents. Rabelais was not alone in exposing and deriding monastic abuses, nor was Erasmus alone in criticizing the aridness of scholasticism and the inadequacies of the clergy.

Anti-papal feelings also increased in the late Renaissance, especially in Germany. The development of this hostility towards the papacy was often linked with the perception that it was dominated by Italians. Hostility to the pope was perhaps greatest among the educated and ruling classes, who resented his interference in local ecclesiastical and political matters; hostility to the clergy was greatest among the ordinary people, especially in the towns, who resented their privileges (such as exemption from taxation) and the oppressive role often played by the clergy as landlords to the German peasants. Studies of this tradition of anti-clerical and anti-papal feeling have pointed to the existence of what might be called an 'ecclesiastical grievance literature'.[5] The list of papal and clerical abuses given by Luther in his famous reforming treatise of 1520s, *Appeal to the German Nobility*, parallels similar lists in circulation in the previous century. Luther appears to have been tapping a tradition of long-standing complaints against the church, in order to gain support for his programme of reform.

In the popular German mind, Luther and others such as Ulrich von Hutten were identified as common liberators from an oppressive church. Furthermore, there is evidence which strongly suggests that German nationalism, fanned by anti-papal and anti-Italian sentiment, reached a peak in the years 1517 to 1521. A popular mythology had developed which saw in Germany a nation chosen by God to fulfil his purposes. Although each mythology was systematically discredited by humanists in the period 1530–60, it seems that many regarded the German Reformation under Luther as divinely guided and inspired. This phenomenon was not restricted to Germany, of course; the Lollard movement in England seems to have displayed much the same characteristics, for example.

One final point must be made concerning the growth of popular religion in the later Middle Ages. In part, popular religion represented an attempt to convert the abstract ideas of theologians into something more tangible. Baptism, marriage and death became events surrounded by popular beliefs and practices – usually referred to as 'folk religion' – which, although originally derived from the textbooks of Christian theologians, often came to bear little relation to them. Popular religion usually centred on the affairs of rural communities, reflecting its rhythms and seasons. The agrarian needs of such a rural community – such as haymaking and harvesting – became firmly enmeshed in popular religious cults. Thus, in the French diocese of Meaux, religious cults arose to ward off animal and infant diseases, the plague and eye trouble, or to ensure that young women found appropriate husbands.

Perhaps the most important element of late medieval popular religion was a cluster of beliefs and practices concerning death, in which participation by a priest was indispensable. The expenses attending such cults of the dead were considerable, a fact reflected in the rise of religious fraternities dedicated to the provision of the appropriate rites of passage for their members. In times of economic hardship, anti-clerical sentiment was an inevitability, as noted earlier (p. 28); for the clergy came to be seen as profiting from the anxiety of the impoverished living concerning their dead kinsfolk. Central to these practices was the concept of purgatory, vividly portrayed by Dante in Book II of his *Divine Comedy*, which expressed the idea that the dead were required to undergo both punishment and purification for their remaining sins, before being allowed to enter into heaven. In effect, it was thought of as a sort of intermediate clearing-house for the dead as they awaited the final judgement. The idea held a particular popular fascination, as can be seen from the growth in the indulgence trade, which seemed to offer at worst an accelerated passage through purgatory and at best its avoidance altogether.

In Germany, trafficking in indulgences was viewed by Luther as a morally outrageous and theologically questionable exploitation of the natural affections of the common people for their dead. His ninety-five theses (31 October 1517) were a direct criticism of those who asserted that a dead soul might be freed instantly from purgatory on payment of an appropriate amount to an authorized ecclesiastical tradesman. For Germans, insult was added to injury in that the fees paid by them eventually found their way to Italy, to finance the extravagances of the Renaissance papacy. Luther took particular exception to the advertising copy of Johann Tetzel, promoting indulgences:

> As soon as the coin in the coffer rings
> The soul from purgatory springs!

Luther's doctrine of justification by faith alone obviated the need for purgatory and indulgences; the dead could rest in peace on account of their faith, which made them right with God, and not on account of the payment of a sweetener to the church. In France, an indulgence campaign had also been arranged by Leo X and Francis I in 1515, with a view to financing a crusade; in 1518, however, the Parisian faculty of theology protested against some of the superstitious ideas to which this campaign gave rise. It condemned as 'false and scandalous' the teaching that 'whoever puts into the collection for the crusade one teston or the value of one soul in purgatory sets that soul free immediately, and it goes unfailingly to paradise'. Yet although regarded as questionable by academic theologians, such beliefs held a deep fascination for ordinary people. An 'unofficial' theology came to develop, largely unrelated to the approved theology textbooks, but deeply rooted in the hopes and fears of society in general.

As the rift between popular belief and theology grew wider, so reform became an increasingly faint possibility. To reform popular belief by bringing it back into line with an 'official' theology presupposed agreement upon what that theology was – and, as we shall see in the following sections, the growth of doctrinal pluralism and confusion effectively ruled out this option. In the end, the reformers cut this Gordian knot by attacking both the popular beliefs and practices *and* the theology upon which they were originally, if increasingly tenuously, based, and by undertaking a massive educational programme. However, the problems facing those who wished to reform popular religion in the later Middle Ages are brought into sharp focus through the relative failure of these massive progammes of the Reformation period: folk religion and popular superstition proved virtually impossible to eradicate.

The Rise of Doctrinal Pluralism

One of the most significant features of medieval religious thought is the growth of 'schools' of theology. Just as the twentieth century witnessed the growth of the Freudian and Adlerian schools in psychoanalysis and the Barthian school in theology, so the Middle Ages saw a number of quite well-defined theological schools of thought establishing themselves. Two such schools may be noted briefly: the Thomist school, based upon the writings of Thomas Aquinas, and the Scotist school, based upon the rather different ideas found in the writings of John Duns Scotus. The Middle Ages was a period of expansion in the universities and schools of Europe. An inevitable result of this expansion was intellectual diversification. In other words, the more academics you have, the more opinions you find in circulation as a result. By the beginning of the sixteenth century, as many as nine such schools had been established within the western European church.[6]

Now each of these schools of thought had rather different understandings of a number of major questions. For example, they were split on a number of issues relating to the doctrine of justification (to which we shall return in chapter 6) – such as what the individual had to do in order to be justified. Similar divisions existed over a whole range of questions of direct importance to both personal religion and ecclesiastical politics. But which of these schools of thought was *right*? Which corresponded most closely to the offical teaching of the church? To use the appropriate technical terms, what was merely 'theological opinion', and what was 'catholic dogma'? It was clearly essential that some way of *evaluating* the reliability of the new doctrines should be brought into play. But, for reasons which we shall explore shortly, no such evaluation was undertaken. The papacy was reluctant to define, and apparently incapable of enforcing, 'true doctrine'. The result was inevitable: confusion. Private opinion and public policy became confused. Nobody could be quite sure exactly what the offical teaching of the church was on certain matters.

As one of those matters was the doctrine of justification, it is perhaps not surprising that this doctrine should have been at the centre of one major movement for reform – that associated with Martin Luther.

The practical consequences of this doctrinal vagueness are easily docu-
mented. An episode from the late Italian Renaissance will serve our purposes
well. During the first decade of the sixteenth century, a small group of young
Italian noblemen met regularly, in order to discuss matters of religion. The
members of this group shared a common concern: how to ensure the salvation of their souls. But how could this be done? What did they have to do
in order to be saved? This direct question appeared to have received no clear-
cut answer from the ecclesiastical authorities. A crisis developed within the
group, reaching its culmination in 1510. The group split into two sections.
One group, convinced that salvation could come about only by a rejection of
the world and personal denial, withdrew to a local monastery, there to work
out their salvation safe from the influences of a fallen world. The second group
chose to remain in the world. Somehow, they reasoned, it must be possible
to remain in the world, and attain salvation. But nobody was entirely sure of
the official position of the church on this major question – a question which
Luther later addressed in his doctrine of justification by faith.

Confusion over the official teaching of the church on justification contributed in no small manner to the origins of Luther's programme of reform
in Germany. The most recent known authoritative pronouncement on the part
of a recognized ecclesiastical body relating to this doctrine dated from 418,
and its confused and outdated statements did little to clarify the position of
the church on the matter in 1518, eleven hundred years later. It seemed to
Luther that the church of his day had lapsed into Pelagianism (see p. 107), an
unacceptable understanding of how an individual entered into fellowship with
God. The church, Luther believed, taught that individuals could gain favour
and acceptance in the sight of God on account of their personal achievements
and status, thus negating the whole idea of grace. Luther may well have been
mistaken in this apprehension – but there was so much confusion within the
church of his day that no one was able to enlighten him on the authoritative position of the church on the matter. Even within the papal sovereign
enclave at Avignon, an anarchy of ideas prevailed. 'Everyone has his own
opinion', wrote Boniface Amerbach, who added further to the chaos during
the 1520s by promoting the ideas of the 'excellent doctor Martin' within this
papal stronghold.

We can speak of a *spectrum* of thought within the late Middle Ages. A
remarkably wide range of doctrines was in circulation. It is all too easy for
twentieth-century writers, with the benefit of hindsight, to recognize the
potential dangers of the ideas being developed by the first reformers – but *at
the time* these ideas attracted little attention from the official defenders of

orthodoxy. The boundary lines between what was orthodox and what was not became so hopelessly confused that it was virtually impossible to treat individuals such as Luther as heretical – and by the time this move became necessary, the Reformation had gained such momentum that it proved difficult to obstruct it. The scene for a future religious confrontation was set by the doctrinal pluralism of the late medieval church.

A Crisis of Authority

A development in the later medieval period which is of central importance to a study of the Reformation is the growing crisis in authority, evident from the fourteenth century onwards. To whom or to what should someone look for an authoritative pronouncement concerning doctrine? Who was in a position to state unequivocally that 'the position of the Catholic church on *this* matter is *that*'? In a period which witnessed a remarkable growth in theological debate, it was essential that someone lay down what was mere theological speculation and what was accepted catholic doctrine. There was a widespread recognition within the church that theological speculation was legitimate – after all, academics had to do something with their spare time, and the church was sufficiently confident in the truth of its teachings to allow them to be subjected to close scrutiny. But there needed to be some means of enforcing orthodoxy (assuming, of course that 'orthodoxy' could be defined, which became increasingly doubtful as time went on). The papacy required the means of coercing those with unorthodox views to abandon them, or at least to stop teaching them.

Two major developments within the late medieval church combined to make the definition and enforcement of orthodoxy virtually impossible in the late fifteenth and early sixteenth centuries. First, the authority of the pope was called into question through the Great Schism and its aftermath. The Great Schism (1378–1417) led to the division of western Christendom on the death of Gregory XI. An Italian faction was led by Urban VI, a French faction by Clement VII. This situation continued until 1417, when the Council of Constance elected Martin V as pope. For a brief period around 1409, there were three claimants to the papacy.

The crucial question was this: how could the dispute concerning who was *really* pope be resolved? It was widely accepted that the final arbiter in all doctrinal disputes within the church was the pope – but *which* pope could settle this dispute? Eventually it was agreed that a Council should meet, with authority to settle the dispute. The Council of Constance (1414–17) was convoked to choose between the three rival candidates for the papacy (Gregory XII, Benedict XIII and John XXII). The Council conveniently resolved the matter by passing over all three, and choosing its own candidate (Martin V). It seemed that an important general principle had been established: councils have authority over the pope. But Martin V thought otherwise.

The scene was thus set for the development of two rival theories of authority within the church: those who held that supreme doctrinal authority resided in a General Council (the 'conciliarist' position) and those who argued that it resided in the person of the pope (the 'curialist' position). As the recognition of the need for reform of the church grew in the fifteenth century, the conciliarist party argued that the only hope for such reform lay in calling a reforming general council. Martin Luther reflected such a position in his 1520 *Appeal to the German Nobility*, in which he argued that the German princes had the right to convoke such a council. The failure of the conciliarist movement is generally regarded as a central cause of the Reformation, for two reasons. First, it led to hopes being raised that the church might be reformed from within – and when such hopes were dashed, many began to look for means of *imposing* reform upon the church, perhaps through an appeal to the secular authorities. Second, it posed a challenge to the doctrinal authority of the pope, thereby contributing to the theological confusion of the later medieval period. As it was not clear who held ultimate doctrinal authority, many theologians developed their theological opinions without asking too many questions concerning their authenticity.

The second major factor concerns the rise in the power of the secular rulers of Europe, who increasingly came to regard the pope's problems as of somewhat limited relevance. Moreover, the popes seem to have been reluctant to make use of the channels already available for enforcing doctrinal orthodoxy. For example, the German diocesan and provincial synods had the power to suppress heresy – but these synods were not convened when required in the early sixteenth century. The attention of many European rulers was focused initially upon the Franco-Italian war and subsequently on the Hapsburg–Valois conflict, at the time when the Reformation *could* have been forcibly suppressed, had the political will been present.

Yet the ability of the popes to call on secular rulers to enforce their religious will was ebbing away. Nationalism became an increasingly important factor in reducing papal authority north of the Alps, as the situation in France demonstrates. The dramatic victory of Francis I over the combined papal and Swiss forces at Marignano in September 1515 established him as a force to be reckoned with in Italian affairs, and enhanced his authority over the French church. The ensuing Concordat of Bologna (1516) gave Francis I the right to appoint all the senior clergy of the French church, effectively weakening the direct papal control over that church. Francis, aware of the need to enforce religious orthodoxy within his realm, delegated responsibility for this matter to the Faculty of Theology of the University of Paris – a body which soon became known simply as 'the Sorbonne'. Francis' gradual move towards absolutism, although temporarily interrupted by his defeat at the battle of Pavia (1525) and subsequent imprisonment at Madrid, led to a corresponding decrease in papal influence over French affairs, whether state or ecclesiastical.

As a result, reforming movements within France were treated as a matter concerning Francis I, rather than the pope. Had the pope wished to intervene in the affairs of the French church, a formidable series of diplomatic and legal obstacles awaited him. Having just defeated the pope in battle, Francis showed relatively little interest in defending papal interests in France, save when they happened to coincide with those of the French monarchy.

A further illustration of the severe restrictions placed upon papal authority by secular rulers can be seen in the case of Henry VIII's attempt to divorce Catherine of Aragon. At the time when Henry petitioned the pope for a divorce (which would normally have been forthcoming without undue difficulty), the pope found himself under enormous pressure from the emperor Charles V – who happened to be related to Catherine of Aragon. As Charles had recently sacked Rome and retained a large military presence in the region, the pope was faced with the choice of offending either the king (who had not, and was never likely to have, armies anywhere near Rome) or the emperor (who had such armies, and was perfectly prepared to use them). The outcome was a foregone conclusion. Henry VIII did not get his divorce.

There was thus a twofold crisis of authority in the later medieval church. There was obvious confusion concerning the nature, location and manner of exercise of *theological* authority, just as there was either a reluctance or an inability to exercise the *political* authority required to suppress the new ideas of the Reformation. In the midst of this ecclesiastical confusion and powerlessness, the Reformation proceeded with increasing pace, until its local suppression was no longer a realistic possibility.

An English Case Study: Lollardy

The Reformation did not bring a church into being from nowhere; throughout Europe, it built upon existing foundations. It is increasingly being recognized that the English Reformation rests on Lollard foundations. Lollardy is therefore included in this analysis of late medieval religion as a single case study, illustrating the way in which elements of popular religion contributed towards the origins and shaping of a local reformation.

Recent studies have demonstrated the complexity of Lollardy, making generalizations concerning its basic beliefs considerably more hazardous that was once the case. For example, although some Lollards were opposed to the idea of purgatory, most appear to have been content to allow it to remain; serious opposition to the concept in England appears to have gained momentum only with the execution of John Frith over the question in 1533. However, a cluster of basic attitudes which appear to have been widespread within the movement can be summarized as follows. Lollards, in general, believed that:

1 The Bible ought to be available in the vernacular.
2 The veneration of images is unacceptable.
3 The practice of pilgrimage is open to serious criticism.
4 Every layperson is a priest.
5 The pope exercises excessive authority.
6 Christ's presence in the communion bread is purely spiritual (as opposed to the medieval doctrine of transubstantiation; see p. 195).

In one sense, this list of beliefs could be argued to be little more than a form of grievance literature. Yet it points to certain attitudes, prevalent within Lollard circles, which gave rise to an enhanced stage of receptivity towards Lutheran ideas when these began to make their appearance in England in the 1520s. For Lutheran doctrines resonated with these attitudes. For example, Luther's doctrine of the 'priesthood of all believers' was consonant with the Lollard dislike of priests and the Lollard belief that all the laity had a right to call themselves priests. Similarly, the Lutheran doctrine of justification by faith seemed (at least, to the Lollards) to imply that there was no longer any need for popes, priests or the institutional church – all of which they cordially detested – in the process of salvation. Each individual could make peace with God, without dragging the detested ecclesiastical hierarchy into the matter.

Movements similar to Lollardy appear to have existed in many parts of Europe, providing fertile seed-beds in which the ideas of the Reformation could germinate and take root. The Lollards developed nothing like the sophisticated doctrines of the priesthood of all believers or justification by faith alone. At best, they were possessed of attitudes, or a general outlook, which was severely critical of the church of their day. But Lutheran ideas, when they came, made a lot of sense to Lollardy. They resonated with these attitudes, reinforced their arguments, adding intellectual sophistication to Lollard enthusiasm and giving a new theological foundation to their criticisms of the English church.

This, then, is a brief overview of the pressures building up within the late medieval church. Instability was on the increase. It is clear that some kind of shake-up was inevitable. In the end, it took the form of the Reformation, as we now know it. A significant additional element within this process of desta-bilization of existing medieval religious beliefs and practices was the rise of Renaissance humanism. It was not long before the new methods of human-ism were raising serious questions about aspects of medieval doctrine. We shall explore this development in the following chapter.

For further reading

The following works offer good surveys of European culture and society around the time of the Reformation:

B. Moeller, *Imperial Cities and the Reformation: Three Essays* (Philadelphia, 1972).

K. von Greyerz (ed.), *Religion and Society in Early Modern Europe 1500–1800* (London, 1984).

E. I. Kouri and T. Scott (eds), *Politics and Society in Reformation Europe* (London, 1987).

F. Oakley, *The Western Church in the Later Middle Ages* (Ithaca, NY, 1979).

S. E. Ozment, *The Age of Reform 1250–1550: An Intellectual and Religious History of Late Medieval and Reformation Europe* (New Haven, CT, 1980).

For an excellent survey of recent literature on religion in the late Middle Ages, see:

F. Oakley, 'Religious and Ecclesiastical Life on the Eve of the Reformation', in *Reformation Europe: A Guide to Research,* ed. Steven Ozment (St Louis, 1982), pp. 5–32.

On anti-clericalism, see:

H. J. Cohn, 'Anti-Clericalism in the German Peasants' War 1525', *Past and Present* 83 (1979), pp. 3–31.

C. Haigh, 'Anticlericalism and the English Reformation', *History* 68 (1973), pp. 391–407.

R. N. Swanson, *Church and Society in Late Medieval England* (Oxford, 1989).

For the importance of doctrinal diversity in the later Middle Ages, see:

Alister E. McGrath, *The Intellectual Origins of the European Reformation* (Oxford, 1987), pp. 9–31.

Jaroslav Pelikan, *The Christian Tradition: A History of the Development of Doctrine. 4. Reformation of Church and Dogma (1300–1700)* (Chicago/London, 1984), pp. 10–22.

On Lollardy, see:

M. Aston, *Lollards and Reformers: Images and Literacy in Late Medieval Religion* (London, 1984).

J. F. Davis, 'Lollardy and the Reformation in England', *Archiv für Reformationsgeschichte* 73 (1982), pp. 217–37.

A. Hudson, *The Premature Reformation: Wycliffite Texts and Lollard History* (Oxford, 1988).

K. B. McFarlane, *Lancastrian Kings and Lollard Knights* (Oxford, 1972).

3

Humanism and
the Reformation

Of the many tributaries which contributed to the flow of the Reformation, by far the most important was Renaissance humanism. Although the Reformation began in the cities of Germany and Switzerland, there are excellent reasons for suggesting that it may well have been the inevitable outcome of developments in fourteenth-century Italy as the movement we now know as the 'Italian Renaissance' gained momentum. The present chapter will survey the ideas and methods of Renaissance humanism, in order that their relevance to the Reformation may be understood.

When the word 'humanism' is used by a twentieth-century writer, we are usually meant to understand an anti-religious philosophy which affirms the dignity of humanity without any reference to God. "Humanism' has acquired very strongly secularist – perhaps even atheist – overtones. But in the sixteenth century, the word 'humanist' had a quite different meaning, as we shall see shortly. Humanists of the fourteenth, fifteenth or sixteenth centuries were remarkably religious, if anything concerned with the *renewal* rather than the *abolition* of the Christian church. The reader, then, is asked to set aside the modern sense of the word 'humanism' in preparing to meet this phenomenon in its late Renaissance setting.

One important terminological point must also be made before beginning our discussion of humanism and the Renaissance as they relate to the Reformation. The reader is likely to encounter reference, even in English-language works, to the Italian terms *Trecènto, Quattrocènto* and *Cinquecènto* (often with the accent omitted). These refer, respectively, to the 1300s, the 1400s and the 1500s – in other words, to the *fourteenth, fifteenth* and *sixteenth* centuries. Similarly, a *quattrocentísta* is a fifteenth-century figure, and a *cinquecentísta* a sixteenth-century figure. Many English-speaking readers wrongly assume that the *Quattrocènto* is the *fourteenth* century, and find themselves hopelessly confused as a result.

The Concept of 'Renaissance'

Although the French term 'Renaissance' is now universally used to designate
the literary and artistic revival in fourteenth- and fifteenth-century Italy, contemporary writers tended to refer to the movement by means of other terms:
'restoration', 'revival', 'awakening' and 're-flowering'.[1] ('Italy', of course, here
designates a geographical rather than a political entity.) In 1546 Paolo Giovio
referred to the fourteenth century as 'that happy century in which Latin letters
are conceived to have been reborn (*renatae*)', anticipating this development.
Certain historians, most notably Jacob Burckhardt, have argued that the
Renaissance gave birth to the modern era. It was in this era, Burckhardt
argued, that human beings first began to think of themselves as *individuals*.
The communal consciousness of the medieval period gave way to the individual consciousness of the Renaissance. Florence became the new Athens,
the intellectual capital of a brave new world, with the river Arno separating
the old and the new worlds.[2]

In many ways, Burckhardt's definition of the Renaissance in purely indi-
vidualist terms is highly questionable, in view of powerful evidence for the
strongly collective values of aspects of Italian Renaissance humanism – for
example, a collective approach to city life (seen in Florentine civic humanism), to politics (for example, the *parte Guelfa*), to commerce (seen in the wool
guild) and to family life. But in one sense, Burckhardt is unquestionably
correct: *something* novel and exciting developed in Renaissance Italy, which
proved capable of exercising a fascination over generations of thinkers.

It is not entirely clear why Italy in general, or Florence in particular, became
the cradle of this brilliant new movement in the history of ideas. A number
of factors have been identified as having some bearing on the question:

1   Italy was saturated with visible and tangible reminders of the great-
    ness of antiquity. The ruins of ancient Roman buildings and mon-
    uments were scattered throughout the land. As Roberto Weiss points
    out in his *Renaissance Discovery of Classical Antiquity*, these ruins rep-
    resented vital links with a great past. They appear to have kindled
    interest in the civilization of ancient Rome at the time of the
    Renaissance, and acted as a vital stimulus to its thinkers to recover
    the vitality of classical Roman culture at a time which they regarded
    as being culturally arid and barren.
2   Scholastic theology – the major intellectual force of the medieval
    period – was never particularly influential in Italy. Although many
    Italians achieved fame as theologians (such as Thomas Aquinas and

Gregory of Rimini), they were generally active in the universities of northern Europe. There was thus an intellectual vacuum in Italy during the fourteenth century. Vacuums tend to be filled – and it was Renaissance humanism which filled this particular gap.

3 The political stability of Florence depended upon the maintenance of her republican government. It was thus natural to turn to the study of the Roman Republic, including its literature and culture, as a model for Florence.

4 The economic prosperity of Florence created leisure, and hence a demand for literature and the arts. Patronage of culture and the arts was seen as a suitable use for surplus wealth.[3]

5 As Byzantium began to crumble – Constantinople finally fell in 1453 – there was an exodus of Greek-speaking intellectuals westward. Italy happened to be conveniently close to Constantinople, with the result that many such emigrés settled in her cities. A revival of the Greek language was thus inevitable, and with it a revival of interest in the Greek classics.

The Concept of 'Humanism'

The term 'humanism' is a nineteenth-century invention. The German word *Humanismus* was first coined in 1808, to refer to a form of education which placed emphasis on the Greek and Latin classics. In English, the word 'humanism' began to appear somewhat later. Its first recorded appearance dates from the writings of Samuel Coleridge Taylor (1812), in which it is used to designate a Christological position – the belief that Jesus Christ was purely human. The word is first used in its cultural sense in 1832.

It is important to appreciate that the term 'humanism' was not used at the time of the Renaissance itself, although we find frequent use of the Italian word *umanista*. This word refers to a university teacher of *studia humanitatis* – 'human studies', or 'liberal arts', such as poetry, grammar and rhetoric.[4] (The English word 'humanist', which first appears in 1589, has the sense of 'a literary scholar, especially someone versed in Latin studies'.) The observation that the word 'humanism' dates from so late suggests that Renaissance writers themselves did not recognize the existence of a common outlook or worldview known by this name. Modern readers tend to assume that 'humanists' were individuals who subscribed to a common body of beliefs, attitudes and values known as 'humanism', in much the same way as Marxists are individuals who subscribe to Marxism. Yet there is little historical evidence for this assumption. As we shall see, it proves remarkably difficult to define what this common body of beliefs, attitudes and values was.

This present section is chiefly concerned with the problem of defining humanism. The term is still used widely in Renaissance and Reformation studies, often with an irritating degree of fluidity. What is meant by the term 'humanism'? In the recent past, two major lines of interpretation of the movement were predominant. First, humanism was viewed as a movement devoted to classical scholarship and philology. Second, humanism was the new philosophy of the Renaissance. As will become clear, both these interpretations of humanism have serious shortcomings.

Classical Scholarship and Philology

It is beyond doubt that the Renaissance witnessed the rise of classical scholarship. The Greek and Latin classics were widely studied in their original languages. Although some early studies suggested that humanism originated outside a university context, the evidence now available points unquestionably to a close link between humanism and the universities of northern Italy. It might therefore seem that humanism was essentially a scholarly movement devoted to the study of the classical period. This, however, would be to overlook the question of *why* the humanists wished to study the classics in the first place. The evidence available makes it clear that such study was regarded as *a means to an end*, rather than *an end in itself*. That end was the promotion of contemporary written and spoken eloquence.[5] In other words, the humanists studied the classics as models of written eloquence, in order to gain inspiration and instruction. Classical learning and philological competence were simply the tools used to exploit the resources of antiquity. As has often been pointed out, the writings of the humanists devoted to the promotion of eloquence, written or spoken, far exceed those devoted to classical scholarship or philology.

The New Philosophy of the Renaissance

According to several recent interpreters of humanism, the movement embodied the new philosophy of the Renaissance, which arose as a reaction to scholasticism. Thus it was argued that the Renaissance was an age of Platonism, whereas scholasticism was a period of Aristotelianism. Others argued that the Renaissance was essentially an anti-religious phenomenon, foreshadowing the secularism of the eighteenth-century Enlightenment. Hans Baron has argued that humanism was basically a republican movement, which studied Cicero in order to benefit from his political ideas.[6]

Two major difficulties confronted these rather ambitious interpretation of humanism. First, as we have seen, humanists appear to have been primarily concerned with the promotion of eloquence. While it is not true to say that humanists made no significant contribution to philosophy, the fact remains that they were primarily interested in the world of letters. Thus in comparison with those devoted to the 'pursuit of eloquence', there are remarkably few humanist writings devoted to philosophy – and these are generally somewhat amateurish. Baron's theory concerning the humanist use of Cicero was weakened through the observation that most humanists read Cicero to learn from his style of writing, rather than from his political ideas.[7]

Second, intensive study of humanist writings uncovered the disquieting fact that 'humanism' was remarkably heterogeneous. For example, many humanist writers did indeed favour Platonism – but others favoured Aristotelianism. The stubborn persistence of Aristotelianism (for example, at the University of Padua) throughout the Renaissance is a serious obstacle to those who regard humanism as philosophically homogeneous. Some Italian humanists did indeed display what seem to be anti-religious attitudes – but other Italian humanists were profoundly pious. Some humanists were indeed republicans – but others adopted different political attitudes. Recent studies have also drawn attention to a less attractive side of humanism – the obsession of some humanists with magic and superstition – which is difficult to harmonize with the conventional view of the movement. In short, it has become increasingly clear that 'humanism' lacked any coherent philosophy. No single philosophical or political idea dominated or characterized the movement. Indeed, it seemed to many that the term 'humanism' would have to be dropped from the vocabulary of historians, because it had no meaningful content. Designating a writer a 'humanist' conveys no essential information concerning his philosophical, political or religious views.

In fact, it is clear that the Italian Renaissance is so multi-faceted that just about every generalization concerning its 'characteristic ideas' tends to be a distortion. It is for this reason that the view of humanism developed by Paul Oskar Kristeller is of decisive importance. Kristeller's view of humanism has gained wide acceptance within North American and European scholarship, and has yet to be discredited.

Kristeller's View of Humanism

Kristeller envisages humanism as a cultural and educational movement, primarily concerned with the promotion of eloquence in its various forms. Its interest in morals, philosophy and politics is of secondary importance. To be a humanist is to be concerned with eloquence first and foremost, and with other matters incidentally. Humanism was essentially a cultural programme, which appealed to classical antiquity as a model of eloquence. In art and architecture, as in the written and spoken word, antiquity was seen as a cultural resource, which could be appropriated by the Renaissance. Petrarch referred to Cicero as his father and Virgil as his brother. The architects of the *Quattrocènto* studiously ignored the Gothic style of northern Europe, in order to return to the classical styles of antiquity. Cicero was studied as an orator, rather than a political or moral writer.

In short, humanism was concerned with *how ideas were obtained and expressed*, rather than with *the actual substance of those ideas*. A humanist might be a Platonist or an Aristotelian – but in either case, the ideas involved derived from antiquity. A humanist might be a sceptic or a religious believer – but both attitudes could be defended from antiquity. The enormous attractiveness of Kristeller's view of humanism derives from the fact that it accounts brilliantly for the remarkable diversity of the Renaissance. Where Baron identifies one set of ideas as central and Burckhardt another, Kristeller points to the way in which ideas were generated and handled as being central. The diversity of *ideas* which is so characteristic of Renaissance humanism is based upon a general consensus concerning *how to derive and express those ideas*.

It will be obvious that any discussion of the relation of humanism to the Reformation will be totally dependent upon the definition of humanism employed. Kristeller's definition of humanism allows the most reliable assessment of the relation of these two movements now available.

Ad fontes – Back to the Sources

The literary and cultural programme of humanism can be summarized in the slogan *ad fontes* – back to the original sources. The squalor of the medieval period is bypassed, in order to recover the intellectual and artistic glories of the classical period. The 'filter' of medieval commentaries – whether on legal texts or on the Bible – is abandoned, in order to engage directly with the original texts. Applied to the Christian church, the slogan *ad fontes* meant a direct return to the title-deeds of Christianity – the patristic writers and, supremely, the Bible.

The slogan, however, does more than specify the sources to be used in the rebirth of civilization. It also specifies the attitude to be adopted towards those sources. It is necessary to remember that the Renaissance was an era of discovery, both geographical and scientific. The discovery of the Americas fired the imagination of the late Renaissance, as did new insights into the functioning of the human body and the natural world. Likewise, the classical sources were read with a view to rediscovering the experiences they reflected. In his *Aeneid*, Virgil described the discovery of new and strange lands; so late Renaissance readers approached Virgil with a sense of expectation, for they too were in the process of discovering *terrae incognitae*. Galen was read in a new light: he described the gaining of physiological insights to a generation engaged in a similar search in their own day and age. And so it was also with Scripture. The New Testament described the encounters of believers with the risen Christ – and late Renaissance readers approached the text of Scripture with the expectation that they too could meet the risen Christ, a meeting which seemed to be denied to them by the church of their day.

This point is often overlooked, but holds the key to the humanist reverence for ancient texts. For the humanists, classical texts mediated an experience to posterity – an experience which could be regained by handling the text in the right way. The new philological and literary methods developed by the thinkers of the Renaissance were thus seen as a way of recapturing the vitality of the classical period. For the Christian church, this opened up a new, exciting and challenging possibility – that the experience of the first Christians, described in the New Testament, could be regained and transferred to a much later point in history. It is this factor, perhaps more than any other, which helps to explain the remarkably high regard in which humanists were held in Reforming circles throughout Europe. It seemed to many that the sterile form of Christianity associated with the Middle Ages could be replaced with a new, vital and dynamic form, through the study of Scripture. *Ad fontes* was more than a slogan: it was a lifeline to those who despaired of the state of the late medieval church. The Apostolic era, the Golden Age of the church, could once more become a present reality.

It is perhaps difficult for some modern readers to empathize with this sense of excitement and anticipation. Yet to enter into the thought-world of Europe on the eve of the Reformation, we must try to recapture this sense of expectation. To many individuals and groups throughout Europe, it seemed that a new day in the history of the church was about to dawn, in which the risen Christ would be restored to the church. It seemed to many, such as Luther, that God in his providence had given the church the key (in the new humanist textual and philological tools) by which the New Testament experience of Christ could be unlocked and made available.

Northern European Humanism

At this point, we must pause to clarify one important point. The 'humanism' which affected the Reformation is primarily *northern European humanism*, rather than *Italian* humanism. We must therefore consider what form this northern European movement took.

The Northern European Reception of the Italian Renaissance

It is becoming increasingly clear that northern European humanism was decisively influenced by Italian humanism at every stage of its development. If there were indigenous humanist movements in northern Europe which originated independently of their Italian counterpart (which is very doubtful), the evidence unambiguously points to those movements having subsequently been decisively influenced by Italian humanism. This does not mean that northern humanists simply took over Italian ideals in their totality; rather, these ideals were adopted and adapted, as they seemed to relate to the northern situation. Thus the civic humanism associated with, for example, the city of Florence was not adopted extensively in northern Europe, except in a few German and Swiss cities.

Three main channels for the diffusion of the methods and ideals of the Italian Renaissance into northern Europe have been identified.

1 Northern European scholars moving south to Italy, perhaps to study at an Italian university or as part of a diplomatic mission. On returning to their homeland, they brought the spirit of the Renaissance back with them. An excellent example of this is provided by Christoph Scheurl, who studied law at Bologna before returning to the newly founded University of Wittenberg with a doctorate of law and a love of letters. This latter soon expressed itself in major reforms of the curriculum at Wittenberg, which may have been of importance in attracting Martin Luther to teach there.

2 The foreign correspondence of the Italian humanists. Humanism was concerned with the promotion of written eloquence, and the writing of letters was seen as a means of embodying and spreading the ideals of the Renaissance. The foreign correspondence of Italian humanists was considerable, extending to most parts of northern Europe.

3 Printed books, originating from sources such as the Aldine Press in Venice. These works were often reprinted by northern European

presses, particularly those at Basle in Switzerland. Italian humanists often dedicated their works to northern European patrons, thus ensuring that they were taken notice of in potentially influential quarters. The university library at Wittenberg is known to have possessed significant holdings of humanist writings, many personally dedicated to Frederick the Wise.

The Ideals of Northern European Humanism

Although there were major variations within northern European humanism, three ideals seem to have achieved widespread acceptance throughout the movement. First, we find the same concern for *bonae litterae* – written and spoken eloquence, after the fashion of the classical period – as in the Italian Reformation. Second, we find a religious programme directed towards the corporate revival of the Christian church. The Latin slogan *Christianismus renascens*, 'Christianity being born again', summarizes the aims of this programme, and indicates its relation to the 'rebirth' of letters associated with the Renaissance. Although Burckhardt is unquestionably right to state that the Renaissance led to a new emphasis on the subjective consciousness of the individual, northern European humanists supplemented this new emphasis on the individual with a recognition of the need to reform the communities (both church and state) to which the individual belonged. It is worth noting at this point that the Renaissance emphasis upon the subjective consciousness of the individual is specifically linked with the doctrine of justification by faith, to which we shall return in chapter 6. Third, some sections of northern European humanism adopted strongly pacifist attitudes during the early sixteenth century, largely in reaction to the tragedy of the Franco-Italian war. The quest for international peace and mutual understanding was espoused by most humanists at the time, particularly in Switzerland. Distaste for papal political manœuvring was also an important element in the background to the Swiss Reformation.

Eastern Swiss Humanism

Perhaps on account of its geographical position, eastern Switzerland proved especially receptive to the ideas of the Italian Renaissance. The University of Vienna attracted large numbers of students from this region. A palace revolution within the faculty of arts, engineered largely through the influence of Konrad Celtis, ensured that Vienna became a centre of humanist learning in the final years of the fifteenth century, attracting individuals such as the great humanist writer Joachim von Watt, alias Vadian. Vadian, having gained every academic honour possible at Vienna, returned to his native town of St Gallen, becoming its leading citizen (*Burgomeister*) in 1529. The University of Basel achieved a similar reputation in the 1510s, and became the centre of a humanist group (usually known as a 'sodality'), which gathered around such individuals as Thomas Wyttenbach.

Eastern Swiss humanism has been the subject of intensive study, and its basic ethos is fairly well understood. For its leading representatives – Vadian, Xylotectus, Beatus Rhenanus, Glarean and Myconius – Christianity was primarily a way of life, rather than a set of doctrines. They saw reform as indeed needed – but reform related primarily to the morality of the church and to personal moral renewal of individual believers. There was no pressure for a reform of church doctrine.[8]

The ethos of Swiss humanism was strongly moralistic, Scripture being regarded as prescribing correct moral behaviour for Christians, rather than narrating the promises of God. This ethos has a number of significant implications, especially in relation to the doctrine of justification (see pp. 122–4). In the first place, the questions which stimulated Luther's concern for the doctrine were quite absent from Swiss circles, in which justification was something of a non-issue. Second, as it became an issue in Germany, a certain degree of anxiety developed within Swiss humanist circles in the 1520s about Luther's doctrine of justification. To the Swiss humanists, Luther seemed to be developing ideas which were a radical threat to morality, and thus to the distinctive ethos of their movement.

These observations are important in relation to Huldrych Zwingli, educated at the universities of Vienna (1498–1502) and Basel (1502–06). Zwingli's programme of reform at Zurich, initiated in 1519, bears the hallmark of Swiss humanist moralism. Augustine, the 'doctor of grace', does not appear to figure prominently in Zwingli's thought until the 1520s (and even then, his influence relates primarily to Zwingli's sacramental thinking). Eventually Zwingli broke with the moralism of Swiss humanism (probably around 1523, certainly by 1525), but until this point his programme of reform was based upon the moralist educational outlook so characteristic of Swiss humanist sodalities of the period.

French Legal Humanism

In early sixteenth-century France, the study of law was in the process of radical revision. The absolutist French monarchy under Francis I, with its increasing trend towards administrative centralization, regarded legal reform as essential to the modernization of France. In order to speed up the process of legal reform, which eventually led to the formulation of a legal system universally valid throughout France, it patronized a group of scholars, centred on the universities of Bourges and Orléans, engaged in studying the theoretical aspects of general codes of law founded on universal principles. A pioneer among these was Guillaume Budé, who argued for a direct return to Roman law, which was both eloquent and economic, as a means of meeting the new legal needs of France. In contrast with the Italian custom (*mos italicus*) of reading classical legal texts in the light of the glosses (annotations to the text) and commentaries of medieval jurists such as Bartholis and Accursius, the French developed the procedure (*mos gallicus*) of appealing directly to the original classical legal sources in their original languages.

One direct result of the humanist programme of proceeding directly *ad fontes* was a marked impatience with glosses and commentaries. Far from being viewed as useful study tools, these increasingly became regarded as obstacles to engagement with the original text. The interpretations of classical Roman legal texts by writers like Bartholis and Accursius came to be seen as irrelevant. They were like distorting filters, placed between the reader and the text. As humanist scholarship became more confident in its assertions, the reliability of Accursius and others was increasingly called into question by legal humanists. The great Spanish scholar Antonio Nebrija published a detailed account of errors he had detected in Accursius' glosses, while Rabelais wrote scornfully of 'the inept opinions of Accursius'. The foundations of French legal humanism had been well and truly laid.

The importance of this development to the Reformation must be noted. One student at Bourges and Orléans during the heyday of French legal humanism was the future reformer John Calvin, who probably arrived at Orléans in 1528. Through studying civil law at Orléans and Bourges, Calvin came into first-hand contact with a major constituent element of the humanist movement. This encounter turned Calvin into a competent lawyer: when he was subsequently called upon to assist with the codification of the 'laws and edicts' of Geneva, he was able to draw on his knowledge of the *Corpus iuris civilis* for models of contract, property law and judicial procedure. But Calvin learned more than this from French legal humanism.

Budé's literary output points to his conviction not merely that the classical heritage, including its legal institutions and codes, was laden with importance for the present, but also that the study of antiquity is a proper preparation for the gospel of Jesus Christ. Calvin would adopt a similar approach in the great 1559 edition of the *Institutes of the Christian Religion*, allowing Cicero to guide the reader from the natural religion of antiquity towards the superior gospel of Jesus Christ.

The origins of the methods of Calvin, who was perhaps the greatest biblical commentator and preacher of his age, may be argued to lie in his study of law in the advanced atmosphere of Orléans and Bourges. There is every indication that Calvin learned from Budé the need to be a competent philologist, to approach a foundational text directly, to interpret it within the linguistic and historical parameters of its context, and to apply it to the situation of his own day. It is precisely this attitude which undergirds Calvin's exposition of Scripture, especially in his sermons, in which he aims to fuse the horizons of Scripture and the context of his audience. French legal humanism gave Calvin both the incentive and the tools to allow the documents of yesteryear to interact with the circumstances of the city of Geneva in the 1550s.

English Humanism

Three major religious and intellectual elements may be argued to lie behind the English Reformation: Lollardy (see pp. 35–7), Lutheranism and humanism. Each of these elements has been regarded as of central importance by Reformation scholars: for example, Gordon Rupp has argued for the decisive influence of Lutheranism, J. K. McConica for that of humanism, and Donald Smeeton for that of Lollardy. Whatever the eventual outcome of this debate may prove to be, it is clear that each of these three elements was involved, at least to some extent, in the generation of pressure for religious and theological change in England in the 1520s and 1530s. Our concern here is with the form of humanism that proved to be so influential in this debate.

Perhaps the most important centre of humanism in early sixteenth-century England was the University of Cambridge, although the importance of Oxford and London must not be underestimated. Cambridge was the home of the early English Reformation, which centred on the 'White Horse Circle' (named after a now demolished tavern close to Queen's College), a group of individuals such as Robert Barnes who met to devour and discuss the latest writings of Martin Luther during the early 1520s. It was only to be expected that the tavern would soon be nicknamed 'little Germany', just as the King Street area – once home of Cambridge's Communist Party – came to be known as 'little Moscow' during the 1930s.

Since the publication of Frederick Seebohm's *Oxford Reformers* (1867), it has become part of the received tradition of English intellectual history to refer to the flowering of humanism at Cambridge and elsewhere as 'the new learning'. However, contemporary sources suggest that this phrase was used in the 1530s to refer to the ideas of early Protestantism. Thus Hugh Latimer's letter to William Huberdin (1531) refers to the 'new learning' made available to the English church through the activities of the Protestant reformers.

English humanism, far from being an indigenous movement, was, to all intents and purposes, a foreign import. Roberto Weiss has demonstrated beyond reasonable doubt that the origins of English humanism may be traced to fifteenth-century Italy. Poggio Bracciolini visited England in the 1430s, and was followed by a succession of Italian Renaissance thinkers. The University of Cambridge was prone to employ Italians – amongst whose numbers we may note Gaio Auberino, Stefano Surigone and Lorenzo Traversagni – in the late fifteenth and early sixteenth centuries, not on account of any shortage of native English teachers, but on account of the acknowledged excellence of their Italian counterparts. Traversagni, a Franciscan friar from Savarona, delivered what appear to have been very well received lectures on rhetoric at Cambridge, which (by popular demand, we are told) soon appeared in print.

But the traffic of personnel was not unidirectional. Noted English scholars travelled to Italy to absorb the spirit of the Renaissance at first hand. John Gunthorpe and William Selling are early examples of this trend; their Italian peregrinations, dating from the first half of the fifteenth century, set the pattern for those of countless others over the next century. Having imbibed the spirit of Italian humanism, it was inevitable that they should propagate its ideals on their return to England.

Perhaps one appointment in Renaissance Cambridge stands out above all others as a witness to the receptivity of England to Renaissance ideas. In 1511, a noted humanist writer from the Lowlands was appointed to a university lectureship in divinity, which had recently been established by Lady Margaret Beaufort (the centre of a circle of reformist devotion in the early sixteenth century). His name was Erasmus.

Erasmus of Rotterdam

If any figure stands head and shoulders above other northern European humanists, not least in terms of his influence upon both the German and the Swiss reformations, it was Erasmus of Rotterdam. Although the direct influence of Erasmus upon Luther and Calvin is less than might be expected, many other reformers (such as Zwingli and Bucer) were heavily influenced by him. It is therefore essential that his considerable contribution to the thought of the Reformation be considered in some detail.

But first, one point should be noted. Erasmus is often presented as reflecting northern European humanism at its best. While there is much that could be said in support of this suggestion, certain tensions within northern European humanism must be recognized. Two are of particular interest: one concerning the question of national languages, the other concerning the question of national boundaries. As regards language, Erasmus regarded himself as a 'citizen of the world' and Ciceronian Latin as the language of that world. National languages were an obstacle to his vision of a cosmopolitan Europe united by the Latin language. To other humanists, especially in Germany and Switzerland, national languages were to be encouraged as promoting a sense of national identity. For Erasmus, however, the vision of a cosmopolitan Europe was threatened by nationalism, which only served to reinforce out-dated concepts such as a 'sense of national identity' and associated ideas such as national boundaries. Other humanists, by contrast saw themselves as engaged in a struggle to *promote* national identity. Where Erasmus would have preferred to concentrate upon *eliminating* nationalist ideas and values, the Swiss human-ists Glarean, Myconius and Xylotectus saw themselves as having a sacred duty to defend Swiss national identity and culture by literary means. This tension between the 'cosmopolitan' and 'nationalist' humanist visions, between those wishing to *abolish* and those wishing to *consolidate* national identities, reflects the conflicting views current within humanism: it also demonstrates that Erasmus cannot be regarded as a totally representative spokesman for human-ism, as some scholars suggest.

The most influential humanist work to circulate in Europe during the first decades of the sixteenth century was Erasmus' *Enchiridion militis Christiani* ('Handbook of the Christian Soldier').[9] Although the work was first published in 1503, and was then reprinted in 1509, the real impact of the work dates from its third printing in 1515. From that moment onwards, it became a cult work, apparently going through twenty-three editions in the next six years. Its appeal was to educated lay men and women, whom Erasmus regarded as the most important resource that the church possessed. Its amazing popular-ity in the years after 1515 suggests that a radical alteration in lay self-perception may have taken place as a result – and it can hardly be overlooked that the reforming rumbles at Zurich and Wittenberg date from soon after the *Enchiridion* became a best-seller. Erasmus' success also highlighted the importance of printing as a means of disseminating radical new ideas – a point which neither Zwingli nor Luther overlooked, when their turn came to prop-agate such ideas.

The *Enchiridion* developed the attractive thesis that the church of the day could be reformed by a collective return to the writings of the Fathers and Scripture. The regular reading of Scripture is put forward as the key to a new lay piety, on the basis of which the church may be renewed and reformed. Erasmus conceived of his work as a lay person's guide to Scripture; it pro-vided a simple yet learned exposition of the 'philosophy of Christ'. This 'phi-losophy' was really a form of practical morality, rather than an academic philosophy; the New Testament concerns the knowledge of good and evil, in order that its readers may eschew the latter and love the former. The New Testament is the *lex Christi*, 'the law of Christ', which Christians are called to obey. Christ is the example whom Christians are called to imitate. Yet Erasmus does not understand Christian faith to be mere external observance of some kind of morality. His characteristically humanist emphasis upon inner religion leads him to suggest that reading of Scripture *transforms* its readers, giving them a new motivation to love God and their neighbours.

A number of features of this book are of particular importance. First, Erasmus understands the future vitality of Christianity to lie with the laity, not the clergy. The clergy are seen as educators, whose function is to allow the laity to achieve the same level of understanding as themselves. There is no room for any superstitions which give the clergy a permanent status superior to that of their lay charges. Second, Erasmus' strong emphasis on inner religion results in an understanding of Christianity which makes no reference to the church – its rites, its priests or its institutions. Why bother confessing sins to another human being, asks Erasmus, just because he's a priest, when you can confess them directly to God himself? Religion is a matter of the individual's heart and mind; it is an inward state. Erasmus pointedly avoids any significant reference to the sacraments in his exposition of Christian living. Similarly, he discounts the view that the 'religious life' (in other words, that of a monk or a nun) is the highest form of the Christian life: the lay person who reads Scripture is just as faithful to his or her calling as any monk.

The revolutionary character of Erasmus' *Enchiridion* lies in its daring new suggestion that the recognition of the Christian vocation of the lay person holds the key to the revival of the church. Clerical and ecclesiastical authority is discounted. Scripture should and must be made available to all, in order that all may return *ad fontes*, to drink of the fresh and living waters of the Christian faith, rather than the stagnant ponds of late medieval religion.

Erasmus came to recognize, however, that there were serious obstacles in the path of the course he proposed, and he was responsible for a number of major developments to remove them. First, there was a need to be able to study the New Testament in its original language, rather than in the inaccurate Vulgate translation. This required two tools, neither of which was then available: the necessary philological competence to handle the Greek text of the New Testament and direct access to that text itself.

The first tool became available through Erasmus' discovery of Lorenzo Valla's fifteenth-century notes on the Greek text of the New Testament. These notes, which had languished in the archives of a local monastery, were discovered and published by Erasmus in 1505. The second was made available through the publication by Erasmus of the first printed Greek New Testament, the *Novum Instrumentum omne*, which rolled off Froben's presses at Basle in 1516. Although a superior version of the same text had been set up in type at Alcalá in Spain two years earlier, publication of this version (the so-called Complutensian Polyglot) was delayed, probably for political reasons, until 1520. Erasmus' text was not as reliable as it ought to have been: Erasmus had access to a mere four manuscripts for most of the New Testament and only one for its final part, the Book of Revelation. As it happened, that manuscript left out five verses, which Erasmus himself had to translate into Greek from the Latin of the Vulgate. Nevertheless, it proved to be a literary milestone. For the first time, theologians had the opportunity to compare the original Greek text of the New Testament with the later Vulgate translation into Latin.

Drawing on Lorenzo Valla's work, Erasmus showed that the Vulgate translation of a number of major New Testament texts could not be justified. As a number of medieval church practices and beliefs were based upon these texts, Erasmus' allegations were viewed with consternation by many conservative catholics (who wanted to retain these practices and beliefs) and with equally great delight by the reformers (who wanted to eliminate them). Some examples will indicate the relevance of Erasmus' biblical scholarship.

The Christian church has always attached particular importance to certain rites, or forms of worship, which are referred to as *sacraments* (see pp. 169–70). Two such sacraments were recognized by the early church as 'dominical' (in other words, as having been authorized by Jesus Christ himself). These were baptism and the sacrament now known by a variety of names, such as 'the Mass', the Lord's supper', the 'breaking of the bread' or 'the eucharist'. In his exposition of the parable of the Good Samaritan (Luke 10:25–37), the great patristic theologian Augustine argued that the two silver coins given by the Samaritan to the innkeeper (10:35) were an allegory of the two sacraments of the gospel given by Christ to his church.

By the end of the twelfth century, however, this number had increased to seven. The development and consolidation of the sacramental system of the church is one of the most important aspects of medieval theology, and is due in part to a major work of medieval theology – Peter Lombard's *Four Books of the Sentences*. The seven sacraments now recognized by the church were eucharist, baptism, penance, confirmation, marriage, ordination, extreme unction.

Erasmus' new translation of the New Testament seemed to many to call this entire system into question. The noted English scholar Thomas Linacre, who gave up the practice of medicine in order to become a priest, is reported to have spoken the following words after reading the gospels for the first time in their original Greek: 'Either this is not the gospel, or we are not Christians.' It will be helpful to consider some of the things which may have moved Linacre to make such a statement.

Much medieval theology justified the inclusion of matrimony in the list of sacraments on the basis of a New Testament text which – at least in the

Vulgate translation – spoke of marriage being a *sacramentum* (Ephesians 5:31–32). Erasmus followed Valla in pointing out that the Greek word (*musterion*) here translated as 'sacrament' simply meant 'mystery'. There was no reference whatsoever to marriage being a 'sacrament'. One of the classic proof texts used by medieval theologians to justify the inclusion of matrimony in the list of sacraments was thus rendered virtually useless.

Similarly, the Vulgate translated the opening words of Jesus' ministry (Matthew 4:17) as '*Do penance*, for the Kingdom of heaven is at hand'. This translation suggested that the coming of the kingdom of heaven had a direct connection with the sacrament of penance. Erasmus, again following Valla, pointed out that the Greek should be translated as '*Repent*, for the Kingdom of heaven is at hand'. In other words, where the Vulgate seemed to refer to an outward practice (the sacrament of penance), Erasmus insisted that the reference was to an inward psychological attitude – that of 'being repentant'. Once more, an important justification of the sacramental system of the church was challenged.

Another area of theology which medieval theologians had developed far beyond the modest views of the early church relates to Mary, the mother of Jesus. For many later medieval theologians, Mary was a bit like a reservoir of grace, which could be tapped when needed. In part, this view rested on the medieval understanding of grace as a kind of substance – an understanding that was abandoned at the time of the Reformation (see pp. 102–3). It also rested upon the Vulgate translation of Gabriel's words to Mary (Luke 1:28) as 'the one who is full of grace (*gratia plena*)', thus suggesting the image of a reservoir full of a liquid (grace). But, as Erasmus and Valla both pointed out, the Greek simply meant 'favoured one', or 'one who has found favour'. Once more, an important feature of medieval theology seemed to be contradicted by humanist New Testament scholarship.

There was thus a general loss of confidence in the reliability of the Vulgate, the 'official' Latin translation of the Bible.[10] No longer could 'Scripture' and 'the Vulgate text' be regarded as one and the same thing. For the reformers, however, these developments were nothing less than providential. As we have seen, the reformers wanted to return to the beliefs and practices of the early church – and if Erasmus' new translation of the New Testament helped demolish medieval additions to those beliefs and practices, then so much the better. Humanist biblical scholarship was therefore regarded as an ally in the struggle for the return to the simplicity of the apostolic church.[11] Much of the complex network of religious ideas and customs of the late Middle Ages could thus be set to one side, as distortions of (or additions to) an earlier and simpler form of Christianity.

Erasmus' programme of reform also required ready access to the writings of the Fathers. This necessitated the production of reliable editions of the writings of theologians such as Ambrose, Augustine and Jerome (Erasmus' favourite patristic writer). Erasmus was responsible for a remarkable feat of editorial work, producing a series of patristic editions which were the marvel of the age. Although Erasmus' edition of the writings of Augustine compares unfavourably with the great eleven-volume Amerbach edition of 1506, his edition of the works of Jerome was widely regarded as an intellectual wonder of the world.

It must not be thought that the theologians of the medieval period ignored the views of patristic writers such as Augustine. They revered such writings, but did not have access to full and accurate editions. Thus medieval writers tended to quote very short extracts, usually referred to as 'sentences', from the Fathers. These sentences were quoted without reference to their context. Since the full versions of the works from which they were quoted were to be found only in a few manuscripts locked away in monastic libraries, it was virtually impossible to check that a Father's viewpoint was being accurately presented. Augustine in particular was often misunderstood through being quoted out of context. The production of printed editions of these works allowed the context of these sentences to be studies, so it now became possible to gain an understanding of the Fathers at a depth denied to the earlier medieval writers.

Furthermore, a large number of works ascribed to Augustine in circulation in the Middle Ages were found to have been written by somebody else. These 'pseudo-Augustinian' works frequently developed views opposed to those of Augustine, making it remarkably difficult for readers to make sense of his apparently contradictory statements.[12] The arrival of the textual-critical methods of humanist scholarship led to these pseudo-Augustinian works being recognized for what they were, and hence being excluded from definitive editions of Augustine's writings. The way was thus opened to more reliable interpretation of the Fathers, by eliminating spurious 'patristic' writings. The scholarly techniques for identifying spurious writings had been developed by Lorenzo Valla in the fifteenth century, and these were used to demonstrate the inauthenticity of the famous *Donation of Constantine* (a document allegedly drawn up by the emperor Constantine giving certain privileges to the western church).

Thus the editions of the Fathers prepared by humanist scholars such as Erasmus and the Amerbach brothers made the theology of the Fathers available in a fuller, more reliable form than had ever been possible before. As a result, it became possible to discern major differences of emphasis and substance between the views of writers such as Augustine and those of the theologians of the later Middle Ages. In Luther's view, it was necessary to reform the ideas of the medieval church, by returning to the authentic teachings of Augustine, especially in relation to the doctrine of grace. The new editions of the patristic writers thus added further fuel to the demands for reform of the church.

Humanism and the Reformation – An Evaluation

What impact did humanism have upon the Reformation? In order to give a reliable answer to this question, it is necessary to draw a distinction between two wings of the Reformation: the Reformation as it developed at Wittenberg under Martin Luther and the Reformation as it developed at Zurich under Huldrych Zwingli. These two wings had very different characters, and generalizations about 'the Reformation' tend to confuse them. The assumption which underlies some writing about the Reformation – that it was intellectually and culturally homogeneous – is seriously flawed. As we emphasized earlier, although the Wittenberg and Swiss reformations (which ultimately led to the establishment of the Lutheran and the Reformed churches) appealed to much the same theological sources (Scripture and the Fathers) as the basis of their reforming programmes, they did so using very different methods and with correspondingly different results. One of the most striking differences between these wings of the Reformation concerns their very different relation to humanism. We shall consider them individually, before returning to some more general points.

Humanism and the Swiss Reformation

The origins of the Swiss Reformation may be traced back to the rise of humanist groups (usually known as 'sodalities') at the universities of Vienna and Basle in the early 1500s.[13] Swiss students, who in the fifteenth century had tended to study at universities noted for their links with scholastic theology, now showed a marked preference for universities with strongly humanist associations. Switzerland was geographically close to Italy, and appears to have become a clearing-house for the northern European dissemination of the ideas of the Renaissance by the beginning of the sixteenth century. Many of the leading printing houses of Europe – for example, Froschauer in Zurich and Froben and Cratander in Basle) – were Swiss. At a time when Swiss national identity appeared to be threatened by the Franco-Italian war, many Swiss humanists appear to have been inspired by the vision of establishing the literary and cultural identity of Switzerland.

The overall impression gained of early sixteenth-century Swiss intellectual life is that of groups of intellectuals based in the Swiss university cities beginning to develop the vision of *Christianismus renascens*. The turning point for this movement came when one member of a humanist sodality, Huldrych Zwingli, was called to Zurich as a preacher in January 1519. Exploiting his position, Zwingli initiated a programme of reform based on broadly humanist principles, especially the vision of the corporate renewal of church and society on the basis of Scripture and the Fathers.

Zwingli had earlier studied at the humanist universities of Vienna and Basle, and his early works reflect the particular concerns of Swiss humanism. He had met Erasmus while the latter was at Basle in 1516, seeing his Greek New Testament through Froben's presses, and was deeply influenced by his ideas and methods. Erasmus' influence upon Zwingli is evident in the following:

1   Religion is seen as something spiritual and internal; external matters cannot be allowed to become of vital importance. The primary purpose of religion is to inculcate in the believer a set of inner attitudes, such as humility and willing obedience to God. Although Zwingli would argue that any programme of reform worthy of the name would extend to external matters (such as the nature of worship and the manner in which the church should be governed), his primary emphasis appears to fall firmly on the need for inner renewal.

2   Considerable importance is attached to moral and ethical regeneration and reform. To many scholars, the early Swiss Reformation appears to be primarily a *moral* reformation, with emphasis upon the need to regenerate both individual and society.

3   The relevance of Jesus Christ to the Christian is primarily as a moral example. Erasmus developed the idea of Christian faith as an *imitatio Christi*, an 'imitation of Christ', and Zwingli follows him in this respect.

4   Certain of the early church Fathers are singled out as being of particular importance. For both Erasmus and Zwingli, Jerome and Origen are particularly valued. Although Zwingli would later begin to recognize the importance of Augustine, this development dates from the 1520s: the *origins* of Zwingli's reforming programme seem to owe nothing to Augustine.

5   Reformation concerns primarily the life and morals of the church, rather than its doctrine. For most humanists, 'philosophy' was about the process of living, rather than a set of philosophical doctrines (see, for example, Erasmus' concept of the *philosophia Christi*, the 'philosophy of Christ', which is essentially a code of life). Initially, Zwingli does not seem to have regarded refor mation of the church as extending to its doctrine – merely to its life. Thus his first reform-

ing actions concerned the practices of the Zurich church – such as the way in which services were ordered and the manner in which churches were decorated.

6 Reformation is viewed as a pedagogical or educational process. It is an essentially human process, based upon the insights contained in the New Testament and the early church Fathers. It was only in the early 1520s that we find Zwingli breaking away from this idea, to embrace the idea of Reformation as a divine action overruling human weakness.

To summarize, then: the Swiss Reformation was dominated by humanism, which was the only intellectual force of any significance in the region at the time. Zwingli's early programme of reform is thoroughly humanist, drawing on both the characteristic insights of Swiss humanism and those of Erasmus. The influence of humanism upon the Swiss Reformation was nothing less than decisive. This makes the contrast with the Reformation at Wittenberg, to which we now turn, all the more obvious.

Humanism and the Wittenberg Reformation

Although humanism was a fairly important intellectual force in Germany by the early 1500s, its impact on Martin Luther appears to have been limited.[14] Luther was an academic theologian, whose world was dominated by the thought-patterns of scholastic theology. Through a careful reading of the writings of Augustine, Luther became convinced that the form of scholastic theology with which he was familiar was wrong. It failed to do justice to the grace of God, and tended to suggest that the individual could earn his or her own salvation. His task was to oppose this theology. Whereas Zwingli regarded the *morals* of the church as what needed reforming, Luther saw the church's theology as what was in need of reform. Luther's reforming theology is set in an academic context (the University of Wittenberg), and is aimed at an academic target (the theology of 'nominalism', or the *via moderna*, which we shall consider in more detail in the following chapter). Furthermore, Luther's quarrel with scholastic theology centred on the doctrine of justification – a concern which finds no real echo in the Swiss Reformation.

Equally, Luther's concern with *doctrine* as such is without any real parallel in either humanism or the early Swiss Reformation. Humanism saw reformation s concerning the *life and morals* of the church – but not doctrine. Indeed, most humanists seem to have regarded an interest in doctrine as equivalent to an obsession with scholastic theology. With Luther, however, we find a determination to inquire into the teaching of the church, with a view to reforming that teaching in the light of Scripture. It is true, of course, that the later Swiss Reformation – especially under the leadership of Bullinger and Calvin – became much more concerned with matters of doctrine. But at this early stage, under Zwingli's leadership, doctrine was marginalized.

In order to combat scholasticism, Luther drew heavily upon Scripture and the Fathers, supremely Augustine. In doing so, he used the new editions of the Greek New Testament and the writings of Augustine which had been prepared by humanist editors. Luther regarded it as nothing less than providential that these new sources should be available to support his programme of reform. His knowledge of Hebrew, his editions of Augustine, his Greek text of the New Testament – all were provided by humanist editors and educationalists. In many ways, the theological programme developed by Luther and Karlstadt at Wittenberg could be seen as humanist. Luther and the humanists were strongly opposed to scholasticism (although for different reasons, as we shall see below).

Indeed, the impression that Luther was sympathetic to humanism gained ground in the late 1510s, perhaps supremely as a result of the Leipzig Disputation of 1519, in which Luther debated a series of issues with the catholic controversialist Johann Eck. Much of what Luther said during that debate seemed to echo the concerns of humanists. Not surprisingly, reports began to circulate in humanist circles concerning this previously obscure figure who had publicly defended humanist ideals with such bravado. The Leipzig Disputation might have remained an obscure academic debate had not humanists taken up Luther's cause with enthusiasm, convinced that he was one of their number.

There is no real evidence, however, that Luther had any interest in humanism as such; he simply exploited its products for his own ends. The superficial similarities between the two programmes mask profound differences. Luther and his colleagues used only the textual and philological skills of humanism, while remaining hostile to humanist attitudes. In the final section of this chapter, we shall develop this point further.

Tensions between Reformation and Humanism

Although humanism made decisive contributions to the development of the Reformation, as we have just seen, there were, nevertheless, tensions between humanism and both wings of the Reformation. Five areas may be singled out for comment.

1 *Their attitude to scholastic theology.* The humanists, the Swiss reformers and the Wittenberg reformers all had no hesitation in rejecting scholasticism;

yet their reasons for doing so were different. The humanists rejected scholasticism because of its unintelligibility and inelegance of expression; they wanted a simpler and more eloquent theology. Similar attitudes are evident within the Swiss Reformation. The Wittenberg reformers, by contrast (especially Luther and Karlstadt), had no difficulty in *understanding* scholastic theology; their rejection of scholasticism was based on their conviction that its theology was fundamentally wrong. Where the humanists and Zwingli dismissed scholasticism as an irrelevance, the Wittenberg reformers regarded it as the major obstacle in the path of a reforming theology.

2   *Their attitude to Scripture.* All three groups believed that Scripture held the key to reform of the church, in that it bore witness to Christian belief and practice in its original form. For the humanists, the authority of Scripture rested in its eloquence, simplicity and antiquity. The Swiss and Wittenberg reformers, by contrast, grounded the authority of Scripture in the concept of the 'word of God'. Scripture was seen as embodying the commands and promises of God, thus giving it a status over and above any purely human document. The phrase *sola scriptura*, 'by Scripture alone', expresses the basic Reformation belief that no source other than Scripture need be consulted in matters of Christian faith and practice. A further tension exists between the Swiss and the Wittenberg reformers: the former regarded Scripture primarily as a source of moral guidance, whereas the latter regarded it primarily as a record of God's gracious promises of salvation to those who believed.

3   *Their attitudes to the Fathers.* For the humanists the writings of the patristic period represented a simple, comprehensible form of Christianity, lent authority by their antiquity and eloquence. In general, humanists appear to have regarded the Fathers as being of more or less equal value, in that all dated from roughly the same period. Erasmus, however, regarded certain Fathers as of particular importance; in the early 1500s, he singled out Origen (a Greek Father from the third century, noted as much for the unorthodoxy as for the elegance of his writings) for special mention, while by 1515 he had decided to opt for Jerome. His new preference for Jerome is to be explained on the basis of his textual studies of the New Testament, leading to the publication of the Greek edition of the New Testament in 1516. Jerome had earlier undertaken extensive work on the scriptural texts, and Erasmus appears to have regarded Jerome with new interest for this reason. This Erasmian attitude towards the Fathers is also evident within the Swiss Reformation.

The Wittenberg reformers Luther and Karlstadt, by contrast, regarded Augustine as pre-eminent among the Fathers. The humanists employed two criteria in evaluating the Fathers: antiquity and eloquence – hence Erasmus' preference for both Origen and Jerome. The Wittenberg reformers, however, used an explicitly *theological* criterion in evaluating the Fathers: how reliable

were they as interpreters of the New Testament? On the basis of this criterion, Augustine was to be preferred, and Origen to be treated with some suspicion. The humanists were not prepared to use such an explicitly theological
criterion in evaluating the relative merits of the Fathers, thus heightening the
tension between these two movements.

4   *Their attitudes to education.* In that the Reformation witnessed the birth
of a series of new religious ideas (or, at least, ideas which were new to most
people in the sixteenth century, even if the reformers argued that they represented the recovery of older ideas), it was essential to the success of both
the Wittenberg and the Swiss reformations that a major programme of religious education be undertaken. Humanism was essentially an educational and
cultural movement based upon reform of the liberal arts, with the result that
most early sixteenth-century humanists were professional educators. It is therefore interesting to note that most northern European humanists joined the
cause of the Reformation not necessarily because they approved of its *religious*
ideas, but because they were attracted strongly by its *educational ideals*. The
reformers were concerned with the religious ideas being taught, viewing educational methods as the means to that end, whereas the professional humanist educators were primarily concerned with the development of educational
techniques, rather than the ideas being taught.

5   *Their attitude to rhetoric.* As we have seen, humanism was concerned with
eloquence, both written and spoken. Rhetoric was thus studied as a means to
this end. The reformers, in both Germany and Switzerland, were concerned
with the promotion of their religious ideas through the written word (for
example, in books such as Calvin's famous *Institutes of the Christian Religion*)
and the spoken word (for example, in sermons, Luther's eight Wittenberg
sermons of 1522 being an excellent example). Rhetoric was therefore the
means to the end of the propagation of the ideas of the Reformation.
Recent studies, for example, have emphasized how Calvin's style is heavily
influenced by rhetoric. Both humanist and reformer, therefore, regarded
rhetoric highly – but for different reasons. For the humanists, rhetoric promoted eloquence; for the reformers, it promoted the Reformation. Once
more, we encounter superficial similarities between the two groups which
mask profound differences.

On the basis of our discussion so far, it will be clear that the Swiss wing
of the Reformation was influenced by humanism to a far greater extent than
its counterpart at Wittenberg. Even at Wittenberg, however, the new programme of study of the Bible and Augustine appeared to many to be thoroughly humanist in inspiration. With the benefit of hindsight, it is very easy
for us to distinguish Luther and Karlstadt from the humanists – yet *at the time,*

this distinction was virtually impossible to make. To most observers, Luther and Erasmus were engaged in precisely the same struggle.

A famous illustration of this misunderstanding of Luther by humanists may be noted. In 1518 Luther delivered the famous Heidelberg Disputation, in which he developed a radically anti-humanist and anti-scholastic theology. Among his audience was the young humanist Martin Bucer, later to become a leading reformer in the city of Strasbourg. Bucer wrote with enthusiasm to his humanist correspondent Beatus Rhenanus, declaring that Luther merely stated Erasmus' views, but did so more forcefully. As a close comparison of that letter and Luther's own text indicates, Bucer seems to have misunderstood Luther on virtually every point. Again, Luther's stance in the Leipzig Disputation in 1519 – as reflected, for example, in his critique of papal authority – was widely regarded as humanist, and led to his becoming something of a cult figure in humanist circles. Yet Luther's position at Leipzig was not distinctively 'humanist' in any meaningful sense of the word; it echoed reforming ideas which were beginning to gain a widespread hearing in evangelical circles throughout Europe at the time.

The full extent of the tension between humanism and the Reformation only became fully apparent perhaps in 1525. In this year, both Zwingli and Luther composed public attacks on Erasmus, both concentrating their attention on the concept of the 'freedom of the will'. For both reformers, Erasmus' teaching of the total freedom of the human will led to a grossly overoptimistic conception of human nature. With the publication of Zwingli's *Commentary on True and False Religion* and Luther's *On the Bondage of the Will*, the tensions that had always been in existence between humanism and the Reformation became obvious to all.

For further reading

On humanism in general, see:

Paul O. Kristeller, 'Valla', in Kristeller, P. O., *Eight Philosophers of the Italian Renaissance* (Stanford, CA, 1964), pp. 19–36.
——, 'The European Diffusion of Italian Humanism', in Kristeller, P. O., *Renaissance Thought II: Humanism and the Arts* (New York, 1965), pp. 69–88.
——, *Renaissance Thought and Its Sources* (New York, 1979).
Alister E. McGrath, *The Intellectual Origins of the European Reformation* (Oxford, 1987), pp. 32–68.
Nicholas Mann, 'The Origins of Humanism', in *The Cambridge Companion to Renaissance Humanism*, ed. J. Kraye (Cambridge, 1996), pp. 1–19.

Charles G. Nauert, *Humanism and Culture of Renaissance Europe* (Cambridge, 1995).

Albert Rabil (ed.), *Renaissance Humanism: Foundations, Forms and Legacy* (3 vols; Philadelphia, 1988).

C. H. Stinger, *Humanism and the Church Fathers* (Albany, NY, 1977).

James D. Tracey, 'Humanism and the Reformation', in *Reformation Europe: A Guide to Research*, ed. Steven E. Ozment (St Louis, 1982), pp. 33–57.

Roberto Weiss, *The Renaissance Discovery of Classical Antiquity* (Oxford, 1988).

On humanism and the Bible, see:

J. H. Bentley, *Humanists and Holy Writ: New Testament Scholarship in the Renaissance* (Princeton, NJ, 1983).

C. Celenza, 'Renaissance Humanism and the New Testament: Lorenzo Valla's Annotations to the New Testament', *Journal of Medieval and Renaissance Studies* 24 (1994), pp. 33–52.

Alasdair Hamilton, 'Humanists and the Bible', in *The Cambridge Companion to Renaissance Humanism*, ed. J. Kraye (Cambridge, 1996), pp. 100–17.

G. Lloyd Jones, *The Discovery of Hebrew in Tudor England* (Manchester, 1983).

N. G. Wilson, *From Byzantium to Italy: Greek Studies in the Italian Renaissance* (London, 1992).

On northern European humanism, see:

Albert Hyma, *The Brethren of the Common Life* (Grand Rapids, 1950).

R. R. Post, *The Modern Devotion: Confrontation with Reformation and Humanism* (Leiden, 1968).

Lewis W. Spitz, *The Religious Renaissance of the German Humanists* (Cambridge, Mass., 1963).

On Erasmus, see:

Roland H. Bainton, *Erasmus of Christendom* (New York, 1969).

Margaret M. Philipps, *Erasmus and the Northern Renaissance* (London, 1949).

James K. McConica, *Erasmus* (Oxford, 1991).

Erica Rummel, *Erasmus' Annotations on the New Testament* (Toronto, 1986).

James D. Tracy, *The Politics of Erasmus: A Pacifist Intellectual and His Political Milieu* (Toronto, 1978).

On English humanism, see:

B. Bradshaw and E. Duffy (eds), *Humanism, Reform and the Reformation* (Cambridge, 1989).

A. G. Chester, 'The New Learning: A Semantic Note', *Studies in the Renaissance* 2 (1955), pp. 139–47.

Roberto Weiss, *Humanism in Fifteenth-Century England*, 3rd edn (Oxford, 1965).

On the educational methods of the reformers, see:

Gerald Strauss, *Luther's House of Learning: Indoctrination of the Young in the German Reformation* (Baltimore, 1978).

4

Scholasticism and the Reformation

Scholasticism is probably one of the most despised intellectual movements in human history. Thus the English word 'dunce' (fool) derives from the name of one of the greatest scholastic writers, Duns Scotus. Scholastic thinkers – the 'schoolmen' as they were called – are often represented as debating earnestly, if pointlessly, how many angels could dance on the head of a pin. Although this particular debate never actually took place, intriguing though its outcome would unquestionably have been, it summarizes precisely the way in which scholasticism was regarded by most people, especially the humanists, at the beginning of the sixteenth century: as pointless, arid, intellectual speculation over trivia. Erasmus spent some time towards the end of the fifteenth century at the scholasticism-dominated University of Paris. He wrote at length of the many things he detested about Paris: the lice, the poor food, the stinking latrines and the utterly tedious debates which vexed the schoolmen. Could God have become a cucumber instead of a human being? Could he undo the past, by making a prostitute into a virgin? Although serious questions lay behind these debates, Erasmus' waspish wit diverted attention from those questions themselves to the frivolous and ridiculous way in which they were debated.

Most textbooks dealing with the Reformation therefore fell justified in dismissing scholasticism without actually explaining what it is and why it was of fundamental importance to the Wittenberg Reformation. This chapter seeks to explain these two things.

We begin with an attempt to define the word 'scholasticism'.

'Scholasticism' Defined

The very word 'scholasticism' could be argued to be the invention of humanist writers, anxious to discredit the movement which it represented. The phrase 'the Middle Ages' was certainly largely a humanist invention, coined by sixteenth-century humanist writers such as Vadian and Beatus Rhenanus to refer disparagingly to an uninteresting period of stagnation between antiquity (the classical period) and modernity (the Renaissance). The 'Middle Ages' was seen as little more than an intermezzo between the cultural magnificence of antiquity and its revival during the Renaissance. Similarly, the term 'scholastics (*scholastici*)' was used by humanists to refer, equally disparagingly, to the ideas of the Middle Ages. In their concern to discredit the ideas of the medieval period, in order to lend enhanced attraction to their appeal to the classical period, the humanists had little interest in drawing distinctions between the various types of 'scholastics' – such as Thomists and Scotists. The word 'scholasticism' is thus both pejorative and imprecise; yet the historian cannot avoid using it.

How may scholasticism be defined? Like humanism, it is difficult to offer a precise definition, capable of doing justice to the distinctive positions of all the major schools within the Middle Ages. Perhaps the following working definition may be helpful: scholasticism is best regarded as the medieval movement, flourishing in the period 1200–1500, which placed emphasis upon the rational justification of religious beliefs and the systematic presentation of those beliefs. Thus 'scholasticism' does not refer to a *specific system of beliefs*, but to a *particular way of organizing theology* – a highly developed method of presenting material, making fine distinctions, and attempting to achieve a comprehensive view of theology. It is perhaps understandable why, to its humanist critics, scholasticism seemed to degenerate into little more than logical nitpicking.

When the so-called Dark Ages finally lifted from over western Europe, the scene was set for revival in every field of academic work. The restoration of some degree of political stability in France in the late eleventh century encouraged the re-emergence of the University of Paris, which rapidly became recognized as the intellectual centre of Europe. A number of theological 'schools' were established on the Left Bank of the Seine, and on the Île de la Cité, in the shadow of the newly built cathedral of Notre Dame de Paris. Two themes began to dominate theological debate: the need to *systematize* and *expand* Christian theology and the need to *demonstrate the inherent rationality* of that theology. Although most early medieval theology was little more than a replay of the views of Augustine, there was growing pressure to systematize Augustine's ideas and take them further. But how could this be done? By what method? And on the basis of what philosophical system could the rationality of Christian theology be demonstrated?

The answer to these questions came through the rediscovery of Aristotle, in the late twelfth and early thirteenth centuries.[1] By about 1270, Aristotle had become established as 'the Philosopher'. His ideas came to dominate theological thinking, despite fierce opposition from more conservative quarters. Through the influence of writers such as Thomas Aquinas and Duns Scotus, Aristotle's ideas became established as the best means of establishing and developing Christian theology. The ideas of Christian theology were thus arranged and correlated systematically, on the basis of Aristotelian presuppositions. Equally, the rationality of Christian faith was demonstrated on the basis of Aristotelian ideas. Thus some of Thomas Aquinas' famous 'proofs' for the existence of God actually rely on principles of Aristotelian physics, rather than any distinctively Christian insights.[2]

For example, consider his argument from motion. Aquinas argues, on the basis of an Aristotelian axiom, that everything which moves is moved by something else. For every motion, there is a cause. Things don't just move – they are moved. (Duns Scotus disagreed here; angels, he argued, had access to independent means of motion.) Now each cause of motion must itself have a cause. And *that* cause must have a cause as well. And so Aquinas argues that there are a whole series of causes of motion underlying the world as we know it. Now unless there are an infinite number of these causes, Aquinas argues, there must be a single cause right at the origin of the series. From this original cause of motion, all other motion is ultimately derived. This is the origin of the great chain of causality which we see reflected in the way the world behaves. From the fact that things are in motion, Aquinas thus argues for the existence of a single original cause of all this motion – and this Prime Unmoved Mover, he concludes, is God himself. Yet, as his later critics pointed out, this rested on the dangerous and unproved assumption that the Prime Unmoved Mover and the God of Christianity were identical. It seemed to those critics, among whose number we must include Martin Luther, that the gods of Aristotle and Christianity were actually radically different.

This, then, is the essence of scholasticism: the demonstration of the inherent rationality of Christian theology by an appeal to philosophy and the demonstration of the complete harmony of that theology by the minute examination of the relationship of its various elements. Scholastic writings tended to be long and argumentative, frequently relying upon closely argued distinctions. Thus Duns Scotus, generally known as the 'subtle doctor', is obliged to distinguish as many as fifteen senses of the Latin word *ratio*, 'reason', in order to justify his views on its role in theology.

The noted medieval historian Etienne Gilson has aptly described the great scholastic systems as 'cathedrals of the mind'. Each scholastic system tried to embrace reality in its totality, dealing with matters of logic, metaphysics and theology. Everything was shown to have its logical place in a totally comprehensive intellectual system. In what follows, we shall look briefly at the main types of scholasticism encountered in the Middle Ages. But first, we should consider the milieu in which scholasticism flourished.

Scholasticism and the Universities

For obvious reasons, the influence of scholasticism was at its greatest in the medieval universities. Unlike *Quattrocènto* humanism, which both flourished in the universities and enjoyed enormous influence in society, scholasticism had a very limited sphere of influence. Humanism made its appeal to the world of education, art and culture, whereas scholasticism could at best make a limited appeal (in bad Latin) to those who enjoyed dialectics. In an age in which rhetoric and dialectic were seen as mutually incompatible, the superior appeal of the former virtually guaranteed the decline of the latter. In the late fifteenth century, a confrontation between humanism and scholasticism developed in many universities.[3] The University of Vienna, of fundamental importance to the development of the Swiss Reformation, witnessed precisely such a humanist revolt against scholasticism in the final decade of the fifteenth century. In the early sixteenth century, many students seem to have begun avoiding universities traditionally dominated by scholasticism in favour of those with humanist educational programmes. Thus the influence of scholasticism was gradually being eroded even in its academic strongholds as the sixteenth century dawned.

Although on the wane as an academic force, however, the fact remains that Martin Luther's theological development took place in reaction against scholastic theology. Whereas scholasticism was a negligible intellectual force in Switzerland, it was still of major importance in Germany, particularly at the University of Erfurt, at which Luther was educated. Luther's early work as a theological reformer was carried out in a university context, fighting against an academic opponent. In marked contrast, the Swiss reformers were, as we have seen, humanists, bent on reforming the life and morals of the church of their day; they had no need to pay any attention to scholasticism. Luther, by contrast, was forced to enter into dialogue with the major force on his intellectual horizon, scholasticism. The Swiss reformers could afford to ridicule scholasticism, for it posed no threat to them – but Luther had to engage with it directly.

This serves to emphasize the differences between the Swiss and the Wittenberg reformations, whose totally different contexts are too often overlooked. Zwingli began by reforming a city (Zurich); Luther began by reforming a university faculty of theology (Wittenberg). Zwingli began by opposing the life and morals of the pre-Reformation Zurich church; Luther began by opposing a particular form of scholastic theology. Initially Zwingli had no need to propose a reformation of the doctrine of the church, whereas for Luther, doctrinal reformation was the essential springboard of his pro-

gramme of reform. In a later chapter, we shall consider Luther's reaction
against scholastic theology. Our attention now turns to the types of scholasticism encountered in the later Middle Ages.

Types of Scholasticism

The reader must accept an apology before proceeding any further. I have
found it impossible to simplify any further the material which follows. My
experience of teaching Reformation theology suggests that many readers will
probably be gripped by a sense of utter tedium as I try to explain some of
the leading ideas of scholasticism. (This actually goes some considerable way
towards explaining why humanism proved so attractive at the time of the
Reformation.) To understand Luther's theological development, however, it is
necessary to become acquainted with at least the basics of two major movements in late medieval scholasticism.

Realism versus Nominalism

In order to comprehend the complexities of medieval scholasticism, it is necessary to grasp the distinction between 'realism' and 'nominalism'. The early
part of the scholastic period (*c.* 1200–*c.* 1350) was dominated by realism, the
later part (*c.* 1350–*c.* 1500) by nominalism. The difference between the two
systems may be summarized as follows. Consider two white stones. Realism
affirms that there is a universal concept of 'whiteness' which these two stones
embody. These particular stones possess the universal characteristic of 'whiteness'. But whereas the white stones exist in time and space, the universal of
'whiteness' exists on a different metaphysical plane. Nominalism, by contrast,
asserts that the universal concept of 'whiteness' is unnecessary, and instead
argues that we should concentrate on particulars. There are these two white
stones – and there is no need to start talking about 'a universal concept of
whiteness'.[4]

The idea of a 'universal', used here without definition, needs to be explored
further. Consider Socrates. He is a human being, and is an example of humanity. Now consider Plato and Aristotle. They are also human beings and examples of humanity. We could go on doing this for some time, naming as many
individuals as we liked, but the same basic pattern would emerge: individual
named people are examples of humanity. Realism argues that the abstract idea
of 'humanity' has an existence of its own. It is a universal; and particular people

– such as Socrates, Plato and Aristotle – are individual examples of this universal. The common feature of humanity which unites these three individuals has a real existence of its own.

This debate may strike many readers as typical of scholasticism: pointless and pedantic. Nevertheless, it is important for the reader to appreciate that the term 'nominalism' refers to a debate concerning universals. *It has no direct theological relevance, and defines no specific theological opinion.* We shall return to this point shortly.

Two major scholastic 'schools' influenced by realism dominated the earlier medieval period. These were *Thomism* and *Scotism*, derived from the writings of Thomas Aquinas and Duns Scotus respectively. Neither of these schools had any major influence upon the Reformation, and need not, therefore, be discussed any further.[5] Two later forms of scholasticism, however, appear to have had a major influence upon the Reformation, and thus merit careful attention. These are the *via moderna* and the *schola Augustiniana moderna*.

Many textbooks dealing with the Reformation refer to a confrontation between 'nominalism' and 'Augustinianism' on the eve of the Reformation, and interpret the Reformation as the victory of the latter over the former. In recent years, however, considerable progress has been made in understanding the nature of late medieval scholasticism, leading to a rewriting of the intellectual history of the early Reformation. In what follows, I shall indicate the situations as established by most recent scholarship.

An earlier generation of scholars writing in the period 1920–65 regarded 'nominalism' as a religious school of thought which captured most northern European university faculties of theology in the later Middle Ages. It proved remarkably difficult, however, to identify the exact features of this theology. Some 'nominalist' theologians (such as William of Ockham and Gabriel Biel) seemed to be very optimistic about human abilities, suggesting that it was possible for a human being to do everything that was necessary to enter into a relationship with God. Other 'nominalist' theologians (such as Gregory of Rimini and Hugolino of Orvieto) appeared to be profoundly pessimistic about those same abilities, suggesting that without the grace of God, humanity was totally unable to enter into such a relationship. In desperation, scholars began to speak of 'nominalistic diversity'. Eventually, however, the real solution to the problem emerged: namely, that there were actually *two* different schools of thought, whose sole common feature was anti-realism. Both schools adopted a nominalist position in matters of logic and the theory of knowledge – but their theological positions differed radically. Earlier, we noted that the term 'nominalism' referred strictly to the question of universals and did not designate any particular theological position. Thus both schools rejected the necessity of universals – but thereafter could agree on virtually nothing. One was highly optimistic concerning human abilities, the other considerably more pessimistic. These two schools are now generally known as the *via moderna*, 'the modern way', and the *schola Augustiniana moderna*, 'the modern Augustinian school'. We shall consider these two schools presently. But first, attention is claimed by the terms 'Pelagian' and 'Augustinian', which are invariably encountered in any discussion of late medieval scholasticism. In what follows, I shall explain what is meant by these terms.

'Pelagianism' and 'Augustinianism'

The doctrine of justification, which assumed particular importance within the Lutheran Reformation, concerns the question of how an individual enters into a relationship with God. How can a sinner be accepted by a righteous God? What must the individual do in order to be acceptable to God? This question was debated with some intensity in the early fifth century during the debate between Augustine and Pelagius. This controversy is known as the 'Pelagian controversy', and Augustine's writings concerning the doctrines of grace and justification which arose out of it are known as the 'anti-Pelagian writings'.[6] In many ways, this controversy was replayed in the fourteenth and fifteenth centuries, with the *via moderna* tending towards the position of Pelagius and the *schola Augustiniana moderna* towards that of Augustine. In what follows, I shall give a brief outline of each position.

A central theme of Augustine's thought is the *fallenness* of human nature. The imagery of 'the Fall' derives from Genesis 3, and expresses the idea that human nature has 'fallen' from its original pristine state. The present state of human nature is thus not what it was intended to be by God. The created order no longer corresponds directly to the 'goodness' of its original integrity. It has lapsed. It has been spoiled or ruined – but not irredeemably, as the doctrines of salvation and justification affirm. The image of a 'Fall' conveys the idea that creation now exists at a lower level than that intended for it by God.

According to Augustine, it follows that all human beings are now contaminated by sin from the moment of their birth. In contrast to many twentieth-century existentialist philosophies (such as that of Martin Heidegger), which affirm that 'fallenness (*Verfallenheit*)' is an option which we choose (rather than something which is chosen for us), Augustine portrays sin as inherent to human nature. It is an integral, not an optional, aspect of our being. This insight, which is given more rigorous expression in Augustine's doctrine of original sin, is of central importance to his doctrines of sin and salvation. In that all are sinners, all require redemption. In that all have fallen short of the glory of God, all require to be redeemed.

For Augustine, left to its own devices and resources, humanity could never enter into a relationship with God. Nothing that a man or woman could do could ever be sufficient to break the stranglehold of sin. To use an image which Augustine was fortunate enough never to have encountered, it is like a narcotic addict trying to break free from the grip of heroin or cocaine. The situation cannot be transformed from within; hence, if transformation is to take place, it must come from outside the human situation. According to Augustine, God has intervened in the human dilemma. He need not have done so, but out of his love for fallen humanity, he has entered into the human situation in the person of Jesus Christ in order to redeem it.

Augustine lays such emphasis on 'grace' that he is often referred to as *doctor gratiae*, 'the doctor of grace'. 'Grace' is the unmerited or undeserved gift of God, by which God voluntarily breaks the hold of sin on humanity. Redemption is possible only as a divine gift. It is not somethind which we can achieve ourselves, but is something which must be done for us. Augustine thus emphasizes that the resources of salvation are located outside humanity, in God himself. It is God who initiates the process of salvation, not men or women.

For Pelagius, however, the situation looked very different. Pelagius taught that the resources of salvation are located within humanity. Individual human beings have the capacity to save themselves. They are not trapped by sin, but have the ability to do all that is necessary to be saved. Salvation is something which is earned through good works, which place God under an obligation to humanity. Pelagius marginalizes the idea of grace, understanding it in terms of demands made of humanity by God in order that salvation may be achieved – such as the Ten Commandments or the moral example of Christ. The ethos of Pelagianism could be summed up as 'salvation by merit', whereas Augustine taught 'salvation by grace'.

It is obvious that the two different theologies have very different understandings of human nature. For Augustine, human nature is weak, fallen and powerless; for Pelagius, it is autonomous and self-sufficient. For Augustine, it is necessary to depend upon God for salvation; for Pelagius, God merely indicates what has to be done if salvation is to be attained, and then leaves men and women to meet those conditions unaided. For Augustine, salvation is an unmerited gift; for Pelagius, salvation is a justly earned reward.

One aspect of Augustine's understanding of grace needs further comment. Since human beings are incapable of saving themselves, and since God has given the gift of grace to some (but not all), it follows that God has 'preselected' those who are to be saved. Using hints of this idea to be found in the New Testament, Augustine developed a doctrine of predestination. The term 'predestination' refers to God's original or eternal decision to save some, and not others. It was this aspect of Augustine's thought which many of his contemporaries, not to mention his successors, found unacceptable. It need hardly be said that there is no direct equivalent in Pelagius' thought.[7]

In the ensuing controversy within the western church, Augustine's position was recognized as authentically Christian, and Pelagius' views were censured as heretical. Two important councils established Augustine's views as normative: the Council of Carthage (418) and the Second Council of Orange (529). Interestingly, Augustine's views on predestination were diluted somewhat, even though the remainder of his system was enthusiastically endorsed. The term 'Pelagian' hence came to be pejorative as well as descriptive, meaning 'placing excessive reliance upon human abilities, and insufficient trust in the grace of God'. At the time of the Reformation, Luther was convinced that most of the western church had lost sight of the idea of the 'grace of God' and had come to rely upon human self-sufficiency. He therefore regarded it as his duty to recall the church to the views of Augustine, as we shall see in chapter 6.

We must now consider the fourteenth- and fifteenth-century replay of this controversy between the *via moderna* and *schola Augustiniana moderna*, the former assuming broadly the role of Pelagius, the latter that of Augustine.

The Via Moderna *('Nominalism')*

The term *via moderna* is now becoming generally accepted as the best way of referring to the movement once known as 'nominalism', which included among its adherents such fourteenth- and fifteenth-century thinkers as William of Ockham, Pierre d'Ailly, Robert Holcot and Gabriel Biel. During the fifteenth century, the *via moderna* began to make significant inroads into many northern European universities – for example, at Paris, Heidelberg and Erfurt. In addition to its philosophical nominalism, the movement adopted a doctrine of justification which many of its critics branded as 'Pelagian'. In view of the importance of this form of scholasticism to Luther's theological breakthrough, I shall explain its understanding of justification in some detail.[8]

The central feature of the soteriology, or doctrine of salvation, of the *via moderna* is a covenant between God and humanity. The later Middle Ages saw the development of political and economic theories based upon the concept of a covenant (for example, between a king and his people), and the theologians of the *via moderna* were quick to realize the theological potential of this idea. Just as a *political* covenant between a king and his people defined the obligations of king to people and people to king, so a *religious* covenant between God and his people defined God's obligations to his people and their obligation to God.[9] This covenant was not negotiated, of course, but was unilaterally imposed by God. The theologians of the *via moderna* were able to develop this theme – already familiar to readers of the Old Testament – using ideas borrowed from their own political and economic world.

According to the theologians of the *via moderna*, the covenant between God and human beings established the conditions necessary for justification. God has ordained that he will accept an individual on condition that this individual first fulfils certain demands. These demands were summarized using the Latin tag *facere quod in se est*, literally 'doing what lies within you', or 'doing your best'. When individuals met this precondition, God was obliged, by the terms of the covenant, to accept them. A Latin maxim was often used to express this point: *facienti quod in se est Deus non denegat gratiam*, 'God will not deny grace to anyone who does what lies within them'. The noted late medieval theologian Gabriel Biel, who is known to have influenced Luther through his writings, explained that 'doing your best' meant rejecting evil and trying to do good.

At this point, the parallels between the *via moderna* and Pelagius become obvious. Both assert that men and women are accepted on the basis of their own efforts and achievements. Both assert that human works place God under an obligation to reward them. It would seem that the writers of the *via moderna* were simply reproducing the ideas of Pelagius, using a more sophisticated covenantal framework. At this point, however, the theologians of the *via moderna* drew upon contemporary economic theory to argue that they were doing nothing of the sort. Their use of late medieval economic theory is fascinating, in that it illustrates the extent to which medieval theologians were prepared to exploit ideas drawn from their social context. We shall consider their argument in some detail.

The classic example invariably cited by these theologians to illustrate the relation between good works and justification is the king and the small lead coin.[10] Most medieval coinage systems used gold and silver coins. This had the advantage of guaranteeing the value of the coins, even if it also encouraged the practice of 'clipping' precious metal from the coins' sides. The introduction of milled edges to coins represented an attempt to prevent removal of gold or silver in this way. Occasionally, however, kings found themselves in a financial crisis, through war for example. A standard way of meeting this was to recall gold and silver coins and melt them down. The gold and silver thus retrieved could be sued to finance a war.

In the meantime, however, currency of some sort was still required. To meet this need, small leaden coins were issued, which bore the same face value as the gold and silver coins. Although their *inherent* value was negligible, their *ascribed* or *imposed* value was considerable. The king would promise to replace the lead coins with their gold or silver equivalents once the financial crisis was past. The value of the lead coins thus resided in the king's promise to redeem them at their full ascribed value at a later date. The value of a gold coin derives from the gold; but the value of a lead coin derives from the royal covenant to treat that coin *as if it were gold*. A similar situation exists, of course, in most modern economies. For example, paper money is of negligible inherent value. Its value derives from the promise of the issuing bank to honour its notes to their full face value.

The theologians of the *via moderna* used this economic analogy to counter the charge of Pelagianism. To the suggestion that they were exaggerating the value of human works (in that they seemed to be making them capable of meriting salvation), they replied that they were doing nothing of the sort. Human works were like lead coins, they argued – of little inherent value. But God had promised, through the covenant, to treat them as if they were of much greater value, in just the same way as a king could treat a lead coin as if it were gold. Pelagius, they conceded, certainly treated human works as if they were gold, capable of purchasing salvation. But *they* were arguing that human works were like lead and that the only reason why they were of any value was that God had graciously undertaken to treat them as if they were much more valuable. The theological exploitation of the difference between the inherent and the imposed value of coins thus served to get the theologians of the *via moderna* out of a potentially awkward situation, even if it did not satisfy their more severe critics, such as Martin Luther.

It is this 'covenantal' understanding of justification which underlies Martin Luther's theological breakthrough, to which we shall return in a later chapter. Our attention now turns to the late medieval scholastic theology which re-embraced the ideas of Augustine, in deliberate opposition to the *via moderna*.

The Schola Augustiniana Moderna *('Augustinianism')*

One of the strongholds of the *via moderna* in the early fourteenth century was the University of Oxford.[11] A group of thinkers, largely associated with Merton College, developed the ideas on justification noted above, characteristic of the *via moderna*. And it was at Oxford that the first backlash against the *via moderna* occurred.[12] The individual responsible for this backlash was Thomas Bradwardine, later to become archbishop of Canterbury. Bradwardine wrote a furious attack on the ideas of the Oxford *via moderna*, entitled *De causa Dei contra Pelagium*, 'The case of God against Pelagius'. In this book he charged his Merton colleagues with being 'modern Pelagians', and developed a theory of justification which represents a return to the views of Augustine, as they are found in the anti-Pelagian writings.

Important though Oxford was as a theological centre, the Hundred Years War led to it becoming increasingly isolated from the continent of Europe. Although Bradwardine's ideas would be developed in England by John Wycliffe, they were taken up on the mainland of Europe by Gregory of Rimini at the University of Paris. Gregory had one particularly significant advantage over Bradwardine: he was a member of a religious order (the Order of the Hermits of St Augustine, generaliy referred to as the 'Augustinian Order'). And just as the Dominicans propagated the views of Thomas Aquinas and the Franciscans those of Duns Scotus, so the Augustinians promoted the ideas of Gregory of Rimini. It is this transmission of an Augustinian tradition, deriving from Gregory of Rimini, within the Augustinian Order which is increasingly referred to as the *schola Augustiniana moderna*, 'the modern Augustinian school'. What were these ideas?

First, Gregory adopted a nominalist view on the question of universals. Like many thinkers of his time, he had little time for the realism of Thomas Aquinas or Duns Scotus. In this respect, he had much in common with thinkers of the *via moderna*, such as Robert Holcot and Gabriel Biel. Second, Gregory developed a soteriology, or doctrine of salvation, which reflected the influence of Augustine. We find an emphasis on the need for grace, on the fallenness and sinfulness of humanity, on the divine initiative in justification and on divine predestination. Salvation is understood to be *totally* a work of God, from its beginning to its end. Where the *via moderna* held that humans could initiate their justification by 'doing their best', Gregory insisted that only God could initiate justification. The *via moderna* held that most (but not all) necessary soteriological resources were located *within* human nature. The merits of Christ were an example of a resource lying outside humanity; the ability to desist from sin and turn to righteousness was, for a writer such as Biel, an example of a vital soteriological resource located within humanity. In marked contrast, Gregory of Rimini argued that such resources were located exclusively *outside* human nature. Even the ability to desist from sin and turn to righteousness arose through the action of God, not a human action. It is obvious that these represent two totally different ways of understanding the human and divine roles in justification.

Although this academic Augustinianism was particularly associated with the Augustinian Order, not every Augustinian monastery or university school seems to have adopted its ideas. Nevertheless, it seems that a school of thought which was strongly Augustinian in cast was in existence in the late Middle Ages on the eve of the Reformation. In many ways, the Wittenberg reformers, with their particular emphasis on the anti-Pelagian writings of Augustine, may be regarded as having rediscovered and revitalized this tradition. As the views of some leading reformers, such as Luther or Calvin, seem to parallel those of this academic Augustinianism, the question has often been asked: were the reformers influenced, directly or indirectly, by this Augustinian tradition? We shall explore this question in the following section.

The Impact of Medieval Scholasticism upon the Reformation

It is beyond doubt that the two leading lights of the Reformation were Martin Luther and John Calvin. In what follows, we shall consider the possible influences of forms of scholastic theology upon them, noting how their educational environments exposed them to central ideas of late medieval scholasticism.

Luther's Relation to Late Medieval Scholasticism

There can be no doubt that Luther was well versed in scholastic philosophy and theology. During his period at the University of Erfurt (1501–5), the faculty of arts was dominated by representatives of the *via moderna*. He would have gained a deep appreciation of the basic features of this nominalist philosophy during his time there. After his decision to enter an Augustinian monastery (1505), he is known to have become immersed in the theology of the *via moderna*, devouring the writings of leading representatives of the movement, such as William of Ockham, Pierre d'Ailly and Gabriel Biel. Biel's *Commentary on the Canon of the Mass* was a standard theological textbook for those preparing for ordination, and there is ample evidence that Luther studied this work and absorbed its contents.

In the autumn of 1508 Luther went to teach philosophical ethics at the newly founded University of Wittenberg. Earlier that year important changes had been introduced in the university statutes, especially those relating to the faculty of arts. Up to that point, members of that faculty were permitted to teach only according to the *via Thomae* and *via Scoti* – in other words, only Thomist and Scotist ideas were allowed, not those of the *via moderna*. According to the new statutes, however, they were now also permitted to teach according to the *via Gregorii*. But what is this hitherto unknown *via*? Earlier scholars had regarded it as simply another way of referring to the *via moderna*, thus bringing Wittenberg into line with other German universities of the period.

We know that the *via moderna* was known by a number of different descriptions at various universities. For example, at Heidelberg the school was described as the *via Marsiliana*, after Marsilius of Inghens, a noted representative of the movement. The *via Gregorii* might refer to Gregory of Rimini, who was a noted exponent of the philosophy of the *via moderna*, even though his theology was radically Augustinian. The coventional view was that the term *via Gregorii* was just a local way of referring to the *via moderna*. But in an important essay published in 1974, Heiko A. Oberman argued that a very different interpretation was to be placed upon the phrase.[13]

Accordign to Oberman, the *via Gregorii* referred to the *schola Augustiniana moderna*, which derived from Gregory of Rimini (the 'Gregorius' of the *via Gregorii*). It was Gregory's theological – not his philosophical – ideas which were being described. Noting a number of ways in which the ideas of this school could have been transmitted to the young Luther, Oberman concludes:

> Taking stock of this cumulative, admittedly circumstantial evidence, we can point to the *schola Augustiniana moderna*, initiated by Gregory of Rimini, reflected by Hugolino of Orvieto, apparently spiritually alive in the Erfurt Augustinian monastery, and transformed into a pastoral reform theology by Staupitz, as the *occasio proxima* – not *causa* – for the inception of the *theologia vera* at Wittenberg.[14]

If Oberman is right, Luther and his 'true theology' stand at the end of a long medieval Augustinian tradition, suggesting that the Lutheran Reformation may represent the triumph of this tradition in the sixteenth century.

Important though Oberman's suggestion unquestionably is, a number of serious difficulties lie in its path. The following may be noted briefly:[15]

1 Luther does not seem to have come across anything written by Gregory of Rimini until 1519 – yet Oberman's hypothesis requires that the reformer should have encountered him by 1508.

2 Johannes von Staupitz, referred to by Oberman as a channel of transmission of this tradition, and who is known to have exercised some influence over Luther's development, cannot be regarded as a representative of the *schola Augustiniana moderna*. Throughout his writings, we find a reluctance to cite any writers (such as Gregory of Rimini or Hugolino of Orvieto) associated with the movement, and a marked preference for quoting from older writers.

3 Gregory of Rimini is specifically identified by the statutes of the University of Paris as a leading representative, along with William of Ockham, of the *via moderna*, suggesting that the *via Gregorii* is indeed nothing more than an alternative way of referring to the *via moderna*.

4 Luther's early theology (1509–14) shows no trace of the radical Augustinianism associated with Gregory of Rimini and the *schola*

Augustiniana moderna. How can this be explained if Luther was as familiar with this theology as Oberman suggests?

5   The Wittenberg statutes of 1508 relate to the faculty of arts, not the faculty of theology. It would therefore be expected that they endorse the philosophical, not the theological, views associated with Gregory of Rimini. As we noted earlier, Gregory's philosophical views are typical of the *via moderna*, even though his theology is radically Augustinian. The statutes therefore appear to allow Gregory's philosophical views to be taught at Wittenberg – that is, the ideas of the *via moderna.* The consensus among most recent studies appears to be that Oberman's hypothesis, although a valuable stimulus to research on Luther's relation to late medieval thought, thus seems to be untenable.

Calvin's Relation to Late Medieval Scholasticism

Calving began his academic career at the University of Paris in the 1520s. As study after study has made clear, the University of Paris – and especially Calvin's college, the Collège de Montaigu – was a stronghold of the *via moderna.* During his four or five years studying at the faculty of arts at Paris, Calvin could not have avoided encountering the leading ideas of this movement.

One especially obvious point of affinity between Calvin and late medieval theology concerns voluntarism – the doctrine that the ultimate grounds of merit lie in the will of God, not in the intrinsic goodness of an action.[16] To explore this doctrine, let us consider a human moral action – for example, giving money to a charity. What is the meritorious value of this action? What is it worth in the sight of God? The relation between the moral (that is, the human) and the meritorious (that is, the divine) value of actions was, of major concern to late medieval theologians. Two distinctive approaches developed: the *intellectualist* and the *voluntarist.*

The intellectualist approach argued that the divine intellect recognized the inherent moral value of an act and rewarded it accordingly. There was a direct connection between the moral and the meritorious. The voluntarist approach rejected this, arguing that it made God dependent on his creatures. The meritorious value of a human action could not be allowed to be predetermined; God had to be free to choose whatever value he liked. There was thus no necessary connection between the moral and the meritorious. So the meritorious value of a human action does not rest upon its inherent value, but is grounded solely in the worth which God chooses to ascribe to it.

This principle is summarized in the maxim of Duns Scotus (usually, though not entirely correctly, regarded as the originator of the trend towards voluntarism in later medieval thought) to the effect that the value of an offering is determined solely by the divine will, rather than by its inherent goodness. The divine will imposed whatever value it chose upon human actions, thereby preserving the freedom of God. In the later Middle Ages, the voluntarist position gained increasing sympathy, especially within radical Augustinian circles. Most theologians of the *via moderna* and *schola Augustiniana moderna* adopted it.

In the *Institutes*, Calvin adopts precisely this voluntarist position in relation to the merit of Christ. Although this is implicit in earlier editions of the work, it is only explicitly stated in the 1559 edition, in the aftermath of Calvin's correspondence with Laelius Socinus on the subject. In 1555, Calvin responded to questions raised by Socinus concerning the merit of Christ and the assurance of faith, and appears to have incorporated these replies directly into the text of the 1559 edition of the *Institutes*.

The death of Christ on the cross is a central focus of Christian thought and worship. But why should the death of Christ have such enormous importance? What justification can be given for its centrality? Why is the death of *Christ* – rather than of any other individual – declared to be of unique significance? In the course of this correspondence, Calvin considers this question, known technically as the '*ratio meriti Christi* (the basis of the merit of Christ)'. Why is Christ's death on the cross sufficient to purchase the redemption of humanity? Is it something intrinsic to the person of Christ, as Luther had argued? For Luther, the divinity of Christ was adequate grounds for declaring that his death was uniquely important. Or was it that God chose to accept his death as sufficient to merit the redemption of humanity? Was this value *inherent* in Christ's death, or was it *imposed* upon it by God? Calvin makes clear his view that the basis of Christ's merit is not located in Christ's offering of himself (which would correspond to an intellectualist approach to the *ratio meriti Christi*), but in the divine decision to accept such an offering as of sufficient merit for the redemption of mankind (which corresponds to the voluntarist approach). For Calvin, 'apart from God's good pleasure, Christ could not merit anything (*nam Christus nonnisi ex Dei beneplacito quidquam mereri potuit*)'. The continuity between Calvin and the late medieval voluntarist tradition will be evident.

In the past, this similarity between Calvin and Scotus has been taken to imply the direct influence of Scotus on Calvin. In fact, however, Calvin's continuity appears to be with the late medieval voluntarist tradition, deriving from William of Ockham and Gregory of Rimini, in relation to which Scotus marks a point of transition. No reason may be given for the meritorious nature of Christ's sacrifice save that God benevolently ordained to accept it as such. The continuity of Calvin with this later tradition is evident.

In 1963 Karl Reuter published a work on Calvin's thought which developed a major hypothesis of Calvin research, which he further elaborated in 1981: namely, that Calvin was decisively influenced by the leading Scottish scholastic theologian John Major (or Mair) then teaching at Paris.[17] Reuter argued that Major introduced Calvin to 'a new conception of anti-Pelagian and Scotist theology, and a renewed Augustinianism' at Paris. It was through the influence of Major, according to Reuter, that Calvin encountered the ideas of writers such as Augustine, Thomas Bradwardine and Gregory of Rimini.

Reuter's hypothesis was subjected to considerable criticism, centring mainly upon the circumstantial nature of the evidence Reuter offered. For example, there is no evidence that Calvin was taught by Major, whatever similarities there may be between their ideas. Equally, Calvin's earlier writings (for example, the 1536 edition of the *Institutes*) make no reference to Major. Nevertheless, it is evident that Calvin does show remarkable affinities with the ideas of the *schola Augustiniana moderna*, and it is possible that Calvin reflects the influence of this tradition, rather than that of one specific individual. Even if Reuter's hypothesis as originally stated is untenable, it seems that there are excellent reasons for suggesting that Calvin may well reflect the influence of a late medieval Augustinian tradition, such as that associated with the *schola Augustiniana moderna*.

An analysis of Calvin's theology will show why this possibility is so plausible. The following seven major features of Calvin's thought have direct parallels with the *schola Augustiniana moderna*:

1   A strict epistemological 'nominalism' or 'terminism'.
2   A voluntarist, as opposed to an intellectualist, understanding of the grounds of human merit and also of the merit of Jesus Christ.
3   The extensive use of the writings of Augustine, particularly his anti-Pelagian works, which concentrate on the doctrine of grace.
4   A strongly pessimistic view of human nature, with the Fall being identified as a watershed in the history of human salvation.
5   A strong emphasis upon the priority of God in the salvation of humanity.
6   A radical doctrine of absolute double predestination (pp. 135–40).
7   A rejection of the role of intermediaries, such as 'created habits of grace', in justification or merit. God can accept individuals *directly* into fellowship with him, without the need for intermediaries of this nature.

This last point is of especial interest, as it represents an example of the application of 'Ockham's razor'. William of Ockham developed the idea, char-

acteristic of nominalism, that intermediate ideas or concepts should be eliminated or reduced to a minimum. For example, the notion of a universal (see.
p. 70) is treated by Ockham as a totally unnecessary intermediary, which can
be dispensed with. It is obvious that Calvin was prepared to shave away many
of the theological ideas of early scholasticism by using this razor.

The Social Context of Scholasticism

In assessing the significance of any intellectual movement, it is essential to
determine the sections of society in which its ideas were transmitted and
developed. For example, we have already seen that humanism was primarily
a cultural and educational movement, whose ideas achieved a wide circulation at the time of the Renaissance in the upper strata of Italian (and, to a
lesser extent, northern European) society, in liberal arts faculties and in educationalist circles. Humanist ideas are also known to have been adopted by
many members of religious Orders.[18] The impression gained is that of an intellectual movement whose ideas were received and transmitted across a number
of important sociological boundaries.

In the case of scholasticism, however, we are faced with a very different
situation. The main scholastic schools were specifically linked with religious
Orders. Thus the Dominicans tended to propagate Thomism and the Franciscans Scotism, although the ideas of the *via moderna* were well established
within both Orders by the fifteenth century. A scholastic would generally be
a member of a religious Order. The University of Padua represents a relatively
rare instance of scholasticism which is not specifically linked with a religious
Order. It is therefore clear that the impact of scholasticism was severely limited
in society. The social mobility so characteristic of humanism is strikingly
absent. Equally, it is obvious that scholasticism was subject to geographical
restrictions: thus, for example, scholasticism was a significant intellectual force
in early sixteenth-century Germany, but not in Switzerland. Thus, while it was
virtually impossible for an educated person to avoid being influenced by
humanism in the early sixteenth century, scholasticism was then an intellectual force on the wane, increasingly confined to certain strongholds in northern Europe.

Two points of relevance to the Reformation will be obvious. First, the
background of the reformers prior to the genesis of their reforming vocation
is of major importance in determining the extent to which they are influenced
by, or feel obliged to enter into argument with, scholasticism. Luther, it may
be noted, is the only major reformer whose origins point to such an encounter
with scholasticism; for he was a member of a religious Order engaged in uni-

versity teaching, whereas Zwingli was simply a parish priest. Also, Luther was German, and Zwingli Swiss. Second, the social mobility associated with humanism allows us to understand how Luther's ideas of 1517–19 achieved such wide circulation. Although Luther's theology at this stage was still remarkably scholastic in form, it was 'productively misunderstood' (Berndt Moeller) by the humanist sodalities as embodying *humanist* values, thus giving those ideas the mobility normally associated only with humanism. The main carrier of the ideals of the Reformation, whether in Germany or Switzerland, was the humanist movement: the essential difference between the two Reformations is that Zwingli's ideas *were* initially humanist, whereas Luther's were *misunderstood* as being humanist.

That Luther was so often misunderstood during the 1520s should not be cause for surprise. Few had the opportunity to read Luther's writings; as studies of the reception of his ideas in Spain and Italy make clear, most people seem to have known about his ideas at second or third hand. As a result, distortion and misunderstanding were inevitable. To give one obvious, if very hackneyed example, German peasants thought that Luther was sympathetic to their cause, and felt themselves to have been betrayed when he made his true position known. Again, Lollardy (pp. 35–7) developed attitudes which were generally strongly anti-priests, anti-sacrament and anti-church, and believed that, as Luther's doctrine of justification seemed to reinforce these attitudes, it followed that Luther himself had no place for priests, sacraments or the institution of the church in his vision of reformed Christianity. Part of Luther's appeal to Lollardy thus rested on a misunderstanding of his position.

In the present chapter we have considered the phenomenon of medieval scholasticism, and indicated its potential relevance to the Reformation. In a later chapter, we shall explore how humanism and scholasticism converged in the theological breakthrough of Martin Luther.

For further reading

An excellent introduction to the phenomenon of 'scholasticism' is:

Josef Pieper, *Scholasticism: Personalities and Problems of Medieval Philosophy* (London, 1960).

On the via moderna, see:

W. J. Courtenay, 'Nominalism and Late Medieval Religion', in *The Pursuit of Holiness in Late Medieval Religion*, ed. C. Trinkaus and H. A. Oberman (Leiden, 1974), pp. 26–59.

——, 'Late Medieval Nominalism Revisited: 1972–1982', *Journal of the History of Ideas* 44 (1983), pp. 159–64.

Alister E. McGrath, *The Intellectual Origins of the European Reformation* (Oxford, 1987), pp. 70–85.

On the schola Augustiniana moderna, see:

McGrath, *Intellectual Origins of the European Reformation*, pp. 86–93.

Heiko A. Oberman, *Masters of the Reformation: The Emergence of a New Intellectual Climate in Europe* (Cambridge, 1981), pp. 64–110.

David C. Steinmetz, *Luther and Staupitz: An Essay in the Intellectual Origins of the Protestant Reformation* (Durham, N.C., 1980), pp. 13–27.

5

The Reformers:
A Biographical Introduction

It is perhaps too easy to overlook the fact that the Reformation was not simply about social forces (a weakness which seriously reduces the value of the model of the Reformation offered by social historians), nor simply about religious ideas (a weakness which can often be detected in more explicitly theological accounts of the Reformation). The thought of the Reformation was generated and developed by a group of highly significant individuals. While there is no doubt that social factors were deeply involved in the manner in which these ideas were received, and the impact which they had upon society at large, this does not permit us to overlook the individuals who contributed so significantly to the genesis and development of the thought of the Reformation.

It is generally agreed that the Reformation had two leading luminaries: Martin Luther and John Calvin. The Swiss reformer Huldrych Zwingli, although widely agreed to have been of major importance in relation to the origins and early development of the Reformation in Switzerland, is generally regarded as the 'third man' of the Reformation. This generally low estimation of Zwingli has often been challenged by scholars anxious to point out the originality of his thought, and his major role in laying the ground for the consolidation of the Reformation within the political sphere of influence of certain leading Swiss cantons. Nevertheless, the general perception remains that Zwingli has, rightly or wrongly, had considerably less influence on the shaping of western Christian thought than Luther or Calvin.

The present chapter offers a biographical overview of five leading reformers. The three figures just noted are supplemented by brief accounts of Luther's colleague Philipp Melanchthon, and the reformer of the great city of Strasbourg, Martin Bucer. It is strongly recommended that you read this chapter before proceeding to engage with the more specifically theological ideas of the Reformation, to be discussed in later chapters. This chapter provides important historical and biographical information which is essential background material to these ideas. We begin by considering the greatest of the first wave of reformers – Martin Luther.

Martin Luther

Martin Luther (1483–1546) is widely regarded as one of the most significant of the reformers. Luther was born on 10 November, 1483 in the German town of Eisleben, and named after Martin of Tours, whose festival fell on 11 November, the day of Luther's baptism. Hans Luder (as the name was spelled at this stage) moved the following year to the neighbouring town of Mansfeld, where he established a small copper mining business. Luther's university education began at Erfurt in 1501. His father clearly intended him to become a lawyer, not unaware of the financial benefits that this would bring the family. In 1505, Luther completed the general arts course at Erfurt, and was in a position to move on to study law.

As events turned out, the study of law never got very far. At some point around 30 June, 1505, Luther was returning to Erfurt from a visit to Mansfeld. As he neared the village of Storterheim, a severe thunderstorm gathered around him. Suddenly, a bolt of lightning struck the ground next to him, throwing him off his horse. Terrified, Luther cried out, 'St Anne, help me! I will become a monk!' (St Anne was the patron saint of miners.) On 17 July, 1505, he entered the most rigorous of the seven major monasteries at Erfurt – the Augustinian priory. Luther's father was outraged at the decision, and remained alienated from his son for some considerable time.

The Erfurt Augustinian monastery had close links with the University of Erfurt, which allowed Luther to wrestle with the great names of late medieval religious thought – such as William of Ockham, Pierre d'Ailly, and Gabriel Biel – in the course of his preparation for ordination. He was ordained priest in 1507. By 1509, he had gained his first major theological qualification. Finally, on 18 October, 1512, he was awarded the degree of Doctor of Divinity, the culmination of his academic studies. By then, however, he had moved from Erfurt, and established himself at the nearby town of Wittenberg, which was the home of one of the newer German universities.

The University of Wittenberg was founded in 1502 by Frederick the Wise. His motives in establishing this seat of learning were not entirely educational: he probably wanted to overshadow the reputation of the neighbouring university of Leipzig. Luther took up a chair of biblical studies at Wittenberg immediately after gaining his doctorate, and remained there (apart from occasional periods of absence) for the rest of his life. He owed this position to Johann von Staupitz, vicar general of the German Observant Augustinian friars, who had held the position before him.

Luther's lectures at Wittenberg are widely regarded as laying the foundations for his subsequent theological development. It is of considerable significance that Luther's emerging theology was forged against the backdrop of a sustained engagement with certain biblical texts. Over the critical period 1513–19, Luther lectured as follows:

1513–15	Psalms (first course of lectures)
1515–16	Romans
1516–17	Galatians
1517–18	Hebrews

At some point during this period, Luther radically changed his theological views. There is intense scholarly debate over both the nature and the date of this breakthrough, and we shall consider this in more detail in the following chapter.

Luther was propelled to fame through a series of controversies. The first such controversy centred on the sale of indulgences. Archbishop Albert of Mainz had given permission for the sales of indulgences in his territories. Johann Tetzel, who was responsible for the sale of these indulgences in the Wittenberg region, irritated Luther considerably, and moved him to write to Archbishop Albert, protesting against the practice and offering 95 Latin theses which he proposed to dispute at the University of Wittenberg. Luther's colleague Philipp Melanchthon subsequently reported that these 95 theses were also 'posted' (that is, nailed for public display) on the door of the castle church at Wittenberg on 31 October, 1517. This date has subsequently been observed by some as marking the beginning of the Reformation. In fact, the theses drew little attention until later, when Luther circulated them more widely and had them translated into German.

The archbishop regarded the thesis as a direct challenge to his authority, and forwarded them with a letter of complaint to Rome. However, this had less impact than might have been expected. The papacy needed the support of Frederick the Wise to secure the election of its favoured candidate to succeed the Holy Roman Emperor Maximillian. As a result, Luther was not summoned to Rome to answer the charges laid against him, but was examined locally in 1518 by the papal legate Cajetan. Luther refused to withdraw his criticisms of the practice of selling indulgences.

Luther's profile was raised considerably in 1519 at the Leipzig Disputation. This disputation pitted Luther and his Wittenberg colleague Andreas Bodenstein von Karlstadt against Johann Eck, a highly regarded theologian from Ingolstadt. During the course of a complicated debate over the nature of authority, Eck managed to get Luther to admit that, in his view, both popes and general councils could err. Even more, Luther indicated a degree of support for Jan Huss, the Bohemian reformer who had been condemned as a heretic some time previously. Eck clearly regarded himself to have won the debate, in that he had forced Luther to state views on papal authority which were unorthodox by the standards of the day.

Others, however, were delighted by Luther's criticisms. Of particular importance was the reaction of many humanists, who saw Luther's criticisms as indicating that he was one of their number. In fact, this was not the case. Nevertheless, this 'constructive misunderstanding' led Luther to be lionized by humanists around this time, and given a high profile within humanist circles. Although Luther's controversy with Erasmus over the period 1524–5 finally ended any notion that Luther was sympathetic to a humanist agenda, he enjoyed at least the tacit support of many humanists (including Erasmus and Bucer) for several years after the Leipzig Disputation.

Luther's brief flirtation with humanism around 1519 can be illustrated from the way in which he styled himself. One of the conceits of the age was that humanist writers would insist on being known by the Latin or Greek versions of their personal names, perhaps in order to lend themselves a little more dignity. Thus Philipp Schwarzerd became 'Melanchthon' (literally, 'black earth'); Johann Hauschein became 'Oecolampadius' (literally, 'house light'). At some point around 1519, Luther himself fell victim to this trend of the age. By then, Luther was gaining a reputation as a critic of the medieval church. His emphasis upon Christian freedom – evident in the 1520 writing *On the Freedom of a Christian* – led him to play around with the original spelling of his family name 'Luder'. He altered this to 'Eleutherius' – literally, 'liberator'. Within what seems to have been a very short period of time, he tired of this pretension. But the new way of spelling his family name remained. Luder had become Luther.

In 1520, Luther published three major works which immediately established his reputation as a major popular reformer. Shrewdly, Luther wrote in German, making his ideas accessible to a wide public: where Latin was the language of the intellectual and ecclesiastical elite of Europe, German was the language of the common people. In the *Appeal to the German Nobility*, Luther argued passionately for the need for reform of the church. In both its doctrine and its practices, the church of the early sixteenth century had cast itself adrift from the New Testament. His pithy and witty German gave added popular appeal to some intensely serious theological ideas.

Encouraged by the remarkable success of this work, Luther followed it up with *The Babylonian Captivity of the Christian Church*. In this powerful piece of writing, Luther argued that the gospel had become captive to the institutional church. The medieval church, he argued, had imprisoned the gospel in a complex system of priests and sacraments. The church had become the master of the gospel, where it should be its servant. This point was further developed in *The Liberty of a Christian*, in which Luther stressed both the freedom and obligations of the believer.

By now, Luther was at the centre of both controversy and condemnation. On 15 June, 1520, Luther was censured by a papal bull, and ordered to retract his views. He refused, adding insult to injury by publicly burning the bull. He was excommunicated in January of the following year, and summoned to appear before the Diet of Worms. Again, he refused to withdraw his views. Luther's position became increasingly serious. Realizing this, a friendly German prince arranged for him to be 'kidnapped', and took him off to the safety of the Wartburg, a castle near Eisenach. During his eight months of isolation, Luther had time to think through the implications of many of his ideas, and to test the genuineness of his motives. By the time he returned to Wittenberg in 1522 to take charge of the Reformation in that town, his ideas were gaining considerable support throughout Europe. By this stage, the Reformation may be said to have begun. In its early phase, it was decisively shaped by Luther.

Luther's influence on the Reformation at this early stage was fundamental. His period of isolation at the Wartburg allowed him to work on a number of major reforming projects, including liturgical revision, biblical translation, and other reforming treatises. The New Testament appeared in German in 1522, although it was not until 1534 that the entire Bible was translated and published. In 1524, Luther argued for the need to establish schools in German towns, and to extend education to women. The two Catechisms of 1529 broke new ground in religious education (see chapter 12).

Serious controversy, however, was not slow to break out. In 1524, Erasmus published a work which was severely critical of his views on human free will. Luther's reply of 1525 was not the most diplomatic of documents, and led to a final break with Erasmus. More seriously, the Peasants' War of 1525 caused Luther's reputation to suffer severely. Luther argued that the feudal lords had every right to end the peasants' revolt, by force where necessary. Luther's writings on this matter – such as his *Against the Thieving and Murderous Hordes of Peasants* – had virtually no impact on the revolt itself, but tarnished his image severely.

Perhaps the most significant controversy erupted over the very different views on the nature of the real presence held by Luther and Huldrych Zwingli (see chapter 9). Luther's strong commitment to the real presence of Christ in the eucharist contrasted sharply with Zwingli's metaphorical or symbolic approach. Although many sought to reconcile the two views, or at least to limit the damage caused by the differences – these eventually came to nothing. The Colloquy of Marburg (1529), arranged by Philip of Hesse, was of particular importance. Its failure can be argued to have led to the permanent alienation of the German and Swiss reforming factions at a time when increasingly adverse political and military considerations made collaboration imperative.

By 1527, it was clear that Luther was not a healthy man. What can now be recognized as Meniere's disease has established itself. Convinced that he had not long to live, Luther married a former nun, Katharina von Bora. Although Luther went on to produce a number of major theological works in his later period (most notably, a commentary on Galatians), his attention was increasingly taken up with his personal health, and the politics of the Reformation struggles. He died in 1546 while attempting to mediate in a somewhat minor quarrel which had broken out between some members of the German nobility in the city of Mansfeld.

Luther's influence on virtually every aspect of Reformation thought is immense. His approaches to biblical interpretation, the doctrine of justification, the church, and the sacraments remain theological landmarks, and will be discussed in detail in this work. His views on the relation of church and state, however, are perhaps not as fully thought through as one might like, and bear the impression of having been forged under the pressure of conflict. Nevertheless, Luther must be considered to be one of the two most significant representatives of the Reformation, and it is imperative that his ideas are examined in some detail.

We now move on to consider the career of a lesser figure – the Swiss reformer Huldrych Zwingli.

Huldrych Zwingli

It is impossible to understand the career and strategy of the Swiss reformer Huldrych Zwingli (1484–1531) without considering his background within the Swiss Confederation. The name 'Switzerland' derives from one of the three original cantons – Schwyz, Uri and Unterwalden – which signed a treaty of mutual defence against the Austrians in 1291. This confederation – known as the 'Helvetic Confederation' (*Confederatio Helvetica*) – was gradually enlarged in the following years. In 1332, Lucerne joined the confederation, followed by Zurich (1351), Glarus and Zug (1352), and Berne (1353). The strength of this confederation was demonstrated at the battle of Nähenfels (1388), at which an historic victory ensured its survival. The great legend of William Tell — a Swiss patriot who fought against the Austrian oppressors – has its origins in the events of this period. In 1481, the cantons of Solothurn and Fribourg joined the confederation, bringing the total membership to ten. In 1501, Basel and Schaffhausen joined, followed by Appenzell in 1513. No further cantons joined the confederation until the aftermath of the French Revolution.

Zwingli was born on New Year's Day, 1484 in the Toggenburg valley in the canton of St Gallen, in the eastern part of modern-day Switzerland. Strictly speaking, St Gallen was not part of the Swiss Confederation. However, in the treaty of 1451, St Gallen had allied itself to some of the Swiss cantons, and Zwingli always appears to have regarded himself as Swiss. After an initial period of education at Berne, Zwingli attended the University of Vienna (1498–1502). Vienna was widely regarded as one of the most exciting universities close to Switzerland, on account of the university reforms then taking place. Under the guidance of leading humanists, such as Conrad Celtis, the university was adopting humanist reforms. He then moved to the University of Basel (1502–6), where he strengthened his humanist position. In 1506, he was ordained priest, and served in this capacity at Glarus for the next ten years, before moving to serve as 'people's priest' at the Benedictine monastery at Einsiedeln in 1516.

During his time as parish priest of Glarus, Zwingli served as a chaplain to Swiss soldiers serving as mercenaries in the Franco-Italian war. He was present at the disaster of Marignano (1515), in which large numbers of Swiss soldiers died. This event confirmed Zwingli's opposition to the mercenary trade, and was also of fundamental importance in the development of Swiss isolationism. In the light of Marignano, it was decided that the Swiss would take no part in other peoples' wars again.

By 1516, Zwingli had become convinced of the need for reform of the church, along the lines suggested by biblical humanists such as Erasmus. He purchased Erasmus' edition of the Greek New Testament, and studied the writings of both the Greek and Latin patristic authors. By the time he left Einsiedeln for Zurich, Zwingli had become convinced of the need to base Christian belief and practice on Scripture, not human traditions.

On 1 January, 1519, Zwingli took up his new position as 'people's priest' at the Great Minster in Zurich. From the outset, his commitment to a program of reform was obvious. He began to preach a course of sermons on Matthew's gospel, ignoring the conventional lectionary altogether. Zwingli's career at Zurich came close to being ended abruptly; he nearly died during an outbreak of the plague at Zurich in the summer of 1519. The influence of his escape on his thinking on providence is well established, and will be considered later in this work (see chapter 7).

It was not long before Zwingli's reforms became more radical. In 1522, he was actively preaching against virtually every aspect of traditional catholic religion, including the cult of the saints, the practice of fasting, and the worship of Mary. His preaching caused controversy within the city, and alarmed the city council. Anxious at the unrest which was growing within the city, the city council determined to settle the matter. In January 1523, a great public disputation was arranged between Zwingli and his catholic opponents. The

City Council sat in judgement, as Zwingli debated his programme of reform with some local catholic clergy. It soon became clear that Zwingli was gaining the upper hand. Able to translate without difficulty from Hebrew, Greek or Latin into the local Zurich dialect, Zwingli displayed a mastery of Scripture which his opponents simply could not match. There could only be one outcome. The City Council decided that a programme of reform based on scripture, such as that outlined by Zwingli, would become official city policy.

In 1525, Zurich city council finally abolished the mass, and substituted Zwingli's version of the Last Supper. Zwingli's views on precisely what took place at the eucharist would prove to be immensely controversial (see chapter 9); indeed, Zwingli is perhaps best remembered for his radical 'memorialist' view of the Lord's Supper, which he regards as a remembrance of Christ's death in his absence.

Encouraged by his reforming successes, Zwingli persuaded other city councils to have public debates along the same lines. A major breakthrough took place in 1528, when the city of Berne decided to adopt the Reformation after a similar public disputation. Berne was a major centre of political and military power in the region. Its political and military support for beleaguered Geneva in 1536 would prove to be decisive in establishing Calvin's influence over the second phase of the Reformation. Calvin's success as a reformer thus owes more to Zwingli than is generally realized.

Zwingli was killed in battle on 11 October, 1531, defending his reformation.

Philipp Melanchthon

One of Luther's closest associates at Wittenberg was Philipp Melanchthon (1497–1560). Melanchthon was born on 16 February, 1497, and went on to attend university at Heidelberg (1509–12) and Tübingen (1512–18). He then moved to a newly-established position at the University of Wittenberg in 1518.

Although Melanchthon's speciality was Greek, he soon developed an interest in theology, encouraged to no small extent by Luther, under whose influence he soon fell. One of Melanchthon's earliest theological emphases related to the authority of Scripture. This is particularly clear from a series of theses which he presented for the degree of Bachelor of Theology in 1519. However, it is generally agreed that this emphasis upon the authority of Scripture is seen at its clearest in a work for which Melanchthon is particularly remembered – the *Loci Communes* ('Commonplaces'), which appeared in its first edition in 1521.

We shall consider the influence of the *Loci Communes* in chapter 12. However, at this stage we may note how Melanchthon constructed the work around a series of biblical themes, particularly relating to the doctrine of justification. The basic intention was to offer a system of Christian theology which was both generated and governed by Scripture. Melanchthon clearly regarded Peter Lombard's *Four Books of the Sentences* – the standard medieval textbook of theology – as deficient in this respect, and wished to move towards an approach which took central themes from Romans as normative. His role as an educationalist was also particularly clear with his finalizing the text of both the Augsburg Confession and its Apology, both of which were published in 1530.

Luther's condemnation by Rome placed severe limitations on his travel. It therefore often fell to Melanchthon to undertake speaking engagements outside electoral Saxony. As a result, the development and diffusion of the Lutheran Reformation often reflected the particular emphases associated with him. In particular, Melanchthon placed an emphasis upon *adiaphora* ('matters of indifference'), believing that it was possible to tolerate disagreement over certain matters. The issue became of particular importance after Luther's death in 1546, when a series of political and military reverses meant that Lutheranism found itself having to adapt to an increasingly unsympathetic situation. Melanchthon's attempt to develop a pragmatic approach, intended to safeguard as much of the Lutheran heritage as possible under the new circumstances, was regarded as tantamount to betrayal by many. The rise of the Gnesio-Lutheran movement can be seen as a reaction against Melanchthon's accommodations.

We now turn to consider another reformer who achieved much at the time, but has generally been neglected subsequently — Martin Bucer.

Martin Bucer

Martin Bucer (1491–1551) was born in Alsace. He joined the Dominican Order at an early age, perhaps wishing to take advantage of the educational opportunities which this offered. Bucer (also known as 'Butzer') went on to study theology at Heidelberg in 1517. He began to develop an admiration for Erasmus; this was both confirmed and significantly redirected in 1518, when he heard Luther speak at the Heidelberg Disputation. Bucer gained the impression that Luther merely stated explicitly what Erasmus hinted at implicitly, and thus came to the view that Luther and Erasmus could be seen as fighting for reform on the basis of a common set of assumptions.

In May 1523, Bucer moved to the imperial city of Strasbourg. The Reformation was under way in the city at this time, although in a somewhat attenuated and uncertain form. Bucer became involved in the movement, and became one of its most important apologists and theoreticians. He was heavily involved in intra-evangelical dialogues, in which he sought to maintain unity within the reforming movement. Although Bucer personally sided with Zwingli in the debate over the real presence, he actively campaigned for reconciliation on this issue, sensing the serious threat which it posed to unity. The 'Wittenberg Concord' (1536) is generally regarded as his greatest achievement in this respect, in that it developed the notion of a common evangelical foundation, on the basis of which variations of emphasis or accentuation might be accepted.

Bucer's greatest impact was on the city of Strasbourg itself. During the 1530s, Bucer was able to establish a viable reformed church, which became a model for others seeking to achieve something similar in other cities. The sojourn of John Calvin in Strasbourg (1538–41) is of particular importance, as we shall note presently. However, Bucer chose to leave Strasbourg in 1549, following the political difficulties which arose through the defeat of the Schmalkaldic League by imperial forces over the period 1546–7. The same events which caused such difficulty for Melanchthon now caused related problems for Bucer.

Bucer emigrated to England. He was appointed Regius Professor of Divinity at Cambridge University by Edward VI, and devoted himself primarily to writing a major treatise on the ideal Christian society. *De regno Christi* ('On the reign of Christ') was published in 1550; it can be regarded as a model of reformed theology, in that it sought to reform both church and society on the basis of the gospel. Bucer died in 1551, without having achieved the reforms which he had sought.

Theologically, Bucer may be regarded as a complex amalgam. His emphasis upon divine sovereignty, expressed particularly in his doctrine of election, may be argued to lie behind many of Calvin's statements on the matter. Although he embraced Luther's reformation with enthusiasm, he preferred the Swiss position on the real presence in the eucharist. He also seemed to suggest that Luther's understanding of justification failed to give a due place to good works; in some ways, Bucer's own approach – which rested on a distinction between the 'justification of the ungodly' through faith and the 'justification of the godly' through works – can be seen as representing an Erasmian position, in which emphasis is placed upon the moral implications of justification.

We shall consider aspects of Bucer's thought at several points during this work. Our attention now turns to the second of the two leading theologians of the Reformation – John Calvin.

John Calvin

For many, the name of John Calvin (1509–64) is virtually synonymous with that of Geneva. Although Geneva is now part of Switzerland, in the sixteenth century it was a small independent city state. Calvin, however, was a Frenchman. He was born on 10 July, 1509 in the cathedral city of Noyon, about seventy miles north-east of Paris. His father was involved in the financial administration of the local diocese, and could rely on the patronage of the bishop to ensure support for his son. At some point in the early 1520s (probably 1523), the young Calvin was sent up to the University of Paris.

After a thorough grounding in Latin grammar at the hands of Mathurin Cordier, Calvin entered the Collège de Montaigu. After completing his rigorous education in the arts, Calvin moved to Orléans to study civil law, probably at some point in 1528. Although Calvin's father had originally intended that his son should study theology, he appears to have changed his mind. His father seems to have realized that the study of law, Calvin later remarked, generally makes people rich. It is also possible that Calvin's father may have lost the patronage of the local bishop on account of a financial wrangle back at Noyon.

It is generally thought that Calvin's detailed study of civil law gave him access to methods and ideas which he would later exploit in his career as a reformer. It was at Orléans that he learned Greek. At some point in 1529 Calvin moved to Bourges, attracted by the fame of the great Italian lawyer Andrea Alciati. Most Calvin scholars consider that Calvin's great clarity of expression is due to the influence of Alciati. Calvin's encounter with French legal humanism is generally thought to have been of fundamental importance in shaping his understanding of the way in which a classical text (such as the Bible or Roman legal texts) could be applied to modern situations.

Soon after graduating in law, Calvin had to return to Noyon. His father was ill, and died in May 1531. He had been excommunicated by the local cathedral chapter. Freed from family obligations (his mother had died while he was a child), Calvin returned to Paris to continue his studies, and became increasingly sympathetic to the reforming ideas then gaining an excited hearing in that city. The university and city authorities, however, were intensely hostile to Luther's ideas. On 2 November, 1533, Calvin was obliged to leave

Paris suddenly. The rector of the university of Paris, Nicolas Cop, had delivered a university address in which he openly supported Luther's doctrine of justification by faith. The Parliament at Paris immediately took action against Cop. A copy of Cop's address exists in Calvin's handwriting, suggesting that he may have composed the address. At any rate, Calvin fled Paris, fearful for his safety.

By 1534 Calvin had become an enthusiastic supporter of the principles of the Reformation. During the following year, he settled down in the Swiss city of Basle, safe from any French threat. Making the best use of his enforced leisure, he published a book destined to exercise a decisive effect upon the Reformation: the *Institutes of the Christian Religion*. First published in May 1536, this work was a systematic and lucid exposition of the main points of the Christian faith. It attracted considerable attention to its author, who revised and expanded the work considerably during the remainder of his life. The first edition of the book had six chapters; the final edition, published in 1559 (and translated by Calvin into his native French in 1560), had eighty. It is generally regarded as one of the greatest works to emerge from the Reformation. We shall consider its development and influence in more detail in chapter 12.

After winding up his affairs in Noyon early in 1536, Calvin decided to settle down to a life of private study in the city of Strasbourg. Unfortunately, the direct route from Noyon to Strasbourg was impassable, due to the outbreak of war between Francis I of France and the Emperor Charles V. Calvin had to make an extended detour, passing through the city of Geneva which had recently gained its independence from the neighbouring territory of Savoy. Geneva was then in a state of confusion, having just evicted its local bishop and begun a controversial programme of reform under the Frenchmen Guillaume Farel and Pierre Viret. On hearing that Calvin was in the city, they demanded that he stay, and help the cause of the Reformation. Calvin reluctantly agreed.

His attempts to provide the Genevan church with a solid basis of doctrine and discipline met intense resistance. Having just thrown out their local bishop, the last thing that many Genevans wanted was the imposition of new religious obligations. Calvin's attempts to reform the doctrine and discipline of the Genevan church were fiercely resisted by a well-organized opposition. After a series of quarrels, matters reached a head on Easter Day 1538: Calvin was expelled from the city, and sought refuge in Strasbourg.

Having arrived in Strasbourg two years later than he had anticipated, Calvin began to make up for lost time. In quick succession he produced a series of major theological works. He revised and expanded his *Institutes* (1539), and produced the first French translation of this work (1541); he produced a major defence of reformation principles in his famous *Reply to Sadoleto* (Cardinal

Sadoleto had written to the Genevans, inviting them to return to the Roman Catholic church); and his skills as a biblical exegete were demonstrated in his *Commentary on the Epistle to the Romans.* As pastor to the French-speaking congregation in the city, Calvin was able to gain experience of the practical problems facing reformed pastors. Through his friendship with Martin Bucer, the Strasbourg reformer, Calvin was able to develop his thinking on the relation between the city and church.

In September 1541, Calvin was asked to return to Geneva. In this absence, the religious and political situation had deteriorated. The city appealed to him to return, and restore order and confidence within the city. The Calvin who returned to Geneva was a wiser and more experienced young man, far better equipped for the massive tasks awaiting him than he had been three years earlier. Although Calvin would still find himself quarrelling with the city authorities for more than a decade, it was from a position of strength. Finally, opposition to his programme of reform died out. For the last decade of his life, he had virtually a free hand in the religious affairs of the city.

During this second period in Geneva, Calvin was able to develop both his own theology and the organization of the Genevan reformed church. He established the Consistory as a means of enforcing church discipline, and founded the Genevan Academy to educate pastors in reformed churches. The period was not without its controversies. Calvin found himself embroiled in serious theological debate with Sebastien Castellion over the correct interpretation of Christ's descent into hell, and whether the Song of Songs was canonical. A furious and very public debate broke out between himself and Jerome Bolsec over the doctrine of predestination. Both Castellion and Bolsec ended up having to leave Geneva. A more serious controversy concerned Michael Servetus, accused by Calvin of heresy, who was finally burned at the stake in 1553. Although Calvin's role in this matter was less significant than some of his critics have implied, the Servetus affair continues to stain Calvin's reputation as a Christian leader.

By the early spring of 1564, it was obvious that Calvin was seriously ill. He preached for the last time from the pulpit of Saint-Pierre on the morning of Sunday 6 February. By April, it was clear that Calvin had not much longer to live. He found breathing difficult, and was chronically short of breath. Calvin died at eight o'clock on the evening of 27 May, 1564. At his own request, he was buried in a common grave, with no stone to mark his grave.

Calvin's theology remains of considerable interest, particularly in relation to his views on predestination and the doctrine of the church. We shall be considering some of those ideas in more detail later in this work.

Having considered something of the background to the leading contributors to the development of Reformation thought, we are now in a position to begin to engage with those ideas in more detail. We begin with a theme which was of central importance to Luther – the doctrine of justification by faith.

For further reading

The works below represent useful introductions in the English language to the life and leading ideas of the five figures discussed in this chapter.

Martin Luther

P. Althaus, *The Theology of Martin Luther* (Philadelphia, 1966).
R. H. Bainton, *Here I Stand: A Life of Martin Luther* (New York, 1950).
G. Ebeling, *Luther: An Introduction to his Thought* (London, 1970).
J. M. Kittelson, *Luther the Reformer: The Story of the Man and His Career* (Minneapolis, 1986).
A. E. McGrath, *Luther's Theology of the Cross* (Oxford: Blackwell, 1985).
H. A. Oberman, *Luther: Man between God and the Devil* (New Haven, 1986).

Huldrych Zwingli

O. Farner, *Zwingli the Reformer: His Life and Work* (Hamden, CT, 1968).
E. J. Furcha and H. W. Pipkin (eds), *Prophet, Pastor, Protestant: The Work of Huldrych Zwingli after Five Hundred Years* (Allison Park, PA, 1984).
G. W. Löcher, *Zwingli's Thought: New Perspectives* (Leiden, 1981).
G. R. Potter, *Zwingli* (Cambridge, 1976).
W. P. Stephens, *The Theology of Huldrych Zwingli* (Oxford, 1986).
R. C. Walton, *Zwingli's Theocracy* (Toronto, 1967).

Philipp Melanchthon

P. Fraenkel, *Testimonia Patrum: The Function of the Patristic Argument in the Theology of Philipp Melanchthon* (Geneva, 1961).
C. L. Manschreck, *Melanchthon: The Quiet Reformer* (New York, 1958).
E. P. Meijering, *Melanchthon and Patristic Thought: The Doctrines of Christ and Grace, the Trinity and the Creation* (Leiden, 1983).

Martin Bucer

M. U. Chrisman, *Strasbourg and the Reform* (New Haven, 1976).
H. Eells, *Martin Bucer* (New Haven, 1931).
C. Hopf, *Martin Bucer and the English Reformation* (Oxford, 1946).

W. P. Stephens, *The Holy Spirit in the Theology of Martin Bucer* (Cambridge, 1970).
D. F. Wright (ed.), *Martin Bucer: Reforming Church and Society* (Cambridge, 1994).

John Calvin

W. Bouwsma, *John Calvin: A Sixteenth-Century Portrait* (New York, 1987).
Q. Breen, *John Calvin: A Study in French Humanism* (Hamden, CT, 1968).
E. A. Dowey, *The Knowledge of God in Calvin's Theology* (New York, 1952).
H. Höpfl, *The Christian Polity of John Calvin* (Cambridge, 1982).
A. E. McGrath, *A Life of John Calvin* (Oxford, 1990).
W. Monter, *Calvin's Geneva* (New York, 1967).
T. H. L. Parker, *John Calvin: A Biography* (London, 1975).
F. Wendel, *Calvin: Origins and Development of His Religious Thought* (London, 1963).

6

The Doctrine of Justification by Faith

The first major theme of Reformation thought to be considered is the doctrine of justification by faith. Before exploring this particular doctrine, it is necessary to consider a central theme in Christian thought, which underlies many of the issues considered in this work. It is impossible to discuss the doctrines of justification, grace, predestination or the sacraments without some understanding of the complex notion of 'redemption through Christ'. The section which follows introduces this theme, and indicates its importance for Reformation thought in general.

A Foundational Theme: Redemption through Christ

The theme of 'redemption through Christ' resonates throughout the New Testament, Christian worship and Christian theology. The basic idea is that God has achieved the redemption of sinful humanity through the death of Christ on the cross.[1] This redemption could be achieved in no other way. The term 'soteriology' (from the Greek word *soteria*, 'salvation') is used in works of Christian theology to refer to the network of ideas and images which centres on the redemption achieved through the death and resurrection of Christ. Five broad components to this network of ideas can be discerned:

1 Images of victory. Christ has gained a victory over sin, death and evil through his cross and resurrection. Through faith, believers may share in that victory, and claim it as their own.
2 Images of changed legal status. Through his obedience on the cross, Christ has obtained forgiveness and pardon for sinners. Those who are guilty can be washed clean of their sin and be justified in the sight of God. They are acquitted of punishment, and given the status of being righteous before God. 'Justification' belongs to this category of images.

3   Images of changed personal relationships. Human sin entails alien-
    ation from God. 'God was in Christ reconciling the world to
    himself' (2 Corinthians 5:19), thus making a renewed relationship
    between himself and humanity possible and available. Just as humans
    who are alienated from one another can draw together again
    through the process of forgiveness and reconciliation, so those who
    are far from God can draw close to God through the death of Christ.
4   Images of liberation. Those who are imprisoned by the oppressive
    forces of evil, sin and the fear of death can be liberated through the
    death of Christ. Just as Christ broke free from the prison of death, so
    believers can, by faith, break free from the bonds of sin, and come to
    life in all its fullness. 'Redemption' belongs to this category of images.
5   Images of restoration to wholeness. Those who are ill on account of
    sin can be made whole again through the cross of Christ. Through
    his cross and resurrection, Christ is able to bind up our wounds and
    heal us, restoring us to wholeness and spiritual health. 'Salvation'
    belongs to this category of images.

'Justification' is a constituent of this network of soteriological terms used
to describe the Christian experience of redemption through Christ. It assumed
a position of special importance at the time of the Reformation partly on
account of the new interest in the writings of St Paul, in which it features
prominently (especially in the letters to the Romans and the Galatians). The
term 'justification' itself has become unfamiliar in a religious context, and
requires some explanation before we proceed any further. The English word
'justification' is an attempt to denote the complex Old Testament idea of being
'right before God'. Through a contorted and complex tradition of translation
and interpretation – from Hebrew to Greek, from Greek to Latin, and finally
from Latin to English – 'justification' has come to refer to the status of being
righteous in the sight of God. It is helpful to paraphrase the word 'justification'
as 'being right with God'. Similarly, 'to be justified' could be paraphrased as
'to be put in a right relationship with God'. At the heart of Luther's Reforming programme lay the question of how sinners are justified. We may begin
our discussion of this question by considering the meaning of the word 'grace'.

The Concept of Grace

As we have seen, the word 'grace' basically means 'the undeserved and unmerited divine favour towards humanity'. Within the New Testament, the idea of

grace is especially associated with the writings of St Paul. Within the history of the Christian church, the writer who developed and defended the concept of the grace of God most powerfully was Augustine of Hippo. Indeed, such was his emphasis upon this concept that he became generally known as *doctor gratiae*, 'the doctor of grace'. As the later Renaissance and Reformation periods witnessed a renewal of interest in the writings of both Paul and Augustine, it is understandable that there should have been renewed interest in the concept of grace at this time.

During the Middle Ages, grace tended to be understood as a supernatural substance, infused by God into the human soul in order to facilitate redemption.[2] One of the arguments underlying this approach made an appeal to the total and unbidgeable gap between God and human nature. There is no way that human beings can enter into a meaningful relationship with God, on account of this gap. Something is needed to bridge it before we can be accepted by God. That 'something' is grace.

Grace was therefore understood as something created within us by God to act as a bridge between pure human nature and divine nature – a kind of middling species. Grace was thus regarded as some sort of bridgehead or middle ground, by which the otherwise absolute gulf between God and humanity could be spanned. Grace was a substance, not an attitude of God; as noted earlier (p. 55), the medieval idea of Mary as a reservoir of grace rested partly on a mistranslation of a crucial biblical passage and partly on the idea of grace as some kind of material. Such ideas of grace had been the subject of severe criticism before the Reformation; by the beginning of the sixteenth century, they had largely fallen into disrepute.

It is the idea of grace as the unmerited favour of God which underlies the doctrine of justification by faith, generally and rightly regarded as underlying the origins of the Lutheran Reformation in Germany. A similar interest in the concept of grace underlies the Swiss Reformation, although this concern was expressed in a very different manner. As we shall see, Zwingli and Calvin laid considerable emphasis upon the related idea of divine sovereignty, which was particularly associated with the doctrine of predestination. We begin by considering Luther's discovery of the doctrine of justification by faith alone.

Martin Luther's Theological Breakthrough

Martin Luther is widely regarded as the most significant personality of the European Reformation. He looms large, not merely in the history of the Christian church, but also in the intellectual, political and social history of

Europe, and especially of Germany. In many ways, he appears as a tragic figure, with magnificent strengths and serious flaws. His stand against the Emperor at the Diet of Worms demonstrates his considerable personal courage, even if it is unlikely that he actually used the famous words attributed to him: 'Here I stand; I can no other.' Yet within a matter of years, his condemnation of the German peasants for revolting against their oppression seemed to many to indicate his political naïvety.

Luther stepped on to the stage of human history on account of an idea. That idea convinced him that the church of his day had misunderstood the gospel, the essence of Christianity. It was necessary to recall it to fidelity, to reform initially its ideology and subsequently its practices. His idea is summarized in the phrase 'justification by faith alone', and it is necessary to explain precisely what is meant by this and why it is of such importance. Luther's theological breakthrough, often referred to as the *Turmerlebnis* ('Tower Experience'), concerned the question of how it was possible for a sinner to enter into a relationship with a righteous God. In view of the enormous importance of this question to the development of the German Reformation, I propose to consider it in some detail.

The Doctrine of Justification

As we noted earlier in this chapter, at the heart of the Christian faith lies the idea that human beings, finite and frail though they are, can enter into a relationship with the living God. This idea is articulated in a number of metaphors and images, such as 'salvation' and 'redemption', initially in the writings of the New Testament (especially the Pauline letters) and subsequently in Christian theological reflection based upon these texts. By the late Middle Ages, one image had come to be seen as especially significant: that of justification. The term 'justification' and the verb 'to justify' came to signify 'entering into a right relationship with God', or perhaps 'being made righteous in the sight of God.' The doctrine of justification came to be seen as dealing with the question of what an individual had to do in order to be saved. As contemporary sources indicate, this question came to be asked with increasing frequency as the sixteenth century dawned. We have already seen (p. ••) how the rise of humanism brought with it a new emphasis upon individual consciousness and a new awareness of human individuality. In the wake of this dawn of the individual consciousness came a new concern with the doctrine of justification – the question of how human beings, *as individuals*, could enter into a relationship with God. A new interest developed in the writings of both Paul and Augustine, reflecting this concern with individual sub-jectivity.[3] This interest is particularly evident in the writings of Petrarch (1304–74).

But what was the church's answer to the crucial question 'What must I do to be saved?' Earlier (pp. 31–3), I drew attention to the doctrinal confusion of the later Middle Ages. It seems that this confusion was perhaps at its great-est in relation to the doctrine of justification. A number of factors contributed to this confusion. First, there had been no authoritative pronouncement from the church on the matter for over a thousand years. In 418, the Council of Carthage discussed the question, and more detailed proposals were set forth by the Second Council of Orange in 529. But for reasons which defy expla-nation, this latter council and its decisions were unknown to the theologians of the Middle Ages. The council appears to have been 'rediscovered' in 1546 – by which time the Reformation had been under way for a generation. Second, the doctrine of justification appears to have been a favourite topic of debate among later medieval theologians, with the result that a dispropor-tionately large number of opinions on the question passed into circulation. But which of these opinions were *right*? The reluctance or inability of the church to evaluate these opinions ensured that an already difficult question became even further confused.

The central question forced upon the church by the rise of humanism – 'What must I, *as an individual*, do to be saved?' – could not be answered with any degree of confidence. Humanism had forced a question upon a church which, as events would demonstrate, was unable to answer it. The scene was set for a tragedy, and Luther happened to wander on to the stage as its chief actor.

Luther's Early Views on Justification

Luther was educated at the University of Erfurt (1501–5), then dominated by the *via moderna*. After a period in which he performed various functions for his Order, Luther was appointed to the chair of biblical studies at Wittenberg, in 1511. In accordance with his job specification, he lectured on various books of the Bible: the Psalms (1513–15), Romans (1515–16), Galatians (1516–17) and Hebrews (1517–18), before returning to the Psalms for a second time (1519–21). We possess the text of Luther's lectures (in various forms) in every case, allowing us to follow the development of his ideas over the period leading up to the ninety-five theses (1517) and the famous Leipzig Disputation (1519).

Our interest especially concerns the first course of lectures on the Psalms, universally known as the *Dictata super Psalterium*. For two or three hours every week over a period of two years, Luther explained the meaning of each Psalm, as he understood it, to an audience which, by all accounts, was entranced by his style. Luther frequently discusses the doctrine of justification in the course of these lectures, allowing us to determine precisely what his early views on this matter were. It turns out that, initially, Luther was a remarkably faithful follower of the views of the *via moderna* (see pp. 74–6).[4] God has established a covenant (*pactum*) with humanity, by which he is obliged to justify anyone who meets a certain minimum precondition (*quod in se est*). In effect, Luther teaches that God gives his grace to the humble, so that all who humble themselves before God can expect to be justified as a matter of course. Two quotations from the *Dictata super Psalterium* will illustrate this principle:

> It is for this reason that we are saved: God has made a testament and a covenant with us, so that whoever believes and is baptized will be saved. In this covenant God is truthful and faithful, and is bound by what he has promised.

> 'Ask and you will receive; seek and you will find; knock and it shall be opened to you. For everyone who asks, receives, etc.' (Matthew 7.7–8) Hence the doctors of theology rightly say that God gives grace without fail to whoever does what lies within them (*quod is se est*).

Because sinners recognize their need for grace and call upon God to bestow it, this places God under an obligation to do so, thereby justifying the sinner. In other words, the sinner takes the initiative, by calling upon God: the sinner is able to do something which ensures that God responds by justifying him or her. As we saw in the previous chapter (pp. 74–6), the covenant between God and humanity established a framework within which a relatively small human effort results in a disproportionately large divine reward. Nevertheless, a definite human effort is required to place God under an obligation to reward the sinner with grace.

Luther's Discovery of the 'Righteousness of God'

Luther found himself faced with impossible difficulties over the idea of *iustitia Dei*, the 'righteousness of God.' This idea is prominent in both the Psalms and the letter to the Romans, upon which Luther lectured in the period 1513–16. We thus find him occasionally dealing with this idea at length in his lectures. At this stage in his development, he understood the 'righteousness of God' to refer to an impartial divine attribute. God judges individuals with complete impartiality. If the individual has met the basic precondition for justification, he or she is justified; if he has not, he or she is condemned. God shows neither leniency nor favouritism: he judges solely on the basis of merit. God is both equitable and just, in that he gives each individual exactly what he or she merits – nothing more and nothing less.[5]

The difficulty of this approach appears to have become increasingly clear to Luther in late 1514 or early 1515. What happens if the sinner is incapable of meeting this basic precondition? What happens if sinners are so crippled and trapped by sin that they cannot fulfil the demand which is made of them? Pelagius and Gabriel Biel, both of whom worked with this idea of the 'righteousness of God',[6] assumed that humans were capable of meeting this precondition without any undue difficulty – but Luther seems to have begun to appreciate the insights of Augustine at this point, arguing that humanity was so trapped in its sinfulness that it could not extricate itself except through special divine intervention.

Luther's comments on his own dilemma are enlightening. He relates how he tried with all his might to do what was necessary to achieve salvation, but found himself more and more convinced that he could not be saved.

> I was a good monk, and kept my rule so strictly that I could say that if ever a monk could get to heaven through monastic discipline, I was that monk. All my companions in the monastery would confirm this . . .

> And yet my conscience would not give me certainty, but I always doubted and said, 'You didn't do that right. You weren't contrite enough. You left that out of your confession.' The more I tried to remedy an uncertain, weak and troubled conscience with human traditions, the more I daily found it more uncertain, weaker and more troubled.

It seemed to Luther that he simply could not meet the precondition for salvation. He did not have the resources needed to be saved. There was no way that God could justly reward him with salvation – only condemnation.

The idea of the 'righteousness of God' thus became a threat to Luther. It could only mean condemnation and punishment. The promise of justification was real enough – but the precondition attached to the promise made its fulfilment impossible. It was as if God had promised a blind man a million dollars, provided that he could see. The idea of the 'righteousness of God' was simply not gospel, not good news, for sinners, in that it spelled nothing but condemnation. Luther's growing pessimism concerning the abilities of sinful humanity led him to despair of his own salvation, which increasingly seemed an impossibility. 'How can I find a gracious God (*Wie kriege ich einen gnädigen Gott*)?', he asked. By the end of 1514, it seems that Luther had failed to find an answer to this question.

This was no mere theological problem of purely academic interest. Luther's growing anxiety regarding it shows a strongly existential dimension. It concerned him, personally; it was no mere textbook difficulty. For Luther, as for so many others, the crucial question of human existence concerned how to clinch one's salvation. Some modern readers may understandably find it difficult to empathize with this concern. However, to enter into Luther's personal situation and hence to appreciate the importance of his 'theological breakthrough', it is necessary to understand how crucial this question was to him. It was *the* central question on his personal agenda.

But then something happened. We shall probably never know exactly what it was or when it occurred. We do not even know where it happened: many scholars refer to the discovery by means of the German term *Turmerlebnis*, 'the tower experience', on account of a later (and somewhat confused) personal recollection of Luther, which seems to imply that his breakthrough took place in a tower of the Augustinian monastery. But whatever it was, and whenever and wherever it happened, it changed Luther's outlook on life completely, and ultimately propelled him into the forefront of the Reformation struggle.

In 1545, the year before he died, Luther wrote a preface to the first volume of the complete edition of his Latin writings in which he described how he came to break with the church of his day. The preface is clearly written with the aim of introducing him to a readership which may not know how he came to hold the radical reforming views linked with his name. In this 'auto-biographical fragment' (as it is usually known), Luther aims to provide those readers with background information about the development of his vocation as a reformer. After dealing with some historical preliminaries which take his narrative up to the year 1519, he turns to describe his personal difficulties with the problem of the 'righteousness of God':

> I had certainly wanted to understand Paul in his letter to the Romans. But what prevented me from doing so was not so much cold feet as that one phrase in the first chapter: 'the righteousness of God is revealed in it' (Romans 1:17). For I hated that phrase, 'the righteousness of God', which I had been taught to understand as the righteousness by which God is righteous, and punishes unrighteous sinners.
>
> Although I lived a blameless life as a monk, I felt that I was a sinner with an uneasy conscience before God. I also could not believe that I had pleased him with my works. Far from loving that righteous God who punished sinners, I actually hated him . . . I was in desperation to know what Paul meant in this passage. At last, as I meditated day and night on the relation of the words 'the righteousness of God is revealed in it, as it is written, the righteous person shall live by faith', I began to understand that 'righteousness of God' as that by which the righteous person lives by the gift of God (faith); and this sentence, 'the right-

eousness of God is revealed', to refer to a passive righteousness, by which the merciful God justifies us by faith, as it is written, 'the righteous person lives by faith'. This immediately made me feel as though I had been born again, and as though I had entered through open gates into paradise itself. From that moment, I saw he whole face of Scripture in a new light . . . And now, where I had once hated the phrase, 'the righteousness of God', I began to love and extol it as the sweetest of phrases, so that this passage in Paul became the very gate of paradise to me.[7]

What is Luther talking about in this famous passage, which vibrates with the excitement of discovery? It is obvious that his understanding of the phrase 'the righteousness of God' has changed radically. But what is the nature of this change?

The basic change is fundamental. Originally Luther regarded the precondition for justification as a human work, something which the sinner had to perform, before he or she could be justified. Increasingly convinced, through his reading of Augustine, that such an act was an impossibility, Luther could interpret the 'righteousness of God' only as a *punishing* righteousness. But in this passage, he narrates how he discovered a 'new' meaning of the phrase – a righteousness which God *gives* to the sinner. In other words, God himself meets the precondition, graciously giving sinners what they require if they are to be justified. An analogy (not used by Luther) may help to bring out the difference between these two approaches.

Let us suppose that you are in prison, and are offered your freedom on condition that you pay a heavy fine. The promise is real – so long as you can meet the precondition, the promise will be fulfilled. Pelagius and, albeit in a slightly different manner, Gabriel Biel work on the presupposition, initially shared by Luther, that you have the necessary money stashed away somewhere. As your freedom is worth far more than the money, you are being offered a bargain. So you pay the fine. This presents no difficulties so long as you have the necessary resources. But Luther increasingly came to share the view of Augustine that sinful humanity just doesn't have the resources. They work on the assumption that, since you don't have the money, the promise of freedom has little relevance to your situation. For both Augustine and Luther, therefore, the good news of the gospel is that you have been *given* the necessary money with which to buy your freedom. In other words, the precondition has been met for you by someone else.

Luther's insight, which he describes in this autobiographical passage, is that the God of the Christian gospel is not a harsh judge who rewards individuals according to their merits, but a merciful and gracious God who bestows righteousness upon sinners as a gift. Earlier (pp. 72–4), we noted the distinction between the Augustinian and Pelagian views on justification. We could say that in his earlier phase Luther adopted something like a Pelagian position, which subsequently gave way to more of an Augustinian position. It is for this reason that Luther scholars tend to put quotation marks round the words 'new' or 'discovery': Luther's ideas may have been new to him, but they were hardly a new discovery for Christianity. Luther's 'discovery' is really a '*re*discovery', or a 'reappropriation', of the insights of Augustine. This is not to say that Luther simply reproduced exactly what Augustine taught; he introduced elements which would have horrified Augustine – for example, he insists that divine righteousness contradicts human ideas of righteousness, whereas for Augustine, the two were complementary. The contrast with Karlstadt is important here: Karlstadt merely repeated Augustine's views, as stated in the anti-Pelagian writings, whereas Luther 'creatively reinterpreted' them on occasion. Nevertheless, the basic *framework* within which Luther now worked was unquestionably Augustinian. True repentance is to be seen as the result, rather than the precondition, of grace.

When did this change take place? On the basis of the evidence of the *Dictata super Psalterium* (1513–15) and the lectures on Romans (1515–16), it seems that the basic change described by Luther in 1545 took place at some point in 1515.[8] Inevitably, there are doubts and uncertainties about this, for a number of reasons. The following may be noted in particular. First, it is possible that Luther's 1545 recollection of events dating back to the 1510s may be slightly confused. After all, Luther was an old man when he wrote these words, and the recollections of old men are not always reliable. In particular, it is possible that Luther may have 'telescoped' his insights, contracting into a small period of time events which actually took place over a longer period. Second, it is not clear whether the 1545 document implies that Luther's breakthrough took place in 1519 or whether it was complete by 1519. The Latin turns of phrase employed by Luther suggest that he is using a kind of 'flashback' technique, similar to that found in *Mildred Pierce* or *Brief Encounter*. In other words, in his narrative of historical events, Luther takes his readers to the year 1519, and then reminisces about events in the past – such as his discovery of the righteousness of God. The general consensus among Luther scholars is that his theology of justification underwent a decisive alteration at some point in 1515. The Luther who posted the ninety-five theses in October 1517 was already in possession of the insights on which he would base his programme of reform.

Central to these insights was the doctrine of 'justification by faith alone', and it is important to understand what was meant by this term. The idea of 'justification' is already familiar (see p. 104). But what about the phrase 'by faith alone'? What is the nature of justifying faith?

The Nature of Justifying Faith

'The reason why some people do not understand why faith alone justifies is that they do not know what faith is'. In writing these words, Luther draws our attention to the need to inquire more closely concerning that deceptively simple word 'faith'. Three points relating to Luther's idea of faith may be singled out as having special importance to his doctrine of justification. Each of these points was taken up and developed by later writers, such as Calvin, indicating that Luther made a fundamental contribution to the development of Reformation thought at this point. These three points are:

1 Faith has a personal, rather than a purely historical, reference.
2 Faith concerns trust in the promises of God.
3 Faith unites the believer to Christ.

We shall consider each of these points individually.

First, faith is not simply historical knowledge. Luther argues that a faith which is content to believe in the historical reliability of the gospels is not a faith which justifies. Sinners are perfectly capable of trusting in the historical details of the gospels; but these facts of themselves are not adequate for true Christian faith. Saving faith concerns believing and trusting that Christ was born *pro nobis*, born for us personally, and has accomplished for us the work of salvation. As Luther puts it:

> I have often spoken about two different kinds of faith. The first goes like this: you believe that it is true that Christ is the person who is described and pro-claimed in the gospels, but you do not believe that he is such a person for you. You doubt if you can receive that from him, and you think: 'Yes, I'm sure he is that person for someone else (like Peter and Paul, and for religious and holy people). But is he that person for me? Can I confidently expect to receive every-thing from him that the saints expect?' You see, this faith is nothing. It receives nothing of Christ, and tastes nothing of him either. It cannot feel joy, nor love of him or for him. This is a faith related to Christ, but not a faith in Christ. . . . The only faith which deserves to be called Christian is this: you believe unreservedly that it is not only for Peter and the saints that Christ is such a person, but also for you yourself – in fact, for you more than anyone else.

The second point concerns faith as 'trust (*fiducia*)'. The notion of trust is prominent in the Reformation conception of faith, as a nautical analogy used by Luther indicates. 'Everything depends upon faith. The person who does not have faith is like someone who has to cross the sea, but is so frightened that he does not trust the ship. And so he stays where he is, and is never saved, because he will not get on board and cross over.' Faith is not merely believing that something is true; it is being prepared to act on that belief and rely on it. To use Luther's analogy, faith is not simply about believing that a ship exists; it is about stepping into it and entrusting ourselves to it.

But what are we being asked to trust? Are we being asked simply to have faith in faith? The question could perhaps be phrased more accurately: *Who* are we being asked to trust? For Luther, the answer was unequivocal: faith is about being prepared to put one's trust in the promises of God and in the integrity and faithfulness of the God who made those promises.

> It is necessary that anyone who is about to confess his sins put his trust only and completely in the most gracious promise of God. That is, he must be certain that the one who has promised forgiveness to whoever confesses his sins will most faithfully fulfil this promise. For we are to glory, not in the fact that we confess our sins, but in the fact that God has promised pardon to those who confess their sins. In other words, we are not to glory on account of the worthiness or adequacy of our confession (because there is no such worthiness or adequacy) but on account of the truth and certainty of God's promises.

Faith is only as strong as the one in whom we believe and trust. The efficacy of faith does not rest upon the intensity with which we believe, but in the reliability of the one in whom we believe. It is not the greatness of our faith, but the greatness of God, which counts. As Luther put it:

> Even if my faith is weak, I still have exactly the same treasure and the same Christ as others. There is no difference. . . . It is like two people, each of whom owns a hundred guldens. One may carry them around in a paper sack, the other in an iron chest. But despite these differences, they both own the same treasure. Thus the Christ who you and I own is one and the same, irrespective of the strength or weakness of your faith or mine.

The *content* of faith thus matters far more than its *intensity*. It is pointless to trust passionately in someone who is not worthy of trust; even a modicum of faith in someone who is totally reliable is vastly to be preferred. Trust is not, however, an occasional attitude. For Luther, it is an undeviating trusting outlook upon life, a constant stance of conviction of the trustworthiness of the promises of God.

In the third place, faith unites the believer with Christ. Luther states this principle clearly in his 1520 writing *The Liberty of a Christian*.

> Faith unites the soul with Christ as a bride is united with her bridegroom. As Paul teaches us, Christ and the soul become one flesh by this mystery

(Ephesians 5:31–2). And if they are one flesh and the marriage is real – in fact, it is the most perfect of all marriages, and human marriages are poor reflections of this one true marriage – then it follows that everything that they have is held in common, whether good or evil. So the believer can boast of and glory in whatever Christ possesses, as though it were his or her own; and whatever the believer has, Christ claims as his own. Let us see how this works and how it benefits us. Christ is full of grace, life and salvation. The human soul is full of sin, death and damnation. Now let faith come between them. Sin, death and damnation will then be Christ's; and grace, life and salvation will be the believer's.

Faith, then, is not assent to an abstract set of doctrines. Rather, it is a 'wedding ring' (Luther's description), pointing to mutual commitment and union between Christ and the believer. It is the response of the whole person of the believer to God, which leads in turn to the real and personal presence of Christ in the believer. 'To know Christ is to know his benefits,' wrote Philipp Melanchthon, Luther's colleague at Wittenberg. Faith makes both Christ and his benefits – such as forgiveness, justification and hope – available to the believer. Calvin makes this point with characteristic clarity. 'Having ingrafted us into his body, Christ makes us partakers, not only of all his benefits, but also of himself.' Christ, Calvin insists, is not 'received merely in the understanding and imagination. For the promises offer him, not so that we end up with the mere sight and knowledge of him, but that we enjoy a true communication of him.'

Thus the doctrine of 'justification by faith' does not mean that the sinner is justified *because* he or she believes, on account of his or her faith – although that is certainly what Luther believed in his earlier period, as we saw. On this view, faith is a human action or work – the precondition for justification. Luther's breakthrough, by contrast, involves the recognition that God provides everything necessary for justification, so that all the sinner needs to do is to receive it. In justification, God is active, and humans are passive. The phrase 'justification *by* grace *through* faith' brings out the meaning of the doctrine more clearly: the justification of the sinner is based upon the grace of God, and is received through faith. Or perhaps we could cite the somewhat rambling title of Heinrich Bullinger's 1554 work on this subject as a comprehensive, if not particularly eloquent, statement of Luther's ideas: *The grace of God that justifies us for the sake of Christ through faith alone, without good works, while faith meanwhile abounds in good works.* God offers and gives; men and women receive and rejoice. The doctrine of justification by faith alone is an affirmation that God does everything necessary for salvation. Even faith itself is a gift of God, rather than a human action. God himself meets the precondition for justification. Thus, as we saw, the 'righteousness of God' is not a righteousness which judges whether or not we have met the precondition for justification, but the righteousness which is given to us so that we may meet that precondition.[9]

This view was regarded by many of Luther's critics as outrageous. It seemed to suggest that God despised morality and had no time for good works. Luther was branded as an 'antinomian' – in other words, someone who has no place for the law (*nomos* in Greek) in the religious life. Perhaps we could use the word 'anarchist' to convey much the same idea. In fact, Luther was simply stating that good works are not the *cause* of justification, but its *result*, a point captured somewhat laboriously in the title of Bullinger's book noted above. In other words, Luther treats good works as the *natural result of having been justified*, rather than the *cause of that justification*. Far from destroying morality, Luther simply saw himself as setting it in its proper context. The believer performs good works as an act of thankfulness to God for having forgiven him, rather than in an attempt to get God to forgive him in the first place.

Causes and Consequences of Luther's Doctrine of Justification

Let us pause briefly to consider how both humanism and scholasticism were implicated in Luther's theological breakthrough. The role of humanism is obvious. The editions of Augustine which gave Luther access to the ideas of this great writer were prepared by humanists. Luther appears to have used the Amerbach edition of Augustine, widely regarded as representing humanist scholarship at its best in the first decade of the sixteenth century (before Erasmus began his editorial work in the 1510s, that is). Similarly, Luther was able to make use of his knowledge of Hebrew as he expounded the Psalms; and both his knowledge of the language and his Hebrew text of some of the Psalms were provided by the humanist Reuchlin. The intense interest which Luther often shows in the intricacies of the text of Scripture probably reflects the humanist emphasis on the importance of the literary form of Scripture as a key to its experiential meaning. Luther appears to have used the tools of humanism, as he wrestled with his theological riddle.

Nevertheless, scholasticism also played a significant role in Luther's theological breakthrough. One of the apparent ironies of Luther's development is that he used a scholastic tool to break free from his original scholastic matrix. The tool in question was a particular method of interpreting Scripture, widespread in the medieval period, known as the *Quadriga*, or 'fourfold sense of Scripture', which will be discussed in detail later (pp. 157–9). This way of approaching a biblical text identified four different meanings of a passage: the *literal* meaning of the text and three *spiritual*, or non-literal, meanings. It was through concentrating on one of these spiritual senses of Scripture (the 'tropo-logical' sense) and playing down the literal sense that Luther was able to wrest his insight concerning the 'righteousness of God'. Considered *literally*, this righteousness might well refer to God's punishment of sinners; but considered *tropologically*, it referred to God's bestowal of righteousness upon the sinner. (Interestingly, no other reformer appears to have made significant use of this scholastic tool of biblical interpretation, indicating Luther's unusually close affinity with medieval scholasticism at this point.) And so the scene was set for Luther's break with the theology of the *via moderna*.

What were the consequences of Luther's breakthrough? Initially, Luther appears to have felt moved to expose the inadequacies of the doctrine of justification associated with the *via moderna*. Working solely within the some-what restricted circle of the Wittenberg university faculty of theology, Luther mounted a sustained attack on scholasticism. The *Disputation against scholastic theology* of September 1517 is actually directed against one scholastic theolo-gian – Gabriel Biel, as representing the *via moderna*.[10] The dean of the faculty of theology at Wittenberg, Andreas Bodenstein von Karlstadt, came to share Luther's views on scholasticism after reading the works of Augustine in early 1517; although he had initially been a champion of scholasticism at Wittenberg, he rapidly became one of its severest critics. Karlstadt and Luther engineering a reform of the theology faculty in March 1518, and succeeded in eliminating virtually everything connected with scholasticism from the cur-riculum. From then on, theological students at Wittenberg would study Augustine and the Bible, not the scholastics.

But there weren't that many theological students at Wittenberg, and Wittenberg was probably near the top of the league table of insignificant European universities. It is necessary to emphasize how utterly *insignificant* Luther's 'new' insights were at this point. All that we are talking about is alter-ations to the theological curriculum of an unimportant university, without any fundamental relevance for church or society. So how did a minor academic debate, of relevance only to scholastics, become the great popular movement of the Reformation? We have already seen how part of that answer lies in the humanist espousal of Luther as a *cause célèbre* in the aftermath of the Leipzig Disputation of 1519 (see pp. 6–7, 88). The remainder of that answer lies in the social dimensions of the doctrine of justification, to which we now turn.

It might be thought that the question of how sin is forgiven could be rel-egated to the appropriate sections of theological textbooks. In the late medieval period, however, sin was regarded as a visible and social matter, some-thing which had to be forgiven in a visible and social way. In many ways, the development of the theory of the sacrament of penance in the Middle Ages may be regarded as an attempt to consolidate the social grounding of forgiveness. Forgiveness is not a private matter between the individual and God; it is a public matter involving that individual, the church and society. In 1215 the Fourth Lateran Council declared that 'All believers of both sexes who have reached the age of discretion must faithfully confess their sins in person to their own priest, and attempt to carry out the penance imposed.' Both priest and penance were thus firmly established as part of the medieval process by which God was understood to forgive sins through appointed human representatives and means on earth.[11]

Ecclesiastical vagueness concerning the precise role of both penitent and priest in penance inevitably led to the development of a number of highly questionable trends in popular belief. Salvation was widely regarded as something which could be earned or merited through good works. The confused and vague theology of forgiveness of the late medieval period lent weight to the suggestion that it was possible to purchase the forgiveness of sins and procure the remission of 'purgatorial penalties' through the purchase of indulgences. In other words, the eternal penalties resulting from sinful actions could be reduced, if not eliminated, by payment of an appropriate sum of money to the appropriate ecclesiastical figure. Thus Cardinal Albrecht of Brandenburg managed to accumulate a remission of purgatorial penalties reckoned to total 39,245,120 years, give or take a few millennia. If such beliefs were contrary to the teaching of the church, no attempt was made by that church to disabuse its members of such ideas. Indeed, there are reasons for thinking that they were tolerated to the point of being unofficially incorporated into the structures of the church. The power and the income of much of the ecclesiastical establishment and its patrons were actually linked with the continuance of such practices and beliefs.

What was an indulgence? Originally, an indulgence seems to have been a gift of money to charity as an expression of thankfulness for forgiveness. By the beginning of the sixteenth century, however, this innocent idea had been transformed into an important source of income for a papacy facing a financial crisis and prepared to be flexible in its theology in order to meet it. Luther's wrath was particularly kindled by the marketing techniques of Johannes Tetzel. For a mere three marks, a sinner could be released from all punishments that he would otherwise face in purgatory – and many found this an offer difficult to refuse at the price. In an age which knew how to enjoy its venial sins, the possibility of being able to do so without any fear of divine punishment was enormously tempting. Tetzel's suggestion that it would be possible to secure the immediate release of the soul of a loved one from its sufferings in purgatory for a reasonable sum (based on a sliding scale according to the individual's wealth) was calculated to make a powerful appeal to the guilt of the living concerning the dead.

In the early sixteenth century, indulgences were a major source of papal revenue; and, as the somewhat sordid trilateral deal between the pope, Albrecht of Brandenburg and the banking house of Fuggers indicates, that income found its way into a number of coffers. In a period when ecclesiastical offices were often purchased, rather than earned, the buyers generally felt justified in looking for a return on their investment – and such practices as paying for masses for the dead were encouraged for this reason. As a result, there were a number of vested interests concerned to ensure that the early sixteenth-century vagueness concerning the doctrine of justification was maintained. The unique and indispensable role of the priest in confession and forgiveness was obviously open to corruption, and the evidence suggests that clerical venality was no small problem on the eve of the Reformation.

Luther's doctrine of justification by faith, with its associated doctrine of the 'priesthood of all believers', thus assumed an importance which far transcended the sphere of academic theology. It cut the ground from under the vested interests we have just noted. Forgiveness was a matter between the believer and God: no others were involved. No priest was required to pronounce that the person had been forgiven; the believer could read in Scripture the promises of forgiveness to those who confessed their sins, and needed no one to repeat them or execute them. No payment of any kind was required to receive divine forgiveness. The concept of purgatory, upon which so much popular superstition and ecclesiastical exploitation were based, was dismissed as a non-scriptural fiction. With the rejection of the existence of purgatory went a whole attitude to death and dying and the practices previously associated with them, such as paying for masses for the dead. The new emphasis on the individual's relation with God, derived partly from Renaissance individualism and partly from the New Testament, effectively marginalized the role of the institutional church. It was not merely income from indulgences which Luther attacked; it was also the view of the role of the church in the granting of forgiveness which lay behind this practice.

Luther's action in posting the ninety-five theses on indulgences on 31 October 1517 (now celebrated as 'Reformation Day' in Germany) was not merely a protest against Tetzel's claims for indulgences, which rivalled those of modern detergent manufacturers in terms of their optimistic claims. Nor was it merely a request that the church clarify its teaching on forgiveness. It marked the appearance of a new theology of forgiveness (or, more accurately, the *re*appearance of an old and apparently forgotten theology of forgiveness) which threatened to take away from the institutional church any role in forgiveness, thereby threatening the vested interests of the pope, many clergy, some princes and one rather important banking house (the Fuggers of Augsburg, which replaced the Medicis as the official church bankers when Leo X, himself a Medici, became pope in 1513). The doctrine of justification by faith alone reaffirmed that God's forgiveness was given, not bought, and was available to all, irrespective of their financial means or social condition. The related doctrine of the 'priesthood of all believers' meant that the believer, with the gracious assistance of God, could do everything necessary to his or her own salvation without having to rely totally upon either priest or church (although Luther believed that both professional ministers and the institution of the church had a significant role to play in the Christian life). It is thus little wonder that Luther's views were regarded with such anxiety by the ecclesiastical establishment and were received with great interest by so many laity at the time.

So whereas Luther's initial controversy is with the academic theology of the *via moderna*, events led to him discarding this limited and rather minor sphere of controversy in order to assume the role of a popular reformer. From 1519 onwards, Luther's views on justification increasingly led him to challenge the doctrines and practices of the church of his day, rather than the ideas of the *via moderna*. Where Luther once concerned himself with the intellectual stratosphere, so to speak, he now came down to earth and grounded his ideas in the life of the church. With the publication of the three great reforming manifestos of 1520,[12] Luther demonstrated the power of an idea to captivate the hearts and minds of men and women. No longer are we dealing with a desk-bound academic, but with a charismatic popular reformer.

The social consequences of Luther's doctrine of justification by faith alone may be illustrated with reference to the fate of the lay fraternities. As we noted earlier (pp. 26–7), lay fraternities were associations of lay persons who undertook to provide their members with full funeral rites. The upper classes were able to endow chantries to ensure continued prayers for their souls in purgatory: for example, in 1483 Count Werner of Zimmern is rumoured to have had a thousand requiem masses said for the safe repose of his soul. The lower classes, not having access to the funds necessary for such extravagances, clubbed together in fraternities to make sure that the proper rites of passage were observed for their members. In addition to this, however, many of the fraternities performed important social roles, such as establishing schools and almshouses for their members and attempting to care for their members' widows and children. Their *raison d'être*, nevertheless, was fundamentally *religious*, based upon belief in purgatory, the veneration of the saints and the intercession of Mary. The doctrine of justification by faith eliminated the necessity of such fraternities by rejecting the network of beliefs concerning death and judgement upon which they were based. The *raison d'être* of the fraternities was thus radically undermined – and with the elimination of any essential *religious* function, the fraternities' *social* roles also collapsed. This development is another example of the manner in which a change in religious ideas can have significant social consequences.

The Concept of 'Forensic Justification'

One of the central insights of Luther's doctrine of justification by faith alone is that the individual sinner is incapable of self-justification. It is God who takes the initiative in justification, providing all the resources necessary to justify the sinner. One of those resources is the 'righteousness of God'. In other words, the righteousness on the basis of which the sinner is justified is not his own righteousness, but a righteousness which is given to him by God. Augustine had made this point earlier: Luther, however, gives it a subtle new twist, which leads to the development of the concept of 'forensic justification'.

The point at issue is difficult to explain, but it centres on the question of the location of justifying righteousness. Both Augustine and Luther are agreed that God graciously gives sinful humans a righteousness which justifies them. But where is that righteousness located? Augustine argued that it was to be found within believers; Luther insisted that it remained outside believers. That is, for Augustine, the righteousness in question is internal; for Luther, it is external.

In Augustine's view, God bestows justifying righteousness upon the sinner in such a way that it becomes part of his or her person. As a result, this righteousness, although originating *outside* the sinner, becomes part of him or her. In Luther's view, by contrast, the righteousness in question remains outside the sinner: it is an 'alien righteousness' (*iustitia aliena*). God treats, or 'reckons', this righteousness *as if* it is part of the sinner's person. In his lectures on Romans of 1515–16, Luther developed the idea of the 'alien righteousness of Christ', imputed – not imparted – to the believer by faith, as the grounds of justification. His comments on Romans 4:7 are especially important:

> The saints are always sinners in their own sight, and therefore always justified outwardly. But the hypocrites are always righteous in their own sight, and thus always sinners outwardly. I use the term 'inwardly' to show how we are in ourselves, in our own sight, in our own estimation; and the term 'outwardly' to indicate how we are before God and in God's reckoning. Therefore we are righteous outwardly when we are righteous solely by the imputation of God and not of ourselves or of our own works.

Believers are righteous on account of the alien righteousness of Christ which is imputed to them – that is, treated as if it were theirs through faith. Earlier, we noted that an essential element of Luther's concept of faith is that it unites the believer to Christ. Justifying faith thus allows the believer to link up with the righteousness of Christ, and be justified on the basis of it. Christians are thus 'righteous by the imputation of a merciful God'.

Through faith, the believer is clothed with the righteousness of Christ in much the same way, Luther suggests, as Ezekiel 16:8 speaks of God covering our nakedness with his garment. For Luther, faith is the right (or righteous) relationship to God. Sin and righteousness thus co-exist; we remain sinners inwardly, but are righteous extrinsically, in the sight of God. By confessing our sins in faith, we stand in a right and righteous relationship with God. From our own perspective we are sinners; but in the perspective of God, we are righteous. Commenting on Romans 4:7, Luther declares that

> the saints are always aware of their sin and seek righteousness from God in accordance with God's mercy. And for this very reason, they are regarded as righteous by God. Thus in their own eyes (and in reality!) they are sinners; but in the eyes of God they are righteous, because God reckons them as such on account of their confession of their sin. In reality they are sinners; but they are righteous by the imputation of a merciful God. They are unknowingly righteous, and knowingly sinners. They are sinners in fact, but righteous in hope.

Luther is not necessarily implying that this co-existence of sin and righteousness is a permanent condition. The Christian life is not static, as if – to use a very loose way of speaking – the relative amounts of sin and righteousness remain constant throughout. Luther is perfectly aware that the Christian life is dynamic, in that the believer (hopefully) grows in righteousness. Rather, his point is that the existence of sin does not negate our status as a Christian. God shields our sin through Christ's righteousness. This righteousness is like a protective covering, beneath which we may battle with our sin. In justification, we are given the status of righteousness while we work with God towards attaining the nature of righteousness. In that God has promised to make us righteous one day, ultimately eliminating our sin, there is a sense in which we are already righteous in God's sight. Luther makes this point as follows:

> It is just like a man who is sick, and who believes the doctor who promises his full recovery. In the meantime, he obeys the doctor's orders in the hope of the promised recovery, and abstains from those things which he has been told to lay off, so that he may in no way hinder the promised return to health . . . Now is this sick person well? In fact, he is both sick and well at the same time. He is sick in reality – but he is well on account of the sure promise of the doctor, whom he trusts, and who reckons him as already being cured.

Obviously enjoying this medical analogy, Luther takes it a stage further. Having established that illness is an analogue of sin and health of righteousness, he concludes:

> So he is at one and the same time both a sinner and righteous. He is a sinner in reality, but righteous by the sure imputation and promise of God that he will

continue to deliver him from sin until he has completely cured him. So he is entirely healthy in hope, but a sinner in reality.

This approach accounts for the persistence of sin in believers, while at the same time accounting for the gradual transformation of the believer and the future elimination of that sin. But it is not necessary to be perfectly righteous to be a Christian. Sin does not point to unbelief or a failure on the part of God; rather, it points to the continued need to entrust one's person to the gentle care of God. Luther thus declares that a believer is 'at one and the same time righteous and a sinner (*simul iustus et peccator*)'; righteous in hope, but a sinner in fact; righteous in the sight and through the promise of God, yet a sinner in reality.

These ideas were subsequently developed by Luther's follower Philipp Melanchthon, resulting in the doctrine now generally known as 'forensic justification'. Whereas Augustine taught that the sinner is *made righteous* in justification, Melanchthon taught that he is *counted as righteous* or *pronounced to be righteous*. For Augustine, 'justifying righteousness' is *imparted*; for Melanchthon, it is *imputed* in the sense of being declared or pronounced to be righteous. Melanchthon drew a sharp distinction between the event of being *declared* righteous and the process of being *made* righteous, designating the former 'justification' and the latter 'sanctification' or 'regeneration'. For Augustine, these were simply different aspects of the same thing. According to Melanchthon, God pronounces the verdict that the sinner is righteous in the heavenly court (*in foro divino*). This legal approach to justification gave rise to the term 'forensic justification', from the Latin word *forum* ('market place' or 'courtyard'), the place traditionally associated with the dispensing of justice in classical Rome.[13]

The importance of this development lies in the fact that it marks a complete break with the teaching of the church up to that point. From the time of Augustine onwards, justification had always been understood to refer to both the event of being declared righteous and the process of being made righteous. Melanchthon's concept of forensic justification diverged radically from this. As it was taken up by virtually all the major reformers subsequently, it came to represent a standard difference between Protestant and Roman Catholic from then on. In addition to differences regarding how the sinner was justified, there was now an additional disagreement on what the word 'justification' designated in the first place. The Council of Trent, the Roman Catholic church's definitive response to the Protestant challenge, reaffirmed the views of Augustine on the nature of justification, and censured the views of Melanchthon as woefully inadequate.

As I hinted above, the concept of forensic justification actually represents a development of Luther's thought. This naturally leads us to ask what other developments and divergences in relation to the question of justification may be discerned within the Reformation.

Divergences among the Reformers on Justification

Popular accounts of the Reformation often create the impression of a monolithic uniformity within the movement in relation to the doctrine of justification. In fact, there are substantial differences of substance and emphasis between individual reformers on the doctrine. This section aims to explore some of those differences.

Justification and the Swiss Reformation

The European Reformation is often portrayed as a homogeneous phenomenon. In other words, it is presented as being consistent in terms of its underlying ideas and emphases. In fact, this is an inaccurate view, and the role played by the doctrine of justification by faith alone in the Swiss Reformation is a particularly important illustration of this point.

Over the period 1515–20, as we have seen, the doctrine of justification came to the fore in Luther's thought. In addition to becoming the centre of his theology, it also became the focus of his programme of reform. Luther's polemical writings, his liturgical innovations and reforms and his sermons of the period all reveal the practical importance of the doctrine of justification by faith to his reforming programme. As noted above, an essential component of Luther's doctrine of justification by faith concerns his understanding of justifying faith itself – a faith which unites the believer to Christ and brings about the real and personal presence of Christ within him or her.

Zwingli, however, faithfully echoes the concerns of the eastern Swiss humanist sodalities during the same period. Ernst Ziegler, in a masterly survey of reforming writings originating in this region of Switzerland around this time, makes the point that, for these writers, the word 'Reformation' designates a reformation of life and morality. The term 'justification by faith' is often conspicuous by its absence from such writings. The moralist ethos of eastern Swiss humanism contrasts sharply with Luther's emphasis upon the unmerited gift of grace, given in advance of and independent of any human moral action. This does not mean that writers such as Vadian or Zwingli defended a doctrine of justification by works, as if salvation came about as a result of human moral achievement. Rather, these reformers chose to place their emphasis on the *moral consequences* of the gospel, with a resulting tendency to play down issues which were of great importance to Luther.

As we saw earlier, Luther's doctrine of justification was directed towards the individual believer, clarifying his relationship with both God and the church, in order that his troubled conscience might be relieved. In many ways, it illustrates Luther's concern with the individual and his subjective consciousness, reflecting the rise of individualism associated with the Renaissance. But what of the Swiss Reformation, where more attention was paid to reformation of the *community*?

Zwingli saw the Reformation as affecting church and society, rather than just the individual. That Reformation was primarily moral in character. Zwingli was concerned with the moral and spiritual regeneration of Zurich along New Testament lines, rather than with any doctrine of justification. He was not concerned with questions about how individuals found a gracious God. Luther's emphasis upon justification by faith was thus absent from Zwingli. Yet the differences between the two on this doctrine in fact extend to matters of substance, as well as of emphasis. For example, Zwingli tends to treat Christ as an external moral example, rather than a personal presence within the believer. It would not be true to say that Zwingli teaches justification by works in his early period – that is to say, that human achievements have a purchasing power capable of attaining salvation. Yet, as Jacques Pollet so masterfully demonstrated, the basic atmosphere of Zwingli's early writings is one of the priority of moral renewal over forgiveness. For writers such as Vadian, the gospel is concerned primarily with the moral renewal and regeneration of individuals and institutions, with justification (although the term, interestingly, is used but rarely) following in the wake of these processes.

During the 1520s, Zwingli's ideas about justification began to become closer to those of Luther, perhaps on account of Zwingli's increased familiarity with the latter's writings. Yet the reader can still discern a fundamental difference between the two writers, reflecting different approaches to justification. For Luther, Scripture declares the promises of God, which reassure and console the believer; it is primarily concerned with narrating and proclaiming what God has done for sinful humanity in Christ. For Zwingli, Scripture sets out the moral demands which God makes of believers; it is primarily concerned with indicating what humanity must do in response to the example provided by Christ.

Even in the 1520s, then, diverging views on justification were evident within the Reformation. The widely differing views of Luther and Zwingli perhaps illustrate two extreme positions. Attempts to mediate between them were eventually forthcoming, and our attention now turns to those associated with Bucer and Calvin.

Later Developments: Bucer and Calvin on Justification

The divergences between Luther and Zwingli may be said to set the scene for extended discussion of the proper understanding of the doctrine of justification in the later Reformation. Two matters required resolution: the role of Christ in justification and the relationship between God's gracious act of justification and human obedience to the divine will. Luther himself, largely through occasional overstatement on the one hand and confusion on the other, managed to convey the impression to many (such as the humanist Georg Spalatin) that once a sinner was justified, he or she was under no obligation at all to perform moral actions. In fact, Luther's basic position was that good works were an entirely appropriate response to God's gracious act of justification, but that they could not – and *must* not – be considered as a cause of that justification. Yet a significant section of his public in the 1520s understood Luther to imply that Christians were dispensed from moral obligation.

Perhaps the most significant attempt to redress the apparent faults in this approach were due to the Strasbourg reformer Martin Bucer. In a series of writings, especially during the 1530s, Bucer developed a doctrine of *double justification*, which seemed to him to get round the difficulty raised by Luther's one-sided stress on the grace of God. Bucer argued that there were two stages in justification. The first stage, which he termed 'justification of the ungodly (*iustificatio impii*)', consisted of God's gracious forgiveness of human sin. (Later Protestant theology simply referred to this stage as 'justification'.) The second stage, which he termed 'justification of the godly (*iustificatio pii*)', consisted of an obedient human response to the moral demands of the gospel. (Later Protestant theology would refer to this process as 'regeneration' or 'sanctification'.) Christ was regarded as an external moral example, graciously provided by God, which justified sinners were required, through the assistance of the Holy Spirit, to imitate.

A causal link was thus established between justification and moral regeneration. Unless both took place, the sinner could not be said to be justified. Since the 'justification of the ungodly' caused the 'justification of the godly', it followed that the absence of moral regeneration in an individual implied that he or she had not been justified in the first place. Bucer thus believed that he had successfully safeguarded both the reality of grace and the necessity of human obedience. Others were not so sure. The theory seemed somewhat artificial, and reduced Christ to an external moral example. What had happened to Luther's emphasis on the real personal presence of Christ within believers?

The model of justification which eventually gained the ascendancy in the later Reformation was formulated by Calvin in the 1540s and 1550s. Calvin's approach avoids the deficiencies both of an external understanding of the role of Christ in justification and the view that justification causes moral renewal. The basic elements of his approach may be summarized as follows. Faith unites the believer to Christ in a 'mystic union'. (Here, Calvin reclaims Luther's emphasis on the real and personal presence of Christ within believers, established through faith.) This union with Christ has a twofold effect, which Calvin refers to as 'a double grace'.

First, the believer's union with Christ leads directly to his or her *justification*. Through Christ, the believer is declared to be righteous in the sight of God. Second, on account of the believer's union with Christ – and *not* on account of his or her justification – the believer begins the process of becoming like Christ through regeneration. Where Bucer argued that justification causes regeneration, Calvin asserts that both justification and regeneration are the results of the believer's union with Christ through faith.

This brief survey of understandings of justification current within the Reformation indicates that the movement was far from uniform on this matter. If space had permitted the views of other significant reformers – such as Wolfgang Capito, Andreas Bodenstein von Karlstadt and Johann Oecolampadius – to be considered, still further differences would have emerged. If the reformers were united in rejecting the view that human beings could achieve their own salvation, this unity did not extend to the precise manner in which God achieved this salvation through Christ. A spectrum of opinions existed in the first generation of the Reformation, with those of Calvin and Melanchthon gradually gaining the ascendancy, through a long process of debate, within the Reformed and Lutheran churches respectively.

The Catholic Response: Trent on Justification

It was obvious that the Catholic church needed to make an official and definitive response to Luther. By 1540, Luther had become something of a household name throughout Europe. His writings were being read and digested with various degrees of enthusiasm, even in the highest ecclesiastical circles in Italy. Something had to be done. The Council of Trent, summoned in 1545, began the long process of formulating a comprehensive response to Luther. High on its agenda was the doctrine of justification.

The Sixth Session of the Council of Trent was brought to a close on 13 January 1547. The Tridentine Decree on Justification, as the substantial product of this session has generally come to be known, probably represents the most significant achievement of this council. Its sixteen chapters set out the Roman

Catholic teaching on justification with a considerable degree of clarity. A series of thirty-three canons condemn specific opinions attributed to opponents of the Roman Catholic church, including Luther. Interestingly, the council seems unaware of the threat posed by Calvin, and directs the vast bulk of its criticisms against views which were known to be held by Luther himself.

Trent's critique of Luther's doctrine of justification can be broken down into four main sections:

1   The nature of justification.
2   The nature of justifying righteousness.
3   The nature of justifying faith.
4   The assurance of salvation.

We shall consider each of these four matters individually.

The Nature of Justification

In his earlier phase, around the years 1515–19, Luther tended to understand justification as a process of *becoming*, in which the sinner was gradually conformed to the likeness of Jesus Christ through a process of internal renewal. Luther's analogy of a sick person under competent medical care points to this understanding of justification, as does his famous declaration in the 1515–16 lectures on Romans: *fieri est iustificatio*, 'justification is about becoming'. In his later writings, however, dating from the mid-1530s and beyond, perhaps under the influence of Melanchthon's more forensic approach to justification (see pp. 121–2), Luther tended to treat justification as a matter of being declared to be righteous, rather than a process of becoming righteous. Increasingly, he came to see justification as an event, which was complemented by the distinct process of regeneration and interior renewal through the action of the Holy Spirit. Justification altered the outer status of the sinner in the sight of God (*coram Deo*), while regeneration altered the sinner's inner nature.

Trent strongly opposed this view, and vigorously defended the idea, originally associated with Augustine, that justification is the process of regeneration and renewal within human nature, which brings about a change in both the outer status and the inner nature of the sinner. Its fourth chapter provided the following precise definition of justification:

> The justification of the sinner may be briefly defined as a translation from that state in which a human being is born a child of the first Adam, to the state of grace and of the adoption of the sons of God through the second Adam, Jesus Christ our Saviour. According to the gospel, this translation cannot come about except through the cleansing of regeneration, or a desire for this, as it is written,

'Unless someone is born again of water and the Holy Spirit, he or she cannot enter into the Kingdom of God' (John 3:5).

Justification thus included the idea of regeneration. This brief statement was amplified in the seventh chapter, which stressed that justification 'is not only a remission of sins but also the sanctification and renewal of the inner person through the voluntary reception of the grace and gifts by which an unrighteous person becomes a righteous person'. This point was given further emphasis through canon 11, which condemned anyone who taught that justification takes place 'either by the sole imputation of the righteousness of Christ or by the sole remission of sins, to the exclusion of grace and charity . . . or that the grace by which we are justified is only the good will of God'.

Justification is closely linked with the sacraments of baptism and penance. The sinner is initially justified through baptism; however, on account of sin, that justification may be forfeited. It can be renewed, however, by penance, as the fourteenth chapter makes clear.

> Those who through sin have forfeited the received grace of justification can be justified again when, moved by God, they exert themselves to obtain through the sacrament of penance the recovery, by the merits of Christ, of the grace which was lost. Now this manner of justification is restoration for those who have lapsed into sin. The holy fathers have properly called this a 'second plank after the shipwreck of lost grace.' For Christ Jesus instituted the sacrament of penance, on behalf of those who lapse into sin after baptism . . . The repentance of a Christian after a lapse into sin is thus very different from that at baptism.

In brief, then, Trent maintained the medieval tradition, stretching back to Augustine, which saw justification as comprising both an event and a process – the event of being declared to be righteous through the work of Christ and the process of being made righteous through the internal work of the Holy Spirit. Reformers such as Melanchthon and Calvin distinguished these two matters, treating the word 'justification' as referring only to the event of being declared to be righteous; the accompanying process of internal renewal, which they termed 'sanctification' or 'regeneration', they regarded as theologically distinct.

Serious confusion thus resulted: Roman Catholics and Protestants used the same word 'justification' to mean very different things. Trent used it to mean what, according to Protestants, was *both* justification *and* sanctification.

The Nature of Justifying Righteousness

Luther stressed the fact that sinners possess no righteousness in themselves. They have nothing within them which could ever be regarded as the basis of

God's gracious decision to justify them. Luther's doctrine of the 'alien righteousness of Christ *(iustitia Christi aliena)'* made it clear that the righteousness
which justified sinners was outside them. It was imputed, not imparted; external, not internal.

Early critics of the Reformation argued, following Augustine, that sinners
were justified on the basis of an internal righteousness, graciously infused or
implanted within their persons by God. This righteousness was itself given as
an act of grace; it was not something merited. But, they argued, there had to
be something within individuals which could allow God to justify them. Luther
dismissed this idea. If God had decided to justify someone, he might as well
do it directly, rather than through an intermediate gift of righteousness.

Trent strongly defended the Augustinian idea of justification on the basis
of an internal righteousness. The seventh chapter makes this point crystal clear:

> The single formal cause (of justification) is the righteousness of God – not the
> righteousness by which God is righteous, but the righteousness by which God
> makes us righteous, so that, when we are endowed with it, we are 'renewed in
> the spirit of our mind' (Ephesians 4:23), and are not only counted as righteous,
> but are called, and are in reality, righteous . . . Nobody can be righteous except
> God communicates the merits of the passion of our Lord Jesus Christ to him
> or her, and this takes place in the justification of the sinner.

The phrase 'single formal cause' needs explanation. A 'formal' cause is the *direct*,
or most immediate, cause of something. Trent is thus stating that the direct
cause of justification is the righteousness which God graciously imparts to us
– as opposed to more distant causes of justification, such as the 'efficient cause'
(God) or the 'meritorious cause' (Jesus Christ). But the use of the word 'single'
should also be noted. One proposal for reaching agreement between Roman
Catholic and Protestant, which gained especial prominence at the Colloquy
of Regensburg (also known as Ratisbon) in 1541, was that *two* causes of
justification should be recognized: an external righteousness (the Protestant
position) and an internal righteousness (the Roman Catholic position). This
compromise seemed to hold some potential. Trent, however, had no time for
it. The use of the word 'single' was deliberate, intended to eliminate the idea
that there could be more than one such cause. The *only* direct cause of
justification was the interior gift of righteousness.

The Nature of Justifying Faith

Luther's doctrine of justification by faith alone came in for severe criticism.
Canon 12 condemned a central aspect of Luther's notion of justifying faith

when it rejected the idea that 'justifying faith is nothing other than confidence in the mercy of God, which remits sin for the sake of Christ'. In part, this rejection of Luther's doctrine of justification reflects the ambiguity, noted above (p. 127), concerning the meaning of the term 'justification'. Trent was alarmed that anyone should believe that they could be justified – in the Tridentine sense of the term – by faith, without any need for obedience or spiritual renewal. Trent, interpreting 'justification' to mean *both* the beginning of the Christian life *and* its continuation and growth, believed that Luther was suggesting that simply trusting in God (without any requirement that the sinner be changed and renewed by God) was the basis of the entire Christian life.

In fact, Luther meant nothing of the sort. He was affirming that the Christian life was begun through faith, and faith alone; good works followed justification, but did not cause that justification in the first place. Trent itself was perfectly prepared to concede that the Christian life was begun through faith, thus coming very close indeed to Luther's position. As chapter 8 of the Decree on Justification declares, 'We are said to be justified by faith, because faith is the beginning of human salvation, the foundation and root of all justification, without which it is impossible to please God.' This is perhaps a classic case of a theological misunderstanding resting upon the disputed meaning of a major theological term.

The Assurance of Salvation

For Luther, as for the reformers in general, one could rest assured of one's salvation. Salvation was grounded in the faithfulness of God to God's promises of mercy; to fail to have confidence in salvation was, in effect, to doubt the reliability and trustworthiness of God. Yet this must not be seen as a supreme confidence in God, untroubled by doubt. Faith is not the same as certainty; although the theological foundation of Christian faith may be secure, the human perception of and commitment to this foundation may waver.

This point is brought out clearly by Calvin, often thought to be the most confident of all the reformers in relation to matters of faith. His definition of faith certainly seems to point in this direction:

> Now we shall have a right definition of faith if we say that it is a steady and certain knowledge of the divine benevolence towards us, which is founded upon the truth of the gracious promise of God in Christ, and is both revealed to our minds and sealed in our hearts by the Holy Spirit.

Yet the *theological* certainty of this statement does not, according to Calvin, necessarily lead to *psychological* security. It is perfectly consistent with a sustained wrestling with doubt and anxiety on the part of the believer.

> When we stress that faith ought to be certain and secure, we do not have in mind a certainty without doubt, or a security without any anxiety. Rather, we affirm that believers have a perpetual struggle with their own lack of faith, and are far from possessing a peaceful conscience, never interrupted by any disturbance. On the other hand, we want to deny that they may fall out of, or depart from, their confidence in the divine mercy, no matter how much they may be troubled.

In his study *Calvin's Doctrine of the Knowledge of God*, Edward A. Dowey writes:

> If the bare words of his definition of faith make it 'steady and certain knowledge', according to Calvin, we must notice that such faith never is realized. We could formulate a description of existing faith for him as 'a steady and certain knowledge invariably attacked by vicious doubts and fears over which it is finally victorious'.

The Council of Trent regarded the reformers' doctrine of assurance with considerable scepticism. Chapter 9 of the Decree on Justification, entitled 'Against the vain confidence of heretics', criticized the 'ungodly confidence' of the reformers. While on one should doubt God's goodness and generosity, the reformers erred seriously when they taught that 'nobody is absolved from sins and justified unless they believe with certainty that they are absolved and justified, and that absolution and justification are effected by this faith alone.' Trent insisted that 'nobody can know with a certainty of faith which is not subject to error, whether they have obtained the grace of God'.

Trent's point seems to be that the reformers seemed to be making human confidence or boldness the grounds for justification, so that justification rested upon a fallible human conviction, rather than on the grace of God. The reformers, however, saw themselves as stressing that justification rested upon the promises of God; a failure to believe boldly in such promises was tantamount to calling the reliability of God into question.

In the present chapter, we have considered the importance of the doctrine of justification to the Reformation. However, important though this doctrine was to the development of the reforming movement, it may be argued that a related doctrine came to have even greater significance in the later phases of that movement. If justification was the way of articulating the grace of God in doctrinal terms that captured the imagination of the first wave of the Reformation, the second wave preferred to speak of grace in terms of predestination, or election. The doctrine of predestination proved to be one of the major distinguishing characteristics of international Calvinism. We shall consider this development in the next chapter.

For further reading

The standard history of the development of the doctrine of justification, which deals at length with sixteenth-century developments within Protestantism and Catholism, is:

Alister E. McGrath, *Iustitia Dei: A History of the Christian Doctrine of Justification*, 2nd edn (Cambridge, 1998).

The following studies are also of importance in clarifying points of detail:

J. P. Donnelly, *Calvinism and Scholasticism in Vermigli's Doctrine of Man and Grace* (Leiden, 1976).

E. J. D. Douglass, *Justification in Late Medieval Preaching* (Leiden, 1966).

M. J. Harran, *Luther on Conversion: The Early Years* (Ithaca, NY, 1983).

A. E. McGrath, *Luther's Theology of the Cross* (Oxford, 1985).

D. C. Steinmetz, *Misericordia Dei: The Theology of Johannes von Staupitz in its Late Medieval Setting* (Leiden, 1968).

T. N. Tentler, *Sin and Confession on the Eve of the Reformation* (Princeton, NJ, 1977).

7

The Doctrine of Predestination

If the Lutheran church arose out of a concern for the doctrine of justification, the Reformed church was born through a new desire to re-establish the scriptural model of the apostolic church, which we shall explore in more detail in chapter 10. Our attention now turns to one of the leading ideas of Reformed theology, of considerable importance to its political and social theories: the concept of the divine sovereignty. The Reformed theologians tended to regard Luther's concern with personal experience as unacceptably subjective and too orientated towards the individual; their concern was primarily with establishing objective criteria on the basis of which society and the church could be reformed – and they found such objective criteria in Scripture. They also had little time for Luther's early preoccupation with scholastic theology, which had never posed a significant threat to the Swiss Reformation.

The doctrine of predestination is often thought of as being the central feature of Reformed theology. For many, the term 'Calvinist' is virtually identical with 'placing great emphasis upon the doctrine of predestination'. How was it that the concept of grace, which for Luther was tied up with the justification of the sinner, came to refer to the sovereignty of God, especially as expressed in the doctrine of predestination? And how did this development take place? In this chapter, we shall be concerned with the understanding of the doctrine of grace associated with the Reformed church.

Zwingli on the Divine Sovereignty

Zwingli began his ministry at Zurich on 1 January 1519. That ministry came close to extinction in August of that same year, when Zurich was struck by the plague. The fact that such outbreaks were commonplace in the early sixteenth century must not be allowed to obscure their seriousness. At least one in four, possibly as many as one in two, died from its effects at Zurich between August 1519 and February 1520. Zwingli's pastoral duties included the consolation of the dying, and it was perhaps inevitable that he himself should contract the disease. As death appeared to be drawing near, Zwingli seems to have been aware that whether he survived or not was a matter for God. We possess a piece of poetry, generally referred to as the *Pestlied*, 'Plague Song', dating from the autumn of 1519. In it, we find Zwingli reflecting on his destiny. We find him making no appeal to the saints for his recovery, and no suggestion that the church can in any way intercede for him. Instead, we find a rugged determination to accept whatever God has in store for him. Whatever God ordains as his lot, Zwingli is prepared to accept:

> Do as you will
> for I lack nothing.
> I am your vessel
> to be restored or destroyed.

It is impossible to read this poem without sensing Zwingli's self-surrender to the divine will. In fact. Zwingli survived his illness. It is probably out of this experience that his conviction arose that he was an instrument in the hand of God, to be used exclusively for God's purposes.

Earlier, we noted that Luther's difficulties concerning the 'righteousness of God' were as much existential as theological. It will be obvious that Zwingli's concern with divine providence also had a strong existentialist dimension. For Zwingli, the question of the omnipotence of God was no longer a textbook question, but an issue which had a direct bearing upon his existence. Whereas Luther's theology is, at least initially, largely shaped by his experience of God's justification of him, a sinner, Zwingli's is almost totally shaped by his sense of the absolute sovereignty of God and of humanity's total dependence upon him.[1] Zwingli's idea of the absolute sovereignty of God was developed in his doctrine of providence, especially in the famous sermon *De providentia*, 'On providence'. Many of Zwingli's more critical readers have noted the similarities between Zwingli's ideas and the fatalism of Seneca, and have suggested that Zwingli merely baptizes Senecan fatalism. This suggestion is lent some credence through Zwingli's interest in and reference to Seneca in *De providentia*. Whether an individual is saved or condemned is totally a matter for God, who freely makes his decision from eternity. However, it seems that Zwingli's emphasis upon the divine omnipotence and human impotence ultimately derives from his reading of St Paul, and is merely reinforced by his reading of Seneca and given existential importance through his close encounter with death in August 1519.

It is instructive to compare Luther's and Zwingli's attitudes to Scripture, which reflect their different approaches to the grace of God. For Luther, Scripture is concerned primarily with the gracious promises of God, culminating in the promise of the justification of the sinner by faith. For Zwingli, Scripture is concerned primarily with the law of God, with a code of conduct, with the demands made by a sovereign God of his people. Luther draws a sharp distinction between 'law' and 'gospel', whereas Zwingli regards the two as essentially the same.

It was Zwingli's growing concern with the sovereignty of God which eventually led to his break with humanism. It is notoriously difficult to say when Zwingli stopped being a humanist and started being a reformer: indeed, there are excellent reasons for suggesting that Zwingli remained a humanist throughout his life. As we saw earlier (pp. 43–4), Kristeller's definition of humanism has to do with its *methods* rather than its *doctrines*; if this definition of humanism is applied to Zwingli, he remained a humanist throughout his career. The same is true of Calvin. But, it may be objected, how can such people be thought of as humanists, when both develop such a rigorous doctrine of predestination? It is certainly true that neither Zwingli or Calvin could be thought of as 'humanist' in the twentieth-century sense of the word – but that is irrelevant to the sixteenth century. When it is recalled that numerous writers of antiquity – such as Seneca and Lucretius – developed strongly fatalist philosophies, it can be seen that the case for treating both reformers as humanists is stronger than might have been thought. Nevertheless, it seems that at some point in his career, Zwingli changed his mind on one central presupposition shared by most of his Swiss humanist contemporaries. If Zwingli remained a humanist after this, he now embraced a somewhat different form of humanism, which many of his humanist colleagues regarded as slightly eccentric.

The programme of reform initiated by Zwingli at Zurich in 1519 was essentially humanist. His use of Scripture was thoroughly Erasmian, as was his style of preaching, although his political views reflected the Swiss nationalism which Erasmus so detested. Most important for our purposes, he saw reformation as an educational process, thus echoing the views of both Erasmus and the Swiss humanist sodalities. Writing to his colleague Myconius on 31 December 1519, reviewing the achievements of his first year at Zurich, Zwingli announced that there were 'more than two thousand more or less enlightened individuals in Zurich'. But in a letter of 27 July 1520, we find Zwingli apparently conceding the failure of this humanist conception of Reformation: something more than the educational insights of Quintillian were needed if the Reformation was to succeed. The fate of humanity in general and the Reformation in particular is determined by divine providence. It is God, and not humanity, who is the chief actor in the reformation process.

Humanist educational techniques are half-measures, incapable of dealing with the root of the problem.

This scepticism concerning the viability of the humanist reforming programme was made public in March 1525, when Zwingli published his *Commentary on True and False Religion*. Zwingli attacked two presuppositions which were central to the Erasmian reforming programme: the idea of 'free will' (*liberum arbitrium*), which Erasmus had defended vigorously in 1524, and the suggestion that educational methods were capable of reforming corrupt, sinful humanity. What was required, according to Zwingli, was providential, divine intervention, without which true reformation was an impossibility. As is well known, of course, 1525 also saw the publication of Luther's violently anti-Erasmian work *De servo arbitrio*, 'On the bondage of the will',[2] which also explicitly attacks Erasmus' doctrine of the 'freedom of the will'. Luther's work is permeated by an emphasis on the total sovereignty of God, linked with a doctrine of predestination similar to Zwingli's. Many humanists found this emphasis upon human sinfulness and divine omnipotence unacceptable, and this led to a certain alienation between Zwingli and many of his former supporters.

Calvin on Predestination

The popular conception of Calvin's religious thought is that of a rigorously logical system centring on the doctrine of predestination. Influential though this popular image may be, it bears little relation to reality; important though the doctrine of predestination may be for later Calvinism (see pp. 140–3), this is not reflected in Calvin's exposition of the subject. Calvin's successors in the later sixteenth century, confronted with the need to impose method on his thought, found that his theology was eminently suited to recasting within the more rigorously logical structures suggested by the Aristotelian methodology favoured by the later Italian Renaissance (p. 43). This has perhaps led to the too easy conclusion that Calvin's thought itself possesses the systematic cast and logical rigour of later Reformed orthodoxy, and has allowed orthodoxy's preoccupation with the doctrine of predestination to be read back into the 1559 *Institutes*. As I shall suggest (pp. 140–3), there is a subtle difference between Calvin and Calvinism at this point, marking and reflecting a significant turning point in intellectual history in general. If Calvin's followers developed Calvin's ideas, it was in response to a new spirit of the age, which regarded systematization and a concern for method as not only intellectually respectable but also highly desirable.

Calvin's thought reflects a concern with human sinfulness and divine omnipotence, a concern which finds its most complete expression in his doctrine of predestination. In his early period, Calvin appears to have held mildly humanist reforming views, perhaps similar to those of Lefevre d'Etaples (Stapulensis). By 1533, however, he appears to have moved to a more radical position. On 2 November 1533, Nicolas Cop, rector of the University of Paris, delivered an oration to mark the beginning of the new academic year. In the course of this, he alluded to several major themes which by then were associated with the Lutheran Reformation. Although the allusions were discreet and were mingled with substantial tracts of traditional Catholic theology, the address provoked an outcry. The rector and Calvin, who appears to have been involved in some way in drafting this oration, were obliged to flee Paris.[3] But how and when did the young humanist become a reformer?

The question of the date and the nature of Calvin's conversion has intrigued generations of Calvin scholars, even if that intrigue has produced remarkably little in the way of concrete findings.[4] It is generally agreed that Calvin switched from a mildly humanist reforming programme to a more radical platform in late 1533 or early 1534. But we do not know why. Calvin appears to be describing his conversion at two points in his later writings, but we lack the wealth of autobiographical detail provided by Luther. It is clear, nevertheless, that Calvin understands his conversion to be due to divine providence. He asserts that he was so deeply devoted to the 'superstitions of the papacy' that nothing less than an act of God could have freed him. He asserts that God 'tamed his heart and reduced it to obedience'. Once more, we find the emphasis characteristic of the Reformation: on the impotence of humanity and the omnipotence of God. It is these ideas which are linked and developed in Calvin's doctrine of predestination.

Although some scholars have suggested that predestination constitutes the centre of Calvin's thought, it is clear that this is not the case. It is simply one aspect of his doctrine of salvation. Calvin's chief contribution to the development of the doctrine of grace is the logical rigour with which he approached it. This is best seen, perhaps, by comparing Augustine and Calvin on the doctrine.

For Augustine, humanity after the Fall is corrupt and impotent, requiring the grace of God to be redeemed. That grace is not given to all. Augustine uses the term 'predestination' to refer to God's action in giving grace to some. It designates the special divine decision and action by which God grants his grace to those who are to be saved. But what, it may be asked, happens to everyone else? God passes them over, according to Augustine. He does not actively decide that they will be damned; he simply omits to save them. Predestination, for Augustine, refers only to the divine decision to redeem, not to the act of abandoning the remainder of fallen humanity.

For Calvin, logical rigour demands that God actively chooses to redeem or to damn. God cannot be thought of as doing something by default: he is active and sovereign in his actions. Therefore God actively wills the salvation of those who will be saved and the damnation of those who will not. Predestination is thus the 'eternal decree of God, by which he determined what he wished to make of every individual. For he does not create all in the same condition, but ordains eternal life for some and eternal damnation for others.' One of the central functions of the doctrine is to emphasize the graciousness of God. For Luther, God's graciousness is reflected in the fact that he justifies sinners, men and women who are totally unworthy of such a privilege. For Calvin, God's graciousness is demonstrated in his decision to redeem individuals irrespective of their merits: the decision to redeem an individual is made without reference to how worthy that individual might be. For Luther, God's graciousness is demonstrated in that he saves sinners *despite* their demerits; for Calvin, that graciousness is demonstrated in that he saves individuals *irrespective* of their merits. Although Luther and Calvin defend the graciousness of God in somewhat different manners, the same principle is affirmed by their respective views on justification and predestination.

Although the doctrine of predestination was not central to the thought of Calvin himself, it became the central nucleus of later Reformed theology through the influence of writers such as Peter Martyr Vermigli and Theodore Beza.[5] From about 1570 onwards, the theme of 'election' came to dominate Reformed theology, and allowed an easy identification of the Reformed congregations with the people of Israel. Just as God had once chosen Israel, so he had now chosen the Reformed congregations as his people. From this moment onwards, the doctrine of predestination began to assume a major social and political function – a function it did not possess under Calvin.

Calvin expounds his doctrine of predestination in Book 3 of the 1559 edition of the *Institutes of the Christian Religion*, as an aspect of the doctrine of redemption through Christ. In the earliest edition of the work (1536), it was treated as an aspect of the doctrine of providence. From the edition of 1539 onwards, it is treated as a topic of importance in its own right.

Calvin's discussion of 'the manner of obtaining the grace of Christ, the benefits which it confers, and the effects which result from it' presupposes that there is a possibility of redemption on account of what Christ achieved by his death on the cross. Having discussed how that death can be the basis of human redemption (see pp. 80–2), Calvin now goes on to discuss how humans can benefit from the benefits which result from it. Thus the discussion shifts from the *grounds* of redemption to the manner in which it is *actualized*.

The order of the topics which follow has puzzled Calvin scholars for some time. Calvin discusses a series of matters in the following order: faith, regeneration, the Christian life, justification, predestination. On the basis of Calvin's discussion of the relation of these entities in the order of salvation, it might be expected that the order would be somewhat different, with predestination preceding justification and regeneration following justification. Calvin's ordering appears to reflect educational considerations, rather than theological precision.

Calvin adopts a distinctly low-key approach to the doctrine of predestination, devoting a mere four chapters to its exposition (chapters 21–4 of Book 3). Predestination is defined as 'the eternal decree of God, by which he determined what he wished to make of every person. For he does not create everyone in the same condition, but ordains eternal life for some and eternal damnation for others' (III.xxi.5). Predestination is something which should induce a sense of awe within us. The *decretum horribile* (III.xxiii.7) is not a 'horrible decree', as a crude translation, insensitive to the nuances of the Latin, might suggest; rather it is an 'awe-inspiring' or 'terrifying' decree.

The very location of Calvin's discussion of predestination in the 1559 edition of the *Institutes* is significant in itself. It follows his exposition of the doctrine of grace. It is only after the great themes of this doctrine – such as justification by faith – have been expounded that Calvin turns to consider the mysterious and perplexing subject of predestination. Logically, predestination ought to precede such an analysis; predestination, after all, establishes the grounds of an individual's election, and hence his or her subsequent justification and sanctification. Yet Calvin declines to be subservient to the canons of such logic. Why?

For Calvin, predestination must be considered in its proper context. It is not the product of human speculation, but a mystery of divine revelation (I.ii.2; III.xxi.1–2). It has been revealed, however, in a specific *context* and in a specific *manner*. That manner relates to Jesus Christ himself, who is the 'mirror in which we may behold the fact of our election' (III.xxiv.5). The context relates to the efficacy of the gospel proclamation. Why is it that some individuals respond to the Christian gospel and others do not? Is the failure of some to respond to be put down to some lack of efficacy, some inherent inadequacy, in that gospel? Or is there some other reason for this divergence in response?

Far from being arid, abstract theological speculation, Calvin's analysis of predestination begins from observable facts. Some do, and some do not, believe the gospel. The primary function of the doctrine of predestination is to explain why some individuals respond to the gospel and others do not. It is an *ex post facto* explanation of the particularity of human responses to grace. Calvin's predestinarianism is to be regarded as *a posteriori* reflection upon the data of human experience, interpreted in the light of Scripture, rather than something which is deduced *a priori* on the basis of preconceived ideas concerning divine omnipotence. Belief in predestination is not an article of faith in its own right, but is the final outcome of scripturally informed reflection on the effects of grace upon individuals in the light of the enigmas of experience.

Experience indicates that God does not touch every human heart (III.xxiv.15). Why not? Is this due to some failure on God's part? Or is there something wrong with the gospel, which prevents it from converting everyone? In the light of Scripture, Calvin feels able to deny the possibility of any weakness or inadequacy on the part of God or the gospel; the observable pattern of responses to the gospel reflects a mystery by which some are predestined to respond to, and others to reject, the promises of God. 'Some have been allocated to eternal life, others to eternal damnation' (III.xxi.5).

This, it must be stressed, is no theological innovation. Calvin is not introducing a hitherto unknown notion into the sphere of Christian theology. As we have seen the 'modern Augustinian school (*schola Augustiniana moderna*)', exemplified by such leading medieval theologians as Gregory of Rimini, also taught a doctrine of absolute double predestination – that God allocates some to eternal life, others to eternal condemnation, without any reference to their merits or demerits. Their fate rests totally upon the will of God, rather than their individualities. Indeed, it is possible that Calvin has knowingly appropriated this aspect of late medieval Augustinianism, which certainly bears an uncanny resemblance to his own teaching.

Salvation thus lies outside the control of the individual, who is powerless to alter the situation. Calvin stresses that this selectivity is not in any way peculiar to the matter of salvation. In every area of life, he argues, we are forced to reckon with the mystery of the inexplicable. Why is it that some are more fortunate than others in life? Why does one person possess intellectual gifts denied to another? Even from the moment of birth, two infants may find themselves in totally different circumstances through no fault of their own: one may find a full breast of milk to suck and thus gain nourishment, while another may suffer malnutrition through having to suck a breast that is nearly dry. For Calvin, predestination is merely a further instance of a general mystery of human existence, in which some are inexplicably favoured with material or intellectual gifts which are denied to others. It raises no difficulties which are not already presented by other areas of human existence.

Does not this idea of predestination imply that God is dispensed from common notions of goodness, justice or rationality? Although Calvin specifically repudiates the conception of God as an absolute and *arbitrary* power, his discussion of predestination raises the spectre of a God whose relationship to his creation is whimsical and capricious and whose conception and exercise of power are not bound to any law or order. At this point, Calvin clearly aligns himself with the late medieval discussion of this contentious issue, particularly within the *via moderna* and the *schola Augustiniana moderna*, concerning the relation of God to the established moral order. God is not subject in any sense to law; for this would place law above God, an aspect of creation – or even something outside God *prior* to creation – above the Creator. God is outside the law, in that God's will is the foundation of existing conceptions of morality (III.xxiii.2). These terse statements reflect one of Calvin's clearest affinities with the late medieval voluntarist tradition.

In the end, Calvin argues that predestination must be recognized to rest in the inscrutable judgements of God (III.xxi.1). We cannot know why God elects some and condemns others. Some scholars have suggested that this position may reveal the influence of late medieval discussions of the 'absolute power of God (*potentia Dei absoluta*)', by which a whimsical or arbitrary God is perfectly at liberty to do whatever God pleases, without being obliged to justify those actions. This suggestion, however, rests on a serious misunderstanding of the role of the dialectic between the two powers – absolute and ordained – of God in late medieval thought. God must be free to choose whom God wills, otherwise God's freedom is compromised by external considerations and the Creator becomes subject to the creation. Nevertheless, God's decisions reflect God's wisdom and justice, which are upheld, rather than contradicted, by the fact of predestination (III.xxii.4; III.xxiii.2).

Far from being a central premises of Calvin's theological 'system' (a quite inappropriate term, in any case), predestination is thus an ancillary doctrine, concerned with explaining a puzzling aspect of the consequences of the proclamation of the gospel of grace. Yet, as Calvin's followers sought to develop and recast his thinking in the light of new intellectual developments, it was perhaps inevitable (if this lapse into a potentially predestinarian mode of speaking may be excused) that alterations to his structuring of Christian theology would occur.

Predestination in Later Calvinism

As I noted earlier, it is not correct to speak of Calvin developing a 'system' in the strict sense of the term. Calvin's religious ideas, as presented in the 1559 *Institute*, are *systematically arranged* on the basis of pedagogical considerations; they are not, however, *systematically derived* on the basis of a leading speculative principle. Calvin regarded biblical exposition and systematic theology as virtually identical, and refused to make the distinction between them which became commonplace after his death.

At that time a new concern for method – that is, the systematic organization and coherent deduction of ideas – gained momentum. Reformed theologians found themselves having to defend their ideas against both Lutheran and Roman Catholic opponents. Aristotelianism, regarded with a certain degree of suspicion by Calvin himself, was now seized upon as an ally. It became increasingly important to demonstrate the internal consistency and coherence of Calvinism. As a result, many Calvinist writers turned to Aristotle, in the hope that his writings on method might provide hints as to how their theology might be placed upon a firmer rational foundation.

Four characteristics of the new approach to theology which resulted may be noted:

1 Human reason was assigned a major role in the exploration and defence of Christian theology.
2 Christian theology was presented as a logically coherent and rationally defensible system, derived from syllogistic deductions based on known axioms. In other words, theology began from first principles, and proceeded to deduce its doctrines on their basis.
3 Theology was understood to be grounded in Aristotelian philosophy, particularly Aristotelian insights into the nature of method; later Reformed writers are better described as philosophical, rather than biblical, theologians.
4 Theology was seen as being concerned with metaphysical and speculative questions, especially as these relate to the nature of God, his will for humanity and creation, and above all the doctrine of predestination.

The starting point of theology thus came to be general principles, not a specific historical event. The contrast with Calvin will be clear. For Calvin, theology centred on and derived from the event of Jesus Christ, as witnessed by Scripture. It is this new concern for establishing a logical starting point for theology which enables us to understand the new importance which came to be attached to the doctrine of predestination. Calvin focused on the specific historical phenomenon of Jesus Christ and then moved out to explore its implications (that is, to use the appropriate technical language, his method was analytic and inductive). By contrast, Beza began from general principles and proceeded to deduce their consequences for Christian theology (that is, his method was deductive and synthetic).

So what general principles did Beza use as a logical starting point for his theological systematization? The answer is that he based his system on the divine decrees of election – that is, the divine decision to elect certain people to salvation and others to damnation. The rest of theology was concerned with the exploration of the consequences of those decisions. The doctrine of predestination thus assumed the status of a controlling principle.

On major consequence of this development may be noted: the doctrine of 'limited atonement' or 'particular redemption'. (The term 'atonement' is often used to refer to 'the benefits resulting from the death of Christ'.) Consider the following question: For whom did Christ die? The traditional answer to this question took the following form: Christ died for everyone. Yet, although his death had the potential to redeem all, it was only effective for those who chose to allow it to have this effect.

This question had surfaced with great force during the great predestinarian controversy of the ninth century, in which the Benedictine monk Godescalc of Orbais (also known as Gottschalk) had developed a doctrine of double predestination similar to that later to be associated with Calvin and his followers. Pursuing with relentless logic the implications of his assertion that God had predestined some to eternal damnation, Godescalc pointed out that it was thus quite improper to speak of Christ dying for such individuals; for if he had, he would have died in vain, since their fate would be unaffected.

Hesitant over the implications of this assertion, Godescalc proposed that Christ died *only for the elect.* The scope of his redeeming work was restricted, limited to those who were predestined to benefit from his death. Most ninth-century writers reacted with disbelief to this assertion. It was to resurface, however, in later Calvinism.

Linked with this new emphasis on predestination was a heightened interest in the idea of election. When exploring the distinctive ideas of the *via moderna* (pp. 74–6), we noted the idea of a covenant between God and believers, similar to the covenant established between God and Israel in the Old Testament. This idea began to assume major importance for the rapidly expanding Reformed church. The Reformed church communities saw themselves as the new Israel, the new people of God, who stood in a new covenant relationship to God.

The 'covenant of grace' laid down God's obligations to his people and his people's obligations (religious, social and political) to him. It defined the framework within which individuals and society functioned. The form which this theology took in England – Puritanism – is of particular interest. The sense of being the 'elect people of God' was heightened as the new people of God entered the new promised land – America.[6] Although this development lies outside the scope of this book, it is important to appreciate that the social, political and religious views which characterized the New England settlers derived from the sixteenth-century European Reformation. The international Reformed social vision was grounded in the concept of divine election and the 'covenant of grace'.

In marked contrast, later Lutheranism marginalized Luther's 1525 insights into divine predestination, preferring to work within the framework of a free human response to God, rather than a sovereign divine election of specific individuals. For later sixteenth-century Lutheranism, 'election' meant a human decision to love God, not God's decision to elect certain individuals. Indeed, disagreement over the doctrine of predestination was one of the two major controversies which occupied polemical writers of both confessions for centuries thereafter (the other controversy concerned the sacraments). Lutherans never had quite the same sense of being the 'elect of God', and were correspondingly modest in their attempts to expand their sphere of influence as a result. The remarkable success of 'international Calvinism', by contrast, reminds us of the power of an idea to transform both individuals and groups – and the Reformed doctrine of election and predestination was unquestionably the driving force behind the great expansion of the Reformed church in the seventeenth century.

The Doctrine of Grace and the Reformation

'The Reformation, inwardly considered, was just the ultimate triumph of Augustine's doctrine of grace over Augustine's doctrine of the church.'[7] This famous remark of Benjamin B. Warfield summarizes with some brilliance the importance of the doctrine of grace to the development of the Reformation. The reformers saw themselves as having recovered Augustine's doctrine of grace from the distortions and perversions of the medieval church. For Luther, Augustine's doctrine of grace, as expressed in the doctrine of justification by faith alone, was the *articulus stantis et cadentis ecclesiae*, 'the article by which the church stands or falls'. And if there were some subtle, and other not so subtle, differences between Augustine and the reformers over the doctrine of grace, the latter felt able to put this down to the superior textual and philological methods at their disposal, regrettably denied to Augustine. For the reformers, especially Luther, the Christian church was constituted by its doctrine of grace; and any compromise or failure on this matter by an ecclesiastical grouping involved the loss of that grouping's claim to be the Christian church. The medieval church had lost its claim to be 'Christian', thereby justifying the action of the reformers in breaking away from it, in order to re-establish the gospel.

Augustine, however, had developed an ecclesiology, or doctrine of the church, which was opposed to any such development. During the Donatist controversy of the early fifth century, Augustine had emphasized the unity of the church, and had argued vigorously against the temptation to form breakaway groups when the main body of the church seemed to be in error. The reformers felt able to disregard Augustine on this point, holding that his views on grace were far more important than his views on the church. The church, they argued, was a product of the grace of God – and so it was the latter that was of primary importance. The opponents of the Reformation disagreed, arguing that it was the church itself which was the guarantor of the Christian faith. The scene was thus set for the debate over the nature of the church, to which we shall return in chapter 10. Our attention is now claimed by the second great theme of Reformation thought: the need to return to Scripture.

For further reading

T. George, *The Theology of the Reformers* (Nashville, TN, 1988), pp. 73–9; 231–4.

P. C. Holtrop, *The Bolsec Controversy on Predestination from 1551 to 1555* (Lewiston, NY, 1993).

R. A. Muller, *Christ and the Decree: Christology and Predestination in Reformed Theology from Calvin to Perkins* (Durham, NC, 1986).

T. H. L. Parker, *John Calvin: A Biography* (London, 1975).

D. A. Penny, *Freewill or Predestination: The Battle over Saving Grace in mid-Tudor England* (London, 1990).

W. P. Stephens, *The Holy Spirit in the Theology of Martin Bucer* (Cambridge, 1970).

F. Wendel, *Calvin: Origins and Development of His Religious Thought* (London, 1963).

P. O. G. White, *Predestination, Policy and Polemic: Conflict and Consensus in the English Church from the Reformation to the Civil War* (Cambridge, 1992).

8

The Return to Scripture

At the heart of most religious systems lies a core of written texts which are regarded as being 'authoritative' – in other words, as having some permanent significance in defining the 'shape' of that religion. In the case of Christianity, the written texts in question are those gathered together as the Bible and often referred to simply as 'Scripture'. (Throughout this book, terms such as 'the Bible' and 'Scripture' and 'biblical' and 'scriptural' are treated as equivalent.) As is well known, the Bible is a central document of western civilization, not only as the source of Christian ideas but also as an influence upon education and culture.[1] The Reformation saw a new importance being attached to Scripture – or, perhaps, an ancient view of the importance of Scripture being recovered. The idea of *scriptura sola*, 'by Scripture alone', became one of the great slogans of the reformers as they sought to bring the practices and beliefs of the church back into line with those of the Golden Age of Christianity. If the doctrine of justification by faith alone was the material principle of the Reformation, the principle of *scriptura sola* was its formal principle. If the reformers dethroned the pope, they enthroned Scripture. Every strand of the Reformation movement regarded Scripture as the quarry from which its ideas and practices were hewn – yet, as we shall see, Scripture proved to be much more difficult to use in this way than might be expected. In this present chapter, we shall consider the Reformation understanding of Scripture in some detail, contextualizing it in the world of thought of the late medieval and Renaissance periods.

Scripture in the Middle Ages

To understand the importance of humanism in relation to the development of the ideas of the Reformation, as well as those ideas themselves, it is necessary to appreciate the way in which Scripture was understood and handled in the medieval period. In this section, I shall sketch an outline of the medieval understanding of the importance of Scripture.

The Concept of 'Tradition'

For most medieval theologians, Scripture was the materially sufficient source of Christian doctrine.[2] In other words, everything that was of essential importance to the Christian faith was contained in Scripture. There was no need to look anywhere else for material relevant to Christian theology. There were certainly matters on which Scripture had nothing to say: for example, who wrote the Apostles' Creed, at what precise moment during the celebration of the eucharist the bread and wine became the body and blood of Christ, or whether the practice of baptism was intended solely for adult believers. On these matters, the church felt at liberty to attempt to work out what Scripture implied, although its judgements were regarded as subordinate to Scripture itself.

By the end of the Middle Ages, however, the concept of 'tradition' had come to be of major importance in relation to the interpretation and authority of Scripture. Heiko A. Oberman has helpfully indicated that two quite different concepts of tradition were in circulation in the late Middle Ages, which he designates 'Tradition 1' and 'Tradition 2'.[3] In view of the importance of these concepts to the Reformation, we shall examine them briefly.

It was not only the orthodox, but also the heretical, who appealed to Scripture for support. John Dryden, writing in the seventeenth century, made this point with force:

> For did not Arius first, Socinus now
> The Son's eternal Godhead disavow?
> And did not these by Gospel texts alone
> Condemn our doctrine and maintain their own?
> Have not all heretics the same pretence,
> To plead the Scriptures in their own defence?

In response to various controversies within the early church, especially the threat from Gnosticism, a 'traditional' method of understanding certain passages of Scripture began to develop. Second-century patristic theologians such as Irenaeus of Lyons began to develop the idea of an authorized way of interpreting certain texts of Scripture, which, he argued, went back to the time of the apostles themselves. Scripture could not be interpreted in a random way; it must be interpreted within the context of the historical continuity of the Christian church. The parameters of its interpretation were historically fixed and 'given'. Oberman designates this understanding of tradition as 'Tradition

1'. 'Tradition' here means simply 'a traditional way of interpreting Scripture within the community of faith'.

In the fourteenth and fifteenth centuries, however, a somewhat different understanding of tradition developed. 'Tradition' was now understood to be a separate, distinct source of revelation, *in addition to Scripture*.[4] Scripture, it was argued, was silent on a number of points. But God had providentially arranged for a second source of revelation to supplement this deficiency: a stream of unwritten tradition, going back to the apostles themselves. This tradition was passed down from one generation to the next within the church. Oberman designates this understanding of tradition as 'Tradition 2'.

To summarize: 'Tradition 1' is a *single-source* theory of doctrine: doctrine is based on Scripture, and 'tradition' refers to a 'traditional way of interpreting Scripture'. 'Tradition 2', by contrast, is a *dual-source* theory of doctrine: doctrine is based upon two quite distinct sources, Scripture and unwritten tradition. A belief which is not to be found in Scripture may thus, on the basis of this dual-source theory, be justified by an appeal to an unwritten tradition. As we shall see, it was against this dual-source theory of doctrine that the reformers primarily directed their criticisms.

The Vulgate Translation of the Bible

When a medieval theologian refers to 'Scripture', he almost invariably means the *textus vulgatus*, the 'common text', drawn up by the great patristic biblical scholar Jerome in the late fourth and early fifth centuries.[5] Although the term 'Vulgate' did not come into general use until the sixteenth century,[6] it is perfectly acceptable to use the term to refer to the specific Latin translation of the Bible prepared by Jerome in the late fourth and early fifth centuries. This text was passed down to the Middle Ages in a number of forms, with considerable variations between them. For example, Theodulf and Alcuin, noted scholars of the Dark Ages, used quite different versions of the Vulgate text. A new period of intellectual activity opened up in the eleventh century, as the Dark Ages lifted. It was clear that a standard version of this text was required to service the new interest in theology which developed as part of this intellectual renaissance. If theologians were to base their theology on different versions of the Vulgate, an equally great, if not greater, variation in their conclusions would be the inevitable result. The need for standardization was met by what appears to have been a joint speculative venture by some Paris theologians and stationers in 1226, resulting in the 'Paris version' of the Vulgate text. By then, Paris was recognized as the leading centre of theology in Europe, with the inevitable result that – despite its many obvious imperfections – the 'Paris version' of the Vulgate became established as normative. This version, it must be emphasized, was not commissioned or sponsored by any ecclesiastical figure; it appears to have been a purely commercial venture. History, however, concerns the fate of accidents, and it is necessary to note that medieval theologians, attempting to base their theology on Scripture, were obliged to equate Scripture with a rather bad commercial edition of an already faulty Latin translation of the Bible. The rise of humanist textual and philological techniques would expose the distressing discrepancies between the Vulgate and the texts it purported to translate – and thus open the way to doctrinal reformation as a consequence.

The Medieval Vernacular Versions of Scripture

During the Middle Ages a number of vernacular versions of Scripture were produced. Although it was once thought that the medieval church condemned this process of translation, it is now known that neither the production of such translations nor their use by clergy or laity was ever explicitly forbidden.[7] An important example of such translations is provided by the Wycliffite versions, produced by a group of scholars who gathered around John Wycliffe at Lutterworth.[8] The motivation for the translation of the Bible into English was partly spiritual, partly political. It was spiritual in that the laity could now have access to 'Goddis lawe' and political in that an implicit challenge was posed to the teaching authority of the church. The laity were enabled to detect the obvious differences between the scriptural vision of the church and its somewhat corrupt English successor, thus setting the agenda for a programme of reform.

Important though such vernacular versions were, their importance must not be exaggerated. All these versions, it must be remembered, were simply *translations of the Vulgate*. They were not based on the best manuscripts of Scripture, in their original languages, but on the Vulgate version, with all its weaknesses and errors. The agenda for the Reformation would be set through the application of textual and philological techniques of a sophistication far beyond that of Wycliffe's circle at Lutterworth. It is to those methods, developed by humanist scholars such as Lorenzo Valla and Erasmus of Rotterdam, that we now turn.

The Humanists and the Bible

We have already seen how important the humanist movement was in relation to the study of Scripture (pp. 53–5). It may be helpful if we bring together the main elements of the humanist contribution to this important question.

1 The great humanist emphasis on the need to return *ad fontes* established the priority of Scripture over later commentaries on its text, particularly those of the Middle Ages. The text of Scripture was to be approached directly, rather than through a complicated system of glosses and commentaries.

2 Scripture was to be read directly in its original languages, rather than in Latin translation. Thus the Old Testament was to be studied in Hebrew (except for those few sections written in Aramaic), and the New Testament was to be read in Greek. The growing humanist interest in the Greek language (which many humanists held to be supreme in its capacity to mediate philosophical concepts) further consolidated the importance attached to the New Testament documents. The late Renaissance scholarly ideal was to be *trium linguarum gnarus*, 'expert in three languages' (Hebrew, Greek and Latin). Trilingual colleges were established at Alcalá in Spain, at Paris and at Wittenberg. The new interest in, and availability of, Scripture in its original languages soon brought to light a number of serious mistakes in translation in the Vulgate, some of them of considerable importance (see pp. 53–5).

3 The humanist movement made available two essential tools for the new method of study of the Bible. First, it made available the printed text of Scripture in its original languages. For example, Erasmus' *Novum Instrumentum omne* of 1516 allowed scholars direct access to the printed text of the Greek New Testament, and Lefèvre d'Etaples provided the Hebrew text of a group of important Psalms in 1509. Second, it made available manuals of classical languages, allowing scholars to learn languages which they otherwise could not have acquired. Reuchlin's Hebrew primer, *De rudimentis hebraicis* (1506), is an excellent example of this type of material. Greek primers were more common: the Aldine Press produced an edition of Lascaris' Greek grammar in 1495; Erasmus' translation of the famous Greek grammar of Theodore of Gaza appeared in 1516; and Melanchthon produced a masterly Greek primer in 1518.[9]

4 The humanist movement developed textual techniques capable of establishing accurately the best text of Scripture. These techniques had been used, for example, by Lorenzo Valla to demonstrate the inauthenticity of the famous *Donation of Constantine* (see p. 56). It was now possible to eliminate many of the textual errors which had crept into the Parisian edition of the Vulgate. Erasmus shocked his contemporaries by excluding a significant part of one verse of the Bible (1 John 5 : 7), which he could not find in any Greek manuscript, as a later addition. The Vulgate version reads as follows: 'For there are three that testify IN HEAVEN: THE FATHER, THE WORD AND THE HOLY SPIRIT,

AND THESE THREE ARE ONE. AND THERE ARE THREE THAT TESTIFY ON EARTH: the Spirit, the water and the blood'. The capitalized section of the verse, omitted by Erasmus, was certainly there in the Vulgate – but not in the Greek texts which it purported to translate. As this text had become an important proof text for the doctrine of the Trinity, many were outraged at his action. Theological conservatism here often triumphed over scholarly progress: even the famous King James Version (also known as the Authorized Version) of 1611, for example, included the spurious verse, despite its obvious inauthenticity.[10]

5   The humanists tended to regard ancient texts as mediating an experience which could be recaptured through appropriate literary methods. Included in the theme *ad fontes* is the notion of recapturing the experience mediated by the text. In the case of the New Testament, the experience in question was that of the presence and power of the risen Christ. Scripture was thus read with a sense of anticipation; it was believed that the vitality and excitement of the Apostolic era could be regained in the sixteenth century, by reading and studying Scripture in the right manner.

6   In his *Enchiridion*, which became enormously influential in 1515, Erasmus argued that a biblically literate laity held the key to the renewal of the church. In his work, both clergy and church were marginalized: the lay reader of Scripture had therein a more than adequate guide to the essentials of Christian belief and especially practice. These views, which achieved wide circulation among the lay intelligentsia of Europe, unquestionably prepared the way for the scriptural reforming programme of Luther and Zwingli in the period 1519–25. Even if Luther adopted a theological approach to Scripture which contrasted with Erasmus' undoctrinaire attitude, he was widely regarded as building on a solidly Erasmian foundation.

The Bible and the Reformation

'The Bible', wrote William Chillingworth, 'I say, the Bible only, is the religion of Protestants.' These famous words of this seventeenth-century English Protestant summarize the Reformation attitude to Scripture. Calvin stated the same principle less memorably, if more fully, thus: 'Let this then be a sure axiom: that nothing ought to be admitted in the church as the Word of God, save that which is contained, first in the Law and the Prophets, and secondly in the writings of the Apostles; and that there is no other method of teaching in the church than according to the prescription and rule of his Word.' For Calvin, as we shall see, the institutions and regulations of both church and society were required to be grounded in Scripture: 'I approve only of those human institutions which are founded upon the authority of God and derived from Scripture.' Zwingli entitled his 1522 tract on Scripture *On the Clarity and Certainty of the Word of God*, stating that 'The foundation of our religion is the written word, the Scriptures of God.' Such views indicate the consistently high view of Scripture adopted by the reformers. This view, as we have seen, is not a novelty; it represents a major point of continuity with medieval theology, which – certain later Franciscan writers excepted – regarded Scripture as the most important source of Christian doctrine. The difference between the reformers and medieval theology at this point concerns how Scripture is *defined* and *interpreted*, rather than the *status* which it is given. We shall explore these points further in what follows.

The Canon of Scripture

Central to any programme which treats Scripture as normative is the delimitation of Scripture. In other words, what *is* Scripture? The term 'canon' (a Greek word meaning 'rule' or 'norm') came to be used to refer to those Scriptures recognized as authentic by the church. For medieval theologians, 'Scripture' meant 'those works included in the Vulgate'. The reformers, however, felt able to call this judgement into question. While all the New Testament works were accepted as canonical – Luther's misgivings concerning four of them gaining little support[11] – doubts were raised concerning the canonicity of a group of Old Testament works. A comparison of the contents of the Old Testament in the Hebrew Bible on the one hand and the Greek and Latin versions (such as the Vulgate) on the other shows that the latter contain a number of books not found in the former. The reformers argued that the only Old Testament writings which could be regarded as belonging to the canon of Scripture were those originally included in the Hebrew Bible.[12] A distinction was thus drawn between the 'Old Testament' and the 'Apocrypha': the former consisted of books found in the Hebrew Bible, the latter of books found in the Greek and Latin Bibles (such as the Vulgate), but *not* in the Hebrew Bible. While some reformers allowed that the apocryphal works were edifying reading, there was general agreement that these works could not be used as the basis of doctrine. Medieval theologians, however, to be followed by the Council of Trent in 1546, defined the 'Old Testament' as 'those Old Testament works contained in the Greek and Latin bibles', thus eliminating any distinction between 'Old Testament' and 'Apocrypha'.

A fundamental distinction thus developed between Roman Catholic and Protestant understandings of what the term 'Scripture' actually meant. This distinction persists to the present day. A comparison of Protestant versions of the Bible – the two most important being the *New Revised Standard Version* (NRSV) and the *New International Version* (NIV) – with Roman Catholic versions, such as the Jerusalem Bible, will reveal these differences. For the reformers, *scriptura sola* thus implied not merely one, but *two*, differences from their catholic opponents: not only did they attach a different status to Scripture, but they disagreed over what Scripture actually was. But what is the relevance of this dispute?

One catholic practice to which the reformers took particular exception was that of praying for the dead. To the reformers, this practice rested on a non-biblical foundation (the doctrine of purgatory), and encouraged popular superstition and ecclesiastical exploitation. Their catholic opponents were able to meet this objection, however, by pointing out that the practice of praying for the dead is explicitly mentioned in Scripture, at 2 Maccabees 12:40–46. The reformers, on the other hand, having declared that this book was apocryphal (and hence not part of the Bible), were able to respond that, in their view at least, the practice was not scriptural. This merited the obvious riposte from the catholic side: that the reformers based their theology on Scripture, but only after having excluded from the canon of Scripture any works which happened to contradict this theology.

One outcome of this debate was the production and circulation of authorized lists of books which were to be regarded as 'scriptural'. The Fourth Session of the Council of Trent (1546) produced a detailed list which included the works of the Apocrypha as authentically scriptural, while the Protestant congregations in Switzerland, France and elsewhere produced lists which deliberately omitted reference to these works or else indicated that they were of no importance in matters of doctrine.

The Authority of Scripture

The reformers grounded the authority of Scripture in its relation to the Word of God. For some, that relation was an absolute identity: Scripture *was* the Word of God. For others, the relation was slightly more nuanced: Scripture *contained* the Word of God. Nevertheless, there was a consensus that Scripture was to be received as if it were God himself speaking. For Calvin, the authority of Scripture was grounded in the fact that the biblical writers were 'secretaries (*notaires authentiques* in the French version of the *Institutes*) of the Holy Spirit'. As Heinrich Bullinger stated it, the authority of Scripture was absolute and autonomous: 'Because it is the Word of God, the holy biblical Scripture has adequate standing and credibility in itself and of itself.' Here was the gospel itself, able to speak for itself and challenge and correct its inadequate and inaccurate representation in the sixteenth century. Scripture was able both to pass judgement upon the late medieval church (and find it wanting) and to provide the model for the new Reformed church which would arise in its wake.

A number of points bring out the importance of the *sola scriptura* principle. First, the reformers insisted that the authority of popes, councils and theologians is subordinate to that of Scripture. This is not necessarily to say that they have *no* authority; as we shall see later, the reformers allowed certain councils and theologians of the patristic era a genuine authority in matters of doctrine. It *is* to say, however, that such authority is *derived from Scripture*, and is thus subordinate to Scripture. The Bible, as the Word of God, must be regarded as superior to both the Fathers and councils. As Calvin put it:

> For although we hold that the Word of God alone lies beyond the sphere of our judgement, and that fathers and councils are of authority only in so far as they agree with the rule of the Word, we still give to councils and fathers such rank and honour as it is appropriate for them to hold under Christ.

Luther tends to defend the *sola scriptura* principle by emphasizing the confusion and incoherence of medieval theology, whereas Calvin and Melanchthon argue that the best catholic theology (such as that of Augustine) supports their views on the priority of Scripture.

Second, the reformers argued that authority within the church does not derive from the status of the office-bearer, but from the Word of God which the office-bearer serves. Traditional catholic theology tended to ground the authority of the office-bearer in the office itself – for example, the authority of a bishop resides in the fact that he is a bishop – and emphasized the historical continuity of the office of bishop with the Apostolic era. The reformers grounded the authority of bishops (or their Protestant equivalent) in their faithfulness to the Word of God. As Calvin stated this point:

> The difference between us and the papists is that they believe that the church cannot be the pillar of the truth unless she presides over the Word of God. We, on the other hand, assert that it is *because* she reverently subjects herself to the Word of God that the truth is preserved by her, and passed on to others by her hands.

Historical continuity is of little importance in relation to the faithful proclamation of the Word of God. The breakaway churches of the Reformation were obviously denied historical continuity with the institutions of the catholic church: no catholic dishop would ordain their clergy, for example. Yet the reformers argued that the authority and functions of a bishop derived ultimately from faithfulness to the Word of God. Similarly, the decisions of bishops (and also of councils and popes) are authoritative and binding to the extent that they are faithful to Scripture. Where catholics stressed the importance of *historical* continuity, the reformers emphasized equally the importance of *doctrinal* continuity. While the Protestant churches could not generally provide historical continuity with the episcopacy (except, as in the case of the English or the Swedish reformations, through defections of catholic bishops), they could supply the necessary fidelity to Scripture – thus, in their view, legitimating the Protestant ecclesiastical offices. There might not be an unbroken historical link between the leaders of the Reformation and the bishops of the early church, but, the reformers argued, since they believed and taught the same faith as those early church bishops (rather than the distorted gospel of the medieval church), the necessary continuity was there none the less.

The *sola scriptura* principle thus involved the claim that the authority of the church was grounded in its fidelity to Scripture. The opponents of the Reformation, however, were able to draw on a dictum of Augustine: 'I should not have believed the gospel, unless I was moved by the authority of the catholic church.' Did not the very existence of the canon of Scripture point to the church having authority over Scripture? After all, it was the church which defined what 'Scripture' was – and this would seem to suggest that the church had an authority over, and independent of, Scripture. Thus Johann Eck, Luther's opponent at the famous Leipzig Disputation of 1519, argued that 'Scripture is not authentic without the authority of the church'. This clearly raises the question of the relation between Scripture and tradition, to which we may now conveniently return.

The Role of Tradition

The *scriptura sola* principle of the reformers would seem to eliminate any reference to tradition in the formation of Christian doctrine. In fact, however, the magisterial reformers had a very positive understanding of tradition, as we shall see.

Earlier, we noted two understanding of tradition characteristic of the late medieval period: 'Tradition 1' and 'Tradition 2' (see p. 147). The *scriptura sola* principle would seem to refer to an understanding of theology which allocates no role whatsoever to tradition – an understanding which we might designate 'Tradition 0'. The three main understandings of the relation between Scripture and tradition current in the sixteenth century can be summarized as follows:

Tradition 0: The radical Reformation
Tradition 1: The magisterial Reformation
Tradition 2: The Council of Trent.

At first, this analysis might seem surprising. Did not the reformers *reject* tradition, in favour of the scriptural witness alone? In fact, however, the reformers were concerned with the elimination of human additions to or distortions of the scriptural witness. The idea of a 'traditional interpretation of Scripture' – embodied in the concept of 'Tradition 1' – was perfectly acceptable to the magisterial reformers, *provided that this traditional interpretation could be justified*.

The only wing of the Reformation to apply the *scriptura sola* principle consistently was the radical Reformation, or 'Anabaptism'. For the radicals (or 'fanatics', as Luther dubbed them), such as Thomas Müntzer and Caspar Schwenkfeld, every individual had the right to interpret Scripture as he pleased, subject to the guidance of the Holy Spirit. For the radical Sebastian Franck, the Bible 'is a book sealed with seven seals which none can open unless he has the key of David, which is the illumination of the Spirit'. The way was thus opened for individualism, with the private judgement of the individual raised above the corporate judgement of the church. Thus the radicals rejected the practice of infant baptism (to which the magisterial Reformation remained committed) as non-scriptural. (There is no explicit reference to the practice in the New Testament.) Similarly, doctrines such as the Trinity and the divinity of Christ were rejected as resting on inadequate scriptural foundations. 'Tradition 0' placed the private judgement of the individual above the corporate judgement of the Christian church concerning the interpretation of Scripture. It was a recipe for anarchy – and, as the history of the radical Reformation sadly demonstrates, that anarchy was not slow to develop.

As has been noted, the magisterial Reformation was theologically conservative. It retained most traditional doctrines of the church – such as the divinity of Christ and the doctrine of the Trinity – on account of the reformers' conviction that these traditional interpretations of Scripture were correct. Equally, many traditional practices (such as infant baptism) were retained, on account of the reformers' belief that they were consistent with Scripture. The magisterial Reformation was painfully aware of the threat of individualism, and attempted to avoid this threat by stressing the church's traditional interpretation of Scripture where this traditional interpretation was regarded as correct. Doctrinal criticism was directed against those areas in which catholic theology or practice appeared to have gone far beyond, or to have contradicted, Scripture. As most of these developments had taken place in the Middle Ages, it is not surprising that the reformers spoke of the period 1200–1500 as an 'era of decay' or a 'period of corruption' which they had a mission to reform. Equally, it is hardly surprising that we find the reformers appealing to the Fathers as generally reliable interpreters of Scripture.[13]

This point is of particular importance, and has not received the attention it merits. One of the reasons why the reformers valued the writings of the Fathers, especially Augustine, was that they regarded them as exponents of a biblical theology. In other words, the reformers believed that the Fathers were attempting to develop a theology based upon Scripture alone – which was, of course, precisely what they were also trying to do in the sixteenth century. Of course, the new textual and philological methods available to the reformers meant that they could correct the Fathers on points of detail; but the reformers were prepared to accept the 'patristic testimony' as generally reliable. Since that testimony included such doctrines as the Trinity and the divinity of Christ and such practices as infant baptism, the reformers were predisposed to accept these as authentically scriptural. It will thus be obvious that this high regard for a traditional interpretation of Scripture (that is, 'Tradition 1') gave the magisterial Reformation a strong bias towards doctrinal conservatism.

This understanding of the *sola scriptura* principle allowed the reformers to criticize their opponents on both sides – on the one side the radicals, on the other the catholics. The catholics argued that the reformers elevated private judgement above the corporate judgement of the church. The reformers replied that they were doing nothing of the sort: they were simply restoring that corporate judgement to what it once was, by combating the doctrinal degeneration of the Middle Ages by an appeal to the corporate judgement of the patristic era. The radicals, however, had no place whatsoever for the 'testimony of the Fathers'. As Sebastian Franck wrote in 1530: 'Foolish Ambrose, Augustine, Jerome, Gregory – of whom not one even knew the Lord, so help me God, nor was sent by God to teach. Rather, they were all apostles of Antichrist.' Tradition 0 had no place for any traditional interpretation of Scripture. The magisterial reformers thus dismissed this radical understanding of the role of Scripture as pure individualism, a recipe for theological chaos.

It will therefore be clear that it is totally wrong to suggest that the magisterial reformers elevated private judgement above the corporate judgement of the church or that they degenerated into some form of individualism. This judgement is unquestionably true of the radical Reformation, the only wing of the Reformation to have been utterly consistent in its application of the *scriptura sola* principle. How often it is that the original, radical ideas of a movement such as the Reformation are rejected in favour of more conservative ideas as that movement develops. It is true that a certain degree of variation can be detected within the mainstream of the Reformation on this point: Zwingli is closer to the radical position than Calvin is, while Luther is closer to the catholic position. But none, it must be emphasized, was prepared to abandon the concept of a traditional interpretation of Scripture in favour of the radical alternative. As Luther gloomily observed, the inevitable result of such an approach was chaos, a 'new Babel'. Perhaps Luther would have had some sympathy for the views of John Dryden in the following century:

> The Book thus put in every vulgar hand,
> Which each presumed he best could understand,
> The common rule was made the common prey
> And at the mercy of the rabble lay.

The Council of Trent, meeting in 1546, responded to the threat of the Reformation by affirming a two-source theory (see pp. 165–6). This affirmation by the Catholic Reformation of Tradition 2 declares that the Christian faith reaches every generation through two sources: Scripture and an unwritten tradition. This extra-scriptural tradition is to be treated as having equal authority with Scripture. In making this declaration, the Council of Trent appears to have picked up the later, and less influential, of the two main medieval understandings of 'tradition', leaving the more influential to the reformers. It is interesting to note that in recent years there has been a certain degree of 'revisionism' within Roman Catholic circles on this point, with several contemporary theologians arguing that Trent *excluded* the view that 'the Gospel is only partly in Scripture and partly in the traditions'.[14]

Methods of Interpreting Scripture

Texts need to be interpreted. There is little point in treating a certain text as authoritative or normative if there is serious disagreement concerning how what that text means. During the later Middle Ages, increasing emphasis came to be placed upon the role of the church as interpreter of Scripture. The authority of Scripture was guaranteed by the authority of its interpreter – the church, under the divine guidance of the Holy Spirit. As we have seen (pp. 31–3), however, there was such doctrinal confusion and disagreement over the nature and location of theological authority in the later medieval period that it was far from clear who had the ultimate authority to interpret Scripture. The pope? A council? Or perhaps even a pious individual who knew his Bible well, as Panormitanus (Nicolo de Tudeschi) suggested, perhaps with his tongue firmly in his cheek. In practice, it seemed to be the pope of the day who held such authority; but there was sufficient confusion concerning this question to allow pluralism to develop virtually unchecked in the later fifteenth century, partly through new approaches to biblical interpretation which laid down a significant challenge to existing views.

The standard method of biblical interpretation used during the Middle Ages is usually known as the *Quadriga*, or the 'fourfold sense of Scripture', as we have seen. The origins of this method lie in the patristic period, although its systematic formulation was part and parcel of the new trend towards theological systematization which accompanied the cultural Renaissance of the twelfth century.

The basic principle underlying this approach is as follows. Scripture possesses a number of different senses. In addition to the literal sense, three non-literal senses could be distinguished: the allegorical, regarding what Christians are to believe; the tropological or moral, regarding what Christians are to do; and the anagogical, regarding what Christians were to hope for. The four senses of Scripture were thus the following:

1   The *literal* sense, whereby the text was taken at face value.
2   The *allegorical* sence, whereby certain passages of Scripture were interpreted so as to produce statements of doctrine. Those passages tended to be either obscure, or to have a literal meaning which was unacceptable, for theological reasons, to their readers.
3   The *tropological or moral* sense, whereby certain passages were interpreted to produce ethical guidance for Christian conduct.
4   The *anagogical* sense, whereby certain passages were interpreted to indicate the grounds of Christian hope, pointing towards the future fulfilment of the divine promises in the New Jerusalem.

A potential weakness was avoided by insisting that nothing should be believed on the basis of a non-literal sense of Scripture unless it could first be established on the basis of the literal sense. This insistence on the priority of the literal sense may be seen as an implied criticism of the allegorical approach adopted by Origen, which virtually allowed interpreters of Scripture to read into any passage whatever 'spiritual' interpretations they liked. As Luther states this principle in 1515: 'In the Scriptures no allegory, tropology or anagogy is valid, unless that same truth is explicitly stated literally somewhere else. Otherwise, Scripture would become a laughing matter.'

Yet the idea of a 'literal' sense of Scripture was regarded by many humanist writers to be imprecise and ill-defined, especially in relation to many passages in the Old Testament. Jacques Lefèvre d'Etaples, writing in the first decade of the sixteenth century, argued that a basic distinction had to be made between two different senses of the term 'literal'. The 'literal historical' sense of Scripture designates the obvious historical sense of a passage. Luther refers to this approach as 'referring to ancient history, rather than to Christ'. The 'literal prophetic' sense of Scripture designates the prophetic sense of a passage – in other words, where a passage points ahead to its fulfilment in the coming of Jesus Christ. As Luther puts it, 'Christ has opened the mind of those who are his, in order that they might understand the Scriptures.' Thus an Old Testament passage could be taken either as a literal historical reference to a series of events in the ancient Near East or as a literal prophetic reference to the coming of Christ. This Christological scheme of interpretation would prove especially important in relation to the Psalter, the Old Testament book which figured so prominently in medieval Christian spirituality and theology, and upon which Luther lectured from 1513 to 1515.

Luther was fully aware of these distinctions, and had no hesitation in using them to the full in his biblical exposition. In his analysis of the Psalter, he distinguished eight senses of the Old Testament. This amazing precision (which may impress some readers as typical of scholasticism) resulted from combining the four senses of Scripture with the insight that each of these senses could be interpreted historically or prophetically.

Luther developed this distinction by arguing that a distinction had to be made between what he termed 'the killing letter (*litera occidens*)' – in other words, a crudely literal or historical reading of the Old Testament – and 'the life-giving spirit (*spiritus vivificans*)' – in other words, a reading of the Old Testament which is sensitive to its spiritual nuances and prophetic overtones. As a worked example, we may consider Luther's analysis of an Old Testament image using this eightfold scheme of interpretation.

The image in question is Mount Zion, which can be interpreted either in a woodenly historical and literal sense as a reference to ancient Israel or as a prophetic reference to the New Testament church. Luther explores the possibilities (perhaps tongue in cheek?) as follows:

1   Historically, according to 'the killing letter':
   (a)   literally: the land of Canaan;
   (b)   allegorically: the synagogue, or a prominent person within it;
   (c)   tropologically: the righteousness of the Pharisees and the Law;
   (d)   anagogically: a future glory on earth.
2   Prophetically, according to 'the life-giving spirit':
   (a)   literally: the people of Zion;
   (b)   allegorically: the church, or a prominent person within it;
   (c)   tropologically: the righteousness of faith;
   (d)   anagogically: the eternal glory of the heavens.

The *Quadriga* was a major component of academic study of the Bible within scholastic theological faculties of universities. But it was not the only option available to biblical interpreters in the first two decades of the sixteenth century. Indeed, it may be argued that Luther was the only reformer to make significant use of this scholastic approach to biblical interpretation. By far the most influential approach to the subject within reforming and humanist circles employed the methods associated with Erasmus of Rotterdam, to which we now turn.

Erasmus' *Enchiridion* made much of the distinction between the 'letter' and the 'spirit' – that is, between the words of Scripture and their real meaning. Especially in the Old Testament, the words of the text are like a shell, containing – but not identical with – the kernel of the meaning. The surface meaning of the text often conceals a deeper, hidden meaning, which it is the task of the enlightened and responsible exegete to uncover. Biblical interpretation, according to Erasmus, is concerned with establishing the underlying sense, not the letter, of Scripture.

Zwingli's basic concern echoes that of Erasmus. The interpreter of the Bible is required to establish the 'natural sense of Scripture' – which is not necessarily identical with the literal sense of Scripture. Zwingli's humanist background allowed him to distinguish various figures of speech, especially *alloiosis*, *catachresis* and *synecdoche*. An example will make this point clear. Take the statement of Christ at the Last Supper, in which, when breaking the bread, he spoke the words 'this is my body' (Matthew 26:26). The literal sense of these words would be 'this piece of bread is my body', but the natural sense is 'this piece of bread signifies my body'.

Zwingli's search for the deeper meaning of Scripture (as contrasted with the superficial meaning) is well illustrated by the story of Abraham and Isaac (Genesis 22). The historical details of the story are too easily assumed to constitute its *real* meaning. In fact, Zwingli argues, the real meaning of that story can only be understood when it is seen as a prophetic anticipation of the story of Christ, in which Abraham represents God and Isaac is a figure (or, more technically, 'type') of Christ.

Most important, perhaps, is the stress placed by Erasmus, Bucer and Zwingli upon the moral or tropological sense of Scripture. Humanist approaches to Christianity never entirely managed to escape from the notion that the gospel primarily designates a way of life, whose moral contours are mapped out by Scripture. It is the task of the exegete to uncover these contours, and thus to allow Scripture to act as an ethical *vade mecum*, guiding believers through the moral maze of life. Whereas Luther tended to treat Scripture as primarily concerned with proclaiming the gracious promises of God to believers, there is a perceptibly more moralist cast to the writings of his three more humanist colleagues, who often portray Scripture as laying down a 'new law'. Similarly, whereas Erasmus and Bucer regard the tropological sense of Scripture as defining what believers must *do*, Luther, in his moment of theological breakthrough (p. 115), interprets that same sense as defining what God *has done* for believers in Christ.

A number of options were thus available for the interpretation of Scripture in the early sixteenth century. The Reformation, however, was not primarily an academic movement, based in universities, but a popular movement which increasingly made its appeal directly to an educated laity. Such academic methods of interpretation were difficult to explain and use at the popular level. It may be argued that the Reformation got under way only with the emphatic declaration that all had the right to interpret Scripture and to call into question existing teachings and practices of the church. In what follows, we shall explore how this development occurred and the weaknesses and inconsistencies which arose in its wake.

The Right to Interpret Scripture

The general consensus of the magisterial Reformation was that Scripture was the container of the Word of God. This Word, although uniquely given at a definite point in the past, could be recovered and appropriated by every generation through the guidance of the Holy Spirit. The early Reformation was characterized by the optimistic belief that it was possible to establish exactly what the Bible said on everything of importance and make this the basis of a reformed Christianity. The archetypal statement of this exegetical optimism may be found in Erasmus' *Enchiridion*: in Erasmus' view, the ploughman may read Scripture and understand it without any great difficulty. Scripture was clear and persuasive, and could serve as the manifesto of the reforming parties within Christendom.

In his great reforming treatise of 1520, *To the Christian Nobility of the German Nation*, Luther declared that the 'Romanists' had eliminated any threat of reform to the church by constructing three defensive walls around themselves:

> In the first place, when pressed by the temporal power, they have made decrees and declared that the temporal power had no jurisdiction over them, but that, on the contrary, the spiritual power is above the temporal. In the second place, when the attempt is made to reprove them with the Scriptures, they raise the objection that only the pope may interpret the Scriptures. In the third place, if threatened with a council, their story is that no one may summon a council except the pope.

Luther seems to have seen himself as a Joshua with a mission to cast down the three walls of this new Jericho (see Joshua 6:1–20). With three blasts of his reforming trumpet, Luther delineates the broad features of his reforming programme. First, the distinction between 'spiritual' and 'temporal' powers is abolished. Second, every believing Christian has the right to interpret Scripture. Third, any Christian (but especially a German prince) has the right to summon a reforming council. Luther's programme of reform is initially founded on these three principles, of which the second is of particular interest to us.

> Their claim that only the pope may interpret Scripture is an outrageous fancied fable . . . The Romanists must admit that there are among us good Christians who have the true faith, spirit, understanding, word, and mind of Christ. Why, then, should we reject the word and understanding of good Christians and follow the pope, who has neither faith nor the Spirit?

Luther appears to suggest that the ordinary pious Christian believer is perfectly capable of reading Scripture and making perfect sense of what he finds within its pages. A similar position is defended by Zwingli in his important treatise of 1522, *On the Clarity and Certainty of the Word of God*. For Zwingli, Scripture is perfectly clear. 'The Word of God, as soon as it shines upon an individual's understanding, illuminates it in such a way that he understands it.'

Yet, by the end of the 1520s, this exegetical optimism had been discredited to a significant degree, largely through the serious disagreement between Luther and Zwingli over the interpretation of one particular biblical text: *hoc est corpus meum*, 'this is my body' (Matthew 26:26), which was central to the eucharist, and hence of enormous theological importance to reformer and catholic alike. For Luther, this text meant what it said: in other words, the bread in the eucharist *is* the body of Christ. For Zwingli, however, its interpretation was somewhat different: for him, it meant 'this *signifies* my body' – in other words, the bread in the eucharist *represents* the body of Christ. As we shall see in the following chapter, the seriousness of this disagreement between the reformers over the eucharist did more than divide the magisterial Reformation permanently into two movements; it demonstrated how difficult it was to reach agreement over the interpretation of even those passages of Scripture which Luther regarded as most straightforward. The exegetical optimism of the late 1510s and early 1520s was also evident in the suggestion that the ordinary Christian could understand Scripture – but by the 1530s, it was considered that ordinary Christians could be relied upon to understand Scripture only if they were fluent in Hebrew, Greek and Latin and were familiar with the complexities of linguistic theories.

For the catholic, Scripture was difficult to interpret – and God had providentially supplied a reliable and authoritative interpreter in the form of the Roman Catholic church. The radical reformers rejected this totally, as we have seen: every individual believer had the right and the ability to interpret Scripture as seemed right to him. The magisterial reformers found themselves in something of a quandary at this point. They had conceded that Scripture is obscure at certain points, and thus requires interpretation. Their commitment to Tradition 1 rather than Tradition 0, however, required that they invoke the whole Christian community in the authoritative interpretation of Scripture at these points. But how could they do this, without conceding that this authority really lay with the Roman Catholic church? How could an authoritative communal *Protestant* interpretation of Scripture be given? We shall examine two means by which the Reformation attempted to overcome this difficulty.

The first might be designated the 'catechetical' approach. Protestant readers of Scripture were provided with a filter, by means of which they might interpret Scripture. One example of such a 'filter' is Luther's *Lesser Catechism* (1529), which provided its readers with a framework by which they could make sense of Scripture. The most famous guide to Scripture, however, was Calvin's *Institutes*, especially the definitive version of 1559. Calvin is known to have initially modelled this work on Luther's catechism. In the preface to the French edition of 1541, he states that the *Institutes* 'could be like a key and an entrance to give access to all the children of God, in order that they might really understand Holy Scripture'. In other words, the reader is expected to use Calvin's *Institutes* as a means to interpret Scripture. As the history of the development of the Reformed church in France and the Lowlands indicates, Calvin's approach was remarkably successful. The reader need only have two books – the Bible and Calvin's *Institutes* – to gain full access to the Reformed faith. Calvin's use of Scripture in the *Institutes* was so persuasive that it seemed to many that this book held the key to the proper interpretation of Scripture. The complex medieval hermeneutical schemes could be dispensed with, in favour of this elegantly written, lucid work.

The second means of dealing with the problem of the interpretation of Scripture might be designated 'the political hermeneutic', and was specifically associated with Zwingli's Reformation at Zurich. This method is of particular importance in relation to the political history of the Reformation. At some point in 1520, the Zurich city council required all clergy in the city to preach according to Scripture, avoiding 'human innovations and explanations'. In effect, the decree committed Zurich to the *scriptura sola* principle. By 1522, however, it had become clear that this decree had little meaning: for how was Scripture to be interpreted? A minor crisis arose in Lent 1522, when some of Zwingli's followers broke the fast traditionally observed at this time of year.[15] During a period in which it was traditional to eat only vegetables or fish, it seems that some of Zwingli's supporters succumbed to the forbidden pleasures of some sort of sausage. A few weeks later, on 9 April, the city council reaffirmed its commitment to the observance of the Lenten fast, and fined Froschauer a trivial amount for allowing it to be broken in his house. There the matter might have rested, had not Zwingli, seven days later, published (on

Froschauer's presses) a treatise arguing that nowhere in Scripture was it said that believers should abstain from meat during Lent. A similar debate developed the same year concerning clerical marriage. As tension began to grow in Zurich, it became clear that some means of resolving such ambiguities was needed.

The central difficulty concerned how Scripture was to be interpreted. On 3 January 1523 the city council announced that, as the body entrusted with control of public preaching, it had arranged a public disputation for later that same month to determine whether Zwingli's sixty-seven *Schlussreden*, or 'key theses', were in accordance with Scripture. This debate is now known as the 'First Zurich Disputation'. The debate, apparently modelled on academic disputations, took place at Zurich town hall on 29 January. It was a personal triumph for Zwingli. More significant, however, was the outcome for the city council, which emerged from the debate as the body entitled to determine what was in accordance with Scripture and what was not.[16]

For Zwingli, the city and the church at Zurich were effectively one and the same body – a point which is of particular importance in relation to his theology of the church and the sacraments, as we shall see in the following chapter. The city council, therefore, had a right to be involved in theological and religious matters. No longer was the Zurich Reformation to be detained by questions concerning the proper interpretation of Scripture. The city council effectively declared that *it* – not the pope or an ecumenical council – had the right to interpret Scripture for the citizens of Zurich, and gave notice that it intended to exercise that right. Scripture might indeed be ambiguous, but the political success of the Reformation at Zurich was virtually guaranteed by the unilateral decision of the city council to act as its interpreter. Similar decisions reached at Basle and Berne on the basis of the Zurich model consolidated the Reformation in Switzerland, and, by allowing Geneva political stability in the mid-1530s, indirectly led to the success of Calvin's Reformation.

It will be obvious that the power struggles within early Protestantism concerned the question of who had the authority to interpret Scripture. Whoever was recognized as possessing that authority was *de facto* in control of the ideology – and hence the social and political views – of the various factions of the Reformation. The pope's secular authority was linked with his role as the authoritative interpreter of Scripture for Roman Catholics in much the same way. This observation allows us some important insights concerning the social and political dimensions of the Reformation. For example, the radical Reformation axiom, that the enlightened individual had full authority to interpret Scripture for himself, is linked with the communism often associated with the movement. All individuals must be regarded as equal. Similarly, the failure of the radical Reformation to produce any first-class theologians – a factor of some importance in relation to the movement's premature degeneration into ideological chaos – reflects a reluctance to allow that any one individual has a right to lay down what others should think or how they should interpret Scripture.

The magisterial Reformation initially seems to have allowed that every individual had the right to interpret Scripture; but subsequently it became anxious concerning the social and political consequences of this idea. The Peasants' Revolt of 1525 appears to have convinced some, such as Luther, that individual believers (especially German peasants) were simply not capable of interpreting Scripture. It is one of the ironies of the Lutheran Reformation that a movement which laid such stress upon the importance of Scripture should subsequently deny its less educated members direct access to that same Scripture, for fear that they might misinterpret it (in other words, reach a different interpretation from that of the magisterial reformers). For example, the school regulations of the duchy of Württemberg laid down that only the most able schoolchildren were to be allowed to study the New Testament in their final years – and even then, only if they studied it in Greek or Latin. The remainder – presumably the vast bulk – were required to read Luther's *Lesser Catechism* instead. The direct interpretation of Scripture was thus effectively reserved for a small, privileged group of people. To put it crudely, it became a question of whether you looked to the pope, to Luther or to Calvin as an interpreter of Scripture. The principle of the 'clarity of Scripture' appears to have been quietly marginalized, in the light of the use made of the Bible by the more radical elements within the Reformation. Similarly, the idea that everyone had the right and the ability to interpret Scripture faithfully became the sole possession of the radicals.

The Catholic Response: Trent on Scripture

The Council of Trent reacted forcefully to what it regarded as Protestant irresponsibility in relation to the questions of the authority and interpretation of Scripture. The Fourth Session of the Council, which concluded its deliberations on 8 April 1546, laid down the following challenges to the Protestant position:

1 Scripture could not be regarded as the only source of revelation; tradition was a vital supplement, which Protestants irresponsibly denied. 'All saving truths and rules of conduct . . . are contained in the written books and

in the unwritten traditions, received from the mouth of Christ himself or from the apostles themselves.'

2 Trent ruled that Protestant lists of canonical books were deficient, and published a full list of works which it accepted as authoritative. This included all the books rejected as apocryphal by Protestant writers.

3 The Vulgate edition of Scripture was affirmed to be reliable and authoritative. The council declared that 'the old Latin Vulgate edition, which has been used for many centuries, has been approved by the Church, and should be defended as authentic in public lectures, disputations, sermons or expositions, and that no one should dare or presume, under any circumstances, to reject it'.

4 The authority of the church to interpret Scripture was defended, against what the Council of Trent clearly regarded as the rampant individualism of Protestant interpreters, thus:

> To check reckless spirits, this council decrees that no one, relying on his or her own judgement, in matters of faith and morals relating to Christian doctrine (distorting the Holy Scriptures in accordance with their own ideas), shall presume to interpret Scripture contrary to that sense which Holy Mother Church, to whom it belongs to judge of their true sense and interpretation, has held and now holds.

5 No Roman Catholic was to be allowed to publish any work relating to the interpretation of Scripture, unless it had first been vetted by his or her superiors and declared that publication had been approved. In particular, the writing, reading, circulation or possession of anonymous books (such as the remarkably successful and influential *Beneficio di Cristo*, which propagated reforming views in the early 1540s) was totally forbidden.

> It shall not be lawful for anyone to print, or have published, any books whatsoever, dealing with sacred doctrinal matters without the name of the author, or in future to sell them, or even to have them in one's possession, unless they have first been examined and approved . . . The approval of such books shall be given in writing, and shall appear properly at the beginning of the book.

On the basis of these five measures, the Council of Trent was able to restore order within its own ranks. Once more, the Catholic church was able to speak with a single voice on matters of doctrine and biblical interpretation. The price paid, however, was high. It would be centuries before Roman Catholic biblical scholarship recovered from this setback. One of the major contributing causes to the superiority of Protestant biblical scholarship in the nineteenth and early twentieth centuries was that their Roman Catholic counterparts were virtually forbidden to express any views about Scripture unless they had received prior approval from the authorities. That situation has now, happily, changed for the better, not least through the wisdom of the Second Vatican Council.

On the basis of the material presented in the present chapter, it will be clear that the Reformation programme of a return to Scripture ended up being considerably more complex than at first had seemed to be the case. The slogan *scriptura sola* turned out to mean something rather different from what might have been expected, with the radical Reformation alone conforming to the popular stereotype of the Reformation on this point. Some of the questions raised in this discussion will be highlighted by the Reformation debate over the church and sacraments, to which we now turn.

For further reading

For a general introduction to the place of the Bible in Christianity, especially in western European thought, see:

The Cambridge History of the Bible, ed. P. R. Ackroyd et al. (3 vols; Cambridge, 1963–9).

For excellent studies of the role of Scripture in the medieval period, see:

Gillian R. Evans, *The Language and Logic of the Bible: The Earlier Middle Ages* (Cambridge, 1984).
Beryl Smalley, *The Study of the Bible in the Middle Ages*, 3rd edn, (Oxford, 1983).

For the role of Scripture in the Reformation, see:

Roland H. Bainton, 'The Bible in the Reformation', in *The Cambridge History of the Bible*, vol. 3, pp. 1–37.
Gillian R. Evans, *The Language and Logic of the Bible: The Road to Reformation* (Cambridge, 1985).
H. Jackson Forstmann, *Word and Spirit: Calvin's Doctrine of Biblical Authority* (Stanford, 1962).
Alister E. McGrath, *The Intellectual Origins of the European Reformation* (Oxford, 1987), pp. 122–74 (with detailed discussion of exegetical and critical methods).
Jaroslav Pelikan, *The Christian Tradition: A History of the Development of Doctrine*, Vol. 4: *Reformation of Church and Dogma (1300–1700)* (Chicago/London, 1984), pp. 203–17.

Also of interest is the role assigned to Scripture in sixteenth-century Protestant Confessions (i.e. articles of faith). These Confessions are conveniently brought together, in English translation, in *Reformed Confessions of the Sixteenth Century*, ed. Arthur Cochrane (Philadelphia, 1966). It is important to observe that the early Reformed Confessions place affirmation of faith in Scripture before faith in God, reflecting the belief that it is only through Scripture that a true faith in God is possible. On the canon of Scripture, see French Confession (1559), articles 3, 4 (pp. 144–5); Belgic Confession (1561), articles 4, 6 (pp. 190–1); Second Helvetic Confession, article 1 (p. 226). On the authority of Scripture, see First Helvetic Confession (1536), articles 1, 2 (pp. 100–1); Geneva Confession (1536), article 1 (p. 120); French Confession (1559), article 5 (pp. 145–6); Belgic Confession (1561), articles 3, 5, 7 (pp. 190–2); Second Helvetic Confession (1566), articles 1, 2 (pp. 224–7).

9

The Doctrine of
the Sacraments

This chapter may raise difficulties for some readers, in that the term 'sacrament' may be unfamiliar. The word comes from the Latin term *sacramentum*, meaning 'something which is consecrated', and has come to refer to a series of church rites or clerical actions which are regarded as having special spiritual qualities, such as the ability to convey the grace of God. Duns Scotus defined a sacrament as 'a physical sign, instituted by God, which efficaciously signifies the grace of God, or the gracious action of God'. Other definitions made much the same point, but more briefly. The basic idea was that sacraments were visible signs of invisible grace which somehow acted as 'channels' or grace. The medieval period witnessed a consolidation of the theology of the sacraments, particularly in the writings of Peter Lombard. Seven sacraments were recognized – baptism, the eucharist, penance, confirmation, marriage, ordination, and extreme unction – and a complex theology developed to justify and explain their importance.

By the early 1520s, it was clear that the sacramental system of the medieval church was becoming the subject of considerable criticism from reforming factions. The reformers mounted a sustained attack on medieval understandings of the number, nature and function of sacraments, and reduced the number of authentic sacraments from seven to two (baptism and the eucharist). But why should the reformers have been so preoccupied with the theology of the sacraments? To many, it seems a remarkably obscure and irrelevant subject. However, reflection on the context in which the reformers operated will help explain why this question was so important for them. Two factors emerge to explain the significance attached to this area of theology by the reformers.

First, the theology of the sacraments was seen by the reformers as representing all that was bad about medieval theology. It seemed to concentrate the vices of scholasticism. The theology of the sacraments was regarded as relatively unimportant by most early Christian writers (with the possible exception of Augustine) until the dawn of the Middle Ages. In many ways, the development of an intricate sacramental theology may be regarded as one of the most important achievements of the scholastic writers.

Now a significant part of the Reformation agenda centred on eliminating medieval additions to earlier – and simpler – versions of Christian theology. Here was an obvious – and, as time showed, a highly vulnerable – target for the general reforming programme of eliminating scholastic distortions to the gospel. To the reformers, the elaborate scholastic theology of the sacraments seemed to be an obvious case of a theological plant in need of radical pruning. So they sharpened their knives.

In the second place, the sacraments represented the publicly visible face of the church. To reform the sacraments would thus be to make obvious changes to the life of the church and the community. For most lay persons, the main point of contact with the church, as well as the wider world, was through church services on Sundays. The pulpit was one of the most important public platforms of the medieval period for this very reason – hence the desire of both reformers and city councils to control what was said from the pulpit.

The main service of the medieval church was the Mass. This service was said according to a set form of words, in Latin, known as 'the liturgy'. The reformers objected to this specific liturgy, for two reasons. First, the Mass was said in Latin, which most lay people couldn't understand. Indeed, it has often been suggested that some of the clergy didn't understand the words either: late Renaissance humanists, fully competent in Latin, occasionally grumbled about priests who couldn't tell the difference between an accusative and an ablative case. But second, and more seriously, the way in which the Mass was celebrated appeared to involve a number of assumptions that the reformers found unacceptable. They disliked the theory known as 'transubstantiation', which held that the bread and wine in the Mass, when consecrated, retain their outward appearances but are in fact transformed into the substance of the body and blood of Jesus Christ. And they resented the implication that priests who celebrated the Mass were performing some kind of good work. To reform the liturgy was thus to help change the way people thought about the gospel.

One of the most effective ways of promoting the cause of the Reformation was therefore to rewrite the liturgy in the vernacular (so that all could understand what was going on), altering it where necessary to eliminate ideas which the reformers found unacceptable. By attending Sunday services, the laity would thus be exposed to the ideas of the Reformation from two sources: the sermon and the liturgy. Altering the ideas contained in the liturgy meant, of course, altering the theology of the sacraments, which is precisely what we find happening in the first decade of the Reformation.

And it is at this point that we find what is generally agreed to have been the most serious disagreement between the magisterial reformers developing.

Luther and Zwingli, the leaders of the two wings of the magisterial Reformation, found themselves totally unable to agree in their views on the sacraments. A number of factors combined to bring about this disagreement: for example, differences in the way in which Scripture was interpreted and the different social contexts of the Wittenberg and Zurich reformations. In what follows, I shall outline their different understandings of the sacraments, and indicate the importance of these differences for the history of the Reformation.

Before going any further, a difficulty in terminology must be noted. The Reformation gradually witnessed a rejection of the term 'Mass' without any agreement being reached on what to call the evangelical equivalent. The Christian service at which bread and wine were consecrated and consumed came to be known by various names, including 'Mass' (a term retained by Luther), 'the bread', 'communion', 'the memorial', 'the Lord's Supper', or 'eucharist'. In view of this disagreement, it is difficult to know which to pick. In the end, the word 'eucharist' has been selected to identify the Protestant equivalent of the Mass, on account of its recent use in major Protestant ecumenical documents; but the reader should note the variety of terms which could also be used.

The Sacraments and the Promises of Grace

A central theme to the Reformation emphasis upon the importance of the sacraments to an evangelical spirituality is that of *divine accommodation to human weakness*. The idea is especially associated with Calvin, who is usually regarded as its most lucid expositor. Calvin argues as follows. All good speakers know and understand the limitations of their audiences. And they adapt their way of speaking accordingly. They modify their language to suit the needs and limitations of their listeners, avoiding difficult words and ideas where necessary and using more appropriate ways of speaking in their place. This 'principle of accommodation' also extends to the use of analogies and visual aids. Many people find ideas and concepts difficult to handle, forcing responsible public speakers to use stories and illustrations to make their point.

So it is with God, Calvin argues. God accommodates himself to our limitations. God comes down to our level, using powerful images and ways of speaking which enable him to reveal himself to a wide range of individuals. No one is excluded from learning about God on account of their educational abilities. That God can use lowly ways of revealing himself does not reflect any weakness or shortcoming on his part; the necessity of adopting lowly ways reflects a weakness on our part, which God graciously acknowledges and takes into account. God is able to deploy a wide range of resources in creating and sustaining faith – words, concepts, analogies, models, signs and symbols. The sacraments are to be seen as an important element in this arsenal of resources.

For the first generation of reformers, the sacraments were God's response to human weakness. Knowing our difficulty in receiving and responding to his promises, God has supplemented his Word with visible and tangible signs of his gracious favour. They are an accommodation to our limitations. The sacraments represent the promises of God, mediated through objects of the everyday world. In his *Propositions on the Mass* (1521), Philipp Melanchthon stressed that sacraments were primarily a gracious divine accommodation to human weakness. In a series of sixty-five propositions, Melanchthon put forward what he regarded as a reliable and responsible approach to the place of the sacraments in Christian life. 'Signs are the means by which we may be both reminded and reassured of the word of faith.' Not every sign is a sacrament; a sacrament is an *instituted and authorized* sign of grace, the credentials of which rest upon a firm evangelical foundation. They are not signs of our own choosing; they have been chosen for us.

In an ideal world, Melanchthon suggests, human beings would be prepared to trust God on the basis of his Word alone. However, one of the weaknesses of fallen humanity is its need for signs (Melanchthon appeals to the story of Gideon as he makes this point). For Melanchthon, sacraments are signs: 'What some call sacraments, we call signs – or, if you prefer, sacramental signs.' These sacramental signs enhance our trust in God. 'In order to mitigate this distrust in the human heart, God has added signs to the word.' Sacraments are thus signs of the grace of God added to the promises of grace in order to reassure and strengthen the faith of fallen human beings. Where scholastic theories of the sacraments stressed their ability to convey grace, the reformers emphasized their ability to confirm and convey the promises of God.

Luther made a similar point, defining sacraments as 'promises with signs attached to them' or 'divinely instituted signs and the promise of forgiveness of sins'. Interestingly, Luther used the term 'pledge (*Pfand*)' to emphasize the security-giving character of the eucharist. The bread and the wine reassure us of the reality of the divine promise of forgiveness, making it easier for us to accept, and having accepted it, to hold firmly to it.

> In order that we might be certain of this promise of Christ, and truly rely on it without any doubt, he has given us the most precious and costly seal and pledge – his true body and blood, given under the bread and wine. These are the very same as those with which he obtained for us the gift and the promise of this precious and gracious treasure, surrendering his life in order that we might receive and accept the promised grace.

The bread and wine of the Mass thus simultaneously remind us of the reality and the cost of the grace of God on the one hand and our response to this grace in faith on the other.

God's promises are thus both real and costly. The death of Christ is a token of both the trustworthiness and the costliness of the grace of God. Luther develops this point by using the idea of a 'testament', understood in the sense of a 'last will and testament'. This point is developed to its full in the 1520 writing *The Babylonian Captivity of the Christian Church*.

> A testament is a promise made by someone who is about to die, in which a bequest is defined and heirs appointed. A testament thus involves, in the first place, the death of the testator, and in the second, the promise of an inheritance and the naming of heirs. . . . We see these things clearly in the words of Christ. Christ testifies concerning his death when he says, 'This is my body, which is given' and 'This is my blood, which is poured out'. He names and designates the bequest when he says 'for the forgiveness of sins'. And he appoints the heirs when he says, 'for you and for many', that is, for those who accept and believe the promise of the testator.[1]

Luther's insight here is that a testament involves promises which become operational only after the death of the person who made those promises in the first place. The liturgy or the Mass or the communion service thus makes three vitally important points.

1 It affirms the promises of grace and forgiveness.
2 It identifies those to whom those promises are made.
3 It declares the death of the one who made those promises.

The Mass thus dramatically proclaims that the promises of grace and forgiveness are now in effect. It is 'a promise of the forgiveness of sins made to us by God, and such a promise as has been confirmed by the death of the Son of God'. By proclaiming the death of Christ, the community of faith affirms that the precious promises of forgiveness and eternal life are now effective for those with faith. As Luther himself put this point:

> So you see that what we call the Mass is a promise of the forgiveness of sins made to us by God, and such a promise that has been confirmed by the death of the Son of God. For the only difference between a promise and a testament is that the testament involves the death of the one who makes it. . . . Now God made a testament. Therefore it was necessary that he should die. But God could not die unless he became a human being. Thus the incarnation and the death of Christ are both included explicitly in this one word 'testament'.

As noted above, a central function of the sacraments is to reassure believers that they are truly members of the body of Christ and heirs of the kingdom of God. Luther developed this point at some length in his 1519 treatise *The Blessed Sacrament of the Holy and True Body of Christ*, stressing the psychological assurance that it makes available to believers:

> To receive this sacrament in bread and wine, then, is nothing else than to receive a sure sign of this fellowship and union with Christ and all the saints. It is as if a citizen were given a sign, a document, or some other token, to assure him that he is indeed a citizen of the city, and a member of that particular community. . . . In this sacrament, therefore, a person is given a sure sign from God himself that he or she is united with Christ and the saints, and has all things in common with them, and that Christ's suffering and life are his own.

This emphasis upon the sacraments as tokens of belonging to the Christian community is perhaps more characteristic of Zwingli than Luther (see pp. 180–1); nevertheless, it is a significant element of Luther's thought at this point.

But how can such mean and common things as water, bread or wine come to have such importance for the Christian life? Surely this represents an unjustified lapse into some kind of nature religion or misguided materialism? Surely the whole point of Christianity is to direct our attention away from material objects, towards the greater reality of God himself? Why bother with material objects when we have the word of God at our disposal? Luther deals with this important question as follows.

> In the sacraments we see nothing wonderful – just ordinary water, bread and wine, and the words of a preacher. There is nothing spectacular about that. But we must learn to discover what a glorious majesty lies hidden beneath these despised things. It is precisely the same with Christ in the incarnation. We see a frail, weak and mortal human being – yet he is nothing other than the majesty of God himself. In precisely the same way, God himself speaks to us and deals with us in these ordinary and despised materials.

We have already touched on Luther's views on the sacraments; we must now consider them in more detail.

Luther on the Sacraments

In his reforming treatise of 1520, *The Babylonian Captivity of the Church*, Luther launched a major attack on the Catholic understanding of the sacraments.

Taking advantage of the latest humanist philological scholarship, he asserted that the Vulgate use of the term *sacramentum* was largely unjustified on the basis of the Greek text. Where the Roman Catholic church recognized seven sacraments, Luther initially recognized three (baptism, eucharist, and penance), but shortly afterwards only two (baptism and eucharist). The transition between these two views can be seen in *The Babylonian Captivity* itself, and we may pause to examine this change and determine its basis. (Incidentally, at his own request, Henry VIII of England gained from the pope the title *Fidei Defensor*, 'defender of the faith', through his anti-Lutheran work *Assertio septem sacramentorum*, 'I assert that there are seven sacraments'. This title, which still appears on British coins in the abbreviated form *F. D.*, represents a riposte to the views developed by Luther in *The Babylonian Captivity of the Church*).

The work opens with a powerful statement of principle, which sets to one side the medieval consensus regarding the sacraments:

> I deny that there are seven sacraments, and for the present maintain that there are only three: baptism, penance and the bread. All three have been subjected to a miserable captivity by the Roman authorities, and the church has been robbed of all her freedom.

By the end of the work, however, Luther has come to place considerable emphasis upon the importance of a visible physical sign. Luther signalled this significant change in his views with the following statement:

> Yet it has seemed right to restrict the name of sacrament to those promises of God which have signs attached to them. The remainder, not being connected to signs, are merely promises. Hence, strictly speaking, there are only two sacraments in the church of God – baptism and the bread. For only in these two do we find the divinely instituted sign and the promise of the forgiveness of sins.

Penance thus ceased to have sacramental status, according to Luther, because the two essential characteristics of a sacrament were the Word of God and an outward sacramental sign (such as water in baptism and bread and wine in the eucharist). The only true sacraments of the New Testament church were thus baptism and eucharist; penance, having no external sign, could no longer be regarded as a sacrament.

Luther further argued that the medieval sacramental system gave a totally unjustified prominence to the role of the priest. In theory, this development should not have taken place, on account of the sacramental theology which developed in response to the Donatist controversy of the late fourth and early fifth centuries. The point at issue in this controversy concerned whether an immoral priest (such as one who had collaborated with the Roman authorities during a time of persecution) should be allowed to baptize or celebrate the eucharist. Two rival theories of the role played by the priest developed.

1 Sacraments work *ex opere operantis* (literally, 'through the work of the one who works'). Here, the efficacy of the sacrament is understood to be dependent on the personal moral and spiritual qualities of the priest. Believers will only benefit from the sacraments if they are administered by a faithful priest.

2 Sacraments work *ex opere operato* (literally, 'through the work that is worked'). Here, the efficacy of the sacrament is understood to depend not on the personal qualities of the priest, but on the inherent quality of the sacrament itself. The ultimate grounds of sacramental efficacy lie in Christ, whose person and benefits are conveyed by the sacraments, not in the priest himself. An immoral priest can thus be permitted to celebrate the sacraments, as the grounds of their validity do not rest in him.

The first view corresponds to the rigorist Donatist position, the second to Augustine's position (and subsequently to that of the Catholic church). Luther and the magisterial reformers had no hesitation in following this majority opinion.

It might therefore be thought that the principle had been firmly established, that the priest does not play a major role in relation to the sacraments. In fact, Luther argued, a number of developments have taken place through which the sacraments were 'held captive by the church'. Luther listed three ways in which this unacceptable situation had arisen:

1 The practice of 'communion in one kind' (in other words, giving the laity bread alone, and not bread and wine). Until the twelfth century, it was the general practice to allow all present at Mass to consume both the consecrated bread and the consecrated wine. However, it seems that during the eleventh century, increasing offence arose through some of the laity being careless with the wine and spilling what was, according to the emerging theology of transubstantiation, the blood of Christ over none too clean church floors. By the thirteenth century, the laity had effectively been banned from receiving the wine.

According to Luther, this was unjustifiable and without scriptural or patristic precedent. Luther declared that the clerical refusal to offer the chalice (the vessel containing the wine) to the laity was sinful. His main reason for taking this position concerned its theological implications: that the laity were prevented from having access to what the wine signified:

> The decisive thing for me is that Christ says: 'This is my blood, which is poured out for you and for many for the forgiveness of sins.' Here you see

very clearly that the blood is given to all those for whose sins it was shed. But who would dare to say that Christ's blood was not shed for the laity? Surely you can see who he is speaking to when he gives the cup? Does he not give it to everyone? Does he not say that it is shed for everyone?

So influential did Luther's attitude become that the practice of offering the laity the chalice became a hallmark of a congregation's allegiance to the Reformation.

2   The doctrine of transubstantiation (which we shall discuss below) seemed to Luther to be an absurdity, an attempt to rationalize a mystery. For Luther, the crucial point was that Christ was really present in the eucharist – not some particular theory as to how he was present. If iron is placed in a fire and heated, it glows – and in that glowing iron, both the iron and heat are present. Why not use some simple everyday analogy such as this to illustrate the mystery of the presence of Christ in the eucharist, instead of rationalizing it using some scholastic subtlety?

> For my part, if I cannot fathom how the bread is the body of Christ, yet I will take my reason captive to the obedience of Christ, and clinging simply to his words, firmly believe not only that the body of Christ is in the bread, but that the bread is the body of Christ. My warrant for this is the words which say: 'He took bread, and when he had given thanks, he broke it and said, 'Take, eat, this (that is, this bread, which he had taken and broken) is my body' (1 Corinthians 11:23–24).

It is not the doctrine of transubstantiation which is to be believed, but simply that Christ really is present at the eucharist. This fact is more important than any theory or explanation.

3   The idea that the priest made an offering or performed a good work or sacrifice on behalf of the people was equally unscriptural. For Luther, the sacrament was primarily a promise of the forgiveness of sins, to be received through faith by the people.

> You see, therefore, that what we call the Mass is a promise of the forgiveness of sins made to us by God, and such a promise as has been confirmed by the death of the Son of God . . . If the Mass is a promise, as has been said, then access to it is to be gained, not with any works, or powers, or merits of one's own, but by faith alone. For where there is the word of the promising God, there must necessarily be the faith of the accepting believer. It is plain therefore, that the beginning of our salvation is a faith which clings to the word of the promising God who, without any effort on our part, in free and unmerited mercy takes the initiative and offers us the word of his promise.

For Luther, sacraments were concerned with the generation and nourishment of the faith of the people of God, whereas the medieval church tended to treat them as some sort of marketable commodity, capable of earning merit.

We have now considered Luther's views concerning the sacraments in general. Our attention now shifts to an aspect of his thought which subsequently proved to be controversial, eventually leading to a division within a hitherto more or less united reforming movement in Germany and Switzerland. The issue at stake concerns the 'real presence' – that is, the question of whether, and in what manner, Christ can be thought of as being physically present in the eucharist.

Luther's Views on the Real Presence

Luther was ordained a priest in 1507, and celebrated his first Mass at Erfurt on 2 May of that year. In a recollection of this event shared around his dinner table on 5 December 1538, Luther recalled that his chief memories of this great occasion concerned his sense of self-importance and his anxiety in case he accidentally left anything out. We find no hint of any misgivings concerning the traditional catholic understanding of the Mass in his writings, however, until 1519.

We have already noted his 'theological breakthrough' of 1515, in which he made his celebrated discovery of the new meaning of the 'righteousness of God' (see pp. 106–10). Although this discovery seems to have had no effect on his attitude to the sacraments initially, it appears that one aspect of his later critique of the medieval theology of the sacraments is foreshadowed in it. Linked with this discovery, significantly, was a new hostility to the use of Aristotelian ideas in theology. In his *Disputation against Scholastic Theology* of 1517, Luther made clear his total rejection of Aristotelianism in theology.[2]

The importance of this anti-Aristotelian development lies in its relation to the medieval doctrine of transubstantiation. This doctrine had been defined by the Fourth Lateran Council (1215), and rested upon Aristotelian foundations – specifically, on Aristotle's distinction between 'substance' and 'accident'. The *substance* of something is its essential nature, whereas its *accidents* are its outward appearances (for example, its colour, shape, smell and so forth). The theory of transubstantiation affirms that the accidents of the bread and wine (their outward appearance: taste, smell and so forth) remain unchanged at the moment of consecration, while their substance changes from that of bread and wine to that of the body and blood of Jesus Christ. Luther rejected this 'pseudo-philosophy' as absurd, and urged the rejection of the use of such Aristotelian ideas. Aristotle had no place in Christian theology. Nevertheless, it is essential to appreciate that Luther did *not* criticize the underlying basic idea that the bread and wine became the body and blood of Christ: 'No importance attaches to this error, if only the body and blood of Christ are left together with the Word.' Luther's objection was not to the idea of the 'real presence' as such, but to *one specific way of explaining that presence*. For Luther, God is not merely *behind* the sacraments: he is *in* them as well.

Luther's view that the bread and wine really did become the body and blood of Christ was not the result of sheer theological conservatism. Indeed, Luther pointed out that if he could have shown that this view was unbiblical, he would have been the first to abandon it. It seemed to him, however, that this was indeed the obvious meaning of biblical texts, such as Matthew 26 : 26: *hoc est corpus meum*, 'this is my body'. The verse was perfectly clear, and seemed to him to admit no other interpretation. It seemed to Luther that the whole principle of the clarity of Scripture (which he regarded as fundamental to his reforming programme at this point) was at stake over the interpretation of this verse.[3] Andreas Karlstadt, his former colleague at Wittenberg – who eventually became his opponent in the 1520s – thought otherwise: it seemed to him that Christ pointed to himself when saying these words. Luther had little difficulty in dismissing this as a misreading of the text. He had considerably more difficulty in dealing with Zwingli's assertion that the word 'is' was simply a rhetorical figure of speech (known as *alloiosis*), which really means 'signifies' or 'represents', and is not to be taken literally.

In common with all the magisterial reformers, Luther retained the traditional practice of infant baptism. It might be thought that his doctrine of justification by faith alone contradicts this practice. After all, infants could not meaningfully be said to have faith, if faith is understood as a conscious, deliberate response to the promises of God. It must be pointed out, however, that Luther's doctrine of justification by faith does not mean that the individual who has faith is justified for that reason: rather, as we saw earlier (pp. 112–13), it means that God graciously gives faith as a gift. In a paradoxical way, infant baptism is totally consistent with the doctrine of justification by faith, because it emphasizes that faith is not something we can achieve, but something which is given to us graciously. For Luther, the sacraments do not merely strengthen the faith of believers – they are capable of generating that faith in the first place. The sacrament mediates the Word of God, which is capable of evoking faith. Thus Luther finds no difficulty with the practice of infant baptism. Baptism does not presuppose faith: rather, it generates faith. 'A child becomes a believer if Christ in baptism speaks to him through the mouth of the one who baptizes, since it is his Word, his commandment, and his Word cannot be without fruit.'

Zwingli, in marked contrast, held that sacraments demonstrated the existence of faith. This caused him some difficulty, not least because he could not use Luther's arguments to justify the practice of infant baptism. For Zwingli, the sacraments merely confirmed the Word of God, which needed to be preached separately. As we shall see, he was thus obliged to justify the baptism of infants on rather different grounds.

Luther's views on the 'real presence' were regarded with something approaching disbelief by his reforming colleagues in Zurich, Basle and Strasbourg. It seemed to them that Luther was being inconsistent at this point, making unnecessary concessions to his catholic opponents. We shall return to Luther's views shortly. Let us now consider Zwingli's views. This will give us some idea of the astonishing diversity of totally irreconcilable theories of the sacraments current in evangelical circles during the 1520s.

Zwingli on the Sacraments

Like Luther, Zwingli had grave misgivings about the word 'sacrament' itself. He noted that the term had the basic sense of 'oath', and initially treated the sacraments of baptism and eucharist (the remaining five sacraments of the catholic system having been rejected) as signs of God's faithfulness to his people and his gracious promise of forgiveness. Thus in 1523 he wrote that the word 'sacrament' could be used to refer to those things which 'God has instituted, commanded and ordained with his word, which is as firm and sure as if he had sworn an oath to this effect'. Up to this point, there was a certain degree of similarity between the views of Luther and Zwingli on the functions of sacraments (although, as I shall indicate below, the question of the real presence of Christ in the eucharist divided them radically).

This limited agreement, however, had evaporated by 1525. Zwingli retained the idea of a 'sacrament' as an oath or a pledge; but whereas, earlier, he had understood this to be *God's pledge of faithfulness to us*, he now asserted that it refers to *our pledge of obedience and loyalty to one another*. It must be remembered that Zwingli was a chaplain to the army of the Swiss Confederacy (and was present at the disastrous defeat at Marignano in September 1515). Drawing on the military use of oaths, Zwingli argued that a 'sacrament' was basically a declaration of allegiance of an individual to a community. Just as a soldier swears allegiance to his army (in the person of the general), so the Christian swears allegiance to his fellow Christians. Zwingli used the German term *Pflichtszeichen*, 'a demonstration of allegiance', to designate the essence of a sacrament. A sacrament is thus the means 'by which someone proves to the church that he either intends to be, or already is, a soldier of Christ, and which informs the whole church, rather than himself, of his faith'. In baptism, the believer pledges loyalty to the community of the church; in the eucharist, he demonstrates that loyalty publicly.

Zwingli thus developed the idea that the sacraments are subordinate to the preaching of the Word of God.[4] It is this preaching which brings faith into existence: the sacraments merely provide an occasion by which this faith may be publicly demonstrated. The preaching of the Word of God is of central importance, and the sacraments are like seals on a letter – they confirm its substance.

Zwingli developed the meaning of the eucharist with a further military analogy drawn from his experience as a Swiss army chaplain:

> If someone sews on a white cross, he proclaims that he wishes to be a confederate. And if he makes the pilgrimage to Nähenfels and gives God praise and thanksgiving for the victory vouchsafed to our forefathers, he testifies that he is a confederate indeed. Similarly, whoever receives the mark of baptism is the one who is resolved to hear what God says to him, to learn the divine precepts, and to live his life in accordance with them. And whoever in the congregation gives thanks to God in the remembrance or supper testifies to the fact that he rejoices in the death of Christ from the depths of his heart, and thanks him for it.

The reference is to the victory of the Swiss over the Austrians in 1388 near Nähenfels, in the canton of Glarus. This victory is usually regarded as marking the beginning of the Swiss (or Helvetic) Confederation, and it was commemorated by a pilgrimage to the site of the battle on the first Thursday in April. Zwingli makes two points. First, the Swiss soldier wears a white cross (now incorporated into the Swiss national flag, of course) as a *Pflichtszeichen*, demonstrating publicly his allegiance to the Confederacy. Similarly, the Christian publicly demonstrates his allegiance to the church, initially by baptism and subsequently by participating in the eucharist. Baptism is the 'visible entry and sealing into Christ'. Second, the historical event which brought the Confederacy into being is commemorated as a token of allegiance to that same Confederacy. Similarly, the Christian commemorates the historical event which brought the Christian church into being (the death of Jesus Christ) as a token of his commitment to that church. The eucharist is thus a memorial of the historical event leading to the establishment of the Christian church and a public demonstration of the believer's allegiance to that church and its members.

This understanding of the nature of the eucharist is confirmed by Zwingli's treatment of Matthew 26:26: *hoc est corpus meum*, 'this is my body'. These words were spoken by Christ during the Last Supper, on the day before his death, signifying the manner in which he wished to be remembered by his church. It is as if, Zwingli wrote, Christ had said: 'I entrust to you a symbol of this my surrender and testament, to awaken in you the remembrance of me and of my goodness to you, so that when you see this bread and this cup, held forth in this memorial supper, you may remember me as delivered up for you, just as if you saw me before you as you see me now, eating with you.' For Zwingli, Christ's death has the same significance for the church as the battle of Nähenfels has for the Swiss Confederacy. It is the foundational event of the Christian church, central to its identity and self-understanding. Just as the commemoration of Nähenfels does not involve the re-enactment of that battle, so the eucharist involves neither the repetition of the sacrifice of Christ nor his presence at the commemoration. The eucharist is 'a memorial of the suffering of Christ, and not a sacrifice'. For reasons which we shall explore below, Zwingli insisted that the words 'this is my body' cannot be taken literally, thus eliminating any idea of the 'real presence of Christ' in the eucharist. Just as a man, on setting off on a long journey from home, might give his wife his ring to remember him by until his return, so Christ leaves his church a token to remember him by until the day on which he will return in glory.

Zwingli on the Real Presence

The background to Zwingli's views on the real presence of Christ can be traced back to some seemingly insignificant events of the year 1509. In November of that year, a change of personnel at a small library in the Lowlands took place, necessitating the cataloguing of its holdings. The work was entrusted to Cornelius Hoen, who discovered that the library contained a significant collection of the writings of the noted humanist Wessel Gansfort (*c.* 1420–89). One of these was entitled *On the Sacrament of the Eucharist*. Although Gansfort did not actually deny the doctrine of transubstantiation, he developed the idea of a spiritual communion between Christ and the believer. Hoen, apparently attracted by this idea, reworked it into a radical critique of the doctrine of transubstantiation, which he wrote up in the form of a letter. It seems that this letter found its way to Luther at some point in 1521 (although the evidence is not entirely conclusive). By 1523, the letter had reached Zurich, where it was read by Zwingli.

In this letter, Hoen suggested that the word *est* in *hoc est corpus meum* should not be interpreted literally as 'is' or 'is identical with', but rather as *significat*, 'signifies'. For example, when Christ says 'I am the bread of life' (John 6:48), he is clearly not identifying himself with a loaf of bread or bread in general. The word 'is' here must be taken in a metaphorical, or non-literal, sense. The Old Testament prophets may indeed have foretold that Christ would 'become flesh (*incarnatus*)' – but this was to happen once, and only once. 'At no point did the prophets foretell or the apostles preach that Christ would, so to speak, "become bread (*impanatus*)" every day through the actions of any priest offering the sacrifice of the Mass.

Hoen developed a number of ideas which eventually found their way into the eucharistic thought of Zwingli. Two may be noted here. The first is the idea of the eucharist being like a ring given by a groom to his bride to reassure her of his love. It is a *pledge* – an idea that resonates throughout Zwingli's writings on the subject.

> Our Lord Jesus Christ, who promised many times to forgive the sins of his people and to strengthen their souls through the Last Supper, added a pledge to that promise in case there remained any uncertainty on their part – in much the same way as a groom, wishing to assure his bride (if she had any doubts), gives her a ring, declaring, 'Take this, I give myself to you'. And she, accepting that ring, believes that he is hers, and turns her heart from all other lovers and, to please her husband, attaches herself to him, and him alone.

Zwingli deploys the imagery of a ring as a pledge of love with considerable skill at a number of points, and it is not impossible that it was Hoen who planted this powerful image in his mind. The second notion that Hoen employs is that of commemoration of Christ in his absence. Noting that Christ's phrase 'this is my body' is immediately followed by the words 'Do this in remembrance of me', Hoen argues that the second set of words clearly points to commemoration of 'a person who is absent (at least, physically absent)'.

Where Luther reacted with a notable lack of enthusiasm to these ideas, Zwingli was considerably more positive in his reaction. By November and December of 1524 he was promoting Hoen's ideas with some vigour, and the following year he arranged for the letter to be published. In the summer of 1525, the learned Oecolampadius of Basle joined in the discussion, producing a book in which he argued that the writers of the patristic period knew nothing of either transubstantiation or Luther's views on the real presence, but tended towards the view now increasingly being associated with Zwingli.

Zwingli argued that Scripture employed many figures of speech. Thus the word 'is' might at one point mean 'is absolutely identical with', and at another mean 'represents' or 'signifies'. For example, in his treatise on *On the Lord's Supper* (1526), he wrote:

> Thoughout the Bible, we find figures of speech, called in the Greek *tropos*, that is, something that is metaphorical, or to be understood in another sense. For example, in John 15 Christ says 'I am the vine'. This means that Christ is like a vine when considered in relation to us, who are sustained and grow in him

in the same way as branches grow on a vine. . . . Similarly, in John 1 we read 'Behold the Lamb of God, who takes away the sin of the world.' The first part of this verse is a trope, for Christ is not literally a lamb.

After a rather wearisome exploration of text after text, Zwingli concluded that 'there are innumerable passages in Scripture where the word "is" means "signifies" '. The question that must therefore be addressed is

> whether Christ's words in Matthew 26, 'this is my body' can also be taken metaphorically or *in tropice*. It has already become clear enough that in this context the word 'is' cannot be taken literally. Hence it follows that it must be taken metaphorically or figuratively. In the words 'this is my body', the word 'this' means the bread, and the word 'body' means the body which was put to death for us. Therefore the word 'is' cannot be taken literally, for the bread is not the body.

This point was developed by Oecolampadius in 1527, who asserted that 'in dealing with signs, sacraments, pictures, parables and interpretations, one should and one must understand the words figuratively and not understand the words literally'. Luther responded vigorously to such suggestions in his 1527 treatise *That these Words of Christ 'This is my Body' Still Stand Firm against the Fanatics*.

Zwingli's point here concerns the relation between the sign and the thing which is signified. He uses this distinction to argue that it is inconceivable that the bread could be the body of Christ.

> A sacrament is the sign of a holy thing. When I say 'the sacrament of the Lord's body', I am simply referring to that bread which is the symbol of the body of Christ who was put to death for our sakes. . . . But the real body of Christ is the body which is seated at the right hand of God, and the sacrament of his body is the bread, and the sacrament of his blood is the wine, of which we partake with thanksgiving. Now the sign and the thing signified cannot be one and the same. Therefore the sacrament of the body of Christ cannot be that body itself.

A further argument used by Zwingli against Luther, hinted at in the passage just cited, concerns the location of Christ. For Luther, Christ is present in the eucharist. Whoever receives the bread and the wine receives Christ. Zwingli, however, pointed out that both Scripture and the creeds affirm that Christ is now 'seated at the right hand of God'. Now Zwingli had not the slightest idea where this might be, and wasted no time speculating on its location – but, he argued, it did mean that wherever Christ is now, it isn't present in the eucharist. He can't be in two places at once. Luther argues that the phrase 'the right hand of God' is actually a metaphorical expression, not to be taken literally. It really means 'God's sphere of influence' or 'God's rule'. To say that 'Christ is seated at the right hand of God' does not mean that Christ is now located at a definite location in the stratosphere, but simply that Christ is present wherever God rules. Once more, the question of which scriptural passages were to be interpreted literally and which metaphorically emerged as central to the debate on the real presence.

The same applies to the notion of 'feeding on Christ', an image with a distinguished history of use in the Christian church, one traditionally linked with the doctrine of transubstantiation. Because the bread is the body of Christ, by eating the bread the believer may be said to feed on Christ. Zwingli insists that this biblical image must be interpreted figuratively as trusting in God through Christ. His *Exposition of the Faith* (1531), a treatise addressed to Francis I, King of France, makes this especially clear:

> To eat the body of Christ spiritually amounts to trusting with heart and soul in the mercy and goodness of God through Christ – that is, to have the assurance of an unbroken faith that God will grant us the forgiveness of sins and the joy of eternal salvation for the sake of his son, who gave himself for us. . . . So when you come to the Lord's Supper to feed spiritually upon Christ, you thank the Lord for his great favour, for the redemption by which you are delivered from despair, and for the pledge which reassures you of eternal salvation.

So what is different about the communion bread? What makes the bread at a communion service different from any other bread? If it is not the body of Christ, what is it? Zwingli answers this question with an analogy. Consider a queen's ring, he suggests. Now consider that ring in two quite different contexts. In the first context, the ring is merely present. Perhaps you can imagine a ring lying on a table. It has no associations. Now imagine that ring transferred to a new context. It is placed on the finger of a queen, as a gift from her king. It now has personal associations, deriving from its connection with the king – such as his authority, power and majesty. Its value is now far greater than that of the gold of which it is made. These associations arise through transfer from the original context to the new context: the ring itself remains completely unchanged.

Zwingli uses this analogy with particular effect in his *Exposition of the Faith*.

> The ring with which your majesty was betrothed to the queen your consort is not valued by her just as if it were precious gold. It *is* gold, but it is also priceless, as it is the symbol of her royal husband. For this reason, she regards it as the most important of all her rings, and if she were ever to name and value her jewels, she would say: 'This is my king, that is, the ring with which my royal husband was betrothed to me. It is the sign of an indissoluble union and fidelity.'

The ring thus gains its associations and its value through its context; they are not inherent, but acquired.

So it is with the communion bread, Zwingli argues. The bread and the ring are both unchanged in themselves, but their signification alters dramatically. The signification – in other words, the associations of the object – can change, without there being any change in the nature of the object itself. Zwingli suggests that exactly the same process is at work in the case of the bread and the wine. In their ordinary everyday context, they are plain bread and plain wine, with no especial associations. But when they are moved into a new context, they take on new and important associations. When they are placed at the centre of a worshipping community and when the story of the last night of the life of Christ is retold, they become powerful reminders of the foundational events of the Christian faith. It is their context which gives them this meaning; they remain unchanged in themselves.

Zwingli on Infant Baptism

Zwingli was obliged to face an obvious difficulty in relation to infant baptism. How, it was argued, could he justify baptizing infants, when these had no faith which they could publicly demonstrate? The traditional answer to this dilemma rested with original sin. Baptism purged the guilt of original sin. The argument in question went back to Augustine in the early fifth century. Yet Zwingli had hesitations here. Following Erasmus, he had difficulties with the notion of original sin, and inclined towards the view that infants had no inherent original sinfulness which needed to be forgiven. As a result, infant baptism seemed to serve no purpose – unless another theoretical justification for the practice were forthcoming.

Initially, it wasn't. It is clear that Zwingli had misgivings in the late 1510s and early 1520s about continuing the practice. By 1524, however, he appears to have developed a theory of baptism which got round this difficulty altogether.[5] Zwingli pointed out that in the Old Testament infant males were circumcised within days of their birth as a sign of their membership of the people of Israel. Circumcision was the rite laid down by the Old Testament covenant to demonstrate that the circumcised child belonged to the covenant community. The child had been born into a community, to which it now belonged – and circumcision was a sign of belonging to this community.

There had been a long-standing tradition within Christian theology of seeing baptism as the Christian equivalent of circumcision. Zwingli developed this idea, pointing out that baptism is gentler than circumcision, in that it involves no pain or shedding of blood, and more inclusive, in that it embraces both male and female infants. It too was a sign of belonging to a community – in this case, the Christian church. The fact that the child was not conscious of this belonging was irrelevant: it *was* a member of the Christian community, and baptism was the public demonstration of this membership. The contrast with Luther on this point will be obvious.

Zwingli subsequently took this argument a stage further. We noted earlier (pp. 15–18) how cities were seen as organic communities in the late Middle Ages, a factor which appears to have been significant for many cities as they considered whether to accept the Reformation. This same view appears in Zwingli, who treats 'state' and 'church' as virtually equivalent: 'A Christian city is nothing other than a Christian church.' The sacraments thus signified not merely loyalty to the church, but also loyalty to the city community, in this case Zurich. To refuse to allow one's child to be baptized, therefore, was an act of disloyalty to the Zurich city community. The magistrates were thus entitled to expel from Zurich all who refused to allow their children to be baptized.

The Anabaptists, as we have seen, regarded infant baptism as unjustifiable. As the radical Reformation posed a major threat to the Reformation at Zurich in the 1520s, on account of both its religious and political views, Zwingli's understanding of baptism as both an ecclesial and a civic event provided an excellent means of enforcing conformity.[6]

Baptism thus became of central importance to Zwingli, in that it provided a criterion by which two totally different concepts of the church might be distinguished. Zwingli's concept of a state or city church was increasingly challenged by the Anabaptists, whose vision of the church involved a return to the simplicities of the apostolic church. For the radicals, the purity of that church had been totally destroyed through the conversion of the Roman emperor Constantine in the early fourth century, which had led to a close alliance of church and state. The Anabaptists wished to sever this link, whereas Zwingli wished to continue it in the specific form found at Zurich. Thus Zwingli felt justified in declaring that 'the issue is not baptism, but revolt, faction and heresy'. Baptism represented the criterion which determined whether an individual was a loyal citizen of Zurich or a traitor to that city. As Anabaptism became an increasing threat to the city in the 1520s, the magistrates at least appreciated the importance of Zwingli's theology on this point. But this merely emphasizes how closely theology and politics, church and city, were linked in the first era of the Reformation. The very term 'magisterial Reformation' itself points to this close relationship between the magistrates and the Reformation.

Luther versus Zwingli: A Summary and Evaluation

The debate between Luther and Zwingli is somewhat technical, and the reader may have found it difficult to follow. It may be helpful, therefore, to summarize the main points of difference between them, both recapitulating and extending the above discussion.

1   Both reformers rejected the medieval sacramental scheme. Whereas the medieval theology had identified seven sacraments, the reformers insisted that only two sacraments – baptism and the eucharist – were authorized by the New Testament. Luther was perhaps more conservative in this respect than Zwingli, initially allowing that penance might be considered sacramental, before withdrawing this view in 1520.

2   Luther understood the Word of God and the sacraments to be inseparably linked. Both bore witness to Jesus Christ, and both mediated his power and presence. The sacraments were thus capable of creating, as well as supporting or demonstrating, faith. For Zwingli, it was the Word of God which created faith and the sacraments which demonstrated that faith publicly. Word and sacrament were quite distinct, with the former being of greater importance.

3   Although both reformers retained the traditional practice of infant baptism, they did so for very different reasons. For Luther, sacraments could generate faith; and hence baptism could generate faith in an infant. For Zwingli, sacraments demonstrated allegiance to and membership of a community; hence baptism demonstrated that an infant belonged to a community.

4   Luther was considerably more traditional in his approach to the celebration of the eucharist than Zwingli. In his major liturgical reforming work *Concerning the Order of Public Worship* (1523), Luther made it clear that he was prepared to retain the traditional title of 'Mass', provided it was not misunderstood to imply a sacrifice, and to authorize it to be celebrated weekly, preferably in the vernacular, *as the main Sunday service*. Zwingli, however, abolished the title 'Mass', and suggested that the equivalent evangelical rite should be celebrated only three or four times a year. No longer was it the centre of Christian worship. Where Luther included a new emphasis upon preaching within the context of the eucharist, Zwingli insisted that preaching displace the eucharist from its customary weekly Sunday celebration.

5   Luther and Zwingli could not agree on the meaning of the words *hoc est corpus meum* (Matthew 26:26), central to the eucharist. For Luther, *est* meant

'is'; for Zwingli, it meant 'signifies'. Two very different ways of interpreting Scripture underlay this disagreement.

6 Both reformers rejected the medieval doctrine of transubstantiation. Luther did so, however, on the basis of its Aristotelian foundations, and was prepared to accept the basic idea which underlay it – the real presence of Christ in the eucharist. Zwingli rejected both the term and the idea. For him, Christ is remembered in his absence in the eucharist.

7 Zwingli asserted that, since Christ now sits at the right hand of God, he cannot be present anywhere else. Luther dismissed Zwingli's assertion as philosophically unsophisticated, and defended the idea of Christ being present without any limits imposed by space or time. Luther's defence of the 'ubiquity of Christ' rested upon some distinctions associated with William of Ockham, which further persuaded Luther's opponents that he had lapsed into some new form of scholasticism.

The dispute between Luther and Zwingli was important at both the theological and the political levels. At the theological level, it raised the gravest of doubts concerning the principle of the 'clarity of Scripture'. Luther and Zwingli were unable to agree on the meaning of such phrases as 'this is my body' (which Luther interpreted literally and Zwingli metaphorically) and 'at the right hand of God' (which – with apparent inconsistency on both sides – Luther interpreted metaphorically and Zwingli literally). The exegetical optimism of the early Reformation may be regarded as foundering on this rock: Scripture, it seemed, was far from easy to interpret.

At the political level, the dispute ensured the permanent separation of the two evangelical factions of the Reformation. An attempt to mediate between their rival views took place at the Colloquy of Marburg (1529), attended by such luminaries as Bucer, Luther, Melanchthon, Oecolampadius and Zwingli. By this stage, it was becoming increasingly obvious that unless the Reformation could achieve a significant degree of internal unity, at least some of its gains would be reversed. The catholics had been inhibited from taking military action against the cities of the Reformation as a result of the long-standing disputes between Emperor Charles V and Francis I of France on the one hand and Pope Clement VII on the other. In 1529, these two disputes were resolved within weeks of each other.[7] Suddenly, the two wings of the Reformation faced a powerful political and military threat. The most obvious course of action would have been to settle their differences – a procedure urged by Bucer, who suggested that differences should be tolerated among evangelicals provided they agreed to recognize the Bible alone as the normative source of faith. The local Protestant ruler Philip of Hesse, anxious at the implications of the new political situation, brought Luther and Zwingli together in the castle hall of Marburg in an attempt to resolve their differences.[8]

The attempt foundered on one point, and one pint only. On fourteen articles, Luther and Zwingli felt able to agree. The fifteenth six points, on which they were able to reach agreement on five. The sixth posed difficulties. In the words of the agreed text resulting from the Colloquy:

> And although we have no reached an agreement as to whether the true body and blood of Christ are bodily present in the bread and wine, nevertheless each side should show such Christian love to the other as their conscience will allow, and both sides should pray diligently to almighty God that, through his spirit, he might confirm us in the right understanding.

So this one point remained unresolved. For Luther, Christ was really present in the eucharist, whereas for Zwingli he was present only in the hearts of believers. Philip of Hesse's hope of a united evangelical front against the newly regrouped catholic forces was dashed, and the political credibility of the Reformation seriously compromised. By 1530, Charles V had begun to reassert his authority over the German Reformation, helped to no small extent by the political consequences of the differences between Luther and Zwingli concerning the eucharist.

Aware of what was happening, Protestant leaders attempted to heal the resulting wounds as quickly as possible. One major attempt to define a common Protestant position on the sacraments should be noted: the *Consensus Tigurinus*, or 'Consensus of Zurich', a formula of faith agreed on in May 1549. The document, drawn up by major leaders such as John Calvin and Heinrich Bullinger (Zwingli's successor as the leading reformer of the city of Zurich), managed to establish significant common ground within a Protestantism hitherto divided on this issue. But we have yet to consider Calvin's views on this matter, and to this we will now turn.

Calvin on the Sacraments

For Calvin, as for all the magisterial reformers, the sacraments were seen as identity-giving; without sacraments, there could be no Christian church. 'Wherever we find the Word of God preached purely and listened to, and the sacraments administered according to the institution of Christ, we cannot doubt that a church exists.' It is thus not the quality of its members, but the presence of the authorized means of grace, which constitutes a true church. Having thus defined one of the 'marks of the church (*notae ecclesiae*)' as the administration of the sacraments, Calvin was obliged to give a detailed consideration of what the true sacraments of the gospel might be and how they were to be understood. In doing so, Calvin was clearly aware of the divergences between Luther and Zwingli, and he attempted to steer a middle course between their rival viewpoints.

Calvin offered two definitions of a sacrament, as 'an external symbol by which the Lord seals on our consciences his promises of good will towards us, in order to sustain the weakness of our faith', and as a 'visible sign of a sacred thing, or a visible form of an invisible grace'. The former was Calvin's own definition, whereas the latter was due to Augustine (although Calvin saw it as too brief to be of much use). Insisting that a sacrament must be based upon 'a promise and a command of the Lord', he followed his colleagues in rejecting five of the seven sacraments traditionally accepted by the Catholic church, allowing only baptism and the eucharist to remain.

For Calvin, sacraments are gracious accommodations to our weakness. God, knowing our weakness of faith, adapts to our limitations.

> A sacrament is never without a preceding promise, but is joined to it as a kind of appendix, in order to confirm and seal the promise itself, making in more clear to us, and in a sense ratifying it . . . As our faith is weak unless it is supported on every side and sustained by every means, it trembles, wavers, and finally collapses. Here our merciful Lord, according to his infinite kindness, so adjusts himself to our capacity that, since we are creatures who always cling to the earth and cleave to fleshly things, and do not think about or even conceive spiritual matters, he condescends to lead us to himself by just such earthly things, and to set before us in the flesh a mirror of spiritual blessings.

The central debate between Luther and Zwingli concerned the relation between the sacramental sign and the spiritual gift which it signified. Calvin may be regarded as occupying a position roughly midway between the two extremes represented by them. In the sacraments, he argued, there is such a close connection between the symbol and the gift which it symbolizes that we can 'easily pass from one to the other'. The sign is visible and physical, whereas the thing signified is invisible and spiritual; yet, because the connection between the sign and the thing signified is so intimate, it is permissible to apply the one to the other. Thus the thing that is signified is effected by its sign.

> Believers ought always to live by this rule: whenever they see symbols appointed by the Lord, to think and be convinced that the truth of the thing signified is surely present there. For why should the Lord put in your hand the symbol of his body, unless it was to assure you that you really participate in it? And if it is true that a visible sign is given to us to seal the gift of an invisible thing, when we have received the symbol of the body, let us rest assured that the body itself is also given to us.

Calvin could thus maintain the difference between sign and thing signified while insisting that the sign really points to the gift it signifies.

> I therefore say . . . that the sacred mystery of the Lord's Supper consists in two things: physical signs, which, when placed in front of our eyes, represent to us (according to our feeble capacity) invisible things; and spiritual truth, which is at the same time represented and displayed through the symbols themselves.

It might be thought that Calvin's position represented a deliberate attempt to reconcile the views of Zwingli and Luther, an exercise in ecclesiastical diplomacy at an opportune moment in the history of the Reformation. In fact, however, there is little evidence to support this view; Calvin's theology of the sacraments cannot be regarded as a compromise reached on political grounds, but rather reflects his understanding of the way in which the knowledge of God is given to us. So important is this point that we will explore it further.

Throughout his discussion of the relation of God to humanity, Calvin took a single model as normative. The model in question was that made available by the incarnation. The incarnation speaks of the *union* of divinity and humanity in the person of Jesus Christ, but not their *fusion*. Time and time again, Calvin appealed to the Christologically grounded formula *distinctio sed non separatio*; ideas may be *distinguished* but not *separated*.

Thus the 'knowledge of God' and the 'knowledge of ourselves' may be distinguished; but they may not be had in isolation from one another. Just as the incarnation represents a case of this coming together of opposites, so the same pattern is repeated and may be discerned throughout the various aspects of the relationship between God and humanity. For Calvin, theology centred on 'knowledge of God and knowledge of ourselves'. It thus followed that this model of 'distinguishing but not separating' dominated his way of thinking about the relation of God to his world – including the nature of sacramental symbols.

This principle can be seen in operation throughout the *Institutes*: in the relation between the Word of God and the words of human beings in preaching; in that between the believer and Christ in justification, where a real communion of persons exists, but not a fusion of being; and in the relation between the secular and the spiritual power. In the case of the sacraments, the sign and the thing signified may be distinguished, but not separated from each other. They are different, but are none the less inseparable.

Calvin's understanding of baptism may be regarded as combining both Zwinglian and Lutheran elements. Nodding in Zwingli's direction, Calvin argued that baptism is a public demonstration of allegiance to God: 'Baptism is the sign of the initiation by which we are received into the society of the church.' Just as Zwingli had asserted that sacraments are primarily ecclesial events, serving to demonstrate the loyalty of believers to the church or civic community, so Calvin stressed the declaratory role of the sacrament of baptism. However, he also incorporated the characteristically Lutheran stress upon baptism as a sign of the remission of sins and the new life of believers in Jesus Christ: 'Baptism also brings another benefit, for it shows us our being put to death in Christ, and our new life in him . . . Thus the free pardon of sins and the imputation of righteousness are first promised, and then the grace of the Holy Spirit to reform us to newness of life'.

In common with all the magisterial reformers, Calvin upheld the validity of infant baptism. The practice, he argued, was an authentic tradition of the early church, and not a later medieval development. Zwingli had justified the practice by an appeal to the Jewish rite of circumcision. By this rite, he had argued, infant males were shown to be members of the covenant community. In a similar manner, baptism was the mark that an infant belonged to the church, the community of the new covenant. The rising influence of the Anabaptists, which Calvin had experienced at first hand during his Strasbourg period, demonstrated the importance of justifying the practice of infant baptism, which the Anabaptists vigorously rejected. Calvin thus reiterated and extended Zwingli's covenantal justification of infant baptism: if Christian infants cannot be baptized, they are at a disadvantage in relation to Jewish infants, who are publicly and outwardly sealed into the covenant community through circumcision: 'Otherwise, if the testimony by which the Jews were assured of the salvation of their posterity is taken away from us, the coming of Christ would have the effect of making God's grace more obscure and less well attested to us than it was to the Jews before us.' Calvin thus argued that infants should be baptized, and not denied the benefits which this conveys.

In his discussion of the eucharist, Calvin distinguished three aspects of the spiritual truth which is presented (*monstretur*) and offered through the visible elements of bread and wine. The *signification or meaning* is the divine promises, which are included or enclosed within the sign itself; believers are reassured, particularly through the words of institution, that the body and blood of Jesus Christ have been broken and shed for them. The sacrament 'confirms the promise in which Jesus Christ declares that his flesh is food indeed, and his blood drink indeed, and that they feed us with eternal life'. The *substance or matter* of the eucharist concerns our reception of the body of Christ: God communicates to us what he has promised us. In receiving the sign of the body of Christ (in other words, the bread), we are simultaneously receiving the body of Christ itself. Finally, the *virtue or effect* of the eucharist is located in the *beneficia Christi* – the benefits won for the believer by Christ through his obedience. The believer participates by faith in all the benefits of Christ, such as redemption, righteousness and eternal life.

Finally, the sacraments encourage Christians to value the creation. Material elements can signify the grace, generosity and goodness of God. This insight is rigorously grounded in Calvin's doctrine of creation. For Calvin, the creation reflects its Creator at every point. Image after image is flashed in front of our eyes, as Calvin attempts to convey the multiplicity of ways in which the creation witnesses to its Creator: it is like a visible garment, which the invisible God dons in order to make himself known; it is like a book, in which the name of the Creator is written as its author; it is like a theatre, in which the glory of God is publicly displayed; it is like a mirror, in which the works and wisdom of God are reflected.

This gives us a new motivation for *enjoying* nature. Although often portrayed as an ascetic killjoy, determined to stop believers from enjoying themselves at any cost, Calvin is genuinely concerned to stress that creation was fashioned in order that we might rejoice in it, rather than merely survive through it. Quoting Psalm 104:15, Calvin points out that God created wine that makes human hearts glad. Food does not merely allow us to survive; it tastes good.

> God not only provides for our necessities, and bestows upon us as much as we need for the everyday purposes of life – in his goodness, he deals still more generously with us, by cheering our hearts with wine and oil. Nature would certainly be satisfied with water to drink! The addition of wine is thus due to God's overflowing generosity.

Further, the rich and satisfying associations of wine are given new meaning through the communion service, as Calvin pointed out in the 1540 *Treatise on the Lord's Supper*:

> Wen we see wine set forth as a symbol of blood, we must reflect upon the benefits which wine imparts to the human body. We thus come to realize that these same benefits are imparted to us in a spiritual manner by the blood of Christ. These benefits are to nourish, refresh, strengthen and gladden.

Calvin developed this point at length in the *Institutes*, pointing out how we are able to appreciate and enjoy the good things of life. 'All things are made for us, in order that we may know and acknowledge their author, and celebrate his goodness towards us by giving him thanks.' The bread and wine of the eucharist thus point not only to God's act of redeeming the world in Christ, but to his preceding act of creation, by which a world which we can enjoy was brought into being.

The Catholic Response: Trent on the Sacraments

Trent took some time to respond to the views on the sacraments associated with the Reformation. The Seventh Session of the Council of Trent reached its conclusion on 3 March 1547, and issued its 'Decree on the Sacraments'. In many ways, this is best seen as an interim measure, designed to counter Protestant views without providing a detailed Catholic rejoinder. The decree takes the form of a preface, followed by thirteen general canons, each condemning some aspect of 'the heresies that in our turbulent times are directed against the most holy sacraments'. The following canons are of particular importance, in that they explicitly condemn the reformers' views on the number of sacraments and the manner in which they operate. Criticism is in particular directed against the view that sacraments signify grace, which is to be received through faith.

1. If anyone says that the sacraments of the new law were not all instituted by our Lord Jesus Christ, or that there are more or less than seven, namely, baptism, confirmation, eucharist, penance, extreme unction, ordination, and marriage, or that any one of these seven is not truly and intrinsically a sacrament, let them be condemned. . . .
5. If anyone says that these sacraments have been instituted for the nourishment of faith alone, let them be condemned.
6. If anyone says that the sacraments of the new law do not contain the grace that they signify, or that they do not confer that grace upon those who do not place obstacles in its path (as though they were only outward signs of grace or righteousness, received through faith, and certain marks of Christian profession by which believers are, at the human level, distinguished from non-believers), let them be condemned. . . .
8. If anyone says that the sacraments of the new law do not confer grace *ex opere operato* (see p. 176), but that faith alone in the divine promise is sufficient to obtain grace, let them be condemned.

These thirteen canons were then followed by a series of fourteen canons relating to baptism and three relating to confirmation.

It was not until the Thirteenth Session of the council, which concluded its deliberations on 11 October 1551, that Trent finally set forth the positive position of the Roman Catholic church in the 'Decree on the Most Holy Sacrament of the Eucharist'. Up to this point, Trent had merely criticized the reformers, without putting forth a coherent alternative position. This deficiency was now remedied.

The Decree opens with a vigorous attack on those who deny the real presence of Christ. Although Zwingli is not specifically mentioned, the council's allusions to Christ sitting at the right hand of God and the improper use of 'tropes' makes it clear that the Swiss reformer is the object of its attack:

> After the consecration of the bread and wine, our Lord Jesus Christ is truly, really and substantially contained in the venerable sacrament of the Holy Eucharist under the appearance of those physical things. For there is no repugnance in the fact that our Saviour sits at the right hand of the Father in heaven according to his natural mode of existing, while he is sacramentally present to us in his own substance in many other places . . . It is a most contemptible action on the part of some contentious and wicked people to twist them (the words of Christ) into fictitious and imaginary tropes by which the truth of the flesh and blood of Christ is denied.

The Council vigorously defended both the doctrine and the terminology of transubstantiation. 'By the consecration of the bread and wine a change is brought about of the whole substance of the bread into the substance of the body of Christ and of the whole substance of the wine into the blood of Christ. This change the Holy Catholic Church properly and appropriately calls transubstantiation.'

For further reading

On the background to the Reformation debates, see:

Francis Clark, *Eucharistic Sacrifice and the Reformation*, 2nd edn (Devon, 1981).

On the sacramental theology of the Reformers, see:

Timothy George, 'The Presuppositions of Zwingli's Baptismal Theology', in *Prophet, Pastor, Protestant: The Work of Huldrych Zwingli after Five Hundred Years*, ed. E. J. Furcha and H. W. Pipkin (Allison Park, Pa., 1984), pp. 71–87.

Brian A. Gerrish, 'Gospel and Eucharist: John Calvin on the Lord's Supper', in Gerrish, B. A., *The Old Protestantism and the New* (Edinburgh, 1982), pp. 106–17.

Basil Hall, '*Hoc est corpus meum*: The Centrality of the Real Presence for Luther', in *Luther: Theologian for Catholics and Protestants*, ed. George Yule (Edinburgh, 1985), pp. 112–44.

David C. Steinmetz, 'Scripture and the Lord's Supper in Luther's Theology', in Steinmetz, D. C., *Luther in Context* (Bloomington, Ind., 1986), pp. 72–84.

W. P. Stephens, *The Theology of Huldrych Zwingli* (Oxford, 1986), pp. 180–259.

10

The Doctrine of the Church

'The Reformation, inwardly considered, was just the ultimate triumph of Augustine's doctrine of grace over Augustine's doctrine of the church.'[1] We have already seen how both wings of the magisterial Reformation laid claim to the insights of Augustine of Hippo concerning grace. Both Luther's doctrine of justification by faith alone, and the emphasis placed by Zwingli and Calvin upon divine predestination, represent slightly different ways of reading Augustine's antiPelagian writings. As we have seen, the Reformation arose within an intellectual context which placed new emphasis upon the importance of this great Christian writer of the late fourth and early fifth centuries, reflected in the publication of the Amerbach edition of Augustine's works in 1506.

In many ways, the reformers' views on the church represent their Achilles' heel. The reformers were confronted with two consistent rival views of the church whose logic they could not match – those of their catholic and radical opponents. For the former, the church was a visible, historic institution, possessing historical continuity with the apostolic church; for the latter, the true church was in heaven, and no institution of any kind on earth merited the name 'church of God'. The magisterial reformers attempted to claim the middle ground somewhere between these two rival views, and found themselves involved in serious inconsistencies as a result.

The reformers were convinced that the church of their day and age had lost sight of the doctrine of grace, which Luther regarded as the centre of the Christian gospel. Thus Luther declared that his doctrine of justification by faith alone was the *articulus stantis et cadentis ecclesiae*, 'the article by which the church stands or falls'. Convinced that the catholic church had lost sight of this doctrine, he concluded (with some reluctance, it would seem) that it had lost its claim to be considered as the authentic Christian church.

The catholics responded to this suggestion with derision: Luther was simply creating a breakaway faction which had no connection with the church. In other words, he was a schismatic – and had not Augustine himself condemned schism? Had not he placed enormous emphasis upon the unity of the church, which Luther now threatened to disrupt? Luther, it seemed, could only uphold Augustine's doctrine of grace by rejecting Augustine's doctrine of the church. It is in the context of this tension between two aspects of Augustine' thought, which proved to be incompatible in the sixteenth century, that the Reformation understandings of the nature of the church are to be seen.

The Reformation debates over the nature of the church allow us to appreciate the major differences which existed within the Reformation itself, as well as between the Reformation and its Catholic opponents. While both the magisterial and radical Reformations rejected the institutional definition of the church offered by Catholicism, the magisterial Reformation found itself defending a more 'institutional' definition of the church against their radical opponents. In an earlier chapter, we explored the differences between the radical Reformation, the magisterial Reformation and Catholicism over the role of tradition; related differences can be observed over the doctrine of the church.

We must begin our discussion by returning to the question of the legacy of Augustine. The Reformation, at least in part, can be seen as an endorsement of Augustine' theology of grace. But what were Augustine's views on the church – views with which the reformers allegedly found themselves in conflict? To understand the complexities of the sixteenth-century debates, we need to examine the Donatist controversy, in which very similar issues were debated a thousand years before the Reformation. There are remarkable parallels between the Reformation debates over the identity and function of the church and those associated with the Donatist controversy.

The Background to the Reformation Debates: The Donatist Controversy

The 'Donatist controversy' had its origins in North Africa in the third century. In part, the controversy reflected tensions between native north African Christians (the Berbers) and Roman colonials who had settled in the region. The real issue, however, was the status of Christian believers and congregations who had lapsed under the threat of persecution.

Under the Roman emperor Diocletian (284–313), the Christian church was subject to various degrees of persecution. The beginnings of the persecution date from 303; it finally ended with the conversion of Constantine, and the issuing of the Edict of Milan in 313. Under an edict of February 303, Christian books were ordered to be burned and churches demolished. Those Christian leaders who handed over their books to be burned came to be known as *traditores* – 'those who handed over'. The modern word 'traitor' derives from the same root. One such *traditor* was Felix of Aptunga, who later consecrated Caecilian as Bishop of Carthage in 311.

Many local Christians were outraged that such a person should have been allowed to be involved in this consecration, and declared that they could not accept the authority of Caecilian as a result. The hierarchy of the Catholic church was tainted as a result of this development. The church ought to be pure, and should not be permitted to include such people. By the time Augustine returned to Africa from Italy in 388, a breakaway faction had established itself as the leading Christian body in the region, with especially strong support from the local African population. Sociological issues clouded theological debate; the Donatists (so named after the breakaway African church leader Donatus) tended to draw their support from the indigenous population, whereas the Catholics drew theirs from Roman colonists.

The theological issues involved are of considerable importance, and relate directly to a serious tension within the theology of a leading figure of the African church in the third century – Cyprian of Carthage. In his *Unity of the Catholic Church* (251), Cyprian had defended two major related beliefs. First, schism is totally and absolutely unjustified. The unity of the church cannot be broken, on any pretext whatsoever. To step outside the bounds of the church is to forfeit any possibility of salvation. Second, it therefore follows that lapsed or schismatic bishops are deprived of all ability to administer the sacraments or act as a minister of the Christian church. By passing outside the sphere of the church, they have lost their spiritual gifts and authority. They should therefore not be permitted to ordain priests or bishops. Any whom they have ordained must be regarded as invalidly ordained; any whom they have baptized must be regarded as invalidly baptized.

But what happens if a bishop lapses under persecution, and subsequently repents? Cyprian's theory is profoundly ambiguous, and is open to two lines of interpretation.

1   By lapsing, the bishop has committed the sin of apostasy (literally, 'falling away'). He has therefore placed himself outside the bounds of the church, and can no longer be regarded as administering the sacraments validly.
2   By his repentance, the bishop has been restored to grace, and is able to continue administering the sacraments validly.

The Donatists adopted the first such position, the Catholics (as their opponents came to be universally known) the second.

The Donatists believed that the entire sacramental system of the Catholic church had become corrupted. It was therefore necessary to replace *traditores* with people who had remained firm in their faith under persecution. It was also necessary to rebaptize and reordain all those who had been baptized and ordained by *traditores*. Inevitably, this resulted in the formation of a breakaway faction. By the time Augustine returned to Africa, the breakaway faction was larger than the church it had broken away from.

Yet Cyprian had totally forbidden schism of any kind. One of the greatest paradoxes of the Donatist schism is that it resulted from principles which were due to Cyprian – yet contradicted those very same principles. As a result, both Donatists and Catholics appealed to Cyprian as an authority – but to very different aspects of his teaching. The Donatists stressed the outrageous character of apostasy; the Catholics equally emphasized the impossibility of schism. A stalemate resulted. That is, until Augustine arrived, and became Bishop of Hippo in the region. Augustine was able to resolve the tensions within the legacy of Cyprian, and put forward an 'Augustinian' view of the church, which has remained enormously influential ever since.

First, Augustine emphasizes the *sinfulness of Christians*. The church is not meant to be a society of saints, but a 'mixed body' (*corpus permixtum*) of saints and sinners. Augustine finds this image in two biblical parables: the parable of the net which catches many fishes, and the parable of the wheat and the tares. It is this latter parable (Matthew 13: 24–31) which is of especial importance, and requires further discussion.

The parable tells of a farmer who sowed seed, and discovered that the resulting crop included both wheat and tares – grain and weeds. What could be done about it? To attempt to separate the wheat and the weeds while both were still growing would be to court disaster, probably involving damaging the wheat while trying to get rid of the weeds. But at the harvest, all the plants – wheat and tares – are cut down and sorted out without any danger of damaging the wheat. The separation of the good and the evil thus takes place at the end of time, not in history.

For Augustine, this parable refers to the church in the world. It must expect to find itself including both saints and sinners. To attempt a separation in this world is premature and improper. That separation will take place in God's own time, at the end of history. No human can make that judgment or separation in God's place. So in what sense is the church holy? For Augustine, the holiness in question is not that of its members, but of Christ. The church cannot be a congregation of saints in this world, in that its members are contaminated with original sin. However, the church is sanctified and made holy by Christ – a holiness which will be perfected and finally realized at the last judgment.

In addition to this theological analysis, Augustine makes the practical observation that the Donatists failed to live up to their own high standards of morality. The Donatists, Augustine suggests, were just as capable as Catholics of getting drunk or beating people up.

Second, Augustine argues that schism and *traditio* (the handing over of Christian books, or any form of lapse from faith) are indeed both sinful – but that, for Cyprian, schism is by far the more serious sin. The Donatists are thus guilty of serious misrepresentation of the teaching of the great North African martyr bishop.

On the basis of these considerations, Augustine argues that Donatism is fatally flawed. The church is, and is meant to be, a mixed body. Sin is an inevitable aspect of the life of the church in the present age, and is neither the occasion nor the justification for schism. Yet precisely the schism which Augustine feared and detested so much would eventually come about in the sixteenth century, with the formation of breakaway Protestant churches in western Europe as a result of the Reformation. It is to these major developments that we now turn.

The Context of the Reformation Views on the Church

In his period as an academic reformer, Luther shared a profound distaste for schism. Even the row over the 95 theses on indulgences of 31 October, 1517 did not persuade Luther to break away from the church. In the twentieth century, we have become used to the phenomenon of 'denominationalism' – but the very idea of the western church breaking up into smaller parts was completely alien to the medieval period. Schism, to put it bluntly, was unthinkable. As Luther himself wrote in early 1519: 'If, unfortunately, there are things in Rome which cannot be improved, there is not – and cannot be – any reason for tearing oneself away from the church in schism. Rather, the worse things become, the more one should help her and stand by her, for by schism and contempt nothing can be mended.'[2] Luther's views here parallel those of other reforming groups throughout Europe: the church must be reformed from within.

The assumption that the growing alienation of the Wittenberg Reformation from the catholic church was purely temporary seems to underlie much of the thinking of Lutheran writers in the period 1520–41. It seems that the evangelical faction at Wittenberg believed that the catholic church would indeed reform itself, perhaps through convening a reforming council, within a matter of years, thus allowing the Lutherans to rejoin a renewed and reformed church. Thus the Augsburg Confession (1530), setting out the main lines of Lutheran belief, is actually remarkably conciliatory towards catholicism. Such hopes of reunion were, however, dashed in the 1540s. In 1541, the Colloquy of Regensburg seemed to offer the hope of reconciliation, as a group of Protestant and catholic theologians met to discuss their differences.[3] Those discussions ended in failure.

In 1545, the Council of Trent finally met to hammer out the response of the catholic church to the Reformation, and institute a major programme of reform within that church. Some present at that Council, such as Cardinal Reginald Pole, had hoped that it would prove to be conciliatory towards the Protestants: in the event, however, the Council identified and condemned the leading ideas of Protestantism. Any hopes of reconciliation had been dashed. The Protestant churches now had to recognize that their existence as separate entities was permanent, rather than temporary. They had to justify their existence as Christian churches alongside a body which seemed to have a much stronger claim to that title – the Roman Catholic church itself.

On this basis of this historical preamble, it will be obvious that the reformers' particular concern with the theory of the church dates from the 1540s. It was in the aftermath of Regensburg – and especially as it became clear that the evangelical groupings would be permanently excluded from the catholic church – that the question of the true identity of the church became of critical importance. This was thus a question which preoccupied the second, rather than the first, generation of reformers. If Luther was concerned with the question, 'How may I find a gracious God?', his successors were obliged to deal with the question which arose out of this – 'Where can I find the true church?' Theoretical justification had to be given to the separate existence of the evangelical churches. Most influential among second-generation reformers, of course, is John Calvin, and it is in his writings that we find perhaps the most important contributions to this debate. Our attention initially focusses on Luther.

Luther on the Nature of the Church

The early reformers were convinced that the medieval church had become corrupted and its doctrine distorted through a departure from Scripture on the one hand and through human additions to Scripture on the other. Luther's early views on the nature of the church reflect his emphasis on the Word of God: the Word of God goes forth conquering, and wherever it conquers and gains true obedience to God is the church.[4]

Now, anywhere you hear or see [the Word of God] preached, believed, confessed, and acted upon, do not doubt that the true *ecclesia sancta catholica*, a 'holy

Christian people' must be there, even though there are very few of them. For God's word 'shall not return empty' (Isaiah 55:11), but must possess at least a fourth or a part of the field. And even if there were no other sign than this alone, it would be enough to prove that a holy Christian people must exist there, for God's word cannot be without God's people and conversely, God's people cannot be without God's word. For who would preach the word, or hear it preached, if there were no people of God? And what could or would God's people believe, if there were no word of God?

An episcopally ordained ministry is therefore not necessary to safeguard the existence of the church, whereas the preaching of the gospel is essential to the identity of that church. 'Where the word is, there is faith; and where faith is, there is the true church.' The visible church is constituted by the preaching of the Word of God: no human assembly may claim to be the 'church of God' unless it is founded on this gospel.

We have already seen (p. 153) how this understanding of the church is functional, rather than historical: what legitimates a church or its office-bearers is not historical continuity with the apostolic church, but theological continuity. It is more important to preach the same gospel as the apostles than to be a member of an institution which is historically derived from them. A similar understanding of the church was shared by Philipp Melanchthon, Luther's colleague at Wittenberg, who conceived of the church primarily in terms of its function of administering the means of grace.

Alongside this view of the nature of the church, Luther set a new understanding of the role of individual Christians. Whereas the medieval church argued for an absolute distinction between priests and laity, Luther insisted that the distinction in question was functional, not ontological. All Christians are priests by virtue of their baptism, faith and the gospel – a doctrine which is often referred to as the 'priesthood of all believers'. The only distinction that can be recognized between them relates to the different 'office' or 'function' (*ampt*) and 'work' or 'responsibility' (*werck*) with which they are entrusted. Priests are to be reckoned as 'office-holders', whose privileges and functions can only continue for as long as they are accepted by those who appointed or elected them. Luther was thus quite clear that, once priests retire or are dismissed, they revert to the role of lay people.[5]

It is an invention that the Pope, bishop, priests and monks are called 'the spiritual estate' (*geistlich stand*), while princes, lords, craftsmen and farmers are called 'the secular estate' (*weltlich stand*). This is a spurious idea, and nobody should fear it for the following reason. All Christians truly belong to the spiritual estate, and there is no difference among them apart from their office (*ampt*) . . . We all have one baptism, one gospel, one faith, and are all alike Christians, in that it is baptism, gospel and faith which alone make us spiritual and a Christian people. . . . We are all consecrated priests through baptism, as St Peter says: 'You are a royal priesthood and a priestly kingdom' (1 Peter 2:9) . . . Therefore someone who bears the status of a priest (*ein priester stand*) is nothing other than an officeholder (*amptman*). He takes priority for as long as he holds this office; when he is deposed, he becomes a peasant or citizen like all the others . . . It follows from this that there is no basic true difference between lay people, priests, princes and bishops, between the spiritual and the secular, except for their office and work (*den des ampts odder wercks halben*) and not on the basis of their status (*stand*). All are of the spiritual estate, and all are truly priests, bishops, and popes, although they are not the same in terms of their individual work.

Luther's vision of the church possessed the great virtue of simplicity. Simplicity, however, frequently amounts to inadequacy. As it became increasingly clear that Luther and Zwingli could not agree over what the gospel was (their eucharistic disagreement highlighting this point), the credibility of Luther's vision of the church became undermined. In part, Luther's difficulties related to the challenge posed by the radical Reformation, to which we may now turn.

The Radical View of the Church

It is important to note the implications of the term 'Reformation'. For the magisterial reformers, such as Luther and Calvin, the task of the Reformation was to reform a church which had become corrupted or disfigured as a result of developments in the Middle Ages. The essential presupposition underlying this program should be noted carefully: *to reform a church is to presuppose that a church already exists.* Luther and Calvin were both clear that the medieval church was indeed a Christian church. The difficulty was that it had lost its way and required to be reformed.

The radicals, however, did not share this basic assumption. The church had simply ceased to exist. For some, such as Sebastian Franck, the apostolic church had been totally compromised through its close links with the state, dating back to the conversion of the Emperor Constantine. As an institution, the church was corrupted by human power struggles and ambition. Franck wrote thus:[6]

I maintain, against all the doctors, that all external things which were in use in the church of the apostles have been abolished (*abrogata*), and none of them are to be restored or reinstituted, even though they have gone beyond their authorization or calling and attempted to restore these fallen sacraments (*lapsa sacramenta*). For the church will remain scattered among the heathen until the end of the world. Indeed, the Antichrist and his church will only be defeated and swept away at the coming of Christ, who will gather together in his kingdom Israel, which has been scattered to the four corners of the world . . . The works [of those who understood this] have been suppressed as godless heresies and rantings, and pride of place has instead been given to foolish Ambrose, Augustine, Jerome, Gregory – of whom not even one knew Christ, nor was sent by God to teach. But rather all were and shall remain the apostles of Antichrist.

Just as most of the radicals were utterly consistent in their application of the *scriptura sola* principle, so they were equally consistent in their views on the institutional church. The true church was in heaven, and its institutional parodies were on earth.[7]

It will therefore be clear that the radicals were in no mood to speak of the 'reformation' of the church. If the church had ceased to exist, it required *restoratio* rather than *reformation*. The basic theme of the radical reformers was that the true church had ceased to exist. By 'reforming' the medieval church, Luther had merely altered the external appearance of a corrupt institution which had no right to call itself a Christian church. As Menno Simons stressed in his 1552 treatise, *The Confession of Distressed Christians*:[8]

The brightness of the sun has not shone for many years . . . However, in these latter days, the gracious, great God by the rich treasures of his love has again opened the windows of heaven and let drop the dew of his divine word, so that the earth once more as of yore produces its green branches and plants of righteousness which bear fruit unto the Lord and glorify his great and adorable name. The holy word and sacraments of the Lord rise up again from the ashes.

It will therefore be clear that the radical view of the church is much closer to the Donatist than the Augustinian view. For Menno Simons, the church is a society of saints, a pure body which is not contaminated by sin in any way. In contrast to those false churches which are recognized by the state, and enjoy its privileges, the true church is totally pure and regenerate.[9]

They are the true congregation of Christ who are truly converted, who are born from above of God, who are of a regenerate mind by the operation of the Holy Spirit through the hearing of the divine word, and have become the children of God, have entered into obedience to him, and live unblamably in his holy commandments, and according to his holy will all their days, or from the moment of their call.

It is therefore important to note that the issue of church discipline is highly significant to radical church leaders. Discipline is the means by which doctrinal and moral purity may be enforced within the church. The 'ban' (p. 220) serves to ensure the purity of the church, and remove any who might contaminate or compromise the congregation at this point.

The radical view of the church was highly coherent, and posed a serious challenge to mainline reformers, such as Luther, who worked with a 'mixed body' ecclesiology – that is to say, that they followed Augustine's view that the church, as a matter of fact, included both saints and sinners. We shall consider some of those difficulties in the following section.

Tensions within Luther's Doctrine of the Church

As we have seen, Luther was forced to deal with two difficulties relating to his understanding of the church. If the church was not defined institutionally, but by the preaching of the gospel, how could he distinguish his views from those of the radicals? He himself had conceded that 'the church is holy even where the fanatics [Luther's term for the radicals] are dominant, so long as they do not deny the word and the sacraments'.

Alert to the political realities of his situation, Luther countered his radical critics at this point by asserting the need for an institutional church. Just as he tempered the radical implications of the *scriptura sola* principle by an appeal to tradition (see pp. 154–7), so he tempered his potentially radical views on the nature of the true church by insisting that it had to be viewed as an historical institution. The institution of the church is the divinely ordained means of grace. But in countering the radicals by asserting that the church was indeed visible and institutional, Luther found himself, having difficulty in distinguishing his views from those of his catholic opponents. He himself fully appreciated this problem:

> We on our part confess that there is much that is Christian and good under the papacy; indeed, everything that is Christian and is good is to be found there and has come to us from this source. For instance, we confess that in the papal church there are the true Holy Scriptures, true baptism, the true sacrament of the altar, the true keys to the forgiveness of sins, the true office of the ministry, the true catechism in the form of the Lord's Prayer, the Ten Commandments and the articles of the Creed.

Luther is thus obliged to assert that 'the false church has only the appearance, although it also possesses the Christian offices'. In other words, the medieval church may have looked like the real thing, but it was really something rather different.

The logic of the situation became impossible, especially when Luther was confronted with two further problems. The first was posed by St Paul's letters in the New Testament to the Corinthians and Galatians. St Paul wrote to these churches, accusing them of having departed from the gospel – yet he still addresses them as Christian churches. How could Luther go futher than Paul in this matter? At worst, the Roman church was like the Galatian church – having departed from the gospel at points, it could still be treated as a Christian church.

The second problem was posed by an aspect of Augustine's theory of the church, going back to the Donatist controversy of the early fifth century, which we noted earlier.[10] The Donatists were a breakaway movement in the north African church, who insisted that the catholic church of their day had become compromised through its attitude to the Roman authorities during a period of persecution. Only those who had not compromised their personal religious integrity could be recognized as members of the true church. It can be seen that this corresponds closely to the radical view of the church.

Augustine argued the catholic case: the church must be recognized as having a mixed membership, both saints and sinners. The righteous and the wicked coexisted within the same church, and no human had the authority to weed out the wicked from the church. Augustine drew upon what is often known as 'the parable of the tares' (Mattew 13:24–31) to support this point. In this parable, the owner of a field arrives one morning to find both wheat and weeds ('tares', in older English) growing side by side. Selective herbicides being unknown, he is reluctant to try to remove the weeds: by doing so, he would inevitably damage some of the wheat as well. His solution to the problem is to wait until the wheat is ready to harvest, and then separate them. According to Augustine, this parable applies to the church. Like the field in the parable, the church contains both wheat and weeds, the just and the wicked, which coexist until the day of judgement. On that day, God will judge between them – and no human is permitted to pre-empt God's judgement. The church will thus contain both good and evil until the end of time. Augustine argues that the term 'catholic' (which literally means 'whole'), as applied to the church, describes its mixed membership of saints and sinners.

Luther followed Augustine in adopting a 'mixed body' ecclesiology. But this raised a serious problem. Luther had argued that the moral failings of the medieval church called into question its credentials. Yet his acceptance of the Augustinian church seemed to many to necessarily imply that there will *always* be corruption in the true church, on account of the fact that it is a mixed body of saints and sinners. On the basis of Augustine's theory, corruption in the catholic church does not necessarily mean that it is a 'false church'.

In practice, the force of this second point was reduced by Luther's insistence on the priority of theology over morals, Luther tended to see his criticisms of the morals of the medieval church as being secondary to its theological deficiencies. Yet the considerations set out in this section will make it clear that the magisterial Reformation at times found itself experiencing difficulties with its concept of the church. The Catholic and radical views of the church possessed a considerable degree of internal consistency and coherence which, at times, seemed absent from Luther's viewpoint.

It is in the writings of John Calvin that we find a more considered and rigorous approach to this important doctrine.

Calvin on the Nature of the Church

If any reformer wrestled with the problem posed by the doctrine of the church, it was Calvin. The first major discussion of the theory of the church is to be found in the second edition of his Institutes of the Christian Religion, published in 1539. Although Calvin deals with the subject in the first edition of the Institutes (1536), he was then quite innocent of any experience of ecclesiastical management or responsibility, which accounts for the curiously unfocused nature of his discussion. By the time of the second edition of this work, Calvin had gained more experience of the problems presented to the new evangelical churches.

The Two Marks of the Church

For Calvin, the marks of the true church were that the Word of God should be preached, and that the sacraments be rightly administered. Since the Roman Catholic church did not conform even to this minimalist definition of the church, the evangelicals were perfectly justified in leaving it. And as the evangelical churches conform to this definition of a church, there was no justification for further division within them. This point is of particular importance, reflecting Calvin's political judgement that further fragmentation of the evangelical congregations would be disastrous to the cause of the Reformation. The text in which Calvin sets out these principles merits careful study:[11]

> Wherever we see the Word of God purely preached and listened to, and the sacraments administered according to Christ's institution, it is in no way to be doubted that a church of God exists. For his promise cannot fail: 'Wherever two or three are gathered in my name, there I am in the midst of them' (Mattew

18:20). . . . If the ministry has the Word and honours it, if it has the administration of the sacraments, it deserves without doubt to be held and considered a church. . . . When the preaching of the gospel is reverently heard and the sacraments are not neglected, there for the time being no false or ambiguous form of the church is seen; and no one is permitted to ignore its authority, flout its warnings, resist its counsels, or make light of its chastisements – much less to break away from it and wreck its unity. . . . When we say that the pure ministry of the Word and pure mode of celebrating the sacraments are a sufficient pledge and guarantee by which we may recognize as a church any society, we mean where both these marks exist, it is not to be rejected, even if it is riddled with faults in other respects.

Notice how Calvin identifies two elements as essential to a Christian church, while at the same time indicating flexibility in other areas.

By 1543, Calvin had gained considerably more experience of ecclesiastical responsibility, particularly during his period at Strasbourg. Bucer, the intellectual force behind the Reformation at Strasbourg, had a considerable reputation as an ecclesiastical administrator, and it is probable that Calvin's later theory of the church reflects his personal influence. The fourfold office of pastor, doctor (or teacher), elder and deacon owes its origins to Bucer, as does the distinction between the visible and the invisible church (explored below). Nevertheless, Bucer's suggestion that ecclesiastical discipline was an essential feature (technically, a 'note' [*nota*] or 'mark') of the church is not echoed by Calvin. Although Calvin includes 'example of life' among the 'certain sure marks' of the church in the 1536 edition of the Institutes, later editions lay stress upon the proper preaching of the word of God and the administration of the sacraments. Discipline strengthens the nerve of the church – but the saving doctrine of Christ establishes its heart and soul.

Calvin argues that there are specific scriptural directions regarding the right order of ministry in the visible church, so that a specific form of ecclesiastical order now becomes an item of doctrine. In other words, he includes a specific form of ecclesiastical administration (and he here borrows the term *administratio* from the filed of secular government) in 'the gospel purely preached'.

The importance of the external administration of the church had been recognized for some time within Reformed circles. The First Helvetic Confession (1536), drawn up at Zurich, stressed that the church was distinguished by certain external signs:[12]

It is the fellowship and congregation of all saints which is Christ's bride and spouse, and which He washes with His blood and finally presents to the Father without blemish or any stain. And although this Church and congregation of Christ is only open and known to God's eyes, yet it is not only known but also gathered and built up by visible signs, rites and ordinances, which Christ Himself has instituted and appointed by the Word of God as a universal, public and orderly discipline. Without these marks (speaking generally and without a special permission revealed by God) no one is numbered with this Church.

Calvin's minimalist definition of the church now takes on a new significance. The true church is to be found where the gospel is rightly preached, and the sacraments rightly administered – and understood to be included within this definition is a specific form of ecclesiastical institution and administration. Calvin refers to the 'order by which the Lord willed his church to be governed', and develops a detailed theory of church government based upon his exegesis of the New Testament, drawing extensively upon the terminology of the imperial Roman administration. Contrary to what the radicals asserted, Calvin insists that a specific form of church structure and administration is laid down by Scripture. Thus Calvin held that the ministerial government of the church is divinely ordained, as is the distinction between 'minister', 'elder', 'deacon' and 'people'.

Whereas Luther regarded the organization of the church as a matter of historical contingency, not requiring theological prescription, Calvin held that a definite pattern of church government was prescribed by Scripture. So what is the importance of this new development in the theory of the church? It will be recalled that Luther had defined the church in terms of the ministry of the Word of God, which was of little help in distinguishing the magisterial Reformation from the catholic position on the one hand, and the position of the radicals on the other. Calvin, while retaining an emphasis on the importance of the ministry of the Word of God, now insisted that this same Work of God specified one particular form of church government. This was a bold new step in the interpretation of Scripture; it also gave Calvin a criterion by which to judge (and find wanting) his catholic and radical opponents. Where Luther was vague, Calvin was precise. By the time of Calvin's death (1564), the Reformed church was as institutionalized as its catholic rival, and had become its most formidable opponent. No small part of that success was due to the role of the Consistory, perhaps the most distinctive and innovative aspect of Calvin's plan for structuring his church.

Calvin on Church and Consistory

If the Institutes of the Christian Religion were the muscles of Calvin's reformation, his ecclesiastical organization was its backbone. The Ecclesiastical Ordinances (1541), which gave the Genevan church its characteristic shape and identity, were drawn up by Calvin virtually immediately on his return to

Geneva from his period of exile in Strasbourg. Convinced of the need for a disciplined, well-ordered and structured church, Calvin proceeded to lay down detailed guidelines governing every aspect of its existence. The establishment of an ecclesiastical apparatus appropriate to Calvin's goals must be regarded as one of the most significant aspects of his ministry, and lends added weight to the case for comparing Calvin to Lenin; both were admirably aware of the importance of institutions for the propagation of their respective revolutions, and lost no time in organizing what was required. The most distinctive and controversial aspect of Calvin's system of church government was the Consistory. This institution came into being in 1542, with twelve lay elders (selected annually by the magistrates), and all the members of the Venerable Company of Pastors (nine in 1542, nineteen in 1564). The body was intended to meet weekly on a Thursday, with the purpose of maintaining ecclesiastical discipline. The origins of this institution are unclear; it seems that existing matrimonial courts, such as Zurich's *Ehegericht*, may have served as a model, and that a prototype had actually been established in Geneva during Calvin's exile in Strasbourg. It is certainly significant that one of the early activities of the Consistory centred on marital problems, viewed as a pastoral, as much as a legal, difficulty; this may well reflect the role of already existing matrimonial courts (which were predominantly lay in character).

The question of ecclesiastical discipline had much exercised the authorities in the reformed Swiss cities. If any dominant general pattern may be said to have emerged by the 1530s, it was the Zwinglian view of the subordination of ecclesiastical discipline to the secular magistrates. Under Zwingli's successor, Heinrich Bullinger, the city of Zurich regarded excommunication as a civil matter, to be handled by magistrates rather than clergy. Basle also had serious reservations concerning the propriety of a purely ecclesiastical tribunal being entitled to excommunicate individuals. If the city of Berne is in any sense an exception to this rule, it is because it did not excommunicate members of its churches.

The origins of a rival theory may be traced to Basle in 1530, when Johann Oecolampadius argued before Basle city council that there was a fundamental difference between civil and ecclesiastical authority. It was necessary to introduce an ecclesiastical court, whose brief was to deal with sin, while secular magistrates would continue to deal with criminal offences. The former should have the right to excommunicate offenders, in order to encourage them to amend their ways and avoid disrupting the unity and life of the church. The Basle city council disagreed, and there the matter rested.

Nevertheless, the idea of a specifically ecclesiastical court gained support during the 1530s. Although Martin Bucer wrote to Zwingli on 19 October, 1530, indicating his hostility towards the idea of such a court, he appears to have shifted ground shortly afterwards. It is not impossible that this reflects

Bucer's alienation from Zwingli, as a result of the latter's letter of 12 February, 1531, in which he accused Bucer of betraying evangelical truth in the interests of political expediency. In 1531, Bucer supported the suggestion that the city of Ulm should have an ecclesiastical court, composed of both laity and pastors, to deal with matters of church discipline. The seizing of Mü[um]nster by the radicals in February 1534 brought home to Strasbourg city council the need to enforce church discipline and orthodoxy, if Strasbourg – by then with an established reputation as a haven for radicals – was to avoid the fate of Münster. However, the council rejected Bucer's preference for a specifically ecclesiastical court; control of church discipline was to remain firmly in the hands of the civil authorities. It was Bucer's ideas, rather than Strasbourg's practice, which appear to have fired the imaganation of Calvin during his sojourn in the city. The articles for the organization of the church at Geneva, drawn up by Farel and Calvin in January 1537, anticipate virtually every aspect of the *Ordonnances ecclésiastiques* of 1541 – with the notable exception of the Consistory. This suggests that it was during his Strasbourg period that Calvin developed the notion.

Calvin conceived of the Consistory primarily as an instrument for the 'policing' of religious orthodoxy. It was the guarantor of the discipline which Calvin's experience at Strasbourg had led him to recognize as essential to the survival of reformed Christendom. Its primary function was to deal with those whose religious views were sufficiently devious to pose a threat to the established religious order at Geneva. Persons whose behaviour was regarded as unacceptable for other reasons, pastoral or moral, were to be treated in the same way. Such individuals were, in the first instance, to be shown the error of their ways; should this fail, the penalty of excommunication was available as a deterrent. This, however, was an ecclesiastical rather than a civil penalty; the miscreant might be denied access to one of the four annual communion services at Geneva, but he could not be subjected to any civil penalty by the Consistory itself. The city council, perennially jealous of its authority, had insisted that 'all this is to take place in such a manner that the ministers have no civil jurisdiction, nor use anything but the spiritual sword of the Word of God . . . nor is the Consistory to detract from the authority of the Seigneurie or ordinary justice. Civil power is to remain unimpeded.'

The importance of church structures, such as the Consistory, to the international development of Calvinism can perhaps be appreciated best by comparing the very different situations within which Lutheranism and Calvinism came to be established in western Europe and North America. Lutheranism generally advanced through the sympathy of monarchs and princes, perhaps not totally unaware of the important ecclesiastical role alloted to them by Luther's doctrine of the 'Two Kingdoms'.

Although Calvin was aware of the potential of winning over monarchs to his ideas (his particular ambition being to gain a sympathetic hearing within the French court), Calvinism generally had to survive and advance in distinctly hostile situations (such as France in the 1550s), in which both monarch and the existing church establishment were opposed to its development. Under such conditions, the very survival of Calvinist groups was dependent upon a strong and well-disciplined church, capable of surviving the hostility of its milieu. The more sophisticated Calvinist church structures proved capable of withstanding considerably more difficult situations than their Lutheran equivalents, providing Calvinism with a vital resource for gaining ground in what might at first sight seem thoroughly unpromising political situations.

Calvin on the Role of the Church

Why is there any need for a church – understood, that is, as an institution, rather than a building – in the first place? Just as God redeemed human beings within the historical process through the incarnation, so he sanctifies them within that same process by founding an institution dedicated to that goal. God uses certain definite earthly means to work out the salvation of his elect; although he is not absolutely bound by these means, he normally works within them. The church is thus identified as a divinely-founded body, within which God effects the sanctification of his people. As Calvin puts it:

> I shall begin then, with the church, into the bosom of which God is pleased to gather his children, not only so that they may be nourished by her assistance and ministry while they are infants and children, but also so that they may be guided by her motherly care until they mature and reach the goal of faith. 'For what God has joined together, no one shall divide' (Mark 10:9). For those to whom God is Father, the church shall also be their mother.

Calvin confirms this high doctrine of the church by citing the two great ecclesiological maxims of Cyprian of Carthage: 'You cannot have God as your father unless you have the church for your mother', used above, and 'Outside the church there is no hope of remission of sins nor any salvation'.

Calvin's doctrine of the church reminds us that it is seriously inadequate to portray the reformers as rampant radical individualists, with no place for corporate conceptions of the Christian life. We have already seen (pp. 152–7) how mainline Reformation biblical interpretation lacks the individualism often projected onto it by its critics; the same is true of the Reformation understanding of the Christian life. The image of the 'church as mother' (which Calvin gladly borrows from Cyprian of Carthage) underscores the corporate dimensions of Christian faith. Note how Calvin stresses its importance.

> Let us learn from this simple word 'mother' how useful (indeed, how necessary) it is to know her. There is no other way to life, unless this mother conceives us in her womb, nourishes us at her breast, and keeps us under her care and guidance.

Powerful theological imagery nestles within this way of speaking, above all that of the word of God which conceives us within the womb of the church. But it is the practical aspects of this way of thinking about the church which command our attention at this point. The institution of the church is a necessary, helpful, God-given and God-ordained means of spiritual growth and development.

Calvin draws an important distinction between the visible and invisible church. At one level, the church is the community of Christian believers, a visible group. It is also, however, the fellowship of saints and the company of the elect – an invisible entity. In its invisible aspect, the church is the invisible assembly of the elect, known only to God; in its visible aspect, it is the community of believers on earth. The former consists only of the elect; the latter includes both good and evil, elect and reprobate. The former is an object of faith and hope, the latter of present experience. Calvin stresses that all believers are obliged to honour and to remain committed to the visible church, despite its weaknesses, on account of the invisible church, the true body of Christ. Despite this, there is only one church, a single entity with Jesus Christ as its head.

The distinction between the visible and invisible churches has two important consequences. In the first place, it is to be expected that the visible church will include both the elect and the reprobate. Augustine of Hippo had made this point against the Donatists, using the parable of the tares (Matthew 13:24–31) as his basis. It lies beyond human competence to discern their difference, correlating human qualities with divine favour (in any case, Calvin's doctrine of predestination precludes such grounds of election). In the second, however, it is necessary to ask which of the various visible churches corresponds to the invisible church. Calvin thus recognizes the need to articulate objective criteria by which the authenticity of a given church may be judged. Two such criteria are stipulated: 'Wherever we see the Word of God preached purely and listened to, and the sacraments administered according to the institution of Christ, we cannot doubt that a church exists'. It is thus not the quality of its members, but the presence of the authorized means of grace, which constitutes a true church. Interestingly, Calvin does not follow Bucer, and make discipline a mark of the true church; although passionately concerned with the need for charitable discipline of church members, Calvin did not regard this as essential to the definition or evaluation of the credentials of a church.

The Debate over the Catholicity of the Church

The Nicene Creed affirms belief in 'one holy, catholic and apostolic church'. Each of these four characteristics (often referred to as the 'four notes of the church') has been the subject of considerable discussion within Christian theology, with the Donatist controversy having given considerable impetus to the issues involved. At the time of the Reformation, particular attention was directed towards the meaning of the term 'catholic'. What did it mean to affirm belief in the catholicity of the church? And were Protestant churches able to affirm such a belief, when they had broken away from the mainstream medieval church?

In modern English, the term 'catholic' is often confused, especially in non-religious circles, with 'Roman Catholic'. Although this confusion is understandable, the distinction must be maintained. It is not only Roman Catholics who are catholic, just as it is by no means Easter Orthodox writers who are orthodox in their theology. Indeed, many Protestant churches, embarrassed by the use of the term 'catholic' in the creeds, have replaced it with 'universal'.

The word 'catholic', however, comes from the Greek phrase *kath' holou* ('referring to the whole'). The Greek words subsequently found their way into the Latin word *catholicus*, which came to have the meaning 'universal' or 'general'. This sense of the word is retained in the English phrase 'catholic taste', meaning 'a wide-ranging taste' rather than 'a taste for things that are Roman Catholic'. Older versions of the English Bible often refer to some of the New Testament letters (such as those of James and John) as 'catholic epistles', meaning that they are directed to all Christians (rather than those of Paul, which are directed to the needs and situations of individual identified churches, such as those at Rome or Corinth).

At no point does the New Testament use the term 'catholic' to refer to the church as a whole. The New Testament uses the Greek work *ekklesia* to refer to local churches or worshipping communities, which it nevertheless understands to represent or embody something which transcends that local body. While an individual church is not the church in its totality, it nevertheless shares in that totality. It is this notion of 'totality' which is subsequently encapsulated in the term 'catholic'. The term is introduced in later centuries, in an attempt to bring together central New Testament insights, and attach them to a single term.

The first known use of the phrase 'the catholic church' occurs in the writings of Ignatius of Antioch, who was martyred at Rome around 110: 'Where Jesus Christ is, there is the catholic church'. Other writings of the second century use the term to refer to the existence of a universal church alongside local congregations.

The meaning of the term changed fundamentally with the conversion of Constantine. By the end of the fourth century, the term 'the catholic church' came to mean 'the imperial church' – that is, the only legal religion within the Roman empire. Any other form of belief, including Christian beliefs which diverged from the mainline, were declared to be illegal. Further expansion of the church in this period contributed to a developing understanding of the term. By the beginning of the fifth century, Christianity was firmly established throughout the entire mediterranean world. In response to this development, the term 'catholic' came to be interpreted as 'embracing the entire world'. These general themes can be found in the writings of Thomas Aquinas, who set out the medieval consensus on 'catholicity' as follows:[13]

> The church is catholic, i.e., universal, first with respect to place, because it is throughout the entire world, against the Donatists. See Romans 1:8: 'Your faith is proclaimed in all the world'; Mark 16:15: 'Go into all the world and preach the gospel to the whole creation.' In ancient times, God was known only in Judea, but now throughout the entire world. This church, moreover, has three parts. One is on earth, another is in heaven, and the third is in purgatory. Secondly, the Church is universal with respect to the condition of people, because no one is rejected, whether master or slave, male or female. See Galatians 3:28: 'There is neither male nor female.' Thirdly, it is universal with respect to time. For some have said that the church should last until a certain time, but this is false, because this church began from the time of Abel and will last to the end of the world. See Matthew 28:20: 'And I am with you always, to the close of the age.' And after the close of the age it will remain in heaven.

On the basis of this understanding of catholicity, it was argued that continuity with the apostolic church could only be maintained *institutionally* – that is, through direct historical continuity with the early church. To break with the historic institution of the church, represented by its bishops, was to step outside the church. Cyprian of Carthage had argued that there was no salvation outside the church; to place oneself outside the institution of the church was therefore to forfeit any hope of salvation.

A fundamental re-examination of the notion of 'catholicity' took place at the time of the Reformation. It seemed to many that the catholicity and unity of the church were destroyed simultaneously with the fragmentation of the western European church in the sixteenth century. Catholic opponents of the Reformation declared that Protestants had broken away from the catholic church by introducing innovations (such as the doctrine of justification by faith alone) or by abandoning the traditional structures of the church (such as the papacy and the episcopacy). By breaking with the continuity of the church, the reformers had forfeited any right to call their churches 'Christian'. One of the essential hallmarks of an authentically Christian church was therefore *institutional continuity*. It was clear to the Catholic opponents of the Reformation that this continuity had been destroyed or disregarded by the reformers, with the result that Protestant congregations could not be regarded as Christian churches, in any meaningful sense of the word.

Protestant writers argued that the essence of catholicity lay, not in church institutions, but in matters of doctrine. The fifth-century writer Vincent of Lérins had defined catholicity in terms of 'that which is believed everywhere, at all times, and by all people'. The reformers argued that they remained catholic, despite having broken away from the medieval church, in that they retained the central and universally-recognized elements of Christian doctrine. Historical or institutional continuity was secondary to doctrinal fidelity. For this reason, the mainline Protestant churches insisted they were simultaneously catholic and reformed – that is, maintaining continuity with the apostolic church at the level of teaching, having eliminated spurious non-biblical practices and beliefs. This approach is adopted by Philipp Melanchthon:[14]

> Why is this term added in the article of the creed, so that the church is called catholic? Because it is an assembly dispersed throughout the whole world and because its members, wherever they are, and however separated in place, accept and externally profess one and the same utterance or true doctrine throughout all ages from the beginning until the very end . . . It is one thing to be called catholic, something else to be catholic in reality. Those are truly called catholic who accept the doctrine of the truly catholic church, i.e., that which is supported by the witness of all time, of all ages, which believes what the prophets and apostles taught, and which does not tolerate factions, heresies, and heretical assemblies.

Note how Melanchthon insists that catholicity refers to the universal teaching of the true faith. The reformers may thus claim to teach the true faith without being appended to the institution of the medieval church. This doctrinal interpretation of catholicity led to the institutional connections of a congregation being regarded as having less than fundamental importance. The important thing was to teach what the apostles taught, rather than to have physical evidence of historical continuity (for example, through the laying on of hands).

It will also be clear at this point that the emphasis placed by Luther and Calvin on the preaching of the gospel as a mark of the church is of foundational significance. If the true gospel is preached, a true Christian church is present – irrespective of its historical pedigree. In this way, the reformers were able to blunt the force of the arguments brought against them by their Catholic opponents, while at the same time offering a theological interpretation of the notion of 'catholicity' which allowed the church to be defined *functionally*. The implications of this development for western Christianity are substantial, in that denominational proliferation was given an important theological justification.

For further reading

For the reformers' views on the church, see:

Paul D. L. Avis, *The Church in the Theology of the Reformers* (London, 1981).

Rupert E. Davies, *The Problem of Authority in the Continental Reformers* (London, 1946).

F. H. Littel. *The Anabaptist View of the Church,* 2nd edn (Boston, 1958).

J. T. McNeill, 'The Church in Sixteenth-Century Reformed Theology', *Journal of Religion* 22 (1942), pp. 251–69.

W. P. Stephens, *The Holy Spirit in the Theology of Martin Bucer* (Cambridge, 1970), pp. 156–66.

——, *The Theology of Huldrych Zwingli* (Oxford, 1986), pp. 260–81.

11

The Political Thought of
the Reformation

In the previous chapter, we noted two distinct theological views of the church associated with the Reformation, each resulting in a different sociological role for that body: the Augustinian model, which corresponds sociologically to a 'church', and the Donatist model, which corresponds sociologically to a 'sect' (see pp. 198–201). The magisterial reformers adopted the former model, their radical opponents the latter model.

The Radical Reformation and Secular Authority

The radical Reformation conceived of the church as an 'alternative society' within the mainstream of sixteenth-century European culture. Just as the pre-Constantinian church existed within the Roman Empire, yet refused to conform to its standards, so the radical Reformation envisaged itself existing parallel to, but not within, its sixteenth-century environment. For Menno Simons, the church was 'an assembly of the righteous', at odds with the world. This notion of the church as a faithful remnant in conflict with the world harmonized with the Anabaptist experience of persecution by the forces of Antichrist, personified in the magistracy.

The radical Reformation was generally hostile to the use of coercion, and advocated a policy of non-resistance. Exceptions to this rule may be noted: for example, Balthasar Hubmaier regarded the coercive powers of government (such as the prerogative to engage in warfare and capital punishment) as something of a necessary evil, and held that Christians could hold office as magistrates without compromising their integrity. But this view was not typical of Anabaptism as a whole, which regarded the swearing of oaths, the use of coercive force, and the authority of the magistrate as Satanic. Jakob Hutter gave this apolitical stance a theological justification through an appeal to the example of Christ: 'As all can see, we have no physical weapons, such as spears or muskets. We wish to show, by our words and deeds, that we are true followers of Christ.' Hans Denck appealed to the meekness of Christ and his silence before his accusers in declaring that 'force is not an attribute of God'.

The clearest statement of the general Anabaptist attitude towards secular authority may be found in the Schleitheim Confession (1527), the sixth and seventh articles of which explain and justify the policy of non-involvement in secular affairs and non-resistance to secular authorities. Coercion has its place 'outside the perfection of Christ' (that is, outside the radical community); inside that community, however, physical force has no place.

> The sword is ordained of God outside the perfection of Christ . . . It is not appropriate for a Christian to serve as a magistrate, for the following reasons. The government magistracy is according to the flesh, but the Christian's is according to the Spirit. Their houses and dwelling places are in this world, but the Christian's is in heaven; their citizenship is of this world, but the Christian's is in heaven; the weapons of their war and conflict are physical, and against the flesh, whereas the Christian's weapons are spiritual, against the fortification of the devil. The worldlings are armed with steel and iron, but the Christian is armed with the armour of God, with truth, righteousness, peace, faith, salvation and the word of God.

Anabaptism maintained discipline within its communities through 'the ban', a means by which church members could be excluded from Anabaptist congregations. This means of discipline was regarded as being essential to the identity of a true church. Part of the Anabaptist case for radical separation from the mainstream churches (a practice which continues to this day among the Amish of Lancaster County, Pennsylvania, and elsewhere) was the failure of those churches to maintain proper discipline within their ranks. The Schleitheim Confession grounded its doctrine of the ban on Christ's words, as they are recorded in Matthew 18:15–20:

> The ban shall be used in the case of all those who have given themselves to the Lord, to walk in his commandments, and with all those who are baptized into the one body of Christ and are called brothers or sisters, yet who lapse on occasion, and inadvertently fall into error and sin. Such people shall be admonished twice in secret, and on the third occasion, they shall be disciplined publicly, or banned according to the command of Christ (Matthew 18).

The 'ban' was seen as being both deterrent and remedial in its effects, providing both an incentive for banned individuals to amend their way of life and a disincentive for others to imitate them in their sin. The Polish Racovian Catechism lists five reasons for maintaining rigorous discipline within Anabaptist communities, most of which reflect its policy of radical separation:

1   So that the fallen church member may be healed, and brought back into fellowship with the church.
2   To deter others from committing the same offence.
3   To eliminate scandal and disorder from the church.
4   To prevent the Word of the Lord falling into disrepute outside the congregation.
5   To prevent the glory of the Lord being profaned.

Despite its pastoral intentions, the 'ban' often came to be interpreted harshly, with congregation members often avoiding all social contact with both the banned individual and his or her family.

Where the majority of the radicals, with their rigorous views on church membership, had no time for compromises with the state or city authorities,[1] however, the magisterial reformers depended on precisely such compromises. Indeed, as we have seen, the very phrase 'magisterial Reformation' points to the close co-operation of reformer and magistrate in the propagation and defence of the Reformation.

We have already noted (pp. 34–5) the rise in power of secular governments throughout Europe in the early sixteenth century. The Concordat of Bologna, for example, had given to the King of France the right to appoint all the senior clergy of the French church. The ascendancy of the Catholic church in both France and Spain was maintained primarily through state interests. The political realities of the early sixteenth century demanded a similar liaison between the states or cities and the churches of the Protestant Reformation. So threatening and destabilizing were their social attitudes that radical congregations and thinkers were gradually excluded from the cities, forced into the countryside, and denied any political or social authority. For example, the Thirty-Nine Articles (1571), which laid down the principles governing the reformed Church of England during the reign of Elizabeth I, explicitly stipulate that 'the laws of the realm may punish Christians with death for heinous and grievous offences. It is lawful for Christians, at the command of the magistrate, to carry weapons and serve in wars' (Article 37). The Anabaptist position was thus rigorously excluded. In this, the English state church followed a pattern that was being established throughout Europe.

It must not be thought, however, that the magisterial reformers were political puppets: their understanding of the role of the city or state authorities in reforming the church reflects their theological presuppositions. In what follows, we shall examine the political views of the four major magisterial reformers: Luther, Zwingli, Bucer and Calvin.

Luther's Doctrine of the Two Kingdoms

The medieval period witnessed the development of the 'doctrine of the two estates': the *temporal* and the *spiritual*. According to this view, actively promoted by supporters of papal political manœuvring, the clergy belonged to the 'spiritual estate' and the laity to the 'temporal' estate. These two estates, or realms or spheres of authority, were quite distinct. Although the spiritual estate could (and did) intervene in the affairs of the temporal estate, the latter was not permitted to interfere with the former. Underlying this theory is a long history of conflict between papal and secular authority, particularly during the period of the Avignon papacy.[2]

Viewed pragmatically, this understanding of the spheres of influence of the secular and ecclesiastical powers meant that the reformation of the church was a matter purely for that church itself: laity, whether peasants or secular rulers such as the emperor himself, did not possess the necessary authority to bring about the reform of the church. As we saw earlier (p. 161), this was the first of the 'three walls' of the modern-day Jericho which Luther proposed to demolish. Convinced that the church had become entrenched in corrupted views of priesthood, Luther developed the doctrine of the 'priesthood of all believers' in his famous reforming treatise of 1520, *To the Christian Nobility of the German Nation*:

> It is pure invention that pope, bishop, priests and monks are called the spiritual estate, while princes, lords, artisans and farmers are called the temporal estate . . . All Christians are truly of the spiritual estate, and there is no difference between them except that of office . . . We are all consecrated priests through baptism, as St Peter says in 1 Peter 2:9.

While fully recognizing the need for administration within the church, Luther insists that the difference is purely one of office, not status.

Medieval Catholicism recognized a fundamental distinction between the 'spiritual estate' (that is, the clergy, whether they were priests, bishops or popes) and the 'temporal estate' (that is, everyone else). Luther declared this distinction to be null and void, a human invention rather than an ordinance of God:

> All Christians are truly of the spiritual estate, and there is no difference among them except that of function (*Amt*). Paul says in 1 Corinthians 12:12–13 that we are all one body, with every member having his or her own function by which he or she serves the others. This is because we have one baptism, one gospel and one faith, and are all Christians, just the same as each other; for baptism, gospel and faith alone make us spiritual and a Christian people. . . .

And so it follows that there is no true fundamental difference between lay persons and priests, between princes and bishops, between those living in monasteries and those living in the world. The only difference has nothing to do with status, but with the function and work which they perform.

There was no place in Christianity for any notion of a professional class within the church which is in a closer spiritual relationship to God than their fellows.

Nevertheless, not everyone could be allowed to *act* as a priest. Luther's doctrine of the priesthood of all believers did not entail the abolition of a professional ministry. Luther's fundamental principle was that all Christians share the same priestly status (*Stand*) on account of their baptism; they may, however, exercise different functions (*Amt*) within the community of faith, reflecting their individual God-given gifts and abilities. To be a minister is to stand alongside one's fellow Christians, sharing their status before God; nevertheless, those fellow believers have recognized the gifts of that individual, and invited him or her, directly or indirectly, to exercise that ministerial function amongst them.

Although we are all priests, this does not mean that all of us may preach, teach and exercise authority. Certain ones from within the community must be selected and set apart for such office. Anyone who holds such an office is not a priest by virtue of that office, but is a servant of all the others, who are just as much priests as he is.

The recognition of the *equality* of all believers thus does not imply the *identity* of all believers.

'Through baptism, we are all consecrated priests.' All believers, by virtue of their baptism, belong to the spiritual estate. (Notice that Luther is able to assume that all Germans are baptized.) 'Christ does not have two bodies, one temporal, the other spiritual. There is but one head and one body.' Laity thus have a right to demand a general council to reform the church; and, tongue placed firmly in his cheek, Luther reminds his readers that it was the Roman emperor Constantine (a lay person if ever there was one) who was responsible for calling the most important council in the history of the church (the Council of Nicea, which met in 325). Why should not the German nobility call for a council to reform the church in 1520?

Having thus abolished the medieval distinction between the 'temporal' and 'spiritual' estates, Luther proceeds to develop an alternative theory of spheres of authority, based upon a distinction between the 'Two Kingdoms', or the 'Two Governments'.[3] It is this doctrine of the 'Two Kingdoms' which is central to Luther's social thought and with which we are concerned in the present section.

Luther draws a distinction between the 'spiritual' and the 'worldly government of society. God's *spiritual* government is effected through the Word of God and the guidance of the Holy Spirit. The believer who 'walks by the Spirit' needs no further guidance from anyone as to how he should act: he is perfectly in tune with the divine will, and acts accordingly. Just as a good tree needs no instructions to bear fruit, so the true believer needs no legislation to guide his conduct. Just as a tree bears fruit naturally, so the believer naturally acts morally and responsibly. Luther also emphasizes the difference between human and divine conceptions of 'righteousness' or 'justice', a theme characteristic of his 'theology of the cross'. God's standards of justice call those of the world into question.[4]

God's *worldly* government is effected through kings, princes and magistrates, through the use of the sword and the civil law. These have no authority in matters of doctrine. 'When temporal princes and lords try to change and be master of the Word of God in such a high-handed manner – something which is as forbidden to them as it is to the meanest beggar – they are seeking to be God themselves.' Their proper sphere of authority concerns the affairs of the world, the things of Caesar rather than of God. Although these temporal rulers are involved in the secular world, they are nevertheless performing the work of God. Whether these princes or magistrates are true believers or not, they still perform a divine role (Luther appeals to Romans 13:1–7 and 1 Peter 2:13–14 in support of this contention). God has ordained that order shall be imposed upon creation, for the maintenance of peace and the repression of sin. There are three hierarchies, or 'orders', within a Christian society: the household or family, with the father as the head (reflecting the paternalism of Luther's age); the princes and magistrates, who exercise secular authority; and the clergy, who exercise spiritual authority. All these are founded on the Word of God, and reflect the divine will for the structuring and preservation of the worldly realm.

Luther recognizes that his Augustinian view of the relation between church and society implies that there are 'mouse droppings among the peppercorns, tares among the grain': in other words, the good and the evil coexist within both church and society. This is not to say that 'good' and 'evil' cannot be *distinguished*: it is simply to recognize, with the pragmatism for which Luther is noted, that they cannot be *isolated*. The good can be ruled by the Spirit, but the evil must be ruled by the sword. Luther insisted that the great masses of baptized Germans were not true Christians. Thus Luther recognized that it was utterly unrealistic to hope that society could be governed by the precepts of the Sermon on the Mount. Perhaps everyone ought to be so governed – but not everyone would be. Spirit and sword must coexist in the government of a Christian society.

Nevertheless, Luther's social ethic seems to suggest that two totally different moralities exist side by side: a private Christian ethic, reflecting the rule of love embodied in the Sermon on the Mount and challenging human conceptions of righteousness; and a public morality, based upon force, which endorses human conceptions of righteousness. Christian ethics is grounded in the doctrine of justification by faith alone, in which the believer gratefully responds to God's grace with good works; public morality is based upon coercion, in which the citizen obeys the law for fear of the consequences of failing to do so. The Sermon on the Mount is a splendid moral guide for the individual Christian, but its moral demands are not necessarily applicable to the public morality. It will therefore be obvious that Luther puts the Christian who is also a public figure (such as a prince or a magistrate) in the virtually impossible position of having to employ two different ethics, one for his private life, the other for his public life.

God thus governs the church by the Holy Spirit through the gospel in a manner from which all coercion is excluded; and he governs the world by the sword of secular authority. The magistrates are entitled to use the sword to enforce the law, not because violence is inherently justified, but on account of the intractability of human sinfulness. Were there no human sin, no coercion would be necessary: all would recognize the wisdom of the gospel, and modify their behaviour accordingly. God established political order in order to restrain human greed and wickedness, themselves the result of sinful inclinations.

The spiritual authority of the church is thus persuasive, not coercive, and concerns the individual's soul, rather than his body or goods. The temporal authority of the state is coercive, rather than persuasive, and concerns the individual's body and goods, rather than his soul. Luther's fundamental criticms of the medieval papacy was that it had confused these two separate realms of authority, especially through its system of canon law. Although Luther carefully distinguished these two realms of authority, in terms of both their scope and their source, he insisted that they are not in opposition to one another, but are merely different aspects of the same thing – God's rule over his fallen and sinful world.

Luther's political theology is thus pragmatic. Recognizing the political realities of his situation at Wittenberg and his reliance on the political support of the German princes, Luther reinforced their political authority by grounding it in divine providence. God governs the world, including the church, through the princes and magistrates. The church is in the world, and so must submit itself to the order of the world.

But what happens, it may reasonably be asked, if the state becomes tyrannical? Have Christians the right to intervene and actively oppose the state?

Luther thought not, at least in the 1520s. As the Peasants' Revolt loomed on the horizon, however, it seems that the deficiencies of his political thought became obvious. Secular rulers possessed their office by divine right. Thus in his *Admonition to Peace* (1525), Luther criticized the German lords for their tyranny over the peasants, but upbraided the peasants for even contemplating revolt against their masters. 'The fact that the rulers are wicked and unjust does not excuse disorder and rebellion, for the punishing of wickedness is not the responsibility of everyone, but of the worldly rulers who bear the sword.' The peasants, by assuming the role of judges and avenging what they regarded as wrong, were in effect assuming the place of God:

> It is true that the rulers do wrong when they suppress the gospel and oppress you in temporal matters. But you do far greater wrong when you not only suppress God's word, but tread it underfoot, invade his authority and law, and put yourselves above God. Besides, you take from the rulers their authority and right . . . What do you expect God and the world to think when you pass judgement and avenge yourselves on those who have injured you and even upon your rulers, whom God has appointed.

This understanding of the relation of church and state has been the object of intense criticism. Luther's social ethic has been described as 'defeatist' and 'quietist', encouraging the Christian to tolerate (or at least fail to oppose) unjust social structures. Luther preferred oppression to revolution. It also seemed to draw a cynical distinction between a private morality which is identifiably Christian and a public morality which is not. The Peasants' War seemed to show up the tensions within Luther's social ethic: the peasants were supposed to live in accordance with the private ethic of the Sermon on the Mount, turning the other cheek to their oppressors – while the princes were justified in using violent coercive means to re-establish social order.[5] And although Luther maintained that the magistrate had no authority in the church, except as a Christian believer, the technical distinction involved was so tenuous as to be unworkable. The way was opened to the eventual domination of the church by the state, which was to become a virtually universal feature of Lutheranism. The failure of the German church to oppose Hitler in the 1930s is widely seen as reflecting the inadequacies of Luther's political thought. Even Hitler, it appeared to some German Christians, was an instrument of God.[6]

David C. Steinmetz has helpfully identified five central premisses underlying Luther's confused political theology:[7]

1   Christian ethics, but not human morality, is grounded in the doctrine of justification by faith alone.

2   All Christians have a civic and social responsibility to perform. Some
     Christians may discharge these responsibilities by holding public
     office.
3   The morality of the Sermon on the Mount applies to the life of
     every Christian, but not necessarily to every decision which Chris-
     tians may make if they hold public office.
4   The state has been divinely ordained to achieve certain purposes,
     which the church cannot, and should not attempt to, achieve. In
     other words, their spheres of influence and authority are different,
     and must not be confused.
5   God rules the church through the gospel, but is obliged to rule the
     sinful world through law, wisdom, natural law and coercion.

Luther was no political thinker, and his limited and deficient experiments
in this field are best regarded as an attempt to accommodate himself to
the political realities of his time.[8] For the consolidation of the German Reformation, the full support of the German princes and magistrates was essential.
Luther appears to have been prepared to lend these rulers religious dignity in
return for their continued support for the Reformation. The end justified the
means. Luther appealed to a specific power group; but had a different group
held political power, he would almost certainly have appealed to that group
instead and justified *its* existence. Thus Luther was clearly a monarchist,
whereas Zwingli argued that all monarchs eventually degenerate into tyrants.
For Zwingli, aristocracy (even when it degenerates into oligarchy) is to be
preferred to monarchy. One wonders what would have happened if Luther
had been a reformer in oligarchical Zurich and Zwingli in electoral Wittenberg. The 'ifs' of history, even if unanswerable, are intriguing.

It is interesting to note the position of Martin Bucer on this point. Bucer's
sphere of influence was twofold. The pioneer of the Reformation in the great
imperial city of Strasbourg, he ended his days in Cambridge attempting
to give a new sense of direction to the faltering English Reformation. Now
Strasbourg was governed by a city council, and England by a monarch. Since
Luther's theology reflected a monarchical and Zwingli's an oligarchical form
of government, Bucer was obliged to tread warily, lest he offend either one
of two governments. It is thus perhaps no cause for surprise that we find
Bucer affirming that the precise form of temporal authority adopted is a
matter of indifference. Temporal authority may be individual or corporate,
based on a hereditary monarchy or an elected assembly: the essential point is
that whoever exercises such authority should be godly, open to the guidance
of the Holy Spirit.

A similar position was developed by John Calvin in the 1536 *Institutes*: any
form of government whatever – whether it be a monarchy, an aristocracy or

a democracy – is equally legitimate and equally competent to perform its divinely appointed office. Perhaps aware of the impact his ideas were to have in a variety of different political contexts, Calvin affirmed (despite his obvious misgivings concerning monarchy) that a scripturally determined understanding of the nature of the church was consistent with whatever form of civil government happened to be established.

Zwingli on the State and Magistrate

We have already noted the strong link in Zwingli's thought between the church and state, evident in his baptismal views (see pp. 186–7). From the beginning of his reforming ministry at Zurich, Zwingli appears to have recognized the political realities of the situation: Zurich could not be reformed without the consent and active involvement of the city council. For Zwingli, 'church' and 'state' were simply different ways of looking at the city of Zurich, rather than separate entities.[9] The life of the state does not differ from the life of the church, in that each demands what the other demands. Both the preacher and the ruler are under obligation to God, in that they have both been entrusted with establishing the rule of God over the city. Zwingli regarded Zurich as a theocracy, in the sense that the whole life of the city community was under the rule of God: minister and magistrate alike were charged with expounding and enforcing that rule.

There are obvious parallels between the theories of government associated with Luther and with Zwingli. It may be helpful to list them.

1 Both maintained that the need for such government is the result of sin. As Zwingli put it, 'If everyone rendered to God what they owed him, we should need neither prince nor ruler – indeed, we should never have left paradise.'

2 Both recognized that not all members of the community were Christians. While the proclamation of the gospel may convert some, there are those who will never be converted. (Both Luther and Zwingli, it must be remembered, were strongly predestinarian in their views: see pp. 132–5.) As government takes in the whole community, it is legitimate for the government to use force where necessary.

3 Those who exercise authority within the community do so with the authority of God. God exercises his authority through the magistrates.

4 Against the radicals, both Luther and Zwingli insisted that Christians may hold public office. For the radicals, holding such office involved political compromises which corrupted the Christian. For Luther and Zwingli, by

contrast, a believer was more likely to exercise power responsibily and chari-
tably than anyone else, and should therefore be encouraged to gain office for
that reason. Zwingli insisted that, without the fear of God, a ruler would
become a tyrant. Where Plato wished his kings to be philosophers, Zwingli
wished his aristocrats to be Christians.

5   Both Luther and Zwingli drew a distinction between private and public
morality. The commands of the Sermon on the Mount (for example, not to
resist evil, or to turn the other cheek) apply to the Christian as a private individual, but not to the Christian as the holder of a public office. Thus Zwingli
pointed out that Christ himself attacked the Pharisees, and did not turn his
other cheek when brought before the high priest.

6   Both Luther and Zwingli distinguished the types of righteousness associated with the Christian and the state. Zwingli argued that the gospel is
concerned with the promotion of inner righteousness, arising from the transformation of the individual through the hearing of the gospel, whereas the
state is concerned with the promotion of outward righteousness, arising from
the individual being constrained to keep the law. The gospel alters human
nature, whereas the state merely restrains human greed and evil, having no
positive power to alter human motivation. Luther emphasized the tension
between human and divine righteousness; whereas Zwingli stated that divine
righteousness is interior and human righteousness exterior, Luther suggested
that they are also mutually contradictory. The righteousness which Christians
are commanded to seek is diametrically opposed to the more cynical standards of righteousness employed by rulers.

For Zwingli, the city council derived its authority from God, whose Word
it was not in a position to judge or challenge. This insight appears to have
been of theoretical, rather than practical, importance. The First Zurich Disputation of 19 January 1523 (see p. 163) effectively ensured that the city
council was recognized as having the authority to interpret Scripture. While
Zwingli clearly understood the council to be *under* the Word of God, the city
council appears to have manœuvred itself into a position by which it was
really *over* the Word of God. Whoever interprets the Word of God in effect
has authority over it – whether that interpreter be the pope or a city council.
This led to the complaint that Zwingli allowed 'matters which ought to
belong to the whole church to be dealt with by the Two Hundred (the city
council) when the church of the whole city and neighborhood is seven thousand, more or less'.

But what form of government was to be preferred? Zwingli draws a distinction between three political systems: monarchy, oligarchy and democracy.
In his discussion of these systems, he displays a political realism which seems
to owe virtually nothing to any specifically Christian insight. In many ways,

his discussion of the question reflects similar discussions of antiquity, with an emphasis on historical rather than theoretical analysis. Monarchy is an arbitrary form of government, in which the ruler is selected on the basis of inadequate criteria. Monarchs are prone to degenerate into tyrants, and are difficult to replace when inadequate. And, Zwingli points out, there are obvious shortcomings in entrusting authority to one single individual. Democracy, by contrast, places authority in the hands of the whole people, but can easily degenerate into chaos. When this happens, individual interests are placed above those of the state, and the *res publica* suffers as a result. Aristocracy, however, possesses both a representative element and an accountability to the people, avoiding the shortcomings of both monarchy and democracy. It is the *via media* between these two deficient forms of government.

This position contrasts sharply with Luther's preference for a monarchical form of government. It also allows us to understand Zwingli's more positive attitude towards the resistance of tyranny. For Zwingli, tyranny was not to be tolerated. Although he occasionally denied that rulers may legitimately be killed, there are a number of passages which clearly imply that tyrannicide is acceptable.[10] Christians are under an obligation to obey God, rather than human beings – and that obedience may involve deposing or killing rulers. Zwingli was careful to lay down the conditions under which a ruler may be deposed. Murder, war and uprising were declared to be unacceptable: peaceable means must be employed wherever possible. Since Zwingli favoured an aristocratic (or, at worst, an oligarchic) form of government, he was able to point to a number of peaceful means by which such rulers might be deposed – for example, by the election of a replacement. Luther's situation was somewhat different: one disadvantage of a monarchical system of government is that the prince rules for life, making regicide one of the few options available for his removal. Zwingli, however, was able to advocate less drastic electoral means of deposing unsatisfactory rulers, thus protecting more tender consciences.

Bucer on Magistrate and Ministry

The consolidation of the magisterial Reformation owed much to the close integration of the roles of preacher and magistrate in the imperial city of Strasbourg under Martin Bucer.[11] Having been expelled from Geneva in 1538, it was to Bucer's Strasbourg that Calvin turned to receive both political refuge and ecclesiastical experience. While Bucer's relationship with the city council of Strasbourg was occasionally stormy, he nevertheless regarded that council as entrusted with a God-given task to reform the church. In view of the importance of Bucer's views, we may consider them before passing on to consider those of Calvin himself.

Bucer points out that in the New Testament period, the temporal authorities were non-Christian. God was therefore obliged to use other means – such as the agency of the Holy Spirit – to preserve and develop his church. But, Bucer argues, such has been the impact of the Christian faith since those early days that temporal authorities are now themselves Christian: God therefore uses such authorities in the sixteenth century, even if he used different ones in the first.

> At the time of the apostles and martyrs, the Lord wanted to accomplish everything by the power of his Spirit, so that the whole world might see that the crucified one was Lord, and that he rules in heaven over all. Therefore he allowed kings and all those who were powerful to act in complete defiance against him and his people. But when he had converted the authorities, he wished them truly to serve him with their office and power, which derives from him, and is committed to them only for the good of Christ's flock.

Whereas it is the task of the minister to preach the World of God, it is that of the magistrate to govern according to it. This might seem to suggest that preachers have authority over magistrates: however, in that the magistrates were responsible for the appointment of preachers, the possibility of tension was lessened. For Bucer, it was axiomatic that the magistracy was godly and open to the promptings of the Holy Spirit. In common with most urban reformed theologians, Bucer regarded 'city' and 'church' as so closely linked that this natural instinct for civic self- preservation directly advanced the cause of the Reformation.

Calvin on Magistrate and Ministry

Bucer's ideas were developed by John Calvin on his return from Strasbourg to Geneva in September 1541.[12] The rulers of Geneva, having broken free from external rule in 1536, found themselves without any coherent system of church order. All the ecclesiastical changes of the 1530s had been destructive, eventually leading to something approaching chaos. A comprehensive set of ecclesiastical ordinances was required, and Calvin was recalled to Geneva to help with this task. The magistrates were prepared to let Calvin have his way (within reason) in organizing the Genevan church, provided that their civil authority was not affected (a principle which they eventually regarded as compromised by Calvin's views on the role of the Consistory: see pp. 210–12). Calvin's original idea was that ecclesiastical discipline should rest with the Consistory, made up of pastors and twelve magistrates of their choice. This Consistory would have the right, for example, to excommunicate anyone whose moral conduct or religious beliefs were unacceptable. The magistrates, scenting a challenge to their authority, vigorously affirmed their right over all temporal matters. A compromise was reached, which Calvin interpreted as a recognition of the right of the Consistory to recommend excommunication and which the magistrates interpreted as a recognition of their authority to excommunicate. The history of Geneva over the next fifteen years indicates how unsatisfactory this compromise turned out to be.

For all the compromises made in light of the political realities of Geneva, the fundamental basis of Calvin's understanding of the relation of church and state is clear. While the political authority must not be allowed to abolish the spiritual, the Anabaptist view that the spiritual authority abrogates the political was unequivocally rejected. When the present order passes away at the day of judgement, there will be no need for a political authority – but while human beings remain tied to this earth, the political authority is essential in order 'to foster and maintain the external worship of God, to defend sound doctrine and the condition of the church, to adapt our conduct to human society, to form our manners to civil justice, to reconcile us to one another, to cherish peace and common tranquility'.

Calvin thus assigned to the magistrates two roles: the maintenance of political and ecclesiastical order and the provision of the teaching of right doctrine. Both the political and spiritual authorities were to use the distinctive resources committed to them by God for the disciplining of the same body of people.

> For the church has not the right of the sword to punish or restrain, has no power to coerce, no prison nor other punishments which the magistrate is wont to inflict. Then the object in view is not to punish the sinner against his will, but to obtain a profession of penitence by voluntary chastisement. The two things, then, are widely different, because neither does the church assume anything to herself which is proper to the magistrate, nor is the magistrate competent to do what is done by the church.

The political authority was to use its right to coercion (generally through the threat of exile or execution; Geneva did not have a long-term prison) and the spiritual authority its teaching ministry for the promotion of virtue. Calvin also stated that the ministry had the right to explain to the magistracy what the Word of God required in a given situation, suggesting that the ministry was the legislative and the magistracy the executive arm of the Genevan theocracy. However, the magistracy appears to have felt able to resist the ministry sufficiently frequently to weaken the latter's role in the government of the city.

For Calvin, both magistrates and ministers were committed to the same task, the difference between them lying in the tools they had available and their respective spheres of authority. Their responsibilities were complementary rather than competitive. Both magistrates and ministers were agents and servants of the same God, committed to the same cause, differing only in their spheres and means of action. Where the Anabaptists regarded church discipline as a matter for the church itself,[13] Calvin regarded it as a matter of public concern, within the legitimate authority of the magistracy. Although Calvin's Geneva was troubled more than once through tensions between the two authorities, spiritual and temporal, the strong sense of social organization which became an essential part of 'Calvinism' may be traced back to the political theorizing of Calvin's Geneva. When the Puritans set foot in the New World, they brought with them not merely a religion, but a social vision, whose roots lay in a small town in modern-day Switzerland.

One further aspect of Calvin's political thought is of interest. Like Zwingli, Calvin had a profound mistrust of monarchy. Monarchs are prone to become tyrants; they are motivated by their personal concerns, rather than the well-being of their people. Even the Old Testament kings were prone to this tendency; and their sixteenth-century equivalents are worse. Although Calvin tends to condemn monarchs rather than monarchy,[14] his misgivings concerning the very idea of absolute rule by one individual are unmistakable. The subsequent threat posed by 'Calvinism' to monarchies throughout Europe, evident in the challenge to and subsequent execution of Charles I of England (1649), testifies to the subsequent importance of Genevan political theology. The relative merits of Lutheranism and 'Calvinism' were often assessed on the basis of their political views, the former being regarded as monarchical, the latter as republican. The political circumstances of the founders of these religious systems seem to have become elevated into fundamental beliefs of those systems.

On the basis of the above analysis, it will be obvious that the phrase 'Calvin's Geneva' is misleading. Calvin was no Genevan dictator, ruling the population with a rod of iron. He was not even a citizen of Geneva throughout his time there, and was thus denied access to political authority. His status was simply that of a pastor who was in no position to dictate to the magisterial authorities who administered the city. Indeed, those authorities retained to the end the right to dismiss Calvin, even if they chose not to exercise that right. As a member of the Consistory, he was certainly able to make representations to the magistracy on behalf of the ministers – representations which were frequently ignored, however. In any case, Calvin had no *legal* right to act independently of the ministry, whose collegiality he is known to have valued and respected. Calvin's influence over Geneva rested ultimately not in his formal legal standing (which was insignificant) but in his considerable personal authority as a preacher and pastor.

For further reading

Heinrich Bornkamm, *Luther's World of Thought* (St Louis, Mo., 1958), pp. 218–72.
——, *Luther's Doctrine of the Two Kingdoms* (Philadelphia, 1966).
Harro Höpfl, *The Christian Polity of John Calvin* (Cambridge, 1985).
—— (ed.), *Luther and Calvin on Secular Authority* (Cambridge, 1991).
David C. Steinmetz, 'Luther and the Two Kingdoms', in *Luther in Context* (Blooming-ton, Ind., 1986), pp. 112–25.
W. P. Stephens, *The Theology of Huldrych Zwingli* (Oxford, 1986), pp. 282–310.
T. F. Torrance, *Kingdom and Church: A Study in the Theology of the Reformation* (Edin-burgh, 1956).

12

The Diffusion of the Thought of the Reformation

In previous chapters, we explored some of the major themes of the emerging theology of the Reformation, including some of the debates within the movement that would contribute to its diversification and polarization. Yet this has largely ignored a major question: how were the ideas and practices of the Reformation diffused throughout Europe? The present chapter examines some of the means by which the beliefs and practices of the Reformation were disseminated beyond their original contexts.

The Physical Agencies of Diffusion

In an earlier chapter, we noted the means by which the ideas of the Italian Renaissance were diffused to northern Europe. The three main agencies of transmission were identified as people, books and correspondence (see p. 46–7). Those factors continue to be of importance in relation to the spread of the Reformation. In what follows, we shall look at some general issues concerning the transmission of the ideas of the Reformation, before looking at some more specific items in subsequent sections.

The Vernacular

One of the most distinctive emphases of the Reformation was the use of the vernacular. Luther published his major reforming treatises of 1520 in German, to ensure a wide readership for his ideas. Similarly, Zwingli ensured that his ideas were published in his native Swiss-German, and Calvin in his native French. The result was not merely an enhanced accessibility of the ideas and practices of the Reformation; the shape of most modern western European languages were decisively shaped by the writings of the reformers, particularly through the publication of the Bible in the vernacular. The Reformers were also aware of the importance of preaching in the vernacular, and of ensuring that the liturgy was also understood by all those taking part in worship.

One of the most significant moments in the history of the Reformation is Martin Luther's decision in 1520 to switch from being an academic reformer (arguing in Latin to an academic public) to a popular reformer (arguing in German to a broader public). The Reformation witnessed a major challenge being laid down to existing understandings of the way that the Bible could and should be read, structures of the church, and Christian doctrine. Time and time again, the reformers appealed over the heads of the clergy and theologians to the people. The people, they insisted, must decide. The practice of the Swiss Reformation, in which a public disputation between evangelicals and catholics in the vernacular was followed by a plenary vote by the assembly body of citizens on whether to accept the Reformation, reflects this basic principle.

The decision to use the vernacular was closely linked with the publication of books, such as Calvin's 1541 French edition of the *Institutes of the Christian Religion*, written in the vernacular. This naturally leads us to consider the importance of books as agents of transmission of the thought of the Reformation.

Books

The invention and widespread adoption of printing revolutionized the transmission of ideas. The diffusion of the ideas of both the Renaissance and Reformation was closely linked with printing. There is no doubt that the relative ease with which books and religious pamphlets could be transported across national boundaries contributed significantly to the spread of the Reformation. Luther never visited England; his ideas, however, were surprisingly widely discussed and assessed there, simply because the flow of his books into the country proved virtually impossible to staunch.

A similar situation can be discerned in France. Calvin never returned to France after 1536. (Although Calvin spent 1538–41 in Strasbourg, this imperial city was not, as it is today, part of France). Yet Calvin's works, and especially those published in the French language, found a substantial readership in Paris. A crucial turning point is marked by the publication of the French-language edition of the *Institutes of the Christian Religion* in 1541. Coherently expressed and carefully justified radical reforming doctrines became available within France in a language which most could understand. On 1 July, 1542, the Parisian authorities directed that all works containing heterodox doctrines, especially Calvin's *Institutes*, should be surrendered to the authorities within three days. The visitation of bookshops became an important element of the official attempt to suppress the growing heterodox movement. In the following year the Parisian Faculty of Theology drew up a list of 65 titles, 22 in Latin and 43 in French (although two items are unwittingly duplicated, making 41 in total), which were to be censured with immediate effect. Of the 36 texts which it is possible to identify and date with anything approaching probability, 23 were printed in Geneva. It seems that the trade route between the two French-speaking cities was being used to import leading works of the Reformation into the French capital.

Calvin's *Institutes* were thus seen as the spearhead of a Genevan assault upon the French church, mediated through the printed word. On 23 June, 1545, an extended list of prohibited works was published. Of its 121 titles in French, almost half were printed in Geneva. The reaction from the booksellers of Paris was immediate: they protested that they would be ruined if they were prohibited from selling such books. It seems there was a not inconsiderable market for works which were considered heretical.

Yet the flood of Genevan literature into Paris continued. The attempt to regulate the public sale of books to exclude those originating from Geneva merely forced the trade to go underground. Until the wars of religion finally put a brake on the expansion of the Genevan publishing industry's sector of the French religious market in the years 1565–80, it was not difficult to obtain such works in Paris. Laurent de Normandie, Calvin's friend and bookseller, found the contraband book trade so profitable that he even emigrated to Geneva, in order that he might publish such books, rather than just sell them.

The Interchange of People

In an earlier chapter (pp. 46–7), we noted how one of the major means by which the leading themes of the Italian Renaissance were transmitted to northern Europe was through individual scholars visiting Italy, and taking the ideas of the Renaissance home with them. It should not be any cause for surprise that a similarly important role was played by such individuals in relation to the Reformation. Luther's ideas were taken to England by both William Tyndale and Robert Barnes, the former of which is believed and the latter known to have studied under Luther at Wittenberg.

The repressive policies introduced under Mary Tudor led many English Protestants to seek refuge in European Protestant cities (such as Frankfurt, Geneva and Zurich). On their return to England, these individuals brought the experience of reformed church life back to their homeland, accelerating the pace of Protestant reform under Elizabeth I. Twelve of the eighteen bishops appointed by Elizabeth I in the aftermath of the mass episcopal resignations of 1559 had sought refuge in Europe during Mary's reign.

As noted above, severe limits were placed upon the movements of leading Reformers. Luther, for example, found that the ban placed upon him in the 1520s prevented him from travelling outside his native Saxony. His younger Wittenberg colleague Philipp Melanchthon thus had to travel on his behalf, promoting the Lutheran Reformation elsewhere in Germany. Similarly, Calvin's movements were restricted. While at the peak of his influence, he was virtually confined to his adopted city of Geneva. Yet Calvin was still able to exercise influence by proxy. This influence was perhaps at its greatest in his native France, the target of a major campaign of infiltration organized from Geneva from 1555 onwards.

In response to requests from French-speaking reformed congregations, particularly in the south-east of the country, Calvin arranged for reformed pastors to be smuggled into the region. Secrecy was essential to the entire operation, at both the Genevan and French ends of the operation. Safe houses, complete with hiding places, were established a day's journey apart. An underground network, similar to that employed by the French Resistance during the Second World War, allowed the men from Geneva to slip across the ill-defined frontier into France. The Company of Pastors made every effort to maintain total secrecy, even to the point of concealing its operations from the theoretically all-knowing city council.

By 1557, however, the Company of Pastors realized it could not hope to keep its activities abroad clandestine indefinitely; late that year Calvin appeared before the city council to explain the situation, and request permission to send further agents. The city council was evidently aware of the serious danger posed to the city by these activities: if it were thought that the Genevan government itself was organizing the infiltration of religious activists, it could be held guilty of seditious action against its larger neighbour, with unpredictable (but probably unpleasant) consequences. The council, however, agreed to the secret continuation of the policy, providing that they could not be held to be associated with it. This successful policy was unquestionably one of the factors contributing to the rapid growth of Calvinism in France, which eventually led to the outbreak of the Wars of Religion in the region.

Other Calvinist-minded intellectuals travelled abroad to propagate his ideas, perhaps most successfully in England. Under the reign of Edward VI, leading divines, either Calvinist or sympathetic to Calvinism, were encouraged to settle in England, and give a sense of theological direction to the nascent reformed church. Individuals such as Martin Bucer, Pietro Martire Vermigli (perhaps better known as Peter Martyr) and John à Lasco gave the Church of England a new impetus which moved it away from its earlier flirtations with Lutheranism, and towards at least some of the ideas associated with Calvin's Geneva. In May 1559, John Knox returned to his native Scotland after a period of exile in Geneva; within days of his arrival, riots broke out at Perth, precipitating the Reformation crisis.

Our attention now turns to some of the publications which were responsible for the diffusion of the thought of the Reformation. Having considered some general factors involved in that process, we now turn to deal with some more specific works which are known to have been instrumental in the dissemination of the new theology of this period. We begin by considering the 'catechism', by which the ideas of the Reformation could be taught to a new generation.

The Catechisms

Although what would now be agreed to be 'catechisms' can be found in the medieval church, it is generally agreed that the extensive use of catechisms is especially associated with the Reformation. A visitation of Lutheran churches in Saxony over the period 1528–9 showed that most pastors and just about every layperson were ignorant of basic Christian teachings. Luther was shocked by his findings, and decided to put in place measures to increase public knowledge of basic Christian teachings.

The first result of Luther's new concern in this area made its appearance in April 1529. Although Luther himself termed it a 'German Catechism', it is now more generally known as the 'Greater Catechism'. The work provides a detailed analysis of the Ten Commandments, the Apostles' Creed and the Lord's Prayer. These sections were followed by discussions of the two sacraments of the church – baptism and the 'sacrament of the altar' (or Communion service). The work does not show Luther at his best. It draws upon earlier sermonical material, and was not written specifically for the purpose of catechizing. As a result, it failed to meet up to its goals.

This was followed in May 1529 by what is now known as the *Lesser Catechism*. This work was written specifically for this purpose, and shows a lightness of touch, an ease of communication, and a general simplicity of expression which ensured that it was widely used and appreciated. The work was a remarkable success, and was widely adopted within Lutheran institutions. Its question-and-answer format was ideally suited to learning by rote, and the work was widely adopted within the schools of the region. It is important to note that both Luther's 1529 catechisms were written in German, the language of the people. Luther avoided the use of Latin for this purpose, recognizing the severe limitations which the use of this scholarly language would have on the appeal and readership of the works.

To illustrate the approach Luther adopted, we may consider the following passage from the *Lesser Catechism*. Note particularly the question-and-answer format, designed to facilitate both teaching and learning.[1]

Q.   What is baptism?

A.   Baptism is not just water on its own, but it is water used according to God's command and linked with God's Word.

Q.   What is this Word of God?

A.   Our Lord Christ, as recorded in Matthew 28:19, said, 'Go therefore and make disciples of all nations, baptizing them in the name of the Father and of the Son and of the Holy Spirit'.

Q.   What gifts or benefits does Baptism bring?

A.   It brings about the forgiveness of sins, saves use from death and the devil, and grants eternal blessedness to all who believe, as the Word and promise of God declare.

Q.   What is this Word and promise of God?

A.   Our Lord Christ, as recorded in Mark 16:16, said, 'Anyone who believes and is baptized will be saved; but those who do not believe will be condemned'.

Q.   How can water bring about such a great thing?

A.   Water does not; but it is the Word of God with and through the water, and our faith which trusts in the Word of God in the water. For without the Word of God, that water is nothing but water, and there is no Baptism. But when it is linked with the Word of God, it is a Baptism, that is, a gracious water of life and a bath of new birth in the Holy Spirit.

The Reformed churches were not slow to appreciate the importance of this literary genre, and the educational advantages which it so clearly offered. After some experimentation, Calvin finally produced the 'Geneva Catechism' in French (1542) and Latin (1545). This catechism was widely used within the Reformed constituency until 1563. It was at this point that the 'Heidelberg Catechism' made its appearance. The origins of this major work lie in the growth of the Reformed church within Germany, particularly within the Palatinate. Elector Frederick III commissioned two Reformed theologians (Kaspar Olevianus and Zacharias Ursinus) to produce a catechism suitable for use in his churches. The result was a German language catechism of 129 questions, which could be arranged in 52 blocks of material to permit regular teaching throughout the year. The leading themes of the Reformed faith are set out in the by-now obligatory question-and-answer format. For example, here is a section of material dealing with the question of the use of images within churches:[2]

> Question 96. What does God require in the next commandment?
> Answer: That we should not portray God in any way, nor worship him in any other manner than he has commanded in his Word.

> Question 97. So should we not make any use of images?
> Answer: God cannot and should not be depicted in any way. As for creatures, although they may indeed be depicted, God forbids making use of or having any likeness of them, in order to worship them or to use them to serve him.

> Question 98. But should we allow pictures instead of books in churches, for the benefit of the unlearned?
> Answer: No. For we should not presume to be wiser than God, who does not want Christendom to be taught by means of dumb idols, but through the living preaching of his Word.

The extensive Protestant use of catechisms, and the significant results that they achieved, led their Catholic opponents to develop the format. Earlier Catholic catechisms tended to avoid the question-and-answer format, and offered extensive discussions of points of theological importance. An excellent example of this may be found in Johann Dietenberger's 1537 catechism, which takes the form of a discussion of the Apostles' Creed, the Lord's Prayer, the Ten Commandments, the 'Hail Mary', and the seven sacraments. However, the superiority of the question-and-answer approach became obvious, and was incorporated into Peter Canisius's three catechisms, published over the period 1554–8. This work was published in Latin, as was the more substantial Tridentine Catechism of 1566. While its cumbersome format ensured that it was hardly ever used, the work's appearance in the aftermath of the Council of Trent may be regarded as an important recognition of the significance of the genre.

Confessions of Faith

We have already noted how the Reformation placed considerable emphasis upon the authority of Scripture. Yet the Bible needed to be interpreted. As the controversy between the magisterial and radical reformers made clear, there were issues of interpretation which were both divisive and elusive. There was clearly a need for some form of 'official' means of setting out the ideas of the Reformation, to avoid confusion. This role was played by the 'Confessions of Faith'. In view of the importance of these documents, we may consider their place within the thought of the Reformation.

The magisterial Reformation, while placing considerable emphasis upon the authority of Scripture, also recognized a role for the Christian consensus of the past – an idea which we discussed earlier in terms of 'Tradition 1' (see pp. 146–7). In general terms, Protestant theologians can be thought of as recognizing three levels or strata of authority:

1 *Scripture.* This was regarded by the magisterial Reformers as possessing supreme authority in matters of Christian belief and conduct.

2 *The Creeds of Christendom.* These documents, such as the Apostles' Creed and the Nicene Creed, were regarded by the magisterial reformers as representing the consensus of the early church, and as being accurate and authoritative intrepretations of Scripture. Although they were to be regarded a *derivative* or *secondary* in terms of their authority, they were seen as an important check against the individualism of the radical reformation (which generally declined to regard these creeds as having any authority). The authority of the creeds were recognized by both Protestants and Catholics, as well as by the various constituent elements within the mainline Reformation.

3 *Confessions of Faith.* These documents were regarded as authoritative by specific groupings within the Reformation. Thus the Augsburg Confession (1530) was recognized by early Lutheran churches as possessing authority. Other groups within the Reformation did not, however, regard it in this way. Specific confessions of faith were, for example, drawn up by other groups within the Reformation. Some were linked with the Reformation in specific cities – for example, the First Confession of Basel (1534) and the Geneva Confession (1536).

The basic pattern within the Reformation was thus to acknowledge Scripture as possessing primary and universal authority; the Creeds as secondary and universal authority; and the Confessions as tertiary and local authority (in that such confessions were only regarded as binding by a denomination or church in a specific region). The development of the Reformed wing of the Reformation was complex, with the result that a number of Confessions – each linked with a specific region – came to be influential. The following are of particular importance.

Date	Title	Geographical region
1559	Gallic Confession	France
1560	Scottish Confession	Scotland
1561	Belgic Confession	The Lowlands
1563	Thirty-Nine Articles	England
1566	Second Helvetic Confession	western Switzerland

To illustrate the role of the Confessions, we may consider an extract from the Gallic Confession of Faith, published in French in 1559. (Note, incidentally, the importance of the vernacular.) This extract sets out clearly the characteristic Protestant understanding of the Canon of Scripture. Note how each book is specified by name, with variants of the name being noted – for example, in the case of Proverbs and Revelation. Note also that the letter to the Hebrews is not ascribed to St Paul, but is treated as an independent writing. This is followed by an affirmation of the authority of Scripture, in which the authority in question is clearly stated to be inherent to the Bible, rather than something which is imposed by the church. It should also be noted how the Creeds are recognized as authoritative on account of their consonance with Scripture.[3]

3. This Holy Scripture is contained in the canonical books of the Old and New Testaments, as follows: the five books of Moses, namely Genesis, Exodus, Leviticus, Numbers, Deuteronomy; then Joshua, Judges, Ruth, the first and second books of Samuel, the first and second books of the Kings, the first and second books of the Chronicles, otherwise called Paralipomenon, the first book of Ezra; then Nehemiah, the book of Esther, Job, the Psalms of David, the Proverbs or Maxims of Solomon; the book of Ecclesiastes, called the Preacher, the Song of Solomon; then the books of Isaiah, Jeremiah, Lamentations of Jeremiah, Ezekiel, Daniel, Hosea, Joel, Amos, Obadiah, Jonah, Micah, Nahum, Habakkuk, Zephaniah, Haggai, Zechariah, Malachi; then the holy gospel according to St Matthew, according to St Mark, according to St Luke, and according to St John; then the second book of St Luke, otherwise called the Acts of the Apostles; then the letters of St Paul: one to the Romans, two to the Corinthians, one to the Galatians, one to the Ephesians, one to the Philippians, one to the Colossians, two to the Thessalonians, two to Timothy, one to Titus, one to Philemon; then the letter to the Hebrews, the letter of St James, the first and second letters of St Peter, the first, second, and third letters of St John, the letter of St Jude; and then the Apocalypse, or Revelation of St John.

4. We know these books to be canonical, and the sure rule of our faith, not so much by the common accord and consent of the Church, as by the testimony and inward persuasion of the Holy Spirit (*par le tesmoignage et interieure persuasion du saint espirit*), which enables us to distinguish them from other ecclesiastical books which, however useful, can never become the basis for any articles of faith.

5. We believe that the Word contained in these books has proceeded from God, and receives its authority from him alone, and not from human beings. And in that it is the rule of all truth, containing all that is necessary for the service of God and for our salvation, it is not lawful for anyone, even for angles, to add to it, to take away from it, or to change it. It therefore follows that no authority, whether of antiquity, or custom, or numbers, or human wisdom, or judgments, or proclamations, or edicts, or decrees, or councils, or visions, or miracles,

should be opposed to these Holy Scriptures, but, on the contrary, all things should be examined, regulated, and reformed according to them. And therefore we confess the three creeds as follows: the Apostles', the Nicene, and the Athanasian, because they are in accordance with the Word of God.

We now turn to consider one of the most influential means of transmission of the ideas of the Reformation, in their Reformed embodiment – Calvin's *Institutes of the Christian Religion*.

Calvin's *Institutes of the Christian Religion*

The first edition of the *Institutes of the Christian Religion* was published by the Basle printers Thomas Platter and Balthasar Lasius in March 1536. The translation of the Latin title – *Institutio Christianae Religionis* – poses some problems. The Latin word *Institutio* suggests a parallel with the Institutes of Justinian, a foundational legal code of the classical period, familiar to Calvin from his Orléans period. In terms of its structure or content, however, Calvin's work bears little resemblance to a legal code.

Erasmus employed the same Latin word in a rather different sense, meaning 'instruction', or perhaps even 'primer' (for example, his *Institutio principis Christiani* of 1516, which may have served as an inspiration for Calvin's title). The English word 'Institution' perhaps conveys another of Calvin's concerns – to return to a more authentic form of Christianity than that encountered in the late medieval period. It is Christianity as originally instituted which concerns Calvin, not as it was developed (or deformed, in Calvin's view) in the Middle Ages. In practice, most English translations choose to render the Latin title as *Institutes of the Christian Religion*, despite the alternatives suggested by the Latin original, and we shall follow this practice.

The first edition of the Institutes was modelled on Luther's *Lesser Catechism* (see pp. 239–40) of 1529. Both its structure and substance indicate the extent to which Calvin has drawn upon this major educational work of the early German Reformation. Its 516 small-format pages comprise six chapters, the first four of which are modelled on Luther's catechism. Calvin, however, is able to engage in more detailed discussion of questions than Luther, for the simple reason that his work is not a question and answer catechism which had to be learned by rote. The first chapter is essentially an exposition of the Ten Commandments (or Decalogue); the second is an exposition of the Apostle's Creed. Where Luther's discussion of the creed has three sections (the Father, the Son, and the Holy Spirit), Calvin adds a substantial fourth section on the church, recognizing both the theoretical and practical importance of this question. After expositions of 'The Law', 'Faith', 'Prayer' and 'The Sacraments', Calvin includes two chapters of a more polemical nature on 'false sacraments' and 'the liberty of a Christian'.

The second edition of the Institutes dates from Calvin's Strasbourg period, and was published in Latin in 1539. The most obvious and important difference between the volumes is that of size: the new work is about three times as long as the first edition of 1536, with seventeen chapters instead of six. Two opening chapters now deal with the knowledge of God and the knowledge of human nature. Additional material was added on the doctrine of the Trinity, the relation of the Old and New Testaments, penitence, justification by faith, the nature and relation of providence and predestination, and the nature of the Christian life. Although the work retained much material drawn from the earlier edition, it is evident that its character and status have changed. It is no longer a catechism; it is well on the way to being a definitive statement of the nature of the Christian faith, inviting comparison with the *Summa Theologiae* of Thomas Aquinas.

'My object in this work,' wrote Calvin, 'is to so prepare and train students of sacred theology for the study of the word of God that they might have an easy access into it, and be able to proceed in it without hindrance.' In other words, the book is intended to be a guide to scripture, functioning as a *vade mecum* and commentary to its often intricate and complex depths of meaning.

This is an important point, as Calvin himself later stressed, in that it establishes Calvin's *Institutes* as the primary resource for his religious thought. His other writings – such as biblical commentaries and sermons – are of secondary importance in this respect, whatever their merits might otherwise be. In writing his *Institutes*, Calvin intended to provide what is essentially a doctrinal commentary on scripture, allowing the reader of scripture direct access to its authentic meaning.

A French edition of the *Institutes* was published in 1541. Curiously, the work is not a direct translation of the 1539 edition; there are several points at which material from the 1536 edition, although altered in 1539, has been included, in translation, in that of 1541. This has led to speculation that Calvin may originally have intended to produce a French translation of the 1536 edition, and, abandoning this project, included material already translated into the 1541 edition without the modifications introduced in 1539. The work shows numerous minor alterations, all of which may be explained with reference to the projected readership. Scholarly points likely to cause difficulty are omitted (for example, all Greek words and references to Aristotle are omitted), and additional material likely to be familiar to the intended readership (for example, French proverbs and idioms) are added.

A further Latin edition appeared in 1543, with a French translation in 1545. Now expanded to 21 chapters, it included as its most significant addition a major section on the doctrine of the church. Minor alterations include the addition of two chapters on vows and human traditions, and the creation of a separate chapter for the material relating to angels. The impact of experience upon Calvin's religious reflections is evident in this edition, particularly in the discussion of the importance of ecclesiastical organization.

Despite the obvious merits of this edition, an inherent defect, already noticeable in 1539, now becomes transparently obvious. The work is poorly organized. New chapters are added, without thought being given to the overall impact such addition has upon the structure and organization of the work. Many chapters are impossibly long, without any attempt to subdivide them into sections. The Latin edition of 1550, and the subsequent French translation of 1551, attempted to remedy this deficiency by subdividing their 21 chapters into paragraphs. A few additions may be noted, such as new sections dealing with biblical authority and human conscience. The fundamental flaw remains, however: the edition of 1550, like that of 1543, must be regarded as a remarkably poorly organized work.

Recognizing both the need for total revision and the limited time available in which to achieve this (illness was a recurring feature of Calvin's final years), the reformer decided to recast the entire work. Surprisingly few additions are made; those that were made are generally unattractive, reflecting Calvin's growing irritability and tendency to abuse and vilify his opponents. The most obvious and positive change is the total reordering of the material, which virtually restores unity to what had almost degenerated into a series of unrelated fragments. The material is now distributed among four 'books', arranged as follows:

1   The knowledge of God the creator;
2   the knowledge of God the redeemer;
3   the manner of participation in the grace of Jesus Christ; and
4   the external means or aids which God uses to bring us to Jesus Christ.

The 21 chapters of 1551 are now expanded to 80 chapters, each carefully subdivided for ease of reading, distributed over these four books. It is possible that Calvin adapted the fourfold structure of the edition of 1543 to create the new division of material. An alternative explanation, however, is that he noticed and adopted the fourfold division of material in the *Four Books of the Sentences* of Peter Lombard, a seminal medieval theologian to whom Calvin often refers. Was Calvin setting himself up as the Protestant successor to Peter Lombard, and his *Institutes* as the successor to his great theological textbook? We shall never know. What we do know is that the *Institutes* were now firmly established as the most influential theological work of the Protestant Reformation, eclipsing in importance the rival works of Luther, Melanchthon and Zwingli.

The success of the 1559 *Institutes* reflects its superb organization. As noted earlier, Philipp Melanchthon established the definitive pattern for Lutheran works of systematic theology in 1521, through the publication of his 'Commonplaces' (*Loci Communes*). In its first edition, this work simply treated a number of subjects of obvious relevance to the Lutheran Reformation. Gradually, however, polemical and pedagogical considerations obliged Melanchthon to expand the work considerably. Melanchthon met this challenge in a surprisingly inadequate manner; he merely added additional material, regardless of the impression of a lack of unified structure this created. It soon became evident that this way of handling material was clumsy and disorganized, incapable of achieving the systematic analysis needed for the theological debates of the late sixteenth and seventeenth centuries.

Calvin, however, bequeathed to his heirs an intensely systematic and organized structure, which proved ideally suited not merely to the needs of his own generation, but also for those of at least a century to come. Lutheranism never really recovered from the false start given to it by Melanchthon; the intellectual domination of Protestantism by theologians of the Reformed tradition is due both to the substance and structure of Calvin's final edition of the *Institutes*.

Calvin's *Institutes* were widely read and appreciated in western Europe, often to the point of being cited extensively in other works. The anonymous Italian treatise *The Benefits of Christ* (1541) – which rapidly attained the status of a religious best-seller before being suppressed by the Inquisition – draws heavily upon the 1539 edition of the *Institutes*. Calvin's work was evidently familiar to front-rank Protestant theologians in the Netherlands by the later 1550s. The work rapidly established itself as a neat and elegant one-stop and free-standing introduction to the ideas of the second wave of the Reformation. Where Calvinism took root at the institutional level, it had often been preceded at the intellectual level by the *Institutes*.

The success of Calvin's 1559 *Institutes* gave rise to a publishing spin-off – the 'summary' or 'compendium'. Even in the sixteenth century, numerous abridgements of this work were in circulation, apparently enjoying considerable commercial success. In 1562, Augustin Marlorat published a set of indexes to the work, facilitating the location of subjects and biblical passages within the work. In 1576, Nicolas Colladon, one of Calvin's early biographers, produced an edition which included brief marginal summaries of the contents of significant passages. Thomas Vautrollier, the Huguenot refugee who became on of London's more important religious publishers, printed two study guides to the *Institutes*: Edmund Bunny's *Compendium* (1576) attempted to deal with

Calvin's difficult style and subtleties of argumentation for the benefit of perplexed students. Guillaume Delaune (a Huguenot refugee who Anglicized his name as Williame Lawne) produced a summary of the *Institutes* in a mere 370 pages seven years later. In addition to summarizing Calvin, the work provided flow charts or diagrams to allow the puzzled reader to follow the intricate structure of the work. Other 'study guides' were published by Caspar Olvianus (1586), Johannes Piscator (1589), and Daniel de Coulogne, also known as Colonius (1628). Through their medium, Calvin became increasingly accessible and comprehensible to an ever-widening circle or readers.

For further reading

A. Cochrane (ed.), *Reformed Confessions of the Sixteenth Century* (Philadelphia, 1966).

W. Forrell and J. McCue (eds), *Confessing One Faith: A Joint Commentary on the Augusburg Confession by Lutheran and Catholic Theologians* (Minneapolis, 1982).

W. P. Haugaard, *Elizabeth and the English Reformation* (Cambridge, 1968), pp. 233–90.

R. M. Kingdon (ed.), *The Formula of Concord: Quadricentennial Essays* (Kirksville, MO, 1977).

H. Robinson-Hammerstein (ed.), *The Transmission of Ideas in the Lutheran Reformation* (Blackrock, Co. Dublin, 1989).

T. F. Torrance, *The School of Faith: The Catechisms of the Reformed Church* (London, 1959).

V. Vajta (ed.), *Confessio Augustana: Commemoration and Self-Examination* (Stuttgart, 1980).

13

The Thought of the English Reformation

Much of the discussion in this volume has concentrated on the Reformation in Continental Europe. The Reformation, however, also had an impact in England, in which it took a distinctive course. In view of the considerable interest and importance of the Reformation in England, the present chapter will consider its leading themes. We begin by exploring the origins of the English Reformation.

The Origins of the English Reformation: Henry VIII

Recent studies of English church life on the eve of the Reformation have pointed to its vitality and diversity. There is no doubt that there was some degree of internal dissatisfaction with the state of the English church in the late Middle Ages. Visitation records show a degree of concern being felt at episcopal level over the low quality of the clergy, and misgivings being expressed over various aspects of church life. There were also clear signs of external dissatisfaction. Hostility towards the clergy in many places, most notably in London, was the cause of much concern. Nevertheless, animosity towards the clergy was by no means universal. In parts of England – such as Lancashire and Yorkshire – the clergy were, on the whole, well-liked, and there was no great enthusiasm for any radical change.

Luther's ideas began to be discussed in the early 1520s. Perhaps the greatest interest in his writings at this stage was among academics, particularly at Cambridge University. The 'White Horse' group, which met at a long-vanished tavern of that name, included some of the future leaders of the Reformation in England. Luther's doctrine of justification by faith, along with his criticisms of certain aspects of late medieval catholicism, had considerable appeal. It is entirely possible that the extent of that appeal may have been enhanced through the influence of Lollardy, a pre-reformational movement, indigenous to England, which was severely critical of many aspects of church life (see pp. 35–6).

Nevertheless, the evidence suggests that the origins of the Reformation cannot be convincingly attributed to criticism of the late medieval church, or to Lutheran influence. These factors may well have served as catalysts to that Reformation, once it had begun. The evidence strongly points to the personal influence of Henry VIII having been of fundamental importance to the origins and subsequent direction of the English Reformation.

The background lies in Henry's concern to ensure a smooth transition of power after his death through producing a son as heir to the English throne. His marriage to Catherine of Aragon had produced a daughter, the future queen, Mary Tudor. The marriage had not only failed to produce the requisite son and heir; it also reflected the political realities of an earlier generation, which saw an alliance between England and Spain as essential to a sound foreign policy. The weakness of this assumption had become clear by 1525, when Charles V declined to marry Henry's daughter by Catherine. Henry therefore began the process by which he could divorce Catherine.

Under normal circumstances, this procedure might not have encountered any formidable obstacles. An appeal to the pope to annul the marriage could have been expected to have secured the desired outcome. However, the situation was not normal. Rome was under virtual siege by the army of Charles V, and the pope (Clement VII) was feeling somewhat insecure. Catherine of Aragon was the aunt of Charles V, and it was inevitable that the pope would wish to avoid offending the emperor at such a sensitive moment. The request for a divorce failed. As if to add insult to injury, Clement VII informed Henry that he would be excommunicated if he married again.

Henry's response was to begin a program of persuasion, designed to assert both the independence of England as a separate province of the church, and the autonomy of the English king. On 3 November, 1529, Henry convened a parliament which attempted to reduce the power of both church and clergy. The English clergy initially refused to concede these points, prompting Henry to undertake more severe measures in order to persuade them. The most important of these took place over the period 1530–1, during which Henry argued that the English clergy, by virtue of their support for Rome, were guilty of *praemunire* (a technical offence which can be thought of as a form of treason, in that it involves allegiance to a foreign power – namely, the papacy). With this threat hanging over them, the clergy reluctantly agreed to at least some of Henry's demands for recognition of his ecclesiastical authority.

Henry was presented with an opportunity for advancement of his aims when the Archbishop of Canterbury, William Warham, died in August 1532. Henry replaced Warham with Thomas Cranmer, who had earlier indicated his

strong support for Henry's divorce proceedings. Cranmer was finally consecrated (possibly against his will) on 30 March, 1533. Meanwhile, Henry had
begun an affair with Anne Boleyn. Anne became pregnant in December 1532.
The pregnancy raised all kinds of legal niceties. Henry's marriage to
Catherine of Aragon was annulled by an English court in May 1533, allowing Anne to be crowned queen on 1 June. Her daughter, Elizabeth Tudor, was
born on 7 September.

Henry's divorce of Catherine immediately led to the threat of excommunication. Henry now determined to follow through the course of action on
which he had embarked, by which his supreme political and religious authority within England would be recognized. A series of Acts were imposed in
1534. The *Succession Act* declared that the crown would pass to Henry's children. The *Supremacy Act* declared that Henry was to be recognized as the
'supreme head' of the English church. The *Treasons Act* made denial of Henry's
supremacy an act of treason, punishable by death. This final act led to the execution of two prominent Catholic churchmen, Thomas More and John
Fisher, both of whom refused to recognize Henry as supreme head of the
English church – a title which they believed belonged only to the pope.

Henry now found himself under threat of invasion from neighbouring
catholic states. The mandate of restoring papal authority would have been a
more than adequate pretext for either France or Spain to launch a crusade
against England. Henry was thus obliged to undertake a series of defensive
measures to ensure the nation's safety. These measures reached their climax in
1536. The dissolution of the monasteries provided Henry with funds for his
military preparations. Negotiations with German Lutherans were begun with
the object of entering into military alliances. At this point, Lutheran ideas
began to be adopted in some official formularies of faith, such as the Ten
Articles. Nevertheless, this theological enthusiasm for Lutheranism appears to
have been little more than a temporary political manoeuvre. When it became
clear that there was serious opposition within England to his reforming measures, Henry backtracked. The 1543 'King's Book' shows every evidence of
Henry's desire to avoid giving offence to Catholics. By the time of Henry's
death in January 1547, the religious situation in England was somewhat
ambivalent. Although Henry had made some concessions to Lutheranism, his
own preference appears to have remained for at least some traditional catholic
beliefs and practices. For example, his will made provision for prayers to be
said for his soul – despite the fact that Henry had, less than two years earlier,
tried to close down the chantries, which existed for precisely this purpose!

From this brief account of the origins of the English Reformation under
Henry VIII, it will be clear that there are reasons for supposing that Henry's
aims were of critical importance for the genesis of that Reformation. Henry's
agenda was political, and was dominated by the desire to safeguard the

succession. Through a series of developments, this required a schism with Rome, and an increasingly tolerant attitude towards Lutheranism, both in Germany and England. Yet Henry's tolerance for Lutheranism, which peaked around 1536, does not seem to have been grounded primarily on religious considerations.

This does not mean that Lutheran ideas were without influence in England. As we shall see, many significant English churchmen were sympathetic to the new ideas, and made it a matter of principle to secure a favourable hearing from them in both church and society at large. In fact, there are reasons for arguing that at least some degree of popular support for Lutheran ideas led Henry to pursue his policies in certain manners, rather than others. The point being made is that the *origins* of Henry's reforming policies are not themselves religious in nature.

In the end, the English Reformation has to be recognized as an Act of State. The comparison with the situation in Germany is highly instructive. Luther's reformation was conducted on the basis of a theological foundation and platform. The fundamental impetus was religious (in that it addressed the life of the church directly) and theological (in that the proposals for reform rested on a set of theological presuppositions). In England, the reformation was primarily political and pragmatic. The reformation of the church was, in effect, the price paid by Henry (rather against his instincts) in order to secure and safeguard his personal authority within England.

The Consolidation of the English Reformation: Edward VI to Elizabeth I

With the death of Henry VIII, an important era in the English Reformation came to an end. In many ways, the first phase of the English Reformation was both driven and directed by the personal agenda of Henry, and the various compromises in which this involved him. At the time of his death in January 1547, Henry had failed to make the fundamental changes which would institutionalize his reforms. The diocesan and parish structures of England had been left virtually as they were, particularly in relation to their forms of worship. Thomas Cranmer might well have had ambitious ideas for the reform of the liturgy and theology of the English church; Henry VIII gave him no opportunity to pursue them.

During the final years of Henry's reign, a subtle power struggle had developed within the court, with a clique based on Edward Seymour gradually gaining the ascendancy. The Seymour family had strongly Protestant inclinations. As Edward VI was still a child, his authority was delegated to the Privy Council, which was initially dominated by Seymour (who had by then become Duke of Somerset, and Lord Protector). The Church of England began to move in a distinctively Protestant direction. Cranmer, now able to flex his theological muscles in a manner which had been impossible under Henry VIII, began to introduce a series of reforms.

Of these, the most important is thought to be the revision of the Prayer Books in 1549 and again in 1552. The revisions proved to be of considerable importance, particularly in relation to eucharistic theology. Yet Cranmer was also responsible for a series of further developments, designed to consolidate Protestantism. Recognizing the theological weakness of the reforms introduced to date, Cranmer invited leading Protestant theologians from continental Europe to settle in England, and give a new theological direction and foundation to the English Reformation. Peter Martyr was appointed as Regius Professor of Divinity at Oxford University, and Martin Bucer as Regius Professor of Divinity at Cambridge University. Their arrival pointed to a new determination to align the English Reformation with its European counterpart, particularly its Reformed constituency. The Forty-Two Articles (1553) drawn up by Cranmer were strongly Protestant in orientation, as were the Book of Homilies (a set of approved sermons for delivery in parish churches).

Edward's early death (1553) put an end to this state-sponsored Protestantization of the English national church. Mary Tudor, who succeeded to the throne, put in place a series of measures designed to bring about a restoration of Catholicism within England. She appointed Reginald Pole – a loyal catholic bishop deposed under Henry VIII – as Archbishop of Canterbury. The reversionary measures became particularly unpopular when Cranmer was executed by being publicly burned at Oxford. By then, most Protestants with the ability and means to do so had fled England for refuges in Europe. Some 800 are known to have accepted exile in this way, waiting their chance to return to England and begin the Reformation all over again. Their exile in cities such as Geneva and Zurich brought them directly into contact with the leading representatives of continental Protestantism, and in effect created a theologically literate and highly motivated Fifth Column that was merely awaiting an opportunity to put their ideas into practice.

Perhaps to their surprise, that opportunity came sooner rather than later. Mary Tudor and Reginald Pole both died on 17 November, 1558. Both monarch and primate had been removed from the scene, which was now set for a radical change in direction. Elizabeth I, initially cautious in revealing her religious inclinations, soon put in place measures to establish a 'Settlement of Religion', which would eventually lead to the creation of a more explicitly Protestant state church. Of particular importance was the formulation of the

Thirty-Nine Articles (1563), which gave a distinctive theological identity to the Church of England.

It will be clear from this analysis that theology did not play the major role in shaping the English Reformation that can be observed in, for example, the Lutheran Reformation. Yet the relative lack of influence of theology over developments cannot be taken to mean that there were no theological factors involved in the English Reformation, nor that there was an absence of theological debates at the time. In the following sections, we shall explore two themes of the thought of the continental Reformation which were appropriated by English theologians – the doctrine of justification by faith, and the 'supper-strife' (the debate over the nature of the real presence in the Lord's Supper). The manner in which each debate was conducted offers important insights into the distinctive nature of the English Reformation, not least in indicating its largely derivative character. The English reformers might have added their own harmonies, but the tunes were written in Germany and Switzerland.

Justification by Faith in the English Reformation

As noted in an earlier chapter, the doctrine of justification by faith was of fundamental importance to the first phase of the Reformation. The doctrine can be seen as central to Luther's own theological agenda, and unquestionably shaped the development of the Lutheran reforming movement throughout the 1520s and 1530s. So what of its development and appropriation within England?

In our discussion of the development of the doctrine of justification in the continental Reformation, we noted the emergence of the concept of *forensic justification* (see pp. 119–22). This idea, although arguably implicit in the writings of Luther during the 1520s, was explicitly stated in the Augsburg Confession (1530). In view of the importance of this point to the appropriation of the doctrine in English reforming circles, we may offer a summary of the distinction between Augustine's views on justification and those associated with Philipp Melanchthon. The most significant elements of these understandings have been emphasized, in order to help compare them.

> Augustine: Justification is an *internal process of making righteous*, in which the righteousness of Christ is *imparted* to us.

> Melanchthon: Justification is an *external event of being declared righteous*, in which the righteousness of Christ is *imputed* to us.

Melanchthon drew a distinction between 'justification' and 'regeneration', along the following lines. *Justification* is an external event in which God declares us to be righteous; *regeneration* is an internal process by which God makes us righteous.

The early English Reformation tended to treat justification as 'being made righteous', showing a preference for the Augustinian rather than the Melanchthonian approach to justification. It is not clear whether this reflects a deliberate decision to reject Melanchthon's views, or an implicit assumption that, since the Reformation represented a return to Augustine, it was therefore entirely in order to define justification in Augustinian terms. Although the Lutheran position on justification was set out correctly and fully in the writings of Robert Barnes (who is known to have attended the University of Wittenberg, and who was an enthusiastic advocate of Luther's views from the early 1520s onwards), this proves to be the exception rather than the rule.

To illustrate this point, we may consider the Ten Articles of July 1536. These Articles date from a period in which Henry VIII was actively pursuing closer relationships with German Lutherans for political reasons. It is widely accepted that the political links which were developed around this time were directly reflected in the official theological statements put out on behalf of the English church. Yet justification is still defined in essentially Augustinian terms, with no mention being made of the imputation of the righteousness of Christ.

The King's Book (1543) is widely regarded as representing a retreat from Reformation views, in the light of growing unrest within England. Henry's desire to reassure Catholics within England is clearly reflected in its view of justification, which is defined as 'the making of us righteous afore God, where before we were unrighteous'. This is an explicitly Augustinian definition, suggesting that there was no great official enthusiasm for the continental Reformation views on the nature of justification towards the end of Henry's reign.

With the death of Henry and accession of Edward VI (1547), the scene was set for the development of more explicitly Protestant theological views within the Church of England. The most important document to deal with justification dating from this period is the homily entitled 'A Sermon of the Salvation of Mankind', generally thought to have been composed by Cranmer. The homily sets out a theology of justification which makes virtually no reference to the concept of 'imputed righteousness', so typical of Lutheranism during the 1540s:[1]

Because all men be sinners and offenders against God, and breakers of his law and commandments, therefore can no man by his own acts, works and deeds, seem they never so good, be justified and made righteous before God: but every man of necessity is constrained to seek for another righteousness or justification, to be received at God's own hands, that is to say, the remission, pardon and forgiveness of his sins and trespasses in such things as he has offended. And this justification or righteousness, which we receive by God's mercy and Christ's merits, embraced by faith, is taken, accepted and allowed of God for our perfect and full justification.

Note how justification is defined in terms of forgiveness and receiving righteousness. What is of particular interest is that there are clear indications that Cranmer – assuming that he is the author of this piece – has incorporated material directly from Melanchthon's writings at several points, yet appears to have deliberately omitted his statements on the imputation of righteousness.

The significance of this observation is difficult to assess. Virtually every aspect of the Lutheran doctrine of justification by faith alone is incorporated into this homily; the one exception is an explicit statement of the notion of imputed righteousness. Was this simply a misunderstanding? Or were there some deeper issues involved? For example, was there an anxiety that the notion of 'imputed righteousness' might lead to moral laxity – a fear which is known to have been expressed in Swiss reforming circles in the 1520s?

From the above discussion, it will be clear that Cranmer had a high regard for Luther's doctrine of justification by faith, particularly as he found it in the writings of Melanchthon. The fact that Cranmer married a German Lutheran can either be seen as a reflection or as a cause of this positive evaluation! Yet this did not mean that Cranmer held an equally high regard for every aspect of Luther's thought. As we shall see, Cranmer rejected Luther's views on the real presence in favour of the more radical views of Zwingli and Oecolampadius. In the following section, we shall explore this matter in a little more detail.

The Real Presence in the English Reformation

The most significant statements of the English Reformation concerning the real presence are found in the writings of Thomas Cranmer (1489–1556). Born in Nottinghamshire in 1489, Thomas Cranmer went up to Jesus College, Cambridge, in 1503. He first came to Henry VIII's attention in 1529, when he became involved in the attempt to gain international recognition for Henry's proposed divorce from Catherine of Aragon. Henry VIII invited

Cranmer to succeed William Warham as Archbishop of Canterbury on the latter's death in 1532. Cranmer eventually accepted, apparently with some reluctance. Although his opportunities to influence the course and shape of the English Reformation under Henry VIII were somewhat limited, a new situation developed under Edward VI. Cranmer's influence was at its height during Edward's reign, as noted above (pp. 252–3).

One of his most significant tasks was the revision of the Prayer Book. Recognizing that one of the most effective ways of changing what people think is to change the way they worship, Cranmer saw the revision of the Prayer Book as a vitally important means of consolidating the principles of the Reformation, and bringing them into direct contact with the parish clergy and the laity. The revisions which Cranmer introduced are of considerable intrinsic interest; our attention here will focus on his views on the real presence, which can be inferred clearly from the Prayer Books of 1549 and 1552.

The 1549 Prayer Book adopted a fairly traditional view of the real presence, showing strong resonance with the position of Luther. This was to be expected. Cranmer had already shown himself to be a strong opponent of the kind of 'memorialist' views which were associated with Zwingli. He presided over the public execution of John Frith in 1533, in response to the latter's denial of the real presence in the eucharist. He was also severely critical of the memorialist views of the Swiss reformer Joachim von Watt (Vadian). The 1549 Prayer Book, drawn up by Cranmer, includes material which points to a generally Lutheran understanding of the real presence. For example, the following words are directed to be spoken to those about to receive the communion: 'The Body [Blood] of our Lord Jesus Christ, which was given for thee, preserve the body and soul unto everlasting life'. These words, however, would be dropped in the 1552 Prayer Book, which sets out Cranmer's mature position on the matter – a position which does not include any notion of a physical 'real presence'.

Cranmer's mature eucharistic views are set out with particular clarity in his *Defence of the True and Catholic Doctrine of the Sacrament*, first published in 1550. For Cranmer, the Lord's Supper serves three central functions:

1   It is a memorial of Christ's sacrifice.
2   It represents a 'sacrifice of praise' for that sacrifice.
3   It stresses the importance of 'spiritually feeding upon Christ'.

Cranmer's mature view is remarkably close to that developed by Zwingli and Oecolampadius. Cranmer rejects what he terms the 'papistical doctrine of transubstantiation' as 'directly contrary to God's word'. Although Cranmer's early views can be argued to be something similar to transubstantiation (perhaps reflecting a familiarity with Luther's views), it is clear that his later position is significantly different.

Cranmer is aware that one of the issues under debate is the nature of the language used by the New Testament. As we noted earlier (pp. 178–85), the precise interpretation of the phrase 'this is my body' was intensely debated in the 1520s, with Luther arguing for a literal interpretation of the phrase, and Zwingli for a metaphorial or symbolic reading of the text. Cranmer makes it clear that he prefers Zwingli's approach:[2]

> And marvel not, good reader, that Christ at that time spoke in figures, when he did institute that sacrament, seeing that it is in the nature of all sacraments to be figures. And although the Scripture can be full of schemes, tropes and figures, yet specially it uses them when it speaks of sacraments.

Having established that the New Testament uses "tropes' and other non-literal modes of expression, particularly in relation to the sacraments, it is only a small step for Cranmer to argue that the eucharist represents a memorial of Christ's saving death.[3]

> Christ calls the bread his body (as the old authors report) because it represents his body, and signifies to them which eat that bread according to Christ's ordinance, that they do spiritually eat his body, and be spiritually fed and nourished by him. And yet the bread remains still there, as a sacrament to signify the same.

In other words, the bread does not change; it remains as it was. Note how Cranmer speaks of 'the old authors' – meaning the patristic writers, who had been cited by Oecolampadius in support of his memorialist view of the eucharist.

Among the arguments which Cranmer marshalls in support of his memorialist view of the eucharist, we may note one in particular. Cranmer argues – following Zwingli, and particularly Zwingli's English discipline John Frith – that Christ is now sitting at God's right hand. If he is indeed at God's right hand, he cannot be anywhere else. Therefore, Christ cannot be present in the eucharist:[4]

> [The Lord] now sits at the right hand of his Father, and there shall remain until the last day, when he shall come to judge the quick and the dead.

Cranmer also insists that the Lord's Supper offers no benefits to those who do not have faith. All people, whether they have faith or not, may physically consume the sacramental elements. Yet the benefits which they represent or signify are only applied to those who believe.[5]

It is evident and manifest that all men, good and evil, may with their mouths visibly and sensibly eat the sacrament of Christ's body and blood; but the very body and blood themselves be not eaten but spiritually, and that of the spiritual members of Christ, which dwell in Christ, and have Christ dwelling in them, by whom they be refreshed, and have everlasting life.

Cranmer's essentially Zwinglian views on the real presence would not have been welcomed by either Lutherans or Catholics. Under Edward VI, this was not an especially important issue. However, things were very different under Elizabeth I. Faced with a complex political agenda at home and abroad on her accession, Elizabeth judged that a 'Settlement of Religion' was a matter of priority. Alterations were introduced to the 1552 Prayer Book to make it more acceptable across a broad spectrum of theological positions. For example, consider the words spoken to those about to receive communion:

1549: 'The Body [Blood] of our Lord Jesus Christ, which was given for thee, preserve thy body and soul unto everlasting life'.

1552: 'Take and eat [drink] this is remembrance that Christ died for thee, and feed on him in thy heart with thanksgiving'.

1559: 'The Body [Blood] of our Lord Jesus Christ, which was given for thee, preserve thy body and soul unto everlasting life. Take and eat [drink] this is remembrance that Christ died for thee, and feed on him in thy heart with thanksgiving'.

The 1549 words reflect an essentially Lutheran position; the 1552 words a more Zwinglian stance. The 1559 statement brings the two together, without attempting any form of theological resolution. Both Lutheran and Zwinglian found something which they could approve, and there, it seems, it was hoped the matter would rest. The Elizabethan 'Settlement of Religion' was essentially pragmatic rather than theological. Perhaps this could be seen as the most distinctive characteristic of the English Reformation under Elizabeth: a desire to reconcile all parties within the theologically and socially fragmented nation, and recover a sense of national unity.

For further reading

P. N. Brooks, *Thomas Cranmer's Doctrine of the Eucharist*, 2nd edn (Rochester, NY, 1993).
P. Collinson, *Archbishop Grindal 1519–1583: The Stuggle for a Reformed Church* (London, 1979).
C. Cross, *Church and People 1450–1660: The Triumph of the Laity in the English Reformation* (London, 1976).
A. G. Dickens, *The English Reformation*, 2nd edn (London, 1989).

E. Duffy, *The Stripping of the Altars: Traditional Religion in England, c. 1400–c. 1580* (New Haven, CT, 1992).

W. P. Haugaard, *Elizabeth and the English Reformation* (Cambridge, 1968).

N. L. Jones, *Faith by Statute: Parliament and the Settlement of Religion* (London, 1982).

D. MacCulloch, *Thomas Cranmer* (New Haven, CT, 1996).

A. E. McGrath, *Iustitia Dei: A History of the Christian Doctrine of Justification*, 2nd edn (Cambridge, 1998), pp. 285–92.

R. Rex, *Henry VIII and the English Reformation* (Basingstoke, 1993).

D. Starkey, *The Reign of Henry VIII* (London, 1991).

14

The Impact of Reformation Thought upon History

Everyone studying a subject likes to be reassured that it has a relevance beyond its own narrow confines. This concluding section aims to explore some of the ways in which the religious ideas of the Reformation may be argued to have changed history, whether by laying the foundations for new attitudes and outlooks or by clearing away intellectual obstacles to these developments. It will trace the trajectory of some of the ideas developed during the period, and consider their longer-term impact upon western culture. As we shall see, it may be argued that the Reformation injected a creative impulse into history, with major results for the shaping of our own world.

A failure to realize the extent to which values, attitudes and actions rest upon *doctrinal* foundations has undoubtedly contributed much to the shallowness of some historical writing in recent years. The new outlooks and attitudes associated with the Reformation were not arbitrary, or a response to purely social or economic forces. The positive and committed attitude towards the secular order so characteristic of the Reformation and charged with such importance for the shaping of modern western culture rests upon a series of theological assumptions.

We may begin, however, by considering two unacceptable understandings of the manner in which theory and practice, thought and social existence, interact. Some scholars of the Reformation, especially during the nineteenth century, took refuge in what we might call 'Romantic idealism', which assumed that religious ideas were the sole motivating force in western history in the sixteenth century. The notion of 'pure religious causation' rests on the indefensible assumption that religious ideas operate in complete abstraction or detachment from social or material factors.

In fact, religious ideas are sometimes deeply affected by the social context in which they develop. An example may illustrate this point. One of the most distinctive features of John Calvin's views on Christian ministry in the city of Geneva, as set out in 1541, is the 'four orders of ministry' – doctors, elders, pastors and deacons. The fourth such order of ministry – the deacons, or 'the diaconate', to use a more technical term – is of especial interest. By the end of the medieval period, the diaconate had come to be seen as little more than an apprenticeship for the priesthood, allowing a decent interval to pass before an individual was finally consecrated priest. Calvin insisted that the diaconate should be a separate lay ministry, with a distinct set of functions and responsibilities in its own right. In part, this insistence upon the distinctive role of the diaconate was founded on Calvin's reading of the New Testament: in commenting on Acts 6:1–6, Calvin linked the diaconate with the apostolic responsibility of caring for the poor.

The idea may indeed have been thoroughly biblical; but the manner in which it was worked out in practice was thoroughly Genevan. Here, as elsewhere, Calvin's ordering of the church at Geneva in the *Ordonnances ecclésiastiques* of 1541 represented an accommodation to existing Genevan civic structures. Calvin laid down that there should be five deacons, four of whom were to be *procureurs* and one a *hospitallier*. But where did he get these very precise ideas from?[1]

Before the Reformation, Geneva had established an institution known as the *Hôpital-Général*, which was responsible for the programme of social welfare within the city. The city appointed six individuals, based at this institution, to administer poor relief within the city; five were to be *procureurs*, responsible for the general administration of the social welfare programme; the sixth was designated *hospitallier*, charged specifically with the supervision of the *hôpital* itself. Apart from a very slight alteration to the number of *procureurs*, Calvin has simply taken over an existing secular practice into his religious thought. This illustrates neatly the way in which Geneva influenced Calvin just as much as Calvin influenced Geneva – and how social structures influence ideas.

Others in the more recent past have adopted a quasi-Marxist analysis, suggesting (with varying degrees of conviction and enthusiasm) that ideas are basically a superstructure erected on a socio-economic sub-structure. The latter determines the former. In its more committed versions, the suggestion is made that radical restructuring of society would eliminate religious ideas altogether, in that their socio-economic foundation would be destroyed. Although this approach is regarded with increasing scepticism, it remains influential indirectly, through what Franziska Conrad refers to as 'a sociologism which fails to do justice to the spiritual and religious components of the Reformation era'.[2]

To discard an *exclusively* theological or religious approach to the Reformation is not to suggest that theology or religion played no significant role in that movement; it is to recognize the complexity of the mutual interplay of ideas and practice within the social situation of the time. Ideas are affected by history; history is affected by ideas. It is the complexity of this mutual interplay of ideas and history which is so irritating to those who, for one reason or another, want to ignore either religious ideas on the one hand or the historical context of those ideas on the other. In the remainder of this chapter, we shall explore some of the cultural consequences of the religious ideas developed at the time of the Reformation.

An Affirmative Attitude towards the World

The noted Reformation scholar Roland H. Bainton once remarked that when Christianity takes itself seriously, it must either renounce the world or master it. If the former attitude was characteristic of much medieval Christianity, the latter dominated the thought of the reformers. The Reformation witnessed a remarkable turnabout in attitudes towards the secular order. Monastic Christianity, which had been the source of virtually all the best Christian theology and spiritual writings during the Middle Ages, treated the world and those who lived and worked in it with a certain degree of disdain. *Real* Christians would withdraw from the world, and enter the spiritual security of a monastery. Yet, for the reformers, the real vocation of a Christian lay in serving God in the world. Monasteries were something of an irrelevance to this task. The real business of Christian living was in the cities, marketplaces and council chambers of the secular world, not in the splendid isolation of the monastic cell.

The importance of this shift in outlook cannot be overstated. It might be thought that monastic Christianity was only one component – and perhaps not even the most significant component – of medieval Christianity. Yet Ernst Curtius is one of the many scholars who have emphasized that it is a conveniently neglected matter of historical fact that much of what we refer to as 'medieval Christianity' is actually *virtually totally monastic in its character and origins*. As a result, medieval Christianity was characterized by a strongly anti-secular attitude. To live in the everyday world was a second-rate option; to value the everyday world was seen as a spiritual absurdity, which could lead to all kinds of spiritual degeneration.

During the Middle Ages, the monasteries became increasingly isolated from ordinary people. Increasingly firmly wedded to the fading medieval world, the monasteries seemed unable to relate to the new interest in religion among the laity and the technological advance of printing. Monastic approaches to the Christian life came to have a minimal impact outside the monasteries, even upon the clergy. The everyday life of the laity was often virtually untouched by what went on behind monastic walls. Monastic attitudes to Christian living envisaged a lifestyle and outlook quite alien to lay people.

An illustration will bring out this point. The most famous writing of the movement generally known as the *Devotio Moderna is* Thomas à Kempis' *De imitatione Christi*. The full title of this work, in English, is *On the Imitation of Christ and Contempt for the World*. A positive response to Jesus Christ is seen as entailing a negative response to the world. For à Kempis, the world is basically little more than a nuisance. It distracts monks from other-worldly contemplation. If the monk wishes to gain experience of the world, he need do nothing more than look around his cell. We are pilgrims on this earth, in the process of travelling to heaven; to develop a commitment to, or even an interest in, the present world is potentially to put at risk the goal of the entire monastic life – holiness in this world and salvation in the next.

This is not an isolated example; but it illustrates deeply seated attitudes within most monastic orders. The monk was to seek solitude, not merely from the world, but also from other human beings. Whenever possible, he was to remain within his cell. William of St Thierry was one of many medieval spiritual writers who made puns on the Latin word for cell, *cella*. The cell hides (*celare*, the Latin root from which the English word 'conceal' is derived) the monk from the world, and opens up heaven (*coelum*) to him. Geert Groote, widely regarded as the founder of the *Devotio Moderna*, renounced all material possessions and academic pursuits, in order to withdraw totally from the world to seek God.

With the Reformation, the formative centres of Christian thought and life gradually shifted from the monasteries to the marketplace, as the great cities of Europe became the cradle and crucible of new modes of Christian thinking and acting. Mirrored in this shift are the political, social, economic and ecclesiastical changes which lie at the heart of the formation of modern western culture. The mainstream Reformation rejected the monastic impulse to withdraw from the word – but primarily on the basis of *theological*, not *social*, considerations.

Two of these theological considerations may be noted briefly.

1   *A new emphasis on the doctrines of creation and redemption.* Calvin's impressively world-affirming theology may be said to rest upon asserting the utter ontological distinction between God and the world, while denying the possibility of separating the two. The theme *distinctio sed non separatio* (see p. ••), which underlies so many aspects of Calvin's theology, reappears in his understanding of the Christian's relationship to society. A knowledge of God the Creator cannot be isolated from knowledge of his creation; Christians are expected to show respect, concern and commitment to the world on account of a loyalty, obedience and love for God its creator. The world does not have a direct claim to a Christian's loyalty; it is an indirect claim, resting on a recognition of the unique relation of origin which exists between God and his cre-

ation. In revering nature as God's creation, one is worshipping God, not wor-shipping nature.

To be a Christian thus does not – indeed, *cannot* – mean renouncing the world; for to renounce the world is to renounce the God who so wondrously created it. The world, though fallen, is not evil. The Christian is called to work in the world, in order to redeem the world. Commitment to the world is a vital aspect of the working out of the Christian doctrine of redemption. A failure to commit oneself to and work in the world is tantamount to declar-ing that it cannot, and should not, be redeemed.

2   *A recovery of the idea of the calling of a Christian.* Although the monastic idea of calling entailed leaving the world behind, the reformers vigorously repudiated this idea. God calls his people not just to faith, but to express that faith in quite definite areas of life. A person is called, in the first place, to be a Christian, and in the second, to live out his or her faith in a quite definite sphere of activity in the world. The impact of Reformation thought in this respect may be judged from the fact that the term *vocatio*, 'calling', has now come to mean 'a worldly activity or career'. Behind this modern habit lies an idea which achieved wide acceptance in the sixteenth-century Reformation – that the Christian is called to serve God in the world.

This idea, linked with the central doctrine of the priesthood of all believ-ers (pp. 222–3), gave a vital new motivation for committing oneself to the everyday world. As we have seen, the reformers rejected the vital medieval distinction between the 'sacred' and the 'secular'. There was no genuine dif-ference of status between the 'spiritual' and the 'temporal' order (see p. 222). All Christians are called to be priests, and that calling extends to the every-day world. They are called to purify and sanctify its everyday life from withing. Luther stated this point succinctly: 'What seem to be secular works are actu-ally the praise of God and represent an obedience which is well pleasing to him.' There were no limits to this notion of calling. Luther even extolled the religious value of housework; declaring that although 'it had no obvious appearance of holiness, yet these very household chores are more to be valued than all the works of monks and nuns'. Again, 'God pays no attention to the insignificance of the work being done, but looks at the heart which is serving him in the work. This is true even of such everyday tasks as washing dishes or milking cows.' Luther's English follower William Tyndale, picking up this idea, insisted that while the 'washing of dishes and preaching the word of God' represented different human activities, 'as touching to please God', there was no difference.

'Every individual's way of life is, as it were, a position assigned to him by the Lord.' In Calvin's view, God places individuals where he wants them to be. (This point, incidentally, is of importance to Calvin's critique of human ambition, which he argues rests on an unwillingness to accept the sphere of action which God has allocated to us.) The social status of this location is an irrelevance, a human invention of no spiritual significance. One cannot allow the human (for example, the monastic) evaluation of the status of an occupation to be placed above the judgement of God. All human work is capable of 'appearing truly respectable and being considered highly important in the sight of God'. No occupation, no calling, is too mean or too lowly not to be graced by the presence of God.

This point will be developed further, since it is a vital aspect of the Protestant work ethic – unquestionably one of the most significant contributions of the Reformation to the shaping of western culture.

The Protestant Work Ethic

To appreciate the significance of the work ethic which emerged at the time of the Reformation, it is necessary to understand the intense distaste with which the early Christian tradition, illustrated by the monastic writers, regarded work. For Eusebius of Caesarea, the perfect Christian life was one devoted to serving God, untainted by physical labour. Those who chose to work for a living were second-rate Christians. To live and work in the world was to forfeit a first-rate Christian calling, with all that this implied. The early monastic tradition appears to have inherited this attitude, with the result that work often came to be seen as a debasing, demeaning activity, best left to one's social – and spiritual – inferiors. If the social patricians of ancient Rome regarded work as below their status, it has to be said that a spiritual aristocracy appears to have developed within early Christianity, with equally negative and dismissive attitudes towards manual labour. Such attitudes probably reached their height of influence during the Middle Ages.

This is not to say that medieval writers denied the importance of work; rather, it is to note that it was seen as necessary, but demeaning. Christians who committed themselves to living and working in the everyday world were, by definition, second-rate Christians. As Adriano Tilgher concluded in his definitive study of work in the western world, monastic spirituality never regarded everyday work in the world as anything of value. Those who chose to live and work in the world were at best 'regarded with indulgent charity'. Work was, in short, not a serious option for a real Christian. Erasmus reacted with scorn to this idea: was not the work of the humble ploughman more pleasing to God than monastic ritual?

The Reformation changed such attitudes, decisively and irreversibly. To illustrate this change in attitude, we may consider the German word *Beruf* ('calling'), as it was used by Martin Luther. In the Middle Ages, the term *Beruf* meant a monastic or clerical calling – in other words, a vocation to a professional ecclesiastical function. Luther began to use the same word to refer to worldly duties. By using the term *Beruf* to refer to activity in the everyday world, Luther applied the religious seriousness of the monastic vocation to activity in the world. One is called by God to serve him in certain specific ways in the world. Here, the modern use and sense of the word 'vocation' or 'calling' may be seen emerging at the time of the Reformation, through a new approach to work. The languages of every area of Europe affected by the Reformation show a decisive shift in the meaning of the word for work during the sixteenth century: German (*Beruf*), English (*calling*), Dutch (*beroep*), Danish (*kald*), Swedish (*kallelse*) and so forth.

A similar development can be seen in relation to the word 'talent'. The word talent – as used in the parable of the talents (Luke 19:11–27) – literally refers to bars of silver or gold, not to the human expertise which we would now call 'talent'. Medieval sermons based on this parable interpreted the talents metaphorically, as spiritual gifts or graces bestowed by God upon certain pious Christians. Calvin, however, interpreted talents in terms of the worldly calling of Christians and the abilities and aptitudes given to them by God in order that they might function more effectively in the world. Once more, the modern meaning of a work-related word can be seen emerging through the new, positive attitudes to work which emerged from the Reformation.

For the reformers, it was the person who works, as much as the resulting work, which was of significance in the sight of God. There was no distinction between spiritual and temporal, sacred and secular work. All human work, however lowly, was capable of glorifying God. Work was, quite simply, an act of praise – a potentially productive act of praise. As Luther remarked, 'The whole world could be filled with the service of God – not just the churches, but the home, the kitchen, the cellar, the workshop and the fields.' Significantly, Luther and Calvin both noted the importance of productive activity for Christian self-esteem. By doing things for God, Christians are able to gain a sense of satisfaction and self-esteem, unattainable by other means.

For the reformers, the ultimate motivation for human activity was to be located in a God-ward direction. The particular emphasis might differ from one reformer to another, but the underlying theme was constant: work is a natural response to God's gracious initiative towards us, by which we demonstrate our thankfulness to him and simultaneously glorify and serve him in his world. Work is something which glorifies God; it is something which serves the common good; it is something through which human creativity can express itself. The last two benefits, it must be stressed, are embraced by the first. As Calvin's English follower William Perkins put it, 'The true end of our lives is to do service to God in serving of man.' For Calvin himself, the common human obligation is to labour in the garden of the Lord, in whatever manner is commensurate with one's God-given gifts and abilities on the one hand and the needs of the situation on the other. The common obligation to work is the great social leveller, a reminder that all human beings are created equal by God.

The historical transformation of the status of work through this ethic is quite remarkable. Calvin's theology led directly from a view of work as a socially demeaning, if pragmatically necessary, activity, best left to one's social inferiors, to a view of it as a dignified and glorious means of praising and affirming God in and through his creation, while adding further to its well-being. It is no accident that those regions of Europe which adopted Protestantism soon found themselves prospering economically – a spin-off, rather than an intended and premeditated consequence, of the new religious importance attached to work. This beings us to the economic impact of Reformation thought and the celebrated Weber thesis concerning the relation of Protestantism to capitalism.

Reformation Thought and the Origins of Capitalism

The popular version of the Weber thesis declares that capitalism is a direct result of the Protestant Reformation. This is historically untenable, and, in any case, is not what Weber actually said. In his *Protestant Ethic and the Spirit of Capitalism,* Weber stressed that he had

> no intention whatsoever of maintaining such a foolish and doctrinaire thesis as that the spirit of capitalism . . . could only have arisen as a result of certain effects of the Reformation. In itself, the fact that certain important forms of capitalistic business organizations are known to be considerably older than the Reformation is a sufficient refutation of such a claim.

The operations of the great medieval catholic banking houses, such as the Medicis or the Fuggers, are clear evidence of capitalist assumptions and methods in the period prior to the Reformation. On the eve of the Reformation, cities such as Antwerp, Augsburg, Liège, Lisbon, Lucca and Milan were all centres of capitalism in its medieval forms. Nor can the religious importance of capitalism prior to the Reformation be ignored. The Medici family were eventually able to purchase the papacy outright. The Fuggers could control virtually every major episcopal appointment in Germany, Poland and Hungary; they even financed the election of Charles V as emperor. Such events point to the importance of capitalism as a religious force on the eve of the

Reformation. Furthermore, the pioneering studies during the second quarter of the twentieth century of Raymond de Roover, a historian with a then rare knowledge of medieval accounting practices, demonstrated that capitalist assumptions and methods were deeply ingrained in medieval society as a whole.

So what did Weber actually say? First, he noted that capitalism existed long before the Reformation. Capitalist attitudes are as characteristic of the medieval merchant princes as they are of traditional peasant societies. Weber termed the capitalism he discerned in the medieval period 'adventurer capitalism'. This form of capitalism, he argued, was opportunistic and unscrupulous; it tended to consume its capital gains in flamboyant and decadent life-styles. Although medieval society tolerated money-making activities, they were nevertheless generally regarded as unethical. Weber argued that a new 'spirit of capitalism' emerged in the sixteenth century. It is not so much *capitalism* but *a specific form of* capitalism which needs to be explained.

In contrast to medieval 'adventure capitalism,' this modern version of capitalism had a strong ethical basis. While it may have encouraged the acquisition of goods and wealth, it nevertheless adopted an ascetic attitude towards them. This form of capitalism was not, Weber argued, prone to hedonism. Indeed, on the contrary, at times it seemed deliberatly to avoid the direct enjoyment of life. How, Weber asked, could such a dramatic turnabout in attitudes be explained?

On the basis of his studies of fourteenth- and fifteenth-century Florence, Weber suggested that, in the minds of those who accumulated capital at this period, there was a serious conflict between their money-making activities on the one hand and the salvation of their souls on the other. Jakob Fugger, for example, was aware of a serious divergence between his banking activities and those actions which were traditionally regarded by the Catholic church as conducive to attaining salvation. yet in Protestant societies of the sixteenth and early seventeenth centuries, the accumulation of capital was not seen as posing a threat to an individual's salvation. There thus seemed to be a religious explanation for this dramatic turnabout in attitudes.

Weber associated this new attitude with the rise of Protestantism. It was particularly well illustrated by a number of seventeenth-century Calvinist writers such as Benjamin Franklin, whose writings combined commendation of the accumulation of capital through engagement with the world with criticism of its consumption. Capital was to be increased, not consumed. The British historian of Puritanism Christopher Hill summarizes the difference between these Protestant and Catholic attitudes as follows:

> Successful medieval business men died with feelings of guilt, and left money to the church to be put to unproductive uses. Successful Protestant business men

were no longer ashamed of their productive activities whilst alive, and at death left money to help others to imitate them.

Protestantism, Weber argued, generated the psychological preconditions essential to the development of modern capitalism. Indeed, Weber located the fundamental contribution of Calvinism as lying in its generation of psychological impulses on account of its belief systems. Weber laid especial stress on the notion of 'calling', which he linked with the Calvinist idea of predestination. Calvinists, assured of their personal salvation, were enabled to engage in worldly activity without serious anxiety regarding their salvation as a consequence. Provided capital was not obtained by unacceptable means or consumed in a profligate manner, its generation and accumulation were devoid of moral difficulties.

It is not my concern here to provide a critique of the Weber thesis. In some circles, the Weber thesis is regarded as utterly discredited; in others, it lives on. My concern is simply to note that Weber rightly discerned that religious ideas could have a powerful economic and social impact upon early modern Europe. The very fact that Weber suggested that the religious thought of the Reformation was capable of providing the stimulus needed for the development of modern capitalism is itself powerful testimony to the need to study the religious ideas of the period. What other such connections exist? And how can they be detected unless historians are familiar with the language and ideas of their era? To propound and evaluate such theories, a knowledge of Reformation thought and its continuities and discontinuities with what went before is essential.

The Notions of Human Rights and Justifiable Regicide

It may be argued that the Reformation changed the political face of Europe, partly through the political and social changes it brought about and partly on account of some dangerous new ideas which it unleashed on an unsuspecting Europe. A number of beliefs which had hitherto contributed to the political and social stability of western Europe were called into question. One such belief relates to the 'givenness' of existing social structures. It has been argued by political theorists such as Quentin Skinner that the Reformation, and more specifically the development of Calvinism, was instrumental in effecting the transition from a medieval notion of worldly order, founded upon 'an order imagined to be natural and eternal', to a modern order 'founded upon change'. In other words, the medieval world-view was static: one was allocated a position within society on the basis of birth and tradition, and it was not possible to alter this situation. Calvinism, however, offered an 'ideology of transition', in that the individual's position within the world was declared to rest, at least in part, upon his or her efforts. The attractiveness of such a suggestion to French peasants – or, indeed, to the *bourgeoisie* throughout Europe – will be evident. To a social class frustrated by its inability to make significant headway in a society dominated by tradition and familial ties, the doctrine of the fundamental *changeability* of existing social orders had considerable attraction. The use made of this principle by the English Calvinists John Ponet and Christopher Goodman, who developed theories of justifiable regicide on its basis, demonstrates a fundamental break with the medieval notion that existing power structures are somehow ordained by God, and are thus inviolable and unalterable.

Similar ideas developed in France in the aftermath of the St Bartholomew's Day massacre of 1572, when a significant number of French Protestants were murdered during orchestrated public demonstrations of anti-Protestant feeling. Initially, French Calvinism had limited its political reflections to the general area of liberty of conscience. Throughout the 1550s, as Calvinist influence in France grew steadily more significant, French Calvinist political agitation increasingly focused on religious toleration. There was, it was suggested, no fundamental contradiction between being a Calvinist and being French; to be a Frenchman and a Calvinist (or a Huguenot, for the terms are more or less interchangeable) implied no disloyalty to the French crown. The logic and persuasiveness of this position, which commended it to Calvin among others, were shattered in May 1560 through the Conspiracy of Amboise, in which an attempt was made, apparently aided and abetted by a number of Calvinist pastors (to Calvin's irritation), to kidnap Francis II. It was, however, the St Bartholomew's Day massacre (1572) which precipitated a radical shift in French Calvinist political thinking.

The emergence of monarchomachs – people who wished to place severe restrictions upon the rights of kings and to uphold the *duty* (not merely the *right*) of the people to resist tyrannical monarchs – was a direct response to the atmosphere of shock which persisted in the aftermath of the 1572 massacre. In 1559, Calvin – perhaps beginning to recognize the practical and political importance of the question – had conceded that rulers might exceed the bounds of their authority by setting themselves against God; by doing this, he suggested, they had abrogated their own power.

The Lord is the king of kings . . . We are subject to those who have been placed over us, but only in him. If they command anything that is contrary to his will, it must be as nothing to us. We should, in such a case, ignore all the dignity possessed by the magistrates. There is no injustice in compelling this dignity to be subject to the true, unique and supreme power (*summa potestas*) of God. It is for this reason that Daniel (Daniel 6:33) denied that he was guilty of any offence against the king when he disobeyed an ungodly law which the latter had made. For the king had transgressed the limits set to him by God, and had not only wronged human beings, but rebelled against God – and by doing so, abrogated his own power.

Calvin, in effect, lays down that any ruler who exceeds the bounds of his or her authority, ordained by God, ceases to be a ruler for that reason, and can no longer exercise the rights and privileges of that rule. Calvin thereby suggests that the magistrates (but not private individuals) may be in a position to take some (unspecified) action against him. Vague though such reflections were, they prompted others to develop them further – most notably, his French followers, in response to the shocking events of 1572. François Hotman produced the celebrated *Franco-Gallia*, Théodore de Bèze his *Droits des Magistrats*, Philippe Duplessis-Mornay his *Vindiciae contra tyrannos*, and other minor writers produced pamphlet after pamphlet, all making the same point: tyrants are to be resisted. The duty to obey God is to be placed above any obligation to obey a human ruler.

These radical new theories, forged within the crucible of French Calvinism, may be seen as marking an important point of transition between feudalism and modern democracy, with the notion of natural human rights being articulated and defended on theological grounds. Although most French Calvinists abandoned outright opposition to monarchy during the reign of Henry IV, particularly after the promulgation of the Edict of Nantes, important new political theories had been let loose in the French political arena. It has been argued that it was these ideas, in purely secular forms, which resurfaced in the French Enlightenment, when the notion of natural human rights, shorn of its theological trimmings, was amalgamated with the republicanism of Calvin's Geneva in Jean-Jacques Rousseau's *thèse républicaine* which – in opposition to Voltaire's modernized *thèse royale* and Montesquieu's *thèse nobilaire* – declared that sixteenth-century Geneva was an ideal republic, which could serve as a model for eighteenth-century France. Thus Calvin's Geneva became a vibrant and potent ideal, which seized the imagination of pre-revolutionary France. Perhaps the French revolution of 1789 could be seen as the final flowering of the Genevan revolution of 1535.

But even if this *political* revolution does not owe its inspiration to Calvin, the *scientific* revolution of the late sixteenth and early seventeenth centuries rests firmly upon the religious ideas which came into being at the time of the Reformation, as we shall see in the following section.

Reformation Thought and the Emergence of the Natural Sciences

One of the most distinctive features of the modern world is the high profile of the natural sciences. The origins of modern natural science are both complex and controversial. Theories which attempt to explain the remarkable development of the natural sciences in terms of one single controlling factor are ambitious and generally unconvincing; it is clear that not one, but a number of contributing factors are involved. One of those is unquestionably religious, and is due to John Calvin.

A large body of sociological research, stretching back more than a century, has shown that there are consistent differences between the abilities of the Protestant and the Roman Catholic traditions within Christianity to produce first-class natural scientists. An example of this work is Alphonse de Candolle's major study of the foreign membership of the Parisian *Académie des Sciences* over the period 1666–1883. These differences, which are broadly consistent across a wide range of periods and countries, can be summarized thus: Protestants seem to be much better at fostering the study of the natural sciences than Roman Catholics. the Reformation thus appears to be implicated in the promotion of attitudes favourable to the natural sciences.

At first sight, this might seem improbable. For the last hundred years, the attitude of reformers such as Calvin to Copernicus' heliocentric theory of the solar system has been the subject of ridicule. In his vigorously polemical *History of the Warfare of Science with Theology* (1968), Andrew Dickson White wrote:

> Calvin took the lead, in his *Commentary on Genesis*, by condemning all who asserted that the earth is not at the centre of the universe. He clinched the matter by the usual reference to the first verse of the ninety-third Psalm, and asked, 'Who will venture to place the authority of Copernicus above that of the Holy Spirit?'

This assertion is repeated by writer after writer on the theme of 'religion and science'. Nobody seems to have bothered to check their sources. For Calvin wrote no such words, and expressed no such sentiments in any of his known writings. The assertion that he did is first to be found, characteristically unsubstantiated, in the writings of the nineteenth-century Anglican dean of Canterbury, Frederick William Farrar (1831–1903), a writer known to rely excessively on his often unreliable memory for his sources.

Calvin, in fact, may be regarded as making two major contributions to the appreciation and development of the natural sciences: first, the positively encouraged the scientific study of nature; second, he eliminated a major obstacle to the development of that study. His first contribution is specifically linked with his stress upon the orderliness of creation; both the physical world and the human body testify to the wisdom and character of God.

> In order that no one might be excluded from the means of obtaining happiness, God has been pleased, not only to place in our minds the seeds of religion of which we have already spoken, but to make known his perfection in the whole structure of the universe, and daily place himself in our view, in such a manner that we cannot open our eyes without being compelled to observe him . . . To prove his remarkable wisdom, both the heavens and the earth present us with countless proofs – not just those more advanced proofs which astronomy, medicine and all the other natural sciences are designed to illustrate, but proofs which force themselves on the attention of the most illiterate peasant, who cannot open his eyes without seeing them.

Calvin thus commends the study of both astronomy and medicine. They are able to probe more deeply than theology into the natural world, and thus uncover further evidence of the orderliness of the creation and the wisdom of its creator.

It may thus be argued that Calvin gave a new religious motivation to the scientific investigation of nature. This was now seen as a means of discerning the wise hand of God in creation, and thus enhancing both belief in his existence and the respect in which he was held. The *Confessio Belgica* (1561), a Calvinist statement of faith which exercised particular influence in the Lowlands (an area which would become particularly noted for its botanists and physicists), declared that nature is 'before our eyes as a most beautiful book in which all created things, whether great or small, are as letters showing the invisible things of God to us'. God can thus be discerned through the detailed study of his creation.

These ideas were taken up with enthusiasm by the Royal Society, the most significant organization devoted to the advancement of scientific research and learning in England. Many of its early members were admirers of Calvin, familiar with his writings and their potential relevance to their fields of study. Thus Richard Bentley (1662–1742) delivered a series of lectures in 1692, based on Newton's *Principia Mathematica* (1687), in which the regularity of the universe, as established by Newton, is interpreted as evidence of design. There are unambiguous hints here of Calvin's reference to the universe as a 'theatre of the glory of God', in which humans are an appreciative audience. The detailed study of the creation leads to an increased awareness of the wisdom of its creator.

Calvin's second major contribution was to eliminate a significant obstacle to the development of the natural sciences: biblical literalism. This emancipation of scientific observation and theory from crudely literalist interpretations of Scripture took place at two levels. First, he declared that Scripture is not concerned with detailing the structure of the world, but with proclaiming the gospel of Jesus Christ. Second, he insisted that not all biblical statements concerning God or the world were to be taken literally. We may consider these points individually.

Calvin suggests that the Bible is to be regarded as primarily concerned with the knowledge of Jesus Christ. It is not an astronomical, geographical or biological textbook. Perhaps the clearest statement of this principle is to be found in a paragraph added in 1543 to Calvin's preface to Olivétan's translation of the New testament (1534): the whole point of Scripture is to bring us to a knowledge of Jesus Christ. It does not, and was never intended to, provide us with an infallible repository of astronomical and medical information. The natural sciences are thus effectively emancipated from theological restrictions.

Calvin's second contribution concerns the status of biblical statements concerning scientific phenomena. The importance of his contribution is best appreciated by considering the very different position adopted by Martin Luther. On 4 June 1539, Luther commented caustically upon Copernicus' theory – to be published in 1543 – that the earth revolved around the sun: did not Scripture insist that the contrary was the case? Did not Joshua speak of the sun standing still at one point? And so the heliocentric theory of the solar system was dismissed by Luther on the basis of the biblical literalism so typical of the German reformer. (As we saw earlier (pp. 178–85) in his controversy with Zwingli over the meaning of the words spoken by Jesus over the bread at the Last Supper – 'this is my body' (Matthew 26:26) – Luther insisted that the word 'is' could only be interpreted as 'is literally identical with'. This struck Zwingli as a religious and linguistic absurdity, totally insensitive to the various levels at which language operated. In this case, 'is' meant 'signifies'.)

Calvin's discussion of the relationship between scientific findings and the statements of the Bible is generally regarded as one of his most valuable contributions to Christian thought. Calvin here develops a sophisticated theory usually referred to by the term 'accommodation'. The word 'accommodation' here means 'adjusting or adapting to meet the needs of the situation and the human ability to comprehend it'.

In revelation, Calvin argues, God adjusts himself to the capacities of the human mind and heart. God paints a portrait of himself which we are capable of understanding. The analogy which lies behind Calvin's thinking at this point is that of a human orator. A good speaker knows the limitations of his audience, and adjusts the way he speaks accordingly. The gulf between the speaker and the hearer must be bridged if communication is to take place. The parables of Jesus illustrate this point perfectly: they use language and illustrations (such as analogies based on sheep and shepherds) perfectly suited to his audience in rural Palestine. Paul also uses ideas adapted to the situation of his hearers, drawn from the commercial and legal world of the cities in which the majority of his readers lived.

Similarly, Calvin argues, God has to come down to our level if he is to reveal himself to us. God scales himself down to meet our abilities. Just as a human mother stoops down to reach her child, so God stoops down to come to our level. Revelation is an act of divine condescension, by which God bridges the gulf between himself and his capacities and sinful humanity and its much weaker abilities. Like any good speaker, God knows his audience – and adjusts his language accordingly.

An example of this accommodation is provided by the scriptural portraits of God. God is often represented, Calvin points out, as if he has a mouth, eyes, hands and feet. That would seem to suggest that God is a human being. It might seem to imply that somehow the eternal and spiritual God has been reduced to a physical human being, like us! (The issue is often referred to as 'anthropomorphism' – in other words, God being portrayed in human form.) Calvin argues that God is obliged to reveal himself in this pictorial manner on account of our weak intellects. Images of God which represent him as having a mouth or hands are divine 'baby-talk', a way in which God comes down to our level and uses images which we can handle. More sophisticated ways of speaking about God are certainly proper – but we might not be able to understand them.

In the case of the biblical story of creation (Genesis 1), Calvin argues that they are accommodated to the abilities and horizons of a relatively simple, unsophisticated people; they are not intended to be taken as *literal* representations of reality. The author of Genesis, he declares, 'was ordained to be a teacher of the unlearned and primitive, as well as the learned; and so could not achieve his goal without descending to such crude means of instruction'. The phrase 'six days of creation' does not designate six periods of twenty-four hours, but is simply an accommodation to human ways of thinking to designate an extended period of time. The 'weater above the firmament' is simply an accommodated way of speaking about clouds.

The impact of both these ideas upon scientific theorizing, especially during the seventeenth century, was considerable. For example, the English writer Edward Wright defended Copernicus' heliocentric theory of the solar system against biblical literalists by arguing, in the first place that Scripture was not concerned with physics, and in the second that its manner of speaking was 'accommodated to the understanding and way of speech of the common people, like nurses to little children'. Both these arguments derive directly from

Calvin, who, it may be argued, made a fundamental contribution to the emergence of the natural sciences at these points.

Conclusion

It is impossible in the limited space available to provide a detailed analysis of the possible influence of the ideas of the Reformation upon the course of subsequent human history. But what has been said in this final chapter indicates that ideas possess the potential to change things. The Reformation, like the Russian Revolution, is a reminder that ideas are not simply the product of societies; on occasion, they bring those societies into being. The telling comparison between Lenin and Calvin, frequent in recent studies of the French reformer, points to the historical importance of people with radical ideas at certain formative points in history. This book has attempted to make some of those ideas intelligible and accessible to a wider public, so that a deeper appreciation of this fascinating period may result.

A history which neglects ideas has not told its story well, and has certainly not told it fully. The Reformation is a movement in which religious ideas played a major role. There were other factors – social, economic, political and cultural – involved in that movement. Those other factors should and must gain a hearing. But to tell the story of the Reformation without allowing for the imaginative power of religious ideas is an absurdity. It may be difficult for some modern secular interpreters of the movement to appreciate the power of religion as a historical force. Since their world has not been directly shaped by religion, they assume that this has always been the case. But it is not so. Perhaps we have yet to learn that most difficult of all historical skills: the ability to immerse ourselves in the world of a culture that is now dead and imagine ourselves in the midst of a world in which religious ideas and attitudes mattered profoundly. This book cannot wholly achieve that aim; but it has tried to draw back the curtain a little, and allow us to understand better what otherwise might remain a complete mystery.

For further reading

On the Weber thesis, see:

H. Lüthy, 'Variations on a Theme by Max Weber', in *International Calvinism 1541–1715*, ed. M. Prestwich (Oxford, 1985), pp. 369–90.

G. Marshall, *In Search of the Spirit of Capitalism: An Essay on Max Weber's Protestant Ethic Thesis* (London, 1982).
Max Weber, *The Protestant Ethic and the Spirit of Capitalism* (London, 1930).

On the political aspects of Reformation thought, see:

Q. Skinner, *The Foundations of Moden Political Thought* (2 vols; Cambridge, 1978), vol. 2, pp. 219–40.

On the relation between Reformation thought and the sciences, see:

J. Dillenberger, *Protestant Thought and Natural Science* (London, 1961).
R. Hooykaas, *Religion and the Rise of Modern Science* (Edinburgh, 1972).
E. Rosen, 'Calvin's Attitude towards Copernicus', *Journal of the History of Ideas* 21 (1960), pp. 431–41.

Appendix 1

A Glossary of Theological and Historical Terms

The standard theological reference work in English, to which the reader is referred for further discussion, is *The Oxford Dictionary of the Christian Church* (Oxford, 3rd edn, 1997). Much useful information may be found in an older reference work: *The New Schaff–Herzog Encyclopedia of Religious Knowledge* (12 vols; Grand Rapids, Mich., 1957), with especially useful information on sixteenth-century Lutheran and Reformed controversies. A specialized glossary of late medieval theological terms may be found in Heiko A. Oberman, *The Harvest of Medieval Theology: Gabriel Biel and Late Medieval Nominalism* (Cambridge, Mass., 1963), pp. 459–76. Glossaries of terms relating to the doctrine of justification may be found in Alister E. McGrath, *Iustitia Dei: A History of the Christian Doctrine of Justification* (2 vols; Cambridge, 1986), vol. 1, pp. 188–90.

adiaphora
  Literally, 'matters of indifference'. Beliefs or practices which the Reformers regarded as being tolerable, in that they were neither explicitly rejected nor stipulated by Scripture. For example, what ministers wore at church services was often regarded as a 'matter of indifference'. The concept is of importance in that it allowed the Reformers to adopt a pragmatic approach to many beliefs and practices, thus avoiding unnecessary confrontation.

Anabaptism
  Literally, 're-baptizer'. A term used to refer to the radical wing of the Reformation, based on thinkers such as Menno Simons or Balthasar Hubmaier. See p. 9.

anti-Pelagian writings
  The writings of Augustine relating to the Pelagian controversy, in which he defended his views on grace and justification. See 'Pelagianism'.

Apostolic era
For humanists and reformers alike, the definitive period of the Christian church, bounded by the resurrection of Jesus Christ (*c.* 35) and the death of the last apostle (*c.*90?). The ideas and practices of this period were widely regarded as normative in humanist and reforming circles.

Augustinianism
A term used in two major senses. First, it refers to the views of Augustine of Hippo concerning the doctrine of salvation, in which the need for divine grace is stressed (see pp. 72–4). In this sense, the term is the antithesis of Pelagianism. Second, it is used to refer to the body of opinion within the Augustinian Order during the Middle Ages, irrespective of whether these views derive from Augustine or not. See further David C. Steinmetz, *Luther and Staupitz: An Essay in the Intellectual Origins of the Protestant Reformation* (Durham, N. C., 1980), also pp. 76–8 above.

Calvinism
An ambiguous term, used with two quite distinct meanings. First, it refers to the religious ideas of religious bodies (such as the Reformed church) and individuals (such as Theodore Beza) who were profoundly influenced by John Calvin or by documents written by him. Second, it refers to the religious ideas of John Calvin himself. Although the first sense is by far the more common, there is a growing recognition that the term is misleading. See p. 8.

catechism
A popular manual of Christian doctrine, usually in the form of question and answer, intended for religious instruction. With its considerable emphasis upon religious education, the Reformation saw the appearance of a number of major catechisms, most notably *Luther's Lesser Catechism* (1529) and the celebrated *Heidelberg Catechism* (1563) (see pp. 239–41).

Christology
The section of Christian theology dealing with the identity of Jesus Christ, particularly the question of the relation of his human and divine natures. Apart from a disagreement between Luther and Zwingli at Marburg in 1529, Christology, like the doctrine of the Trinity, was not debated extensively during the Reformation.

cinquecènto

The 1500s – i.e. the sixteenth century. See p. 39.

confession

Although the term refers primarily to the admission of sin, it acquired a rather different technical sense in the sixteenth century – that of a document which embodies the principles of faith of a Protestant church. Thus the Augsburg Confession (1530) embodies the ideas of early Lutheranism, and the First Helvetic Confession (1536) those of the early Reformed church. The term 'Confessionalism' is often used to refer to the hardening of religious attitudes in the later sixteenth century, as the Lutheran and Reformed churches became involved in a struggle for power, especially in Germany.

Donatism

A breakaway movement, based in Roman North Africa during the late fourth century, which stressed the need for purity and holiness on the part of church members and leaders. Donatism insisted that the church was a community of saints, rather than, as Augustine taught, a mixed body of the righteous and evil. The Donatist controversy raised the question, which re-emerged at the time of the Reformation, of how the mainstream church could be reformed, without the need to form splinter groups.

ecclesiology

The section of Christian theology dealing with the theory of the church (Latin *ecclesia* = 'church'). At the time of the Reformation, controversy centred upon the question of whether the Protestant churches could be regarded as continuous with mainstream Christianity – in other words, were they a reformed version of Christianity or something completely new, having little or no connection with the previous 1,500 years of Christian history?

evangelical

A term used to refer to the nascent reforming movements, especially in Germany and Switzerland, in the 1510s and 1520s. The term was later replaced by 'Protestant' in the aftermath of the Second Diet of Speyer.

évangeliques

A term often used to refer to the French reforming movement, especially in the 1520s and 1530s, centring upon figures such as Margaret of Navarre and Guillaume Briçonnet.

Evangelism

A term often used in English-language scholarship to refer to the Italian reforming movement in the period 1511–45, centring upon figures such as Gasparo Contarini and Reginald Pole.

exegesis

The science of textual interpretation, usually referring specifically to the Bible. The term 'biblical exegesis' basically means 'the process of interpreting the Bible'. See pp. 157–61. The specific techniques employed in the exegesis of Scripture are usually referred to as 'hermeneutics'.

Fathers

An alternative term for 'patristic writers'.

Hermeneutics

The principles underlying the interpretation, or exegesis, of a text, particularly of Scripture. The first phase of the Reformation witnessed the development of a number of ways of interpreting Scripture, deriving from both humanism and scholasticism. Zwingli initially used a hermeneutical scheme deriving from Erasmian humanism, and Luther a scheme deriving from scholastic theology. See pp. 157–61.

Humanism

A complex movement, linked with the European Renaissance, discussed in detail in chapter 3. At the heart of the movement lay not (as the modern sense of the word might suggest) a set of secular or secularizing ideas, but a new interest in the cultural achievements of antiquity. These were seen as a major resource for the renewal of European culture and Christianity during the period of the Renaissance. The impact of humanism upon Reformation thought is considerable, and is discussed in detail at pp. 44–50; 54–7.

Justification by faith, doctrine of

The section of Christian theology dealing with how the individual sinner is able to enter into fellowship with God. See pp. 104–5. Although of major importance to Martin Luther and his colleagues at Wittenberg, the doctrine was of relatively little interest to the Swiss reformers, such as Zwingli. See pp. 122–4.

liturgy

The written text of public services, especially of the eucharist. As liturgy was predetermined by theology in the Reformation, the reform of the liturgy was regarded as being of particular importance. See pp. 169–71.

Lutheranism

The religious ideas associated with Martin Luther, particularly as expressed in the *Lesser Catechism* (1529) and the Augsburg Confession (1530). A series of internal disagreements within Lutheranism after Luther's death (1546) between hardliners (the so-called 'Gnesio-Lutherans' or 'Flacianists') and moderates ('Philippists'), led to their resolution by the *Formula of Concord* (1577), which is usually regarded as the authoritative statement of Lutheran theology.

Magisterial Reformation

A term used to refer to the Lutheran and Reformed wings of the Reformation, as opposed to the radical wing (Anabaptism). See pp. 5–11.

Nominalism

Strictly speaking, the theory of knowledge opposed to realism. The term is, however, still used occasionally to refer to the *via moderna*. See pp. 70–2; 74–6.

patristic

An adjective used to refer to the first centuries in the history of the church, following the writing of the New Testament (the 'patristic period') or thinkers writing during this period (the 'patristic writers'). For the reformers, the period thus designated seems to be *c.*100–451 (in other words, the period between the closing of the New Testament and the Council of Chalcedon). The reformers tended to regard the New Testament and, to a lesser extent, the patristic periods as normative for Christian belief and practice.

Pelagianism

An understanding of how humans are able to merit their salvation which is diametrically opposed to that of Augustine of Hippo and places considerable emphasis upon the role of human works and plays down the idea of divine grace. See pp. 72–4.

Protestantism

A term used in the aftermath of the Diet of Speyer (1529) to designate those who 'protested' against the practices and beliefs of the Roman Catholic church. Prior to 1529, such individuals and groups had referred to themselves as 'evangelicals'.

quattrocènto

The 1400s – i.e. the fifteenth century. See p. 39.

Radical Reformation

A term used with increasing frequency to refer to the Anabaptist movement – in other words, the wing of the Reformation which went beyond what Luther and Zwingli envisaged. See pp. 9–11.

sacrament

In purely historical terms, a church service or rite which was held to have been instituted by Jesus Christ himself. Although medieval theology and church practice recognized seven such sacraments, the reformers argued that only two (baptism and eucharist) were to be found in the New Testament itself. The theory of the sacraments proved intensely divisive, with the reformers unable to reach agreement among themselves concerning what the sacraments actually achieved. See pp. 169–90 for further discussion.

schism

A deliberate break with the unity of the church, condemned vigorously by influential writers of the early church, such as Cyprian and Augustine. The reformers were branded as 'schismatics' by their opponents. The reformers thus found themselves in the difficult situation of upholding Augustine's views on grace, but disregarding his views on schism. See pp. 215–18.

schola Augustiniana moderna

A form of late medieval scholasticism which laid emphasis upon Augustine's doctrine of grace, while adopting a nominalist position on the question of universals. See pp. 76–8.

Scotism
The scholastic philosophy associated with Duns Scotus. See p. 71.

Scripture Principle
The theory, especially associated with Reformed theologians, that the practices and beliefs of the church should be grounded in Scripture. Nothing that could not be demonstrated to be grounded in Scripture could be regarded as binding upon the believer. The phrase *sola scriptura* ('by Scripture alone') summarizes this principle. See pp. 152–7.

Septuagint
The Greek translation of the Old Testament, dating from the third century BC.

Sermon on the Mount
The standard way of referring to Christ's moral and pastoral teaching in the specific form which it takes in chapters 5–7 of Matthew's gospel.

sodality
A term used generally to refer to the humanist groups associated with many northern European cities and universities in the late fifteenth and early sixteenth centuries. For example, the *sodalitas Collimitiana* at Vienna centred around Georg Collimitius, and the *sodalitas Staupitziana* at Nuremberg centred around Johannes von Staupitz.

Soteriology
The section of Christian theology dealing with the doctrine of salvation (Greek: *soteria*).

Thomism, via Thomae
The scholastic philosophy associated with Thomas Aquinas. See p. 71.

transubstantiation
The medieval doctrine according to which the bread and the wine are transformed into the body and blood of Christ in the eucharist, while retaining their outward appearance. See pp. 178–80.

trecènto

The 1300s – i.e. the fourteenth century. See p. 39.

Turmerlebnis

A German term, literally meaning 'tower experience', often used to designate Luther's moment of breakthrough. See p. 104. In a later (confused) reference, Luther mentions that his theological breakthrough took place in a tower of the Augustinian monastery at Wittenberg – hence the reference to the 'tower'.

via antiqua

A term used to designate forms of scholastic philosophy, such as Thomism and Scotism, which adopted a realist position on the question of universals. See pp. 70–1.

via moderna

A term used broadly in two senses. First, forms of scholastic philosophy which adopted a nominalist position on the question of universals, in opposition to the realism of the *via antiqua*. See pp. 70–2. Second, and more important, the form of scholasticism (formerly known as 'Nominalism') based upon the writings of William of Ockham and his followers, such as Pierre d'Ailly and Gabriel Biel. See pp. 74–6.

Vulgate

The Latin translation of the Bible, largely deriving from Jerome, upon which medieval theology was largely based. Strictly speaking, 'Vulgate' designates Jerome's translation of the Old Testament (except the Psalms, which were taken from the Gallican Psalter), the apocryphal works (except Wisdom, Ecclesiasticus, 1 and 2 Maccabees, and Baruch, which were taken from the Old Latin Version), and all the New Testament. The recognition of its many inaccuracies was of fundamental importance to the Reformation. See pp. 147–8.

Zwinglianism

The term is used generally to refer to the thought of Huldrych Zwingli, but is also often used specifically to refer to his views on the sacraments, especially on the 'real presence' (which for Zwingli was more of a 'real absence'). See pp. 182–6.

Appendix 2

English Translations of Major Primary Sources

John Calvin

Calvin's most important work is the 1559 edition of the *Institutes of the Christian Religion*. This is available in a number of English translations, of which the two following are particularly recommended:

Institutes of the Christian Religion, trans. Henry Beveridge (2 vols; Grand Rapids, Mich., 1975).
Institutes of the Christian Religion, ed. J. T. McNeill, trans. Ford Lewis Battles (2 vols; Library of Christian Classics 20–1: Philadelphia/London, 1975).

The 1536 edition of the *Institutes* is also available in English translation: *Institution of the Christian Religion*, trans. F. L. Battles (Atlanta, 1975).

Many of Calvin's remaining works, particularly his tracts and New Testament commentaries, were translated into English by the Calvin Translation Society during the nineteenth century:

Calvin's Tracts (3 vols; Edinburgh, 1844–51).
Calvin's Commentaries (47 vols; Edinburgh, 1843–59).

A new translation of the New Testament commentaries is also available:

Calvin's Commentaries, ed. D. W. Torrance and T. F. Torrance (Edinburgh, 1959–).

The following translations should also be noted:

Calvin's Commentary on Seneca's 'De Clementia', ed. F. L. Battles and A. M. Hugo (Leiden, 1969).
John Calvin and Jacopo Sadoleto: A Reformation Debate. Sadoleto's Letter to the Genevans and Calvin's Reply (New York, 1996).

Jean Calvin: Three French Treatises, ed. F. H. Higman (London, 1970).
Calvin's Theological Treatises, ed. J. K. S. Reid (Library of Christian Classics 22: Philadelphia, 1954).

Desiderius Erasmus of Rotterdam

The most comprehensive English edition of Erasmus' works is *The Collected Works of Erasmus* (81 vols; Toronto, 1969–), still in progress. This series, when complete, will be the definitive English-language edition of Erasmus. The following are of particular interest to the historian of the Reformation: The correspondence (vols 1–22), especially letters 993–1251 (vols 7–8), which deal with the period 1519–21, during which the 'Lutherana tragoedia' began to dominate Erasmus' concerns; and the New Testament Scholarship (vols 41–60), which did much to lay the intellectual foundations of the Reformation. These volumes should be read in conjunction with Erika Rummel, *Erasmus' Annotations on the New Testament: From Philologist to Theologian* (Erasmus Study 8: Toronto, 1986).

Martin Luther

The most widely used English translation of Luther's works is the so-called *American edition: Luther's Works* (55 vols; St Louis/Philadelphia, 1955–75). In addition to a companion volume, this edition includes most of Luther's exegetical works (vols 1–30), as well as tracts, sermons and political writings (vols 31–54). The exegetical works are arranged in the order in which the scriptural books are found in the Bible, rather than in the order in which Luther wrote them.

A useful anthology is *Martin Luther: Selections from his Writings*, ed. John Dillenberger (New York, 1962). The three 'Reformation treatises' of 1520 are conveniently collected together in *Three Treatises* (Philadelphia, 1973).

Huldrych Zwingli

The most complete English translation to date are the three volumes of *The Latin Works of Huldreich Zwingli*, as follows:

The Latin Works and Correspondence of Huldreich Zwingli, vol. I: 1510–1522, ed. S. M. Jackson (New York, 1912).

The Latin Works of Huldreich Zwingli, vol. II, ed. W. J. Hinke (Philadelphia, 1922); reprinted as *Zwingli on Providence and Other Essays* (Durham, N.C., 1983).

The Latin Works of Huldreich Zwingli, vol. III, ed. C. N. Heller (Philadelphia, 1929); reprinted as *Commentary on True and False Religion* (Durham, N.C., 1981).

These have been supplemented by:

Huldrych Zwingli Writings: The Defense of the Reformed Faith, ed. E. J. Furcha (Allison Park, Pa., 1984).

Huldrych Zwingli Writings: In Search of True Religion, ed. H. Wayne Pipkin (Allison Park, Pa., 1984).

Two other collections are worth noting:

The Selected Works of Huldrych Zwingli, ed. S. M. Jackson (Philadelphia, 1901; reprinted 1972).

Zwingli and Bullinger, ed. G. W. Bromiley (Library of Christian Classics 24: Philadelphia, 1953).

Appendix 3

Standard Abbreviations of Major Journals and Sources

The following abbreviations are encountered regularly in the literature dealing with the history and thought of the Reformation period. The situation is made more complicated than necessary through absence of general agreement on the standard abbreviations for certain works. Where several abbreviations are in use, the preferred abbreviation is indicated. The most helpful guide to the abbreviations used to designate the secondary literature is Siegfried Schwertner, *Internationales Abkürzungsverzeichnis für Theologie und Grenzgebiete* (Berlin/New York, 1973). ('International Glossary of Abbreviations for Theology and Related Subjects', often abbreviated as *IATG*).

Primary Sources

The reader will find it helpful to read these notes in conjunction with Appendixes 2 and 4.

CR Corpus Reformatorum (Berlin/Leipzig/Zurich, 1834–). The standard edition of the works of Melanchthon (vols 1–28), Calvin (vols 29–87), and Zwingli (vols 88–). The Calvin section is sometimes (confusingly) referred to as *OC*. See notes on Calvin and Zwingli in Appendix 4.

CWE Complete Works of Erasmus (Toronto, 1969–). This series, which is still in progress, has become the standard English translation of Erasmus' works.

EE Erasmi Epistolae, ed. P. S. Allen (Oxford, 1905–58). The standard edition of Erasmus' correspondence.

LB Desiderii Erasmi Opera Omnia, ed. J. LeClerc (Leiden, 1703–6; reprinted London, 1962). The Leiden (Lugduni Batavorum) edition of Erasmus' works.

LCC Library of Christian Classics (London/Philadelphia, 1953–). Includes useful translations of Bucer, Zwingli and Melanchthon, as well as of Calvin's 1559 *Institutes*.

LW   Luther's Works, ed. Jaroslav Pelikan and Helmut Lehmann (55 vols; St Louis/Philadelphia, 1955–75). The 'American edition' of Luther's works in English translation.

OC   Opera Calvini. An alternative, and somewhat confusing, reference to the Calvin section of *Corpus Reformatorum*: see *CR*.

OS   Opera Selecta Ioannis Calvini, ed. Peter Barth (5 vols; Munich, 1926–36). A useful critical edition of Calvin's major works, including both the 1536 and 1559 editions of the *Institutes*.

S   Huldrich Zwingli's Werke, ed. M. Schuler and J. Schulthess (8 vols; Zurich, 1828–42). The first edition of Zwingli's works, now being supplanted gradually by the *Corpus Reformatorum* edition.

*SS   An alternative abbreviation for the Schuler–Shulthess edition of Zwingli's works: see *S*.

WA   D. Martin Luthers Werke: Kritische Gesamtausgabe, ed. J. K. F. Knaake, G. Kawerau et al. (Weimar, 1883–). The definitive 'Weimar edition' of Luther's works, which also includes his correspondence (*WABr*), his German Bible (*WADB*) and his 'Table-Talk' (*WATr*).

WABr   D. Martin Luthers Werke: Briefwechsel (15 vols; Weimar, 1930–78). The correspondence section of the Weimar edition of Luther's works.

WADB   D. Martin Luthers Werke: Deutsches Bibel (Weimar, 1906–). The 'German Bible' section of the Weimar edition of Luther's works.

WATr   D. Martin Luthers Werke: Tischreden (6 vols; Weimar, 1912–21). The 'Table-Talk' section of the Weimar edition of Luther's works.

Z   Huldreich Zwinglis sämtliche Werke, ed. E. Egli et al. (*Corpus Reformatorum*, vols 88– : Berlin/Leipzig/Zurich, 1905–). The best critical edition of Zwingli's works, still in progress, replacing the Schuler–Schulthess edition of the nineteenth century. Two other methods of referring to this edition should be noted: first, *CR* followed by a volume number of 88 or greater, which refers the reader to the appropriate volume in the section of *Corpus Reformatorum* series devoted to Zwingli; second, *CR (Zwingli)*, which refers the reader to the *Corpus Reformatorum* series, vols 88– . Thus *CR (Zwingli)* 1 is a referene to the first volume in the Zwingli section of the *Corpus Reformatorum* series – i.e. vol. 88. See further Appendix 4.

*ZW   Alternative abbreviation for *Huldreich Zwinglis sämtliche Werke*: preferred abbreviation is *Z*.

Secondary Sources

ADB   Allgemeine Deutsche Biographie (55 vols; Leipzig, 1875–1912; reprinted Berlin, 1967–71).

AGBR *Aktensammlung zur Geschichte der Basler Reformation in den Jahren 1519 bis Anfang 1534* (3 vols; Basle, 1921–37).

AGZR *Aktensammlung zur Geschichte der Zürcher Reformation in den Jahren 1519–33*, ed. Emil Egli (Zurich, 1879; reprinted Aalen, 1973).

ARG *Archiv für Reformationsgeschichte.*

BHR *Bibliothèque d'humanisme et Renaissance.*

CIC *Corpus Iuris Canonici* (2 vols; Leipzig, 1879; reprinted Graz, 1959).

CICiv *Corpus Iuris Civilis* (3 vols; Berlin, 1872–1908).

EThL *Ephemerides Theologicae Louvaniensis.*

FcS *Franciscan Studies.*

FS *Franziskanische Studien.*

HThR *Harvard Theological Review.*

JThS *Journal of Theological Studies.*

QFRG *Quellen und Forschungen zur Reformationsgeschichte* (Gütersloh, 1911–).

RGG *Religion in Geschichte und Gegenwart* (6 vols; Tübingen, 3rd edn, 1957–65).

RGST *Reformationsgeschichtliche Studien und Texte* (Münster, 1906–).

RThAM *Recherches de théologie ancienne et médiévale.*

SJTh *Scottish Journal of Theology.*

SMRT *Studies in Medieval and Reformation Thought*, ed. H. A. Oberman (Leiden, 1966–).

ZKG *Zeitschrift für Kirchengeschichte.*

ZKTh *Zeitschrift für katholische Theologie.*

ZThK *Zeitschrift für Theologie und Kirche.*

Zwa *Zwingliana: Beiträge zur Geschichte Zwinglis, der Reformation, und des Protestantismus in der Schweiz.*

Note that some writers prefer to abbreviate 'Theology' and derived words as 'T' rather than 'Th' – thus *SJTh*, *JThS* and *HThR* are often abbreviated as *SJT, JTS* and *HTR*.

Appendix 4

How to Refer to Major Primary Sources

Major studies of Reformation personalities or ideas frequently assume that their readers know how to interpret references to primary source materials. Experience suggests that this is a wildly optimistic assumption. This appendix aims to enable the reader to handle the most commonly encountered methods of referring to such material for the four major figures for which this is usually necessary: Calvin, Erasmus, Luther and Zwingli.

Abbreviations used in referring to primary sources may be found in Appendix 3. English translations of major works may be found in Appendix 2.

John Calvin

Calvin's *Institutes of the Christian Religion* is almost invariably referred to in the edition of 1559. This edition is divided into four main sections (books), each dealing with a broad general theme. Each book is then divided into chapters, each of which is further subdivided into sections. A reference to the 1559 edition of this work will therefore include *three* numbers, identifying the *book*, the *chapter* and the *section*. The book number is usually given in capital roman numerals, the chapter in small roman numerals, and the section in arabic numerals. Thus book two, chapter twelve, section one, would probably be referred to as II.xii.1, although a reference might read II, 12, 1 or 2.12.1.

In addition, reference may be given to an edition (e.g. the *Corpus Reformatorum* or *Opera Selecta*) or an English translation. For example, the reference *Institutio* III.xi.1; *OS* 4.193.2–5 is a reference to book three, chapter eleven, section one of the 1559 edition of the *Institutes*, specifically the section to be found on lines 2–5 of page 193 of the fourth volume of the *Opera Selecta*. Similarly a reference to *Institutes* IV.v.5; tr. Beveridge, 2.243 is to the fifth section of the fifth chapter of book four of the *Institutes*, as it is found on page 243 of volume two of the celebrated translation by Henry Beveridge (see Appendix 2).

Reference to Calvin's commentaries and sermons usually involves the *Corpus Reformatorum* edition, which is referred to simply by volume and page number. Thus *CR* 50.437 is a reference to page 437 of volume 50. The volume number will be in the range 1–59. Occasionally, unfortunately, confusion can result from an irritating practice, fortunately generally confined to older studies of Calvin. The *Corpus Reformatorum* edition consists of the works of Melanchthon (vols 1–28), Calvin (vols 29–87) and Zwingli (vols 88–). Volume one of Calvin's works is thus volume 29 within the series – and older works sometimes refer to Calvin's works using this higher volume number. If you find reference to this edition of Calvin with a volume number in the region 60–87, you should subtract 28 to obtain the correct volume number. If you find an isolated reference to Calvin, especially in an older work, which doesn't seem to make sense, subtract 28, and try again!

Desiderius Erasmus

The two most commonly encountered editions of Erasmus' Latin works are the LeClerc edition, published at Leiden in 1703 (reprinted in 1963), and the Allen edition of the correspondence.

The LeClerc edition is almost invariably referred to in the following manner. An initial number denotes the *volume*, and a second number the *column* (each page is divided into two columns, numbered individually). This is then followed by a *letter* (A–F), which indicates the position of the section being referred to in the column. These letters are printed on the page of the LeClerc edition for ease of reference. The following references are given to illustrate this: *LB* V.153 F; *LB* X.1754 C–D; and *LB* II.951 A–B. The first reference is to column 153 of volume 5, the letter F indicating that the section is at the bottom of the column. The second reference is to column 1754 of volume 10, the letters C–D indicating that the section being referred to is to be found towards the middle of the column. The final reference is to column 951 of volume 2, the letters A–B indicating that the section is towards the top of the page.

The Allen edition of the correspondence is generally referred to by first identifying the *volume*, followed by the *page* and *line* numbers – thus *EE* 2.491.133–9 refers to lines 133–9 on page 491 of the second of the twelve volumes. Occasionally, reference is made to the *letter number* – thus *EE* 2, no. 541, is a reference to letter number 541 (from Erasmus to Capito, dated 26 February 1517), to be found in the second volume of the Allen edition.

Martin Luther

The only critical edition of Luther's works now generally referred to is the great 'Weimar edition', begun in 1883 as part of the celebrations of the 400th anniversary of the German Reformer's birth. The edition is divided into four main sections:

1 The main body of the work, containing his major theological writings (abbreviated as *WA*).
2 The correspondence (abbreviated as *WABr*). In catalogues, this section is generally designated by the German word *Briefwechsel*.
3 The so-called Table-Talk (abbreviated as *WATr*). In catalogues, this section is generally designated by the German word *Tischreden*. This material was not written by Luther himself, but consists of reports of Luther's meal-time conversations with his friends. The reliability of this material has frequently been challenged.
4 The 'German Bible' (abbreviated as *WADB*). In catalogues, this section is generally designated by the German words *Deutsches Bibel*.

The first stage in deciphering a reference to the Weimar edition is thus to determine which of the four sections of the work is being referred to. For most purposes, it is likely to be the main body of the work.

This is relatively simple to handle. Reference is invariably given by volume number, page number and line number — in that order. There is some variation in the method of referring to the volume number, some writers using roman, others arabic numerals. Thus *WA* 4.25.12–17 and *WA* IV.25.12–17 are both references to lines 12–17 of page 25 of the fourth volume of the main body of the work. The only difficulty to note is that some volumes are divided into parts. Where this applies, the *part* number follows immediately after the *volume* number. Three main systems are encountered for designating the part number. The references *WA* 55 II.109.9, *WA* LV/2.109.9 and *WA* 55^2.109.9 all refer to line nine of page 109 of the second part of volume 55 of the Weimar edition.

The correspondence (*WABr*) and the German Bible (*WADB*) are generally referred to in much the same way. Thus *WABr* 1.99.8–13 is a reference to lines 8–13 of page 99 of the first volume of the correspondence. In the case of the Table-Talk (*WATr*), however, a slightly different means of reference is generally employed. The Table-Talk is divided into nearly 6,000 sections, and the general practice is to refer to the volume number, followed by the section number. Thus *WATr* 2.2068 is a reference to section 2068, which may be found in the second of the six volumes of the Weimar edition of the Table-Talk. On a few rare occasions, these sections are further subdivided: the subdivisions are identified by letter – for example, *WATr* 3.3390b.

Huldrych Zwingli

Reference in all modern studies is to the excellent *Corpus Reformatorum* edition, generally designated simply as *Z* (for other designations, see Appendix 3). Several works not in this modern edition are to be found in the Schuler–Schulthess edition. The student must therefore be able to deal with both these editions.

The *Corpus Reformatorum* edition is referred to by volume number, page number and line number. Volume 6 is subdivided, with the subdivisions usually being designated by lower-case roman numbers. Thus *Z* III.259.32 refers to line 32 on page 259 of volume 3, and *Z* VI iii.182.3–5 to lines 3–5 on page 182 of the third part of volume 6 of the *Corpus Reformatorum* edition. In older works, reference is occasionally made to the Zwingli section of the *Corpus Reformatorum* edition using a volume number of 88 or greater. This is because the *Corpus Reformatorum* edition brings together the works of three Reformers (the others being Melanchthon and Calvin, who take up volumes 1–87). To convert from this older system, subtract 87 from the volume number. Thus *CR* 90.259.32 is equivalent to *Z* III.259.32.

The Schuler–Schulthess edition is referred to by volume number, page number and line number. Volumes 2 and 6 are subdivided, with the subdivisions being designated by lower-case roman numbers. Thus *S* IV.45.26–8 refers to lines 26–8 on page 45 of volume 4; *S* VI i.602.48 refers to line 48 on page 602 of the first part of volume 6.

Appendix 5

Referring to the Psalms in the Sixteenth Century

Several major works of the sixteenth-century Reformers take the form of commentaries on the Psalter or on individual Psalms – for example, Martin Luther's famous lectures of 1513–15, generally known as *Dictata super Psalterium*. The student is likely to be confused by a major difficulty encountered in referring to the Psalms. Most sixteenth-century writers used the Latin version of the Bible known as the Vulgate. For reasons which defy a simple explanation, the numeration of the Psalms in the Vulgate is different from that found in the Hebrew text, and hence in modern English versions following the latter's numeration. Thus when Luther refers to Psalm 70, he means *Psalm 70 according to the numbering used in the Vulgate* – which is Psalm 71 in most modern English editions. This obviously raises two difficulties. First, how can we convert from the Vulgate numbers to those found in the English Bible? And second, how can we refer to the Psalms to take account of this difference in numeration? We shall deal with these questions separately.

The Vulgate Psalm Numbers

We can tabulate the differences between the Vulgate and modern English versions of the Psalter as follows:

Vulgate	English versions
1–8	1–8
9.1–21	9
9.22–39	10
10–112	11–113
113.1–8	114
113.9–26	115
114	116.1–9

115	116.10–19
116–45	117–46
146	147.1–11
147	147.12–20
148–50	148–50

It will thus be clear that the Vulgate and English Psalm numbers are identical only in the case of eleven Psalms (1–8, 148–50).

Thus when Luther refers to Psalm 22, he actually intends what most people know as Psalm 23. Some modern English translations alter references to the Psalms to make allowance for the numeration difference – but when dealing with the original text, the student must be prepared to adjust the Psalm numbers accordingly. If you find a reference to a Psalm which doesn't make sense, try altering the numbers according to the above table.

Referring to Psalms

It is now virtually universal practice within the scholarly literature dealing with the Reformation (and especially Luther) to refer to Psalms in the following manner. If there is a difference between the Psalm numbers in the English and the Vulgate texts, *the Vulgate number is given first, followed by the English number in parentheses.* Thus a discussion of 'Luther's exposition of Psalm 70 (71)' means Psalm 70 *according to the Vulgate numeration* and Psalm 71 *according to the English numeration.* Similarly, a reference to Psalm 22 (23):3 is a reference to verse 3 of Psalm 22 *following the Vulgate numeration*, and Psalm 23 *following the English numeration.* Occasionally the situation is further complicated through some Psalms having different verse numbers in the Vulgate and English versions. A reference to 'Psalm 84:11 (85:10)' thus means Psalm 84, verse 11, in the Vulgate version; Psalm 85, verse 10, in the English version.

Appendix 6

Updating Reformation Bibliographies

The present book includes a comprehensive bibliography of important works dealing with Reformation thought. Bibliographies, however, go out of date quickly, particularly in a field such as Reformation studies, in which so much scholarly activity is taking place. The student may therefore wonder how such a bibliography may be kept up to date. It is hoped that the following suggestions will be helpful.

The *Archiv für Reformationsgeschichte* Literature Supplement

The leading journal in the field of Reformation studies is *Archiv für Reformationsgeschichte* ('Archive for Reformation History'), published annually in October. Since 1972 this journal has included a supplementary Literature Review (*Literaturbericht*), which provides details of several thousand important books or articles published recently relating to the history or the thought of the Reformation. Some are annotated, either in English or in German. The review is divided into sections and subsections, the classification being given in German. An English version of its most important sections follows:

1	General
2	Religion and Culture
2.1	Before the Reformation
2.2	Luther
2.3	Zwingli
2.4	Calvin
2.5	Protestantism
3	Spirit and Culture
3.1	Philosophy and Political Theory
3.2	Humanism
6	The Reformation in European Countries

The student should select the section or subsections of particular interest to him, and work his way through the publications listed thereunder.

Review Articles and Published Bibliographies

A number of review articles or bibliographies are published regularly. The annual *Luther-Jahrbuch*, *Zwingliana*, and the November issue of *Calvin Theological Journal* include invaluable reports on recent works on Luther, Zwingli and Calvin respectively. The journal *Ephemerides Theologicae Louvaniensis* publishes an annual bibliography of works, including many relevant to the study of the Catholic Reformation. The student is also recommended to check library catalogues under the 'Bibliography' sections of noted reformers – such as Luther, Calvin or Zwingli – where works such as the following will be found:

J. Bigane and K. Hagen, *Annotated Bibliography of Luther Studies, 1967–1976* (St Louis, Mo., 1977).
A. Erichson, *Bibliographia Calviniana*, 3rd edn (Nieuwkoop, 1965).
W. Niesel, *Calvin-Bibliographie (1901–1959)* (Munich, 1961).
S. E. Ozment (ed.), *Reformation Europe: A Guide to Research* (St Louis, Mo., 1982).
H. W. Pipkin, *A Zwingli Bibliography* (Pittsburg, Pa., 1972).

It is also useful to look through recent numbers of leading history or theology journals – such as *Church History, Journal of Ecclesiastical History* or *Journal of Theological Studies* – with two objectives in mind. First, look for reviews of recent books. If a book *has* been reviewed by one of these journals, it is likely to be important. Second, look for review articles – in other words, articles which summarize recent work in a given field.
    Examples of such reviews are:

James Atkinson, 'Luther Studies', *Journal of Ecclesiastical History* 23 (1972), pp. 69–77.
L. C. Green, 'Luther Research in English-Speaking Countries since 1971', *Luther-Jahrbuch* 44 (1977), pp. 105–26.
Robert White, 'Fifteen Years of Calvin Studies in French (1965–1980)', *Journal of Religious History* 21 (1982), pp. 140–61.

Finally, the student is recommended to browse through the bibliography section of any recent publication dealing with the Reformation and note works of relevance which appeared recently. Writers using the Harvard (author-date) system make this a particularly easy task, in that the date of publication of the work is immediately obvious.

Journal Literature Searches

A number of major journals publish important articles in English dealing with Reformation thought. You are recommended to gain access to each number of these journals as it is published and note any studies of relevance to your particular interest. The following list of major journals is arranged in descending order of importance:

Archiv für Reformationsgeschichte
Sixteenth Century Journal
Church History
Journal of Ecclesiastical History
Harvard Theological Review
Journal of Theological Studies

Readers with a particular interest in the radical Reformation should also gain access to the *Mennonite Quarterly Review*. *Archiv für Reformationsgeschichte* publishes articles in English and German in about equal number; those published in German, however, helpfully include an abstract in English.

Readers with a knowledge of German should also check the following journals:

Zeitschrift für Kirchengeschichte
Zeitschrift für Theologie und Kirche
Kerygma und Dogmma

Abstracting Services

A number of organizations and journals provide abstracts of articles and/or books, arranged by subject. Two major publications are provided by the American Theological Library Association:

Religion Index One: Periodicals
Index to Book Reviews in Religion

These works are to be found in most North American university and college libraries. The following are also useful:

Guide to Social Science and Religion in Periodical Literature
Religious and Theological Abstracts
Social Sciences and Humanities Index

   Cataloguing practices vary from one library to another. In the event of difficulty in locating these reference works, you should consult your librarian.

Appendix 7

Chronology of Political and Intellectual History

1348	First German university founded at Prague.
1365	University of Vienna founded.
1378–1417	The Great Schism in the western church, with antipopes in Avignon and Rome.
1386	University of Heidelberg founded. Reform of statutes of University of Vienna, leading to dominance of the *via moderna*.
1388	University of Cologne founded.
1392	University of Erfurt founded.
1409	University of Leipzig founded.
1414–18	Council of Constance, ending the Great Schism.
1425	University of Louvain founded.
1453	The Fall of Constantinople: increased migration westwards of Greek-speaking scholars and their manuscripts.
1457	University of Freiburg-im-Breisgau founded.
1460	University of Basle founded.
1472	University of Ingolstadt founded.
1474	Condemnation of the *via moderna* at Paris: migration of those sympathetic to the *via moderna* to German universities.
1477	Outbreak of war between France and the house of Hapsburg.
1481	French decree against the *via moderna* rescinded.
1483	Martin Luther born at Eisleben in the Electorate of Saxony, 10 November.
1484	Huldrych Zwingli born, 1 January. Gabriel Biel appointed to chair at Tübingen.
1491	Johan Froben starts printing at Basle.
1492	Christobal Colon (Columbus) discovers the Americas.
1498	Zwingli begins his studies at University of Vienna.
1501	Luther begins his studies at University of Erfurt.
1502	University of Wittenberg founded by Elector Frederick of Saxony.
1503	First edition of Erasmus' *Enchiridion*.

1505   Luther enters the Augustinian monastery at Erfurt, 17 July.

1506   Publication of Amerbach edition of the works of Augustine.

1508   Reform of statutes of University of Wittenberg. Luther lectures in moral philosophy at University of Wittenberg.

1509   John Calvin born at Noyon, Picardy, 10 July. Erasmus publishes *Enconium Moriae*. Henry VIII assumes English throne.

1512   Luther visits Rome, January–February; begins lecturing on the Bible at Wittenberg. Philipp Melanchthon arrives at Tübingen.

1515   Publication of the *Letters of Obscure Men*, ridiculing the Cologne Dominicans. Publication of third edition of Erasmus' *Enchiridion*. Luther begins his lectures on Romans at Wittenberg. Defeat of the Swiss Confederation at the Battle of Marignano, September: Zurich announces it will henceforth enter into no further foreign alliances.

1516   First edition of Thomas More's *Utopia* published. Publication of Erasmus' *Novum Instrumentum omne*. Luther and Karlstadt clash over the interpretation of Augustine, 25 September.

1517   Karlstadt defends 151 Augustinian theses, 26 April. Luther posts 95 theses on indulgences, 31 October.

1518   Karlstadt reforms theological curriculum at Wittenberg, with new emphasis upon Augustine and the Bible, March. Christoph Froschauer begins printing at Zurich. Luther's Heidelberg Disputation, April. Luther appears before Cajetan at Augsburg, October–November. Zwingli called to Zurich as Leutpriest.

1519   Zwingli begins public preaching at the Grossmu[um]nster, Zurich. Charles V elected Holy Roman emperor. Leipzig Disputation between Luther, Karlstadt and Eck, July. Luther condemned by the University of Cologne, 30 August. Luther condemned by the University of Louvain, 7 November.

1520   Luther condemned by the University of Paris, 15 April. Papal bull *Exsurge Domine* threatens Luther with excommunication, 15 June. Luther publishes his three reforming treatises: *Appeal to the German Nobility, The Babylonian Captivity of the Church, The Freedom of a Christian*. Zurich city council issues mandate declaring that all preaching must be based upon Scripture. Luther publicly burns the papal bull and works of canon law.

1521   Melanchthon publishes first edition of his *Loci Communes*, destined to become the standard format for Lutheran works of systematic theology. Diet of Worms; Luther placed under the ban of the Empire, 8 May. Luther placed in protective custody in the

Wartburg. Riots and iconoclasm at Wittenberg, as Karlstadt takes charge of church affairs in Luther's absence.

1522 Unrest at Wittenberg leads to Luther's return. Breaking of the Lenten Fast at Zurich. Publication of Luther's German translation of the New Testament, September.

1523 First Zurich Disputation, placing city council in charge of scriptural preaching at Zurich, 29 January. Basle city council issues mandate on preaching according to Scripture, based on Zurich's 1520 mandate. Second Zurich Disputation, on the mass and images in churches, 26–28 October.

1524 Battle of Novara, 30 April. Zurich city council issues decree permitting removal of images from churches, 15 June. German Peasants' War breaks out.

1525 Anabaptism becomes an important movement: first baptisms at Zurich, 21 January. Battle of Pavia, 25 February. Zwingli's *Commentary on true and false religion*, criticizing Erasmus, published. *The Twelve Articles of Memmingen* set out the grievances of the German peasantry: mob violence results. Zurich abolishes the mass, 12 April. Luther writes *Against the Murderous and Thieving Hordes of Peasants*, 4 May. Thomas Müntzer and 53 supporters of the Peasants' Revolt publicly executed, 27 May. Luther secretly marries Katharina von Bora, a former nun, 13 June; public ceremony follows, 27 June. Luther's *de servo arbitrio* published, confirming a serious rift with Erasmus.

1526 Diet of Speyer, June–August.

1527 Schleitheim Confession (February); Sack of Rome by the troops of Charles V. Henry VIII seeks divorce from Catherine of Aragon.

1528 Berne accepts Zwinglian Reformation, including the abolition of the mass, 7 February. St Gall abolishes the mass, 17 July. Charles V authorizes death penalty for Anabaptists.

1529 Diet of Speyer, ending toleration of Lutheranism in Catholic districts, 21 February. Protest of six princes and fourteen cities against the Diet of Speyer, giving rise to the term 'Protestant'. Treaty of Barcelona, between Charles V and Pope Clement VII, 29 June. Peace of Cambrai: Francis I of France and Charles V agree peace, 3 August. Philip of Hesse convenes abortive Colloquy of Marburg, 1–4 October. Charles V and Venice agree peace at Bologna, 28 December; Augsburg Confession of Faith promulgated at Imperial Diet of Augsburg.

1530 Pope Clement VII crowns Charles V emperor at Bologna.

1531 Founding of the Schmalkaldic League for the defence of Protestantism, 27 February. Charles V leaves Germany, creating a vacuum which encourages the spread of the Reformation. Death of Zwingli in battle at Cappel, 11 October.

1532   Calvin publishes his commentary on Seneca's *De clementia*. Death of William Warham, Archbishop of Canterbury.

1533   Thomas Cranmer appointed Archbishop of Canterbury. Nicolas Cop's All Saints Day oration at Paris, 1 November. Calvin flees Paris.

1534   Affair of the Placards provokes Francis I to action against French evangelicals, 18 October. Calvin settles in Basel; writes *Institutes*. First edition of Luther's German Bible (including both Old and New Testaments) published. Anabaptists take over the city of Münster, sending shock waves throughout the region. Succession Act, Supremacy Act and Treason Act give Henry VIII power over English church.

1535   City of Geneva declares itself to be a republic.

1536   First edition of Calvin's *Institutes* published, March. Bucer and Luther reach agreement on the eucharist, May. Calvin detained in Geneva by Farel, July. Henry VIII enters into negotiations with German Lutherans. Calvin's intervention at the Lausanne Disputation (October) leads to an enhancement of his authority within Geneva. Genevan Confession published (November).

1538   Calvin expelled from Geneva; takes refuge in Strasbourg.

1539   Second edition of Calvin's *Institutes*. First volume of Luther's complete works appears. *Six Articles* published in England.

1540   Bigamy of Philip of Hesse. Calvin marries the widow Idelette de Bure. The Society of Jesus formally established. Calvin publishes his *Reply to Sadoleto* and his *Commentary on Romans*.

1541   Colloquy of Regensburg (Ratisbon), April–May. First French edition of Calvin's *Institutes*. Calvin returns to establish his theocracy at Geneva, September.

1545   Council of Trent opens, 13 December.

1546   Death of Luther, 18 February. Outbreak of Schmalkaldic War. Fourth Session of Council of Trent (8 April).

1547   Henry VIII dies, succeeded by Edward VI. Sixth Session of Council of Trent (13 January); Seventh Session (3 March); defeat of Schmalkaldic League at Mühlberg, 24 April. *Book of Homilies* published.

1549   First Prayer Book of Edward VI published, written by Cranmer.

1552   Second Prayer Book of Edward VI published, written by Cranmer.

1553   Servetus executed at Geneva for heresy. Edward VI dies, succeeded by Mary Tudor.

1555	Religious Peace of Augsburg recognizes existing religious territorial divisions between Lutherans and Roman Catholics in the Holy Roman Empire. Charles V abdicates.
1556	Thomas Cranmer and others executed.
1558	Charles V dies. Mary Tudor dies, succeeded by Elizabeth I.
1559	Publication of 1559 edition of Calvin's Institutes; establishment of Genevan Academy. Henri II of France dies, leading to domination of the French court by the anti-Protestant Guise family. Elizabethan Settlement of Religion.
1560	The Conspiracy of Amboise points to growing Calvinist influence in France, and increased tension as a result. Final French edition of Calvin's *Institutes*.
1562	French Wars of Religion break out.
1563	Publication of *Heidelberg Catechism*, demonstrating an increased Calvinist presence within German territories. Council of Trent closes. Publication of *Thirty-Nine Articles*.
1564	Death of Calvin, 27 May.

Notes

Chapter 1   Introduction

1   F. M. Powicke, *The Reformation in England* (London, 1941), pp. 1, 34. See further A. G. Dickens, 'The Reformation in England', in *Reformation Studies* (London, 1982), pp. 443–56; J. J. Scarisbrick, *The Reformation and the English People* (Oxford, 1985), pp. 61–84.
2   See the analysis in Alister E. McGrath, *The Genesis of Doctrine* (Oxford/Cambridge, Mass., 1990), pp. 37–52.

Chapter 2   Late Medieval Religion

1   Berndt Moeller, 'Piety in Germany around 1500', in *The Reformation in Medieval Perspective*, ed. Steven E. Ozment (Chicago, 1971), pp. 50–75.
2   The best study is H.-J. Goertz, *Pfaffenhass und gross Geschrei: Die reformatorischen Bewegungen in Deutschland 1517–1529* (Munich, 1987). See also H. J. Cohn, 'Anticlericalism in the German Peasants' War, 1525', *Past and Present* 83 (1979), pp. 3–31.
3   H. Heller, *The Conquest of Poverty: The Calvinist Revolt in Sixteenth-Century France* (Leiden, 1986).
4   M. Edelstein, 'Les origines sociales de l'épiscopat sous Louis XII et François Ier', *Revue d'histoire moderne et contemporaine* 24 (1977), pp. 239–47.
5   Gerald Strauss, *Manifestations of Discontent in Germany on the Eve of the Reformation* (Bloomington, Ind., 1971); A. G. Dickens, 'Intellectual and Social Forces in the German Reformation', in *Reformation Studies* (London, 1982), pp. 491–503.
6   On the origins and impact of doctrinal pluralism, see Alister E. McGrath, *The Intellectual Origins of the European Reformation* (Oxford, 1987), pp. 12–28.

Chapter 3   Humanism and the Reformation

1   Wallace K. Ferguson, *The Renaissance in Historical Thought* (New York, 1948).
2   Jacob Burckhardt, *The Civilization of the Renaissance in Italy* (New York, 1935), p. 143.

3   See the invaluable study of Peter Burke, *The Italian Renaissance: Culture and Society in Italy*, revised edn (Oxford, 1986).

4   See W. Rüegg, *Cicero und der Humanismus* (Zurich, 1946), pp. 1–4; A. Campana, 'The Origin of the Word "Humanist"', *Journal of the Warburg and Courtauld Institutes* 9 (1946), pp. 60–73.

5   Charles Trinkaus, 'A Humanist's Image of Humanism: The Inaugural Orations of Bartolommeo della Fonte', *Studies in the Renaissance* 7 (1960), pp. 90–147; H. H. Gray, 'Renaissance Humanism: The Pursuit of Eloquence', in *Renaissance Essays*, ed. P. O. Kristeller and P. P. Wiener (New York, 1968), pp. 199–216.

6   Hans Baron, *The Crisis of the Early Italian Renaissance: Civic Humanism and Republican Liberty in an Age of Classicism and Tyranny*, revised edn (Princeton, N.J., 1966).

7   Jerrold E. Seigel, 'Civic Humanism or Ciceronian Rhetoric? The Culture of Petrarch and Bruni', *Past and Present* 34 (1966), pp. 3–48.

8   E. Ziegler, 'Zur Reformation als Reformation des Lebens und der Sitten', *Rorschacher Neujahrsblatt* (1984), pp. 53–71.

9   The word *enchiridion* literally means 'something held in the hand', and came to have two meanings: a *weapon* held in the hand (i.e. a dagger) or a *book* held in the hand (i.e. a 'handbook').

10 On the Vulgate, see chapter 8 and R. Loewe, 'The Medieval History of the Latin Vulgate', in *Cambridge History of the Bible II: The West from the Fathers to the Reformation*, ed. G. W. H. Lampe (Cambridge, 1969), pp. 102–54.

11 The full extent of humanist influence upon the reformers goes further than suggested by this brief summary. The reader is referred to Alister E. McGrath, *The Intellectual Origins of the European Reformation* (Oxford, 1987), for a discussion of two major points: (1) the influence of humanism upon the text of Scripture (pp. 122–39) and (2) the influence of humanism upon the interpretation of Scripture (pp. 152–74). On the full importance of the 'patristic testimony' for the Reformation, see ibid. pp. 175–90.

12 Several pseudo-Augustinian works managed to get through the humanists' process of sieving: the Amerbach edition of Augustine's works includes *De vera et falsa poenitentia* ('On True and False Penitence'), which contradicts Augustine at a number of important points.

13 For further details, see McGrath, *Intellectual Origins*, pp. 43–59.

14 For further details, see ibid., pp. 59–68.

Chapter 4   Scholasticism and the Reformation

1   David Knowles, *The Evolution of Medieval Thought* (London, 1976), pp. 71–288; Paul Vignaux, *Philosophy in the Middle Ages* (New York, 1959), pp. 69–90.

2   On Aquinas, see Etienne Gilson, *The Christian Philosophy of St Thomas Aquinas* (New York, 1956).

3   See Charles G. Nauert, 'The Clash of Humanists and Scholastics: An Approach to Pre-Reformation Controversies', *Sixteenth Century Journal* 4 (1973), pp. 1–18; James Overfeld, 'Scholastic Opposition to Humanism in Pre-Reformation Germany', *Viator* 7 (1976), pp. 391–420. A particularly helpful essay on this theme

is A. H. T. Levi, 'The Breakdown of Scholasticism and the Significance of Evangelical Humanism', in *The Philosophical Assessment of Theology*, ed. G. R. Hughes (Georgetown, 1987), pp. 101–28.

4   On the problem of universals, see John Hospers, *An Introduction to Philosophical Analysis*, 2nd revised edn (Englewood Cliffs, N.J., 1976), pp. 354–67. On realism and nominalism in the Middle Ages, see Etienne Gilson, *History of Christian Philosophy in the Middle Ages* (London, 1978), pp. 489–98; M. H. Carré, *Realists and Nominalists* (Oxford, 1946).

5   On Thomism, see Gilson, *History of Christian Philosophy in the Middle Ages*, pp. 361–83. On Scotism, see ibid., pp. 454–71.

6   For the historical development of the Pelagian controversy and the issues involved, see Peter Brown, *Augustine of Hippo: A Biography* (London, 1975), pp. 340–407; Gerald Bonner, *St Augustine of Hippo: Life and Controversies*, 2nd edn (Norwich, 1986), pp. 312–93.

7   See Alister E. McGrath, *Institia Dei: A History of the Christian Doctrine of Justification* (2 vols; Cambridge, 1986), vol. 1, pp. 128–45; Brown, *Augustine of Hippo*, pp. 398–407.

8   For what follows, see McGrath, *Iustitia Dei*, vol. 1, pp. 119–28; 166–72.

9   See Francis Oakley, *The Political Thought of Pierre d'Ailly: The Voluntarist Tradition* (New Haven, 1964).

10   See William J. Courtenay, 'The King and the Leaden Coin: The Economic Background of Sine Qua Non Causality', *Traditio* 28 (1972), pp. 185–209.

11   For the personalities involved, see William J. Courtenay, *Adam Wodeham: An Introduction to his Life and Writings* (Leiden, 1978).

12   See Heiko A. Oberman, *Masters of the Reformation: The Emergence of a New Intellectual Climate in Europe* (Cambridge, 1981), pp. 64–110.

13   Heiko A. Oberman, 'Headwaters of the Reformation: *Initia Lutheri – Initia Reformationis*', reprinted in *The Dawn of the Reformation: Essays in Late Medieval and Early Reformation Thought* (Edinburgh, 1986), pp. 39–83.

14   Oberman, 'Headwaters of the Reformation', p. 77.

15   Alister E. McGrath, *The Intellectual Origins of the European Reformation* (Oxford, 1987), pp. 108–15.

16   Alister E. McGrath, 'John Calvin and Late Medieval Thought: A Study in Late Medieval Influences upon Calvin's Theological Development', *ARG* 77 (1986), pp. 58–78; *idem, Intellectual Origins*, pp. 94–107.

17   Karl Reuter, *Das Grundverständnis der Theologie Calvins* (Neukirchen, 1963); *idem, Vom Scholaren bis zum jungen Reformator: Studien zum Werdegang Johannes Calvins* (Neukirchen, 1981).

18   See P. O. Kristeller, 'The Contribution of Religious Orders to Renaissance Thought and Learning', *American Benedictine Review* 21 (1970), pp. 1–55.

Chapter 6   The Doctrine of Justification by Faith

1   For a full account, see F. W. Dillistone, *The Christian Understanding of Atonement* (London, 1968). (The term 'atonement' is often used to refer to the 'significance

of the death of Christ'.) For a more popular account, see Alister McGrath, *Making Sense of the Cross* (Leicester, 1992).

2 S. Alzeghy, *Nova creatura: la nozione della grazia nei commentari medievali di S. Paolo* (Rome, 1956); J. Auer, *Die Entwicklung der Gnadenlehre in der Hochscholastik* (2 vols; Freiburg, 1942–51).

3 For the background, see Krister Stendahl, 'The Apostle Paul and the Introspective Conscience of the West', in *Paul among Jews and Gentiles* (Philadelphia, 1983), pp. 78–96.

4 See Alister E. McGrath, *Luther's Theology of the Cross: Martin Luther's Theological Breakthrough* (Oxford, 1985), pp. 72–92; 100–28.

5 See ibid., pp. 106–13, for texts and analysis.

6 See Alister E. McGrath, *Iustitia Dei: A History of the Christian Doctrine of Justification* (2 vols; Cambridge, 1986), vol. 1, pp. 51–70.

7 For the full Latin text and an English translation, see McGrath, *Luther's Theology of the Cross*, pp. 95–8. For an English translation only, see *Luther's Works* (55 vols; St Louis/Philadelphia, 1955–75), vol. 34, pp. 336–8. In the 'quotation' in the text, I have paraphrased Luther somewhat, and omitted some of his more technical phrases for the sake of clarity.

8 For the debate, see McGrath, *Luther's Theology of the Cross*, pp. 95–147, esp. pp. 142–7. A significant minority opinion places the breakthrough in 1518–19. A useful essay, worth consulting, is Brian A. Gerrish, 'By Faith Alone: Medium and Message in Luther's Gospel', in *The Old Protestantism and the New: Essays on the Reformation Heritage* (Edinburgh, 1982), pp. 69–89.

9 For details of Luther's doctrine of justification by faith, see McGrath, *Iustitia Dei*, vol. 2, pp. 10–20.

10 As demonstrated by Leif Grane, *Contra Gabrielem: Luthers Auseinandersetzung mit Gabriel Biel in der Disputatio contra scholasticam theologiam* (Gyldendal, 1962).

11 For further discussion, see John Bossy, *Christianity in the West 1400–1700* (Oxford, 1987), pp. 35–56; David C. Steinmetz, 'Luther against Luther', in *Luther in Context* (Bloomington, Ind., 1986), pp. 1–11; Thomas N. Tentler, *Sin and Confession on the Eve of the Reformation* (Princeton, 1977).

12 *Appeal to the German Nobility, The Babylonian Captivity of the Church* and *The Freedom of a Christian.* These works are collected together in *Martin Luther: Three Treatises* (Philadelphia, 1973).

13 On this, see McGrath, *Iustitia Dei*, vol. 2, pp. 1–3, 20–5.

Chapter 7   The Doctrine of Predestination

1 See W. P. Stephens, *The Theology of Huldrych Zwingli* (Oxford, 1986), pp. 86–106.

2 On this work, see Harry J. McSorley, *Luther – Right or Wrong* (New York, 1969).

3 Although doubt was cast on Calvin's role in drafting Nicolas Cop's All Souls' Day oration, new manuscript evidence has been uncovered suggesting that he was positively implicated. See Jean Rott, 'Documents strasbourgeois concernant Calvin. Un manuscrit autographe: la harangue du recteur Nicolas Cop', in *Regards contemporains sur Jean Calvin* (Paris, 1966), pp. 28–43.

4   See e.g. Harro Höpfl, *The Christian Polity of John Calvin* (Cambridge, 1982), pp. 219–26; Alister E. McGrath, *A Life of John Calvin* (Oxford/Cambridge, Mass., 1990), pp. 69–78.

5   For details of this important alteration and an analysis of its consequences, see McGrath, *Life of John Calvin*, pp. 202–18.

6   For Calvinism in England and America at this time, see Patrick Collinson, 'England and International Calvinism, 1558–1640', in *International Calvinism 1541–1715*, ed. M. Prestwich (Oxford, 1985), pp. 197–223; W. A. Speck and L. Billington, 'Calvinism in Colonial North America', in *International Calvinism*, ed. Prestwich, pp. 257–83.

7   B. B. Warfield, *Calvin and Augustine* (Philadelphia, 1956), p. 322.

Chapter 8   The Return to Scripture

1   See the magisterial collection of studies assembled in *The Cambridge History of the Bible*, ed. P. R. Ackroyd et al. (3 vols; Cambridge, 1963–69).

2   Alister E. McGrath, *The Intellectual Origins of the European Reformation* (Oxford, 1987), pp. 140–51. Two major studies of this theme should be noted: Paul de Vooght, *Les sources de la doctrine chrétienne d'après les théologiens du XIVé siècle et du début du XVé* (Paris, 1954); Hermann Schüssler, *Der Primät der Heiligen Schrift als theologisches und kanonistisches Problem im Spätmittelalter* (Wiesbaden, 1977).

3   Heiko A. Oberman, 'Quo vadis, Petre? Tradition from Irenaeus to *Humani Generis*', in *The Dawn of the Reformation: Essays in Late Medieval and Early Reformation Thought* (Edinburgh, 1986), pp. 269–96.

4   George H. Tavard, *Holy Writ or Holy Church? The Crisis of the Protestant Reformation* (London, 1959).

5   J. N. D. Kelly, *Jerome: Life, Writings and Controversies* (London, 1975). Strictly speaking, 'Vulgate' designates Jerome's translation of the Old Testament (except the Psalms, which were taken from the Gallican Psalter), the apocryphal works (except Wisdom, Ecclesiasticus, 1 and 2 Maccabees, and Baruch, which were taken from the Old Latin Version), and all the New Testament.

6   See Raphael Loewe, 'The Medieval History of the Latin Vulgate', in *Cambridge History of the Bible*, vol. 2, pp. 102–54.

7   McGrath, *Intellectual Origins*, pp. 124–5 and references therein.

8   Henry Hargreaves, 'The Wycliffite Versions', in *Cambridge History of the Bible*, vol. 2, pp. 387–415.

9   Basil Hall, 'Biblical Scholarship: Editions and Commentaries', in *Cambridge History of the Bible*, vol. 3, pp. 38–93.

10 Roland H. Bainton, *Erasmus of Christendom* (New York, 1969), pp. 168–71.

11 Roland H. Bainton, 'The Bible in the Reformation', in *Cambridge History of the Bible*, vol. 3, pp. 1–37, esp. pp. 6–9.

12 For further discussion of the problem of the Old Testament canon, see Roger T. Beckwith, *The Old Testament Canon of the New Testament Church* (London, 1985).

13   Pierre Fraenkel, *Testimonia Patrum: The Function of the Patristic Argument in the Theology of Philip Melanchthon* (Geneva, 1961); McGrath, *Intellectual Origins*, pp. 175–90.

14   e.g. Tavard, *Holy Writ or Holy Church?*, p. 208.

15   G. R. Potter, *Zwingli* (Cambridge, 1976), pp. 74–96.

16   Heiko A. Oberman, *Masters of the Reformation* (Cambridge, 1981), pp. 187–209.

Chapter 9   The Doctrine of the Sacraments

1   The passage makes use of a number of biblical texts, most importantly Matthew 26:26–8; Luke 22:19–20; 1 Corinthians 11:24. See also Basil Hall, '*Hoc est corpus meum*: The Centrality of the Real Presence for Luther', in *Luther: Theologian for Catholics and Protestants*, ed. George Yule (Edinburgh, 1985), pp. 112–44, for further details.

2   For an analysis of the reasons underlying Luther's rejection of Aristotle at this point, see Alister E. McGrath, *Luther's Theology of the Cross: Martin Luther's Theological Breakthrough* (Oxford, 1985), pp. 136–41.

3   Other important texts used by Luther include 1 Corinthians 10:16–33; 11:26–34. See David C. Steinmetz, 'Scripture and the Lord's Supper in Luther's Theology', in *Luther in Context* (Bloomington, Ind., 1986), pp. 72–84.

4   See W. P. Stephens, *The Theology of Huldrych Zwingli* (Oxford, 1986), pp. 180–93.

5   Timothy George, 'The Presuppositions of Zwingli's Baptismal Theology', in *Prophet, Pastor, Protestant: The Work of Huldrych Zwingli after Five Hundred Years*, ed. E. J. Furcha and H. W. Pipkin (Allison Park, Pa., 1984), pp. 71–87, esp. pp. 79–82.

6   On this point and its political and institutional importance, see Robert C. Walton, 'The Institutionalization of the Reformation at Zürich', *Zwingliana* 13 (1972), pp. 497–515.

7   Pope Clement VII accepted peace at Barcelona on 29 June; the King of France came to terms with Charles V on 3 August. The Colloquy of Marburg took place on 1–5 October.

8   For an excellent account of the Colloquy of Marburg, see G. R. Potter, *Zwingli* (Cambridge, 1976), pp. 316–42.

Chapter 10   The Doctrine of the Church

1   B. B. Warfield, *Calvin and Augustine* (Philadelphia, 1956), p. 322.

2   See Scott H. Hendrix, *Luther and the Papacy: Stages in a Reformation Conflict* (Philadelphia, 1981).

3   Also known as 'Ratisbon'. For details, see Peter Matheson, *Cardinal Contarini at Regensburg* (Oxford, 1972); Dermot Fenlon, *Heresy and Obedience in Tridentine Italy: Cardinal Pole and the Counter Reformation* (Cambridge, 1972).

4 *On the Councils and the Church* (1539); in D. *Martin Luthers Werke: Kritische Gesamtausgabe*, vol. 50 (Weimar, 1914), p. 630.

5 *Appeal to the German Nobility* (1520); in D. *Martin Luthers Werke: Kritische Gesamtausgabe*, vol. 6 (Weimar, 1888), pp. 406–8.

6 Letter to John Campanus, 1531; in B. Becker, 'Fragment van Francks latijnse
brief aan Campanus', *Nederlands Archief voor Kerkgeschiedenis* 46 (1964–5), pp.
197–205.

7 For a full discussion, see F. H. Littel, *The Anabaptist View of the Church*, 2nd edn
(Boston, 1958).

8 *Complete Writings of Menno Simons*, ed. J. C. Wenger (Scottsdale, PA, 1956), p. 502.

9 *Complete Writings of Menno Simons*, p. 300.

10 See Geoffrey G. Willis, *Saint Augustine and the Donatist Controversy* (London, 1950);
Gerald Bonner, *St Augustine of Hippo: Life and Controversies*, 2nd edn (Norwich,
1986), pp. 237–311.

11 *Institutes* IV.i.9–10; in *Joannis Calvini: Opera Selecta*, ed. P. Barth and W. Niesel, vol.
5 (Munich: Kaiser Verlag, 1936), pp. 13–16.

12 The First Helvetic Confession, 1536, article 14; in E. F. K. Müller (ed.), *Die
Bekenntnisschriften der reformierten Kirche* (Leipzig, 1903), p. 101.

13 *In Symbolum Apostolorum*, 9; in S. *Thomae Aquinitatis Opera Omnia*, vol. 6, ed. R.
Busa (Holzboog, 1980), p. 20.

14 *de appellatione ecclesiae catholicae*; in *Corpus Reformatorum*, vol. 24 (Halis Saxonum,
1845), columns 397–9.

Chapter 11   The Political Thought of the Reformation

1 The case of Thomas Müntzer illustrates this point: see Gordon Rupp, *Patterns
of Reformation* (London, 1969), pp. 157–353. More generally, the development
of the radical Reformation in the Low Countries should be noted: W. E.
Keeney, *Dutch Anabaptist Thought and Practice, 1539–1564* (Nieuwkoop,
1968).

2 See W. Ullmann, *Medieval Papalism: The Political Theories of the Medieval Canonists*
(London, 1949); M. J. Wilks, *The Problem of Sovereignty: The Papal Monarchy with
Augustus Triumphus and the Publicists* (Cambridge, 1963).

3 There is a considerable degree of ambiguity in Luther's use of terms such as
'kingdom' and 'government': see W. D. J. Cargill Thompson, 'The "Two Kingdoms" and the "Two Regiments": Some Problems of Luther's *Zwei-Reiche-Lehre*',
in *Studies in the Reformation: Luther to Hooker* (London, 1980), pp. 42–59.

4 See F. Edward Cranz, *An Essay on the Development of Luther's Thought on
Justice, Law and Society* (Cambridge, Mass., 1959), for a full analysis of this
point.

5 See David C. Steinmetz, 'Luther and the Two Kingdoms', in *Luther in Context*
(Bloomington, Ind., 1986), pp. 112–25.

6 See The famous letter of Karl Barth (1939), in which he asserted that 'The
German people suffer . . . from the mistake of Martin Luther regarding the relation of Law and Gospel, of temporal and spiritual order and power': quoted by

Helmut Thielicke, *Theological Ethics* (3 vols; Grand Rapids, Mich., 1979), vol. 1, p. 368.

7 Steinmetz, 'Luther and the Two Kingdoms', p. 114.

8 See the useful study of W. D. J. Cargill Thompson, 'Luther and the Right of Resistance to the Emperor', in *Studies in the Reformation*, pp. 3–41.

9 R. N. C. Hunt, 'Zwingli's Theory of Church and State', *Church Quarterly Review* 112 (1931), pp. 20–36; Robert C. Walton, *Zwingli's Theocracy* (Toronto, 1967); W. P. Stephens, *The Theology of Huldrych Zwingli* (Oxford, 1986), pp. 282–310.

10 Stephens, *Theology of Huldrych Zwingli*, p. 303, n. 87.

11 W. P. Stephens, *The Holy Spirit in the Theology of Martin Bucer* (Cambridge, 1970), pp. 167–72. On Bucer's political theology in general, see T. F. Torrance, *Kingdom and Church: A Study in the Theology of the Reformation* (Edinburgh, 1956), pp. 73–89.

12 For a careful study, see Harro Höpfl, *The Christian Polity of John Calvin* (Cambridge, 1982), pp. 152–206. Additional information may be found in Gillian Lewis, 'Calvinism in Geneva in the Time of Calvin and Beza', in *International Calvinism 1541–1715*, ed. M. Prestwich (Oxford, 1985), pp. 39–70.

13 K. P. Davis, 'No Discipline, no Church: An Anabaptist Contribution to the Reformed Tradition', *Sixteenth Century Journal* 13 (1982), pp. 45–9.

14 Indeed, Calvin was in the habit of dedicating works to European monarchs, in the hope of winning them to the Reformation cause. Among the dedicatees of Calvin's published works were Edward VI and Elizabeth I of England and Christopher III of Denmark.

Chapter 12 The Diffusion of the Thought of the Reformation

1 Martin Luther, *The Lesser Catechism* (1529); in *D. Martin Luthers Werke: Kritische Gesamtausgabe*, vol. 30, part 1 (Weimar, 1910), 225.20–257.24.

2 Heidelberg Catechism, Questions 96–8; in E. F. K. Müller (ed.), *Die Bekenntnisschriften der reformierten Kirche* (Leipzig, 1903), 710.8–27.

3 Gallic *Confession*, articles 3–5; in E. F. K. Müller (ed.), *Die Bekenntnisschriften der reformierten Kirche* (Leipzig, 1903), 222.5–44.

Chapter 13 The Thought of the English Reformation

1 'A Sermon of the Salvation of Mankind', in *The Two Books of Homilies* (Oxford, 1859), p. 24.

2 *Archbishop Cranmer on the True and Catholic Doctrine and Use of the Sacrament of the Lord's Supper*, ed. C. H. H. Wright (London, 1907), p. 156. Note that the spelling has been modernized to facilitate understanding of the meaning of this text.

3 *True and Catholic Doctrine*, p. 36.

4 *True and Catholic Doctrine*, p. 97.

5 *True and Catholic Doctrine*, p. 213.

Chapter 14   The Impact of Reformation Thought upon History

1. Robert M. Kingdon, 'The Deacons of the Reformed Church in Calvin's Geneva', in *Mélanges d'histoire du XVIe siècle* (Geneva, 1970), pp. 81–9.

2 Franziska Conrad, *Reformation in der bäuerlichen Gesellschaft: Zur Rezeption reformatorischer Theologie im Elsass* (Stuttgart, 1984), p. 14.

Select Bibliography

The best reference resource currently available relating to the thought of the Reformation is H. J. Hillerbrand (ed.), *The Oxford Encyclopaedia of the Reformation* (4 vols; Oxford, 1996). This is an essential resource for any concerned with any aspect of the Reformation, and includes substantial bibliographies.

The present bibliography does not aim to be exhaustive; its task is to identify potentially valuable studies in the English language, in order to allow readers of this work to further their study. The scheme of classification is as follows:

1 General Surveys of the Reformation
2 Studies of Aspects of Late Medieval Thought
    2.1 Scholasticism
    2.2 Humanism
3 Studies of Individual Reformers
    3.1 Luther
    3.2 Zwingli
    3.3 Calvin
    3.4 Erasmus
    3.5 Others
4 Studies of Aspects of Reformation Thought
    4.1 Biblical Authority and Interpretation
    4.2 Doctrines of Justification and Predestination
    4.3 Church, Ministry and Sacraments
    4.4 Church and Society
5 Studies of Individual Reforming Movements
    5.1 Lutheranism
    5.2 Calvinism
    5.3 The Radical Reformation
    5.4 The Catholic Reformation
    5.5 The English Reformation

1 General Surveys of the Reformation

Bossy, J., *Christianity in the West 1400–1700* (Oxford, 1987).
Cameron, E., *The European Reformation* (Oxford, 1991).

Chadwick, O., *Pelican History of the Church*, Vol. 3: *The Reformation* (London, 1972).
Elton, G. R. (ed.), *New Cambridge Modern History*, 2nd edn, Vol. 2: *The Reformation 1520–1559* (Cambridge, 1990).
George, T., *The Theology of the Reformers* (Nashville, Tenn., 1988).
Hillerbrand, H. J., *The Protestant Reformation* (New York, 1968).
Léonard, E. G., *A History of Protestantism* (2 vols; London, 1965–7).
Noll, M. A., *Confessions and Catechisms of the Reformation* (Grand Rapids, Mich., 1991).
Ozment, S. E., *The Age of Reform 1250–1550* (New Haven/London, 1973).
Pelikan, J., *The Christian Tradition*, Vol. 4: *Reformation of Church and Dogma, 1300–1700* (Chicago/London, 1984).
Reardon, B. M. G., *Religious Thought in the Reformation* (London, 1981).
Rupp, G., *Patterns of Reformation* (London, 1969).
Spitz, L. W., *The Protestant Reformation 1517–1559* (New York, 1986).

2   Studies of Aspects of Late Medieval Thought

Bolton, B., *The Medieval Reformation* (London/Baltimore, 1983).
Lambert, M. D., *Medieval Heresy: Popular Movements from Bogomil to Hus* (London, 1977).
Leff, G., *Heresy in the Later Middle Ages* (2 vols; Manchester, 1967).
Oakley, F., 'Religious and Ecclesiastical Life on the Eve of the Reformation', in *Reformation Europe: A Guide to Research*, ed. Steven Ozment (St Louis, Mo., 1982), pp. 5–32.
Oberman, H. A., 'Fourteenth Century Religious Thought: A Premature Profile', in *The Dawn of the Reformation: Essays in Late Medieval and Early Reformation Thought* (Edinburgh, 1986), pp. 1–17.
——, 'The Shape of Late Medieval Thought', in *The Dawn of the Reformation*, pp. 18–38.
Ozment, S. E., *The Age of Reform 1250–1550: An Intellectual and Religious History of Late Medieval and Reformation Europe* (New Haven, 1973).
Strauss, G., *Manifestations of Discontent in Germany on the Eve of the Reformation* (Bloomington, Ind., 1971)

2.1   Scholasticism

Coplestone, F., *A History of Christian Philosophy in the Middle Ages* (London, 1978).
Gilson, E., *The Spirit of Medieval Philosophy* (London, 1936).
Janz, D. R., *Luther and Late Medieval Thomism* (Waterloo, Ont., 1983).
Levi, A. H. T., 'The Breakdown of Scholasticism and the Significance of Evangelical Humanism', in *The Philosophical Assessment of Theology*, ed. G. R. Hughes (Georgetown, 1987), pp. 101–28.
Nauert, C. G., 'The Clash of Humanists and Scholastics: An Approach to Pre-Reformation Controversies', *Sixteenth Century Journal* 4 (1973), pp. 1–18.
Oberman, H. A., *The Harvest of Medieval Theology* (Cambridge, Mass., 1963).
——, *Masters of the Reformation* (Cambridge, 1981).
Overfeld, J., 'Scholastic Opposition to Humanism in Pre-Reformation Germany', *Viator* 7 (1976), pp. 391–420.

Pieper, J., *Scholasticism* (London, 1961).
Steinmetz, D. C., *Misericordia Dei: The Theology of Johannes von Staupitz in its Late Medieval Setting* (Leiden, 1968).

2.2 Humanism

Boyle, M. O., *Rhetoric and Reform: Erasmus' Civil Dispute with Luther* (Cambridge, Mass., 1983).
Burckhardt, J., *The Civilization of the Renaissance* (London, 1944).
Burke, P., *The Italian Renaissance: Culture and Society in Italy*, revised edn (Oxford, 1986).
Dowling, M., *Humanism in the Age of Henry VIII* (London, 1986).
Ferguson, W. K., *The Renaissance in Historical Thought* (New York, 1948).
Grassi, E., *Rhetoric as Philosophy: The Humanist Tradition* (University Park, Pa., 1980).
Grossmann, M., *Humanism at Wittenberg 1485–1517* (Nieuwkoop, 1975).
Overfeld, J. H., *Humanism and Scholasticism in Late Medieval Germany* (Princeton, 1984).
Spitz, L. W., *The Religious Renaissance of the German Humanists* (Cambridge, Mass., 1963).
Trinkaus, C., *The Scope of Renaissance Humanism* (Ann Arbor, Mich., 1983).

3 Studies of Individual Reformers

3.1 Luther

Althaus, P., *The Theology of Martin Luther* (Philadelphia, 1966).
Bainton, R. H., *Here I Stand: A Life of Martin Luther* (New York, 1959).
Brendler, G., *Martin Luther: Theology and Revolution* (New York, 1991).
Ebeling, G., *Luther: An Introduction to His Thought* (Philadelphia, 1970).
Hendrix, S. H., *Luther and the Papacy* (Philadelphia, 1981).
Kittelson, J. M., *Luther the Reformer: The Story of the Man and his Career* (Leicester, 1989).
Loewenich, W. von, *Martin Luther: The Man and his Work* (Minneapolis, 1986).
Lohse, B., *Martin Luther: An Introduction to his Life and Writings* (Philadelphia, 1986).
McGrath, A. E., *Luther's Theology of the Cross* (Oxford/New York, 1985).
McSorley, H. J., *Luther – Right or Wrong?* (New York, 1969).
Oberman, H. A., *Luther: Man between God and the Devil* (New Haven, 1989).
Rupp, E. G., *The Righteousness of God* (London, 1953).
Steinmetz, D. C., *Luther in Context* (Bloomington, Ind., 1986).
Watson, P. S., *Let God be God* (London, 1947).

3.2 Zwingli

Courvoisier, J., *Zwingli: A Reformed Theologian* (Richmond, Va., 1963).
Farner, O., *Zwingli the Reformer* (New York, 1952).
Furcha, E. J., and Pipkin, H. W. (eds), *Prophet, Pastor, Protestant: The Work of Huldrych Zwingli* (Allison Park, Pa., 1984).
Gäbler, U., *Huldrych Zwingli: His Life and Work* (Philadelphia, 1986).
Potter, G. R., *Zwingli* (Cambridge, 1976).
Stephens, W. P., *The Theology of Huldrych Zwingli* (Oxford, 1986).

3.3 Calvin

Bouwsma, W. J., *John Calvin: A Sixteenth Century Portrait* (Oxford, 1989).
Ganoczy, A., *The Young Calvin* (Edinburgh, 1988).
George, T. (ed.), *John Calvin and the Church: A Prism of Reform* (Louisville, Ky., 1990).
Leith, J. H., *Calvin's Doctrine of the Christian Life* (Atlanta, Ga., 1989).
McGrath, A. E., *A Life of John Calvin* (Oxford/Cambridge, Mass., 1990).
Parker, T. H. L., *John Calvin* (London, 1976).
Reid, W. S., *John Calvin: His Influence in the Western World* (Grand Rapids, Mich., 1982).
Reist, B. A., *A Reading of Calvin's Institutes* (Louisville, Ky., 1991).
Selinger, S., *Calvin against Himself: An Inquiry in Intellectual History* (Hamden, Conn., 1984).
Stauffer, R., 'Calvin', in *International Calvinism 1541–1715*, ed. M. Prestwich (Oxford, 1985), pp. 15–38.
Wallace, R. S., *Calvin, Geneva and the Reformation* (Edinburgh, 1988).
Wendel, F., *Calvin: The Origins and Development of his Religious Thought* (London, 1963).

3.4 Erasmus

Bainton, R. H., *Erasmus of Christendom* (New York, 1969).
McConica, J. K., *Erasmus* (Oxford, 1991).
Phillips, M. M., *Erasmus and the Northern Renaissance* (London, 1949).
Rummel, E., *Erasmus as Translator of the Classics* (Toronto, 1985).
Schoeck, R. J., *Erasmus of Europe: The Making of a Humanist 1467–1500* (Edinburgh, 1990).

3.5 Others

Baker, J. W., *Heinrich Bullinger and the Covenant: The Other Reformed Tradition* (Athens, Ohio, 1980), pp. 55–140.
Fraenkel, P., *Testimonia Patrum: The Function of the Patristic Argument in the Theology of Philip Melanchthon* (Geneva, 1961).
——, 'Bucer's *Memorandum* of 1541 and a 'lettera nicodemitica' of Capito's', *BHR* 36 (1974), pp. 575–87.
Hobbs, G., 'Martin Bucer on Psalm 22: A Study in the Application of Rabbinical Exegesis by a Christian Hebraist', in *Etudes de l'exégèse au XVIe siècle*, ed. O. Fatio and P. Fraenkel (Geneva, 1978), pp. 144–63.
Kittelson, J. M., *Wolfgang Capito: From Humanist to Reformer* (Leiden, 1975).
Maxcey, C. E., *Bona Opera: A Study in the Development of the Doctrine in Philip Melanchthon* (Nieuwkoop, 1980).
Quere, R. W., *Melanchthon's Christum cognoscere: Christ's Efficacious Presence in the Eucharistic Theology of Melanchthon* (Nieuwkoop, 1977).
Stephens, W. P., *The Holy Spirit in the Theology of Martin Bucer* (Cambridge, 1970).

4 Studies of Aspects of Reformation Thought

4.1 Biblical Authority and Interpretation

The Cambridge History of the Bible, ed. P. R. Ackroyd et al. (3 vols; Cambridge, 1963–9).

Bentley, J. H., *Humanists and Holy Writ: New Testament Scholarship in the Renaissance* (Princeton, N.J., 1983).

Bradshaw, B., 'The Christian Humanism of Erasmus', *JThS* 33 (1982), 411–47.

Evans, G. R., *The Language and Logic of the Bible: The Road to Reformation* (Cambridge, 1985).

Gerrish, B. A., 'The Word of God and the Word of Scripture: Luther and Calvin on Biblical Authority', in *The Old Protestantism and the New: Essays on the Reformation Heritage* (Edinburgh, 1982), pp. 51–68.

Oberman, H. O., 'Quo vadis, Petre? Tradition from Irenaeus to *Humani Generis*', in *The Dawn of the Reformation: Essays in Late Medieval and Early Reformation Thought* (Edinburgh, 1986), pp. 269–96.

Tavard, G. H., *Holy Writ or Holy Church? The Crisis of the Protestant Reformation* (London, 1959).

Tracy, J. D., '*Ad Fontes*: The Humanist Understanding of Scripture as Nourishment for the Soul', in *Christian Spirituality II: High Middle Ages and Reformation*, ed. Jill Raitt (New York, 1988), pp. 252–67.

4.2   Doctrines of Justification and Predestination

Knox, D. B., *Doctrine of Faith in the Reign of Henry VIII* (London, 1961).

McGrath, A. E., *Iustitia Dei: A History of the Christian Doctrine of Justification*, 2nd edn (Cambridge, 1998).

——, 'Justification and the Reformation', *ARG* 81 (1990), pp. 5–20.

Muller, R. A., *Christ and the Decree: Christology and Predestination from Calvin to Perkins* (Grand Rapids, Mich., 1988).

Penny, D. A., *Freewill or Predestination? The Battle over Saving Grace in Mid-Tudor England* (London, 1990).

Santmire, P. H., 'Justification in Calvin's 1540 Romans Commentary', *Church History* 33 (1964), pp. 294–313.

Wallace, D. D., *Puritans and Predestination: Grace in English Protestant Theology, 1525–1695* (Chapel Hill, N.C., 1982).

4.3   Church, Ministry and Sacraments

Avis, P. D. L., *The Church in the Theology of the Reformers* (Basingstoke, 1980).

Brooks, P. N., *Thomas Cranmer's Doctrine of the Eucharist* (London, 1965).

Clark, F., *Eucharistic Sacrifice and the Reformation*, 2nd edn (Devon, 1981).

Eire, C. M. N., *War against the Idols: The Reformation of Worship from Erasmus to Calvin* (Cambridge, 1986).

George, T., 'The Presuppositions of Zwingli's Baptismal Theology', in *Prophet, Pastor, Protestant: The Work of Huldrych Zwingli*, ed. E. J. Furcha and H. Pipkin (Allison Park, Pa., 1984), pp. 71–87.

Gerrish, B. A., 'Gospel and Eucharist: John Calvin on the Lord's Supper', in *The Old Protestantism and the New* (Edinburgh, 1982), pp. 106–17.

Hall, B., '*Hoc est corpus meum*: The Centrality of the Real Presence for Luther', in *Luther: Theologian for Catholics and Protestants*, ed. George Yule (Edinburgh, 1985), pp. 112–44.

McClelland, J., *The Visible Words of God: An Exposition of the Sacramental Theology of Peter Martyr Vermigli* (London, 1957).

Steinmetz, D. C., 'Scripture and the Lord's Supper in Luther's Theology', in *Luther in Context* (Bloomington, Ind., 1986), pp. 72–84.

4.4 Church and Society

Cargill Thompson, W. D. J., 'The "Two Kingdoms" and the "Two Regiments": Some Problems of Luthr's *Zwei-Reiche-Lehre*', in *Studies in the Reformation: Luther to Hooker* (London, 1980), pp. 42–59.

——, *The Political Thought of Martin Luther* (Brighton, 1984).

Cranz, F. E., *An Essay on the Development of Luther's Thought on Justice, Law and Society* (Cambridge, Mass., 1959).

Green, R. W. (ed.), *Protestantism and Capitalism: The Weber Thesis and Its Critics* (Boston, Mass., 1959).

—— (ed.), *Protestantism, Capitalism and Social Science: The Weber Thesis Controversy* (Boston, Mass., 1973).

Höpfl, H., *The Christian Polity of John Calvin* (Cambridge, 1985).

—— (ed.), *Luther and Calvin on Secular Authority* (Cambridge, 1991).

Hunt, R. N. C., 'Zwingli's Theory of Church and State', *Church Quarterly Review* 112 (1931), pp. 20–36.

Marshall, G., *Presbyteries and Profits: Calvinism and the Development of Capitalism in Scotland, 1560–1707* (Oxford, 1980).

O'Donovan, J. L., *Theology of Law and Authority in the English Reformation* (Atlanta, Ga., 1991).

Skinner, Q., *The Foundations of Modern Political Thought*, vol. 2 (Cambridge, 1978).

——, 'The Origins of the Calvinist Theory of Revolution', in *After the Reformation*, ed. B. C. Malament (Philadelphia, 1980), pp. 309–30.

Steinmetz, D. C., 'Luther and the Two Kingdoms', in *Luther in Context* (Bloomington, Ind., 1986), pp. 112–25.

Tonkin, J., *The Church and Secular Order in Reformation Thought* (New York/London, 1971).

Torrance, T. F., *Kingdom and Church: A Study in the Theology of the Reformation* (Edinburgh, 1956).

Zaret, D., *The Heavenly Contract: Ideology and Organization in Pre-Revolutionary Puritanism* (Chicago, 1985).

5 Studies of Individual Reforming Movements

5.1 Lutheranism

Burgess, J. A., *The Role of the Augsburg Confession* (Philadelphia, 1980).

Elert, W., *Structure of Lutheranism* (St Louis, Mo., 1962).

Gritsch, E. W., and Jenson, R. W., *Lutheranism: The Theological Movement and its Confessional Writings* (Philadelphia, 1976).

Maurer, W., *A Historical Commentary on the Augsburg Confession* (Philadelphia, 1976).

5.2   Calvinism

Armstrong, B. G., *Calvinism and the Amyraut Heresy: Protestant Scholasticism and Humanism in Seventeenth Century France* (Madison, Wis., 1969).

Ball, B. W., *A Great Expectation: Eschatological Thought in English Protestantism to 1660* (Leiden, 1975).

Baron, H., 'Calvinist Republicanism and its Historical Roots', *Church History* 7 (1939), pp. 30–42.

Collinson, P., 'Calvinism with an Anglican Face', in *Reform and Reformation: England and the Continent*, ed. D. Baker (Oxford, 1979), pp. 71–102.

Kendall, R. T., *Calvin and English Calvinism to 1649* (Oxford, 1980).

Klauber, M. I., 'Continuity and Discontinuity in Post-Reformation Reformed Theology', *Journal of the Evangelical Theological Society* 33 (1990), pp. 467–75.

Platt, J., *Reformed Thought and Scholasticism: The Arguments for th Existence of God in Dutch Theology, 1575–1670* (Leiden, 1982).

Prestwich, M. (ed.), *International Calvinism 1541–1715* (Oxford, 1985).

Strehle, S., *Calvinism, Federalism and Scholasticism: A Study of the Reformed Doctrine of Covenant* (Berne, 1988).

5.3   The Radical Reformation

Blickle, P., *The Revolution of 1525* (Baltimore/London, 1981).

Clasen, C.-P., *Anabaptism. A Social History 1525–1618* (Ithaca/London, 1972).

Cohn, H. J., 'Anti-Clericalism in the German Peasants' War 1525', *Past and Present* 83 (1979), pp. 3–31.

Keeney, W. E., *Dutch Anabaptist Thought and Practice, 1539–1564* (Nieuwkoop, 1968).

Littel, F. H., *The Anabaptist View of the Church*, 2nd edn (Boston, 1958).

Scriber, R. W., and Benecke, G. (eds), *The German Peasant War 1525: New Perspectives* (London, 1979).

Stayer, J. M., *Anabaptists and the Sword*, 2nd edn (Lawrence, 1976).

——, *The German Peasants' War and Anabaptist Community of Goods* (Montreal, 1991).

Yoder, J. H., *The Legacy of Michael Sattler* (Scottdale, Pa., 1973).

5.4   The Catholic Reformation

Dickens, A. G., *The Counter Reformation* (New York, 1979).

Evennett, H. O., *The Spirit of the Counter Reformantion* (Notre Dame, Ind., 1970).

Fenlon, D., *Heresy and Obedience in Tridentine Italy: Cardinal Pole and the Counter Reformation* (Cambridge, 1972).

Jedin, H., *A History of the Council of Trent* (2 vols; London, 1957–61).

O'Connell, M. R., *The Counter Reformation 1560–1610* (New York, 1974).

5.5   The English Reformation

Clebsch, W. A., *England's Earliest Protestants 1520–1535* (New Haven, 1964).

Dickens, A. G., *The English Reformation*, revised edn (London: Batsford, 1989).

Haigh, C. (ed.), *The English Reformation Revised* (Cambridge, 1987).

Hall, B., 'The Early Rise and Gradual Decline of Lutheranism in England (1520–1600)', in *Humanists and Protestants* (Edinburgh, 1990), pp. 208–36.

Hughes, P. E., *The Theology of the English Reformers* (London, 1965).

O'Day, R., *The Debate on the English Reformation* (London, 1986).

Rupp, E. G., *Studies in the Making of the English Protestant Tradition* (Cambridge, 1947).

Smeeton, D. D., *Lollard Themes in the Theology of William Tyndale* (Kirksville, Mo., 1986).

Index